CITIZEN, INVERT, QUEER

CITIZEN, INVERT, QUEER

QUEER

*Lesbianism and War
in Early Twentieth-Century Britain*

DEBORAH COHLER

UNIVERSITY OF MINNESOTA PRESS

MINNEAPOLIS • LONDON

Chapter 4 was first published as "Sapphism and Sedition: Producing Female Homosexuality in Great War Britain," *Journal of the History of Sexuality* 16, no. 1 (2007): 68–94. Copyright 2007 by the University of Texas Press. All rights reserved.

Published by the University of Minnesota Press
111 Third Avenue South, Suite 290
Minneapolis, MN 55401-2520
http://www.upress.umn.edu

Library of Congress Cataloging-in-Publication Data

Cohler, Deborah.
Citizen, invert, queer : lesbianism and war in early twentieth-century Britain / Deborah Cohler.
p. cm.
Includes bibliographical references and index.
ISBN 978-0-8166-4975-4 (hc : alk. paper) — ISBN 978-0-8166-4976-1 (pb : alk. paper)
1. Lesbianism—Great Britain—History—20th century. 2. Nationalism and feminism—Great Britain—History—20th century. 3. War and society—Great Britain—History—20th century. 4. World War, 1914-1918—Social aspects—Great Britain. I. Title.
HQ75.6.G7C57 2010
306.76´63094109041—dc22
2009045683

17 16 15 14 13 12 11 10   10 9 8 7 6 5 4 3 2

For Barb

CONTENTS

introduction

QUEER NATIONALISMS

In June 2002, transgender author and activist Leslie Feinberg circulated
a broadsheet at U.S. gay pride parades seeking to incite antiwar activism
among participants. "When World War I broke out," it reads in part, "gay
and trans movement leaders backed their own [nation's] rulers in that
bloody inter-imperialist war and it derailed their struggle."[1] In 1928, an
anonymous review of Compton Mackenzie's novel *Extraordinary Women*
headlined "The Vulgarity of Lesbianism" asserted that female homosexuality "is impossible to dismiss . . . quite so confidently in these post-war days
of boy-girls and girl-boys."[2] Whereas Feinberg critiques the nationalist cap-
itulations of early twentieth-century "gay and trans movement leaders," the
1928 review attributes the increasing visibility of gender and sexual variations in the interwar period to "wider causes arising out of the war." These
polemics, separated by more than seventy years and two nations, connect
homosexual identity and gender variation both to wartime cultural transformations generally and to World War I specifically.[3]

Citizen, Invert, Queer takes seriously this rhetorical connection and argues
that in early twentieth-century Britain, discourses of lesbian identity emerged
through the nationalist transformations of World War I ("the Great War").
This book examines the discursive emergence of "boy-girls and girl-boys"
through examining the rhetorical and ideological intersections of nationalism and sexuality in the early years of the twentieth century. The production of modern lesbian subjectivity in the interwar years stems from racial
and imperialist anxieties as well as from shifts in wartime gendered possibilities for women. Whereas in 2002 activist Feinberg distinguishes "gay
and trans" identities from one another, the 1928 book review links the two
categories under the rubric "boy-girls and girl-boys." The review reflects a

common twentieth-century assumption: that women's gender deviance (female masculinity) is a necessary symptom, signal, or sign of their sexual deviance (female homosexuality). Yet this equation of female masculinity and female homosexuality is a relatively recent, rather than a transhistorical, phenomenon.

Citizen, Invert, Queer brings questions of racial, national, and gendered otherness to bear on the construction of whiteness and masculinity in the rise of lesbian identity in Britain. In late nineteenth-century England, gender inversion was primarily a sign of cultural, rather than sexual, transgression. It was not until after the Great War that masculine or mannish women were consistently labeled "homosexual" in British culture. This signification of gender deviance becomes clear when read through public discourses of geopolitics and racial citizenship: at the turn of the twentieth century, masculine women signified a national or eugenic threat more often than a homosexual symptom. The intimate relationship between representations of sexuality and those of empire and nationhood reveals how women's masculinity and female homosexuality became linked in the public imagination. In this book, I read Feinberg's "bloody inter-imperialist war" in relation to the discursive development of a "gay and trans movement," and I parse the connections, in the anonymous 1928 reviewer's words, among "the vulgarity of lesbianism," the Great War, and "boy-girls and girl-boys."

Historians of sexuality have established how conditions in the United States during World War II enabled the formations of lesbian and gay communities during and immediately after that war (through the homosocial environments of home-front industry and urban aggregation, homoerotic intimacies among deployed military men and women, and the formation of postwar gay enclaves at ports of call in San Francisco and New York).[4] *Citizen, Invert, Queer* makes a distinct yet related argument: that the ideological and discursive conditions of home-front England enabled the emergence of a language of female homosexual identity during and immediately after the Great War. Whereas the case study of the United States during World War II takes up the reorganization of individuals into homosocial clusters and is an argument about practices, identity, and community, my case study of the years before, during, and after the Great War in England focuses primarily on ideological change and discursive possibilities. Mine is an argument, in other words, not about lesbian sexual practices but about shifting language and the emergence of new categories through which those practices were classified, organized, resisted, or embraced.

Citizen, Invert, Queer builds on the work of Laura Doan, Jane Garrity, and Gay Wachman in early twentieth-century studies of British lesbian literary culture. Specific debts to each of these path-clearing scholars will be found throughout the book. This study of female masculinity is also indebted to the groundbreaking, though very different, work on that topic by both Judith Halberstam and Jay Prosser. My work on the production of the "English race" in emergent lesbian identities is in dialogue with scholars of U.S. race and sexuality such as Siobhan Somerville as well as with those in the emerging field of transnational feminist cultural studies, exemplified by Caren Kaplan and Inderpal Grewal. By drawing transnational feminist critique into dialogue with queer theories of modernity and literary modernism, *Citizen, Invert, Queer* not only highlights questions of race and war at a key moment in the history of sexual and gendered representation but also models a reading practice that centers questions of empire and nation in the analysis of sexual subjects.

To illustrate both dominant ideologies of female sexuality and emergent rhetorics of homosexual identities and desires, *Citizen, Invert, Queer* examines a range of cultural texts including novels, legal and medical texts, newspaper editorials and cartoons, plays, and reviews. Focusing on questions of public discourse rather than on private documents such as diaries or letters, I analyze nationalist, sexological, imperialist, and gendered rhetorics in texts both marginal and influential, from the obscure or banned to the widely reprinted and mass distributed. In juxtaposing well-known texts with those minimally circulated, common tropes of sexual deviance and imperial citizenship, as well as key ideological and discursive distinctions, emerge. *Citizen, Invert, Queer* focuses less on relative cultural impact and more on representational possibilities that selected texts (both alone and in dialogue) reflect and that are reflected in a particular cultural moment through the juxtaposition of like or unlike representations.

Citizen

The late nineteenth and early twentieth centuries saw intranational and international movements of people, goods, and cultural ideologies. Indeed, such movements can define modernity. Particularly notable for scholars of British and American literary modernism are the transatlantic crossings of artists and art in the first decades of the twentieth century. Literary communities in Paris, New York, London, and Chicago produced a sense of elite cosmopolitanism among British and American writers. Early recuperative work on the lesbian or "Sapphic" modernists charts the particularly lesbian valences of such cosmopolitanism, but it retains a model of communities predicated on mobility—if not of persons, then of ideas, texts, and capital.[5] That women who had erotic desires and relationships with other women did or did not cross national lines, and that those crossings produced and were produced through ideologies of cosmopolitan sexual modernity, are factors crucial to the development of ideas of female homosexuality in relation to categories of the nation, citizenship, and empire. I depart from models of cosmopolitan modernism, not to deny the importance of international communities and connections but to argue for the specific function of the rhetoric of the nation in the production of lesbian identity in British public culture.[6]

Less concerned with the lives of women who had erotic relations with other women (or even with those sexual behaviors themselves) than with emerging public representations of female same-sex desire, I argue that the ideological and rhetorical force of nationalism was central to the production of a widely understood female homosexual subject by the mid-twentieth century in Britain. In examining the rise of lesbian identity through its relation to nationalism, "lesbianism" emerges not as an innocent or purely oppositional category but as a field of representation complicit with and produced through discourses of imperialist nationalism.

In the late nineteenth and early twentieth centuries, ideologies of British bourgeois femininity were infused with the geopolitical and cultural consequences of imperial power. With Britain's long imperial reach came both an administrative need to fill the "empty" geographies of the empire with loyal British subjects and the ideological need to clearly delineate the "domestic" from the "foreign." The late nineteenth century saw an increase in eugenic anxieties about the racial composition of England and the increasing discipline of men and women under British rule both at "home" and in the empire. The ideological and material production of the British "race" positioned bourgeois English women as mothers of the nation: maternity rested at the core of ideologies of femininity, and reproduction defined representations of female sexuality. The nation, in other words, constituted gendered ideologies.[7]

Bourgeois English women responded to the ideological weight of imperial motherhood in various ways at the turn of the twentieth century. Whether explicitly in sympathy with or in opposition to ideologies of imperial expansion, middle-class domestic femininity, and Enlightenment

individualism, women seeking to establish literary, civic, or cultural autonomy in written texts engaged with the legacies of empire as they sought to
define modernity and subjectivity for women. As Jane Garrity remarks of
interwar women writers of experimental fictions, "Because these imperial
tropes—expansiveness, exploration, discovery, mapping, usurpation, appropriation—are so culturally pervasive, so imbricated in popular idioms of
the period, modernist women invariably recapitulate them in their attempt
to re-imagine themselves as full citizens, as legitimate and agency-wielding
daughters rather than as subjugated mothers of England."[8] The gendered
and sexual transformations of representations of British womanhood between the 1890s and the 1920s grapple with questions of "the race" through
the language of reproduction, citizenship, subjectivity, and modernity.

Because of the dominant focus on reproductive citizenship, some feminist analyses of the role of nationalism in gendered subjectivity either elide
questions of female homosexual erotics or collapse discussions of women's
gender deviance and sexual deviance. To gain cultural or political citizenship, many bourgeois women at the turn of the twentieth century appropriated tropes of masculinity to assert female subjectivity. Prior to the Great
War, these masculine strategies were not primarily coded references to
female homosexuality, but rather signals of women's efforts to gain subjectivity, enfranchisement, and access to the public sphere. Thus, some analyses of early twentieth-century lesbian identity misread cultural strategies as
sexual signals. Complicating the relation of women's sexual and gendered
roles, eugenicists at the turn of the twentieth century not only were concerned with "positive" eugenic reproduction by "good" eugenic subjects but
also advocated for "negative" eugenics—preventing reproduction by "poor"
eugenic subjects, including not only people of color and physically "deficient" Britons but also mentally or psychologically "deficient" men and
women. Included in the latter categories were those who exhibited nonnormative sexual desires or behaviors. Here, sexological definitions of normative or deviant sexual desires encountered cultural discussions of race
suicide, national health, and reproductive citizenship. After the Great War,
as novelists, pundits, jurists, and journalists began to represent female
same-sex desires as constituting sexual identities, registers of racial health
and cultural citizenship joined languages of morality and sexology to produce multiple competing models of female homosexuality. *Citizen, Invert,
Queer* argues that the emergence of the dominant model of the masculine
lesbian in the mid-twentieth century should be understood as not only

following the sexological invert but also emerging through discourses of masculine citizenship and racial health.

Invert

Recently, scholars of both transsexual and lesbian communities have looked to early twentieth-century medical and literary texts to construct genealogies of contemporary identities. Both groups of scholars seek to separate gender deviance from sexuality, but they often strive to privilege one category of identity over another. In this book, I argue that we must read gender and sexuality as distinct but intertwined categories. By analytically untangling gender and sexuality, we can read their relations as culturally and historically produced, rather than naturalized, phenomena. Gender inversion becomes a central, but not defining, element of the emergence of female homosexual representations, as it also signals women's assertions of citizenship in the British public sphere before and during the Great War.

By the mid-twentieth century female gender inversion was widely associated with lesbian identity in Britain, but in the late nineteenth century such female gender deviance was not widely equated with female homosexuality. Rather, many forms of female masculinity, often more cultural than sexual, undercut expectations of women.[9] Women's gender nonconformity served a variety of representational ends, including political agitation, social transgression, and libertine and aesthetic experimentation. In the interwar period, rapidly proliferating lesbian representations far exceeded any one model: the "mannish lesbian" was only one trope among many that signaled emergent lesbian identity.

"Inversion" is a concept that was widely used by sexologists from the late nineteenth century to the mid-twentieth century to describe characteristics culturally assigned to one gender or sex that appear in the "opposite" sex. Medical descriptions of inversion focused on the body—men's narrow shoulders, women's broad shoulders or low voices—as well as on cultural markers such as nervous dispositions in both inverted men and women or a penchant for cigarettes in inverted women. Inversion is a trope that participates in ideological and discursive configurations of gendered, sexual, psychic, and social identities. Reading the functions of tropes of inversion can illuminate the transition to modernity as "culture" and "consciousness" began to replace physical bodies as explainers of behaviors and pathology. Whereas by the mid-twentieth century, gender inversion was equated with "sexual inversion" or homosexuality, this was not the widespread case

a generation before. Suffrage women, for example, were considered gender
deviants in the first decades of the twentieth century because of their social,
not anatomical or erotic, gender transgressions. Suffragists' gender inversions changed definitions of "femininity" and "citizenship" through their
actions and their appropriations of "masculine" spaces, words, and actions.
Parsing the intertwined relations of gender inversions and female sexual
subjectivity can complicate medical models of gender inversion as sexual
inversion, and also can allow for a gendered analysis of power, citizenship,
and subjectivity to engage with, rather than be mapped directly onto, debates regarding representations of female sexuality in modernity.

Sexology's classifying framework of inversion has been mobilized as a
foundational model of twentieth-century identities by historians of lesbian
and gay communities as well as by scholars of transsexual and transgender
identities. Havelock Ellis's "congenital invert" has been inscribed as a "fore-
parent" of both lesbians and female-to-male (FTM) transsexuals.[10] Jean
Bobby Noble notes that "some definitions of lesbianism and, recently, FTM
trans-sexuality trace discursive histories back to the late nineteenth- and
early twentieth-century construction/invention of inversion and, curiously,
back to *The Well of Loneliness*."[11] Indeed, Radclyffe Hall's now-canonical
1928 novel *The Well of Loneliness* can invite such a through-line from sexological classification to emergent identity and community (whether that
identity is lesbian or transgender). Yet Hall's novel, written thirty years after
sexologists such Richard von Krafft-Ebing and Havelock Ellis first published
their works on female "inversion," produced only one model of female
homosexuality among many, and engaged not only with the language of
sexology but also with the languages of religion, citizenship, race, and class
to produce her desiring "mythic mannish lesbian." Hall's novel, the subject
of many late twentieth-century cultural claims, also produced its own
genealogy of homosexual subjectivity. Such genealogies work to create transhistorical connections for emergent and established communities and cultures predicated on identity politics. But they also create a direct line from
medical models of bodily inversion to cultural organizations of identities.
Citizen, Invert, Queer seeks to complicate such a direct line from medical
models to widespread public culture by tracing carefully the rhetoric of
gender deviance and female sexuality in culture productions beyond those
which derive primarily from a sexological model.

The production of gender deviance through the rhetorics of nation,
race, and citizenship as well as medicine and pathology disrupts a narrative

of a seamless sexological line from Havelock Ellis to Radclyffe Hall. By the mid-twentieth century, female masculinity was equated with female homosexuality, but this discursive cleavage was neither inevitable nor natural. This book seeks to uncover the more twisted path of emergent lesbian identities in early twentieth-century Britain to illustrate the ideological as well as historical stakes of representations of female homosexual desiring subjects. In particular, the material and rhetorical conditions of the "home front" during the Great War produced widespread changes in conceptions of female sexuality and gender. As Ann Stoler has remarked, "Racial thinking harnesses itself to varied progressive projects and shapes the social taxonomies defining who will be excluded from them."[12] Changing gendered ideologies affected both bodies and nation-states: in my highlighting of the role of racial nationalism in the production of gendered and sexual representations, sexology loses its central place in the narrative of emergent lesbian identities, and subsequently those identities may lose a bit of their ideological innocence.

Queer

Following Foucault's famous invective that, before modernity, "the sodomite had been a temporary aberration; the homosexual was now a species,"[13] many historians of sexuality have turned primarily to medical models to explore the rise of homosexual identities in modernity. Foucault traces the rise of the homosexual from religious to legal to medical (specifically sexological) institutions and discourse. Grounded in analyses of the cultural power of medical and scientific institutions, Foucault's conceptual framework of bio-power is central to his arguments regarding transformations of sexuality in modernity and, indeed, has been crucial to scholars of sexuality, power, and culture who follow him.[14] But science and medicine were not the sole registers through which homosexual identities, and female sexuality more broadly, emerged in modernity. *Citizen, Invert, Queer* illustrates the cultural misreadings that can result from an overemphasis on a medical model and an overestimation of its cultural impact when we trace out the ideological, discursive, and material emergence of sexual subjectivities for women in modernity.

Citizen, Invert, Queer begins by contextualizing the rise of sexology in the late nineteenth century within the imperialist political and intellectual traditions that produced this fledgling "science," in order to point to its mutually constituting rhetorical force in relation to other contemporary cultural discourses. In her reading of Foucault's *History of Sexuality*, Ann Stoler points to the lacuna in his theorization of tropes of nineteenth-century sexual subjectivity. Foucault produces the "masturbating child of the bourgeois family, the 'hysterical woman,' the Malthusian couple, and the perverse adult. But students of empire would surely add at least one more. Did any of these figures exist as objects of knowledge and discourse in the nineteenth century without a racially erotic counterpoint, without reference to the libidinal energies of the savage, the primitive, the colonized—reference points of difference, critique, and desire?"[15] Stoler points to the gap in Foucault's conception of the key figures for "the very production of sexuality."[16] With Stoler, I wish to draw critical attention not only to supplementary nineteenth-century figures (Stoler's savage, primitive, and colonized peoples) but also to the centrality of empire in the construction of female homosexuality a generation after the (male) homosexual became a species, according to Foucault. In analyzing within their imperial, cultural, methodological, and discursive contexts the sexological and classifying theories of erotic behaviors upon which Foucault draws so heavily, the role of sexology can be seen less as a constitutive discourse to the rise of modern sexual identities and more as one generative discourse among many.

In 1990, Eve Sedgwick challenged queer theorists to explore how (much) to theorize "lesbian and gay male identities together. Or separately."[17] When I initially began this project, just a few years after Sedgwick's call, I envisioned the work as a part of emerging studies of "Sapphic modernism," a feminist response and corrective to histories of sexuality that assumed Foucault's sodomite was also a Sapphist, and that set as a historical guidepost the trials of Oscar Wilde, rather than that of Radclyffe Hall twenty years later. Lesbians lagged a bit behind gay men, I hypothesized, because lesbian sex was never criminalized in England as was gay male sex.

Citizen, Invert, Queer has led me to a slightly different conclusion from my early theory of historical lag. Once we understand citizenship, empire, and nation to be just as constitutive of sexual and gendered identities as legal prohibitions and medical discourse, the representational politics of homosexual men and women become far more intertwined than separated. Indeed, they become quite queer. From the uneasy alliances and the rhetorics of empire shared by New Woman and decadent writers in the 1890s, to the tangled relations of seditious behavior by prewar female suffragists and wartime male pacifists, to the feminization of male suffrage advocates and the insistent masculinity of some nationalist women, gendered and nationalist representations of male and female sexuality (both normative and deviant) are not only mutually constituting but also utterly interdependent for their legibility in British public culture. Within novels, suffrage polemics, juridical and legislative arguments, and eugenic and sexological treatises on the relative harm or benefit of nonreproductive sexual behaviors, the hypervisibility of male homosexuality shaped emergent discourses of female homosexuality, and cultural changes in women's gendered positions produced and challenged definitions of masculinity for both male and female subjects. The emergence of female homosexuality in public discourse neither followed directly from men's nor arose in an entirely separate or parallel narrative. Rather, male homosexual representations informed but did not wholly define emergent lesbian identities. The two are mutually productive and related, yet distinct, strands of discursive history.

In her wartime novel *Despised and Rejected,* Rose Allatini's male homosexual protagonist tells his female homosexual friend, "It's a case of 'like to like' with us. . . . And because there's a certain amount of the masculine element in you, and of the feminine element in me, we both have to suffer in the same way."[18] *Citizen, Invert, Queer* challenges a direct "like to like" theory of male and female homosexual representations in the early years of the twentieth century. But Allatini's 1917 characterization of this equivalent relation of male and female homosexual identities is a key moment in the emergence of a legible lesbian subject: a critical threshold in the final months of the Great War in which national, as well as gendered and sexual, identities were radically transformed.

Lesbianism and War in Early Twentieth-Century Britain

Citizen, Invert, Queer invokes gendered and sexual identities at both ends of the twentieth century: the gender invert and sexual invert of the turn of the twentieth century, and queers (both sexual and gendered) of the turn of the twenty-first. The book begins by investigating the impact of empire on discourses of female sexuality and gender deviance in the 1890s. First examining the influence of colonial anthropology and imperialist travel on sexology's classifying logic, chapter 1 seeks both to demystify and to decenter sexology as the origin story for modern sexual identities in Britain by examining it as one discursive home among others for the production of sexual representations that seek to unseat or challenge Victorian gendered and sexual ideologies. Havelock Ellis's first edition of *Sexual Inversion,* Oscar Wilde's banned play *Salomé,* and Victoria Cross's controversial short story

"Theodora: A Fragment" together illustrate the dependence of self-styled sexual renegades on more culturally conservative tropes of racial citizenship and empire.

Chapter 2 examines prewar women's suffrage debates. Here, gender inversion indicates cultural deviance and nationalist tensions, rather than sexual deviance. Both pro- and antisuffragist polemics invoke gender inversion in debates over patriotism and gender conformity, but gender inversion is not a homosexual accusation in this context. Suffrage women fought for inclusion in the national body politic through material and discursive transformations of the meanings associated with women's bodies. By constructing themselves either as (moderate) proper British subjects or as (radical) nationalists, suffrage women mobilized familiar tropes of national, sexual, and racial identity in the service of their agitation for gender parity. Readings of the intersections of sexual, gendered, and national tropes of normalcy and deviance in antisuffrage tracts, *Punch* cartoons, suffrage newspapers, Christabel Pankhurst's *The Great Scourge,* and Virginia Woolf's *Night and Day* complicate current scholarly assumptions about the widespread use of sexological classifications in the first years of the twentieth century. The women's suffrage debates illustrate that although sexuality was a central concern to suffragists and antisuffragists alike, the gender transgressions of suffragists and the accusations of sex war and gender betrayal by "the antis" did not constitute accusations of homosexuality but, rather, contested the gender of the national body.

At the same time that leaders of the women's suffrage movement and antisuffrage supporters leveraged the rhetoric of citizenship, nation, and sexuality in debates over women's gendered and national roles, others were engaging questions of nation and gender in debates over more radical reconfigurations of female sexuality. Chapter 3 examines the prewar discursive politics of topics such as male homosexuality, birth control, free love, and planned reproduction in the pages of Dora Marsden's *Freewoman* journal and among sexual freethinkers from eugenicist Edith Lees Ellis and sexologist Stella Browne to the socialist homosexual Edward Carpenter and members of the British Society for the Study of Sex Psychology. The almost complete absence of any discussions of female same-sex erotic love by these "sex radicals" indicates the discursive slipperiness of female homosexual representations and the dependence of even slight allusions to female same-sex desire on established rhetorics of male homosexuality. In the years prior to the Great War, British men and women concerned with reimagining sexual relations between men and women (and between men) produced (and failed to produce) narratives of female sexual autonomy interlaced with contemporary debates over marriage, eugenics, and cultural citizenship.

Chapter 4 explores the British cultural anxieties and political instabilities during the Great War that produced the first widespread public linkages between representations of female masculinity and female homosexuality in British culture. Having established the dearth of prewar representations of female homosexuality, this chapter examines how such representations did emerge in the final years of the Great War in spaces between signifiers of female nationalism and seditious male homosexuality. English wartime characterizations of male homosexuality such as "Hunnish erotomania" marked male homosexuality as a German phenomenon. Women were simultaneously exhorted to bear masculine responsibilities on the "Home Front" and to guard against homosexual relations in the absence of men. The Great War and its aftermath radically reconfigured sexual and gender relations on the home front and on the battlefield. Cultural anxieties about the transformations of British culture in wartime resulted in emergent discourses of female homosexual identity that were produced by ideas of British cultural supremacy and vulnerability as well as by domestic wartime reconfigurations. Focusing on Rose Allatini's novel of homosexual identity *Despised and Rejected,* which was banned under the Defense of the Realm Act; the notorious "trial of the century" in which actress Maud Allan accused right-wing publisher Noel Pemberton Billing of libelously labeling her a lesbian; and the 1921 parliamentary debates over criminalizing female homosexuality, chapter 4 illustrates how British wartime identities created representational space for female homosexuality that previously had been impossible in the public sphere.

By 1928, discourses of female homosexuality had become so culturally legible that newspaper editorialists, literary reviewers, and pundits of all stripes readily discussed lesbianism in the obscenity trial of Radclyffe Hall's notorious novel. Yet, despite its exalted place in literary and cultural studies as "the classic novel of lesbian love," *The Well of Loneliness* was far from alone in 1928. Hall's tragic gender invert presented only one model of female homosexuality circulating in 1928; why and how did this representation become the dominant one in twentieth-century culture? That is, why do we now often map gender deviance onto homosexuality? Chapter 5 explores the textual and extratextual lives of three British novels, all published within a few months at the end of 1928, each of which takes female same-sex eroticism as its subject. Not only do Radclyffe Hall's *The Well of Loneliness,* Compton Mackenzie's *Extraordinary Women,* and Virginia Woolf's *Orlando* each represent female same-sex eroticism, but each novel also mobilizes tropes of Englishness, nationalism, and cultural difference to produce female homosexuality as a culturally legible identity. Whereas Hall notoriously attempts to position her congenital invert as a rightful inheritor of pastoral nineteenth-century England in contrast to colonial others, Mackenzie constructs his playful Sapphic tourists in opposition to all things British. These nationalist moments are best highlighted not only through close readings of the three novels and their medical, geopolitical, legal, and literary contexts, but also through examinations of the marketing, pricing, production, distribution, and reception of the novels by their intended (and unintended) reading publics in the closing days of the 1920s. By reading the textual and cultural intersections of narratives of nationalism and colonialism with those of gender inversion and sexual deviance, I illustrate the interdependence of national identity and sexual identity in the emerging representation of lesbianism in the interwar years.

The afterword to *Citizen, Invert, Queer* takes the book's methodological imperative—to read emerging sexual and gendered identities through the lens of nationalism—from the turn of the twentieth century in Britain to the turn of the twenty-first in the United States. These concluding pages situate the rise of transgender identities alongside post–September 11, 2001, nationalism and state repression in the United States through a reading of transgender author and activist Leslie Feinberg's novel of "genderqueer" antiwar solidarities *Drag King Dreams.* In this dialectical novel of solidarity and struggle on the streets of New York City following September 11, Feinberg draws nationalist oppressors against a multicultural and multinational mix of genderqueers, drag kings, and straight and gay immigrants. Sexual and gender identities become the means through which U.S.-born characters can work in solidarity with recent immigrants, and their resistance to the state allows articulations of complex gender and sexual identities. Like the wartime and postwar novels discussed earlier in *Citizen, Invert, Queer, Drag King Dreams* relies on structures of nationalism and struggle to produce queer inversions. *Citizen, Invert, Queer* concludes by applying its methodological approach (reading sexual and gendered representations around the Great War through their stakes in nationalism) to a different time and place in which the stakes of nationalism fundamentally affect representations of queer desires and communities.

Foucault teaches us that our histories are products as much of our present as of the past. The novelists, polemicists, sexologists, editors, and pundits analyzed in these pages produced narratives of sexual, gendered, national, and racial identities. My narrative is equally an invested one. *Citizen, Invert, Queer* produces a history of sexuality that foregrounds the relation of sexual subjectivities to the nation-state. Through this invested history, we can grasp some of the cultural and historical stakes of the rise of lesbian identities and understand sexual subjectivity's intractable and often difficult dependence on discourses of race and nation, racism, and empire for its potency and cultural weight.

chapter 1

IMPERIALIST CLASSIFICATIONS: SEXOLOGY, DECADENCE, AND NEW WOMEN IN THE 1890S

In this brief glance at some of the ethnographic, historical and literary aspects of homosexual passion there is . . . the curious fact that we seem to find a special proclivity to homosexuality (whether or not involving a greater frequency of congenital inversion is not usually clear) among certain races and certain regions. On the whole, this proclivity seems more common in the hotter regions of the globe.

—HAVELOCK ELLIS AND JOHN ADDINGTON SYMONDS, *Sexual Inversion*

In 1897, when Havelock Ellis published *Sexual Inversion,* the first of his seven-volume *Studies in the Psychology of Sex,* England was in the throes of cultural, imperial, and gendered transformations. Almost forty years after the publication of *On the Origin of Species,* amid widespread Malthusian and eugenic appropriations of Darwin's work; twelve years following the criminalization of "gross indecencies" between men; five years after Sarah Grand and Ouida coined the term "New Woman" to describe the recently educated and independent women of England's bourgeoisie;[1] and two years before the "disaster" of the Anglo-Boer War (1899–1902) would inaugurate "over a decade of imperial crises for Britain including the efflorescence or resurgence of nationalist and anti-imperialist movements,"[2] Ellis's text entered debates over the sexual, gendered, and racial character of not only the "inverts" referred to in his first volume's title but also English men and women more broadly. By assigning deviance to "the hotter regions of the globe," Ellis's work not only distances "this proclivity" from England's chilly geography but also reflects a broader cultural moment grappling with the effects of empire at home. In this chapter, I interrogate the interconnected politics of empire in three areas of British representation in the 1890s: the early work of the influential sexologist Havelock Ellis; the treatment of female sexuality and empire in Oscar Wilde's "decadent" play *Salomé*; and the writings of a renegade "New Woman" novelist, Victoria Cross. In so doing, I highlight the imperialist foundations of many so-called radical British writings on sexuality in the late nineteenth and early twentieth centuries, whether the writings take as their objects proper British subjects or contemplate the sexual proclivities of those residing in "in the hotter regions of the globe."

This chapter makes no claims to representativeness; indeed, Victoria Cross's work is notable for its departures from many themes of other New Woman writers, just as Wilde's *Salomé* is for its treatment of the popular Salome myth. Rather than making an argument about representativeness or genre, this chapter intervenes in histories of sexuality and studies of imperialist feminism of the turn of the twentieth century by highlighting the dependence on discursive and material effects of empire in texts (even) by self-styled renegades. As Gayatri Spivak remarks, "Every rupture is also a repetition";[3] each text discussed in this chapter produced discursive or cultural rupture. Yet each text also relies on a core foundational structure of late nineteenth-century England: its hegemonic relation to empire. And so we must understand these moments of rupture also as repetition in the congruence and mutual production of imperial, gendered, and sexual representation.

The feminism of late nineteenth-century British middle- and upper-class women was predicated on eugenic motherhood. Popular rhetoric of a declining birthrate in conjunction with nationalist mobilizations of women as "mothers of the nation" created "positive eugenic" pressures on "fit" British women to create racially pure, healthy children for the nation.[4] Eugenic messages about racial hygiene, social purity, and women's reproductive function influenced feminist, as well as nationalist, discourses of womanhood: "Feminists were able to exploit the ideological assumptions about women's superior moral strength to enable themselves to take up imperial service in the name of Victorian womanhood. Women's roles as nurturers, child-carers, preservers of purity, could all be put to use as part of the wider imperialist project. A good deal of feminist argument, in common with imperial discourse, was preoccupied with race preservation, racial purity and racial motherhood."[5] This imperialist discourse infused not only the more conservative sexual politics of writers such as Sarah Grand but also so-called radical or deviant inscriptions of women's sexuality.

Highly sexualized and classificatory writings by Oscar Wilde and his New Woman literary contemporaries evince British fascinations with the Orient and cement a discursive link between late nineteenth-century sexual classifications and the imperialist project.[6] Feminist critics have long noted that English women's economic and cultural independence in the nineteenth century relied in great part on structures of empire and discourses of racial womanhood.[7] Not only did imperialism form a foundation from which certain English women construct citizen identities, but the methodological and rhetorical power of imperial classification also drove the rise of sexological and erotic identities in the British metropole. In reading the imperialist foundations of incendiary sexual thought of the 1890s in Wilde and Cross, as well as in Havelock Ellis's soon-to-be-canonical sexological work, it is clear that the orientalist impulse of British national identity remains foundational, both discursively and ideologically.

British Sexology and Imperialist Classification: Havelock Ellis's *Sexual Inversion*

Neither a doctor nor a scientist by training, Havelock Ellis possessed a primarily literary and reformist background. Throughout his life (1859–1939), Ellis wrote widely on social relations and advocated "the triumph of science, the emancipation of women, and the growth of social democracy."[8] His interest in the psychology and legal rights of homosexual men and women may have originated in membership in the Fellowship of the New Life, where, in the 1880s, he developed his socialist beliefs as well as close friendships with homosexual men such as Edward Carpenter and with women, including his future wife, Edith Lees. Ellis viewed himself as a political advocate for sexual inverts; his work emphasizes the basic humanity of sexual inverts as well as their inability to change their sexuality.

Havelock Ellis remains the most prominent British sexologist of the late nineteenth and early twentieth centuries. Alongside Germans Karl Heinrich Ulrichs, Richard von Krafft-Ebing, and Carl Westphal, Ellis laid the foundations of twentieth-century sexology and psychoanalysis with his classificatory systems of gender and sexual deviance, and of the Western turn to a medical model of sexuality, as distinct from a religious or penal model of sexual behavior. *Studies in the Psychology of Sex* was a living document through the early decades of sexological study: Ellis continually wrote, published, revised, and reissued the seven volumes for more than twenty years. This chapter focuses specifically on the first edition of the first volume—the 1897 edition of *Sexual Inversion,* coauthored with John Addington Symonds. In the late nineteenth century, sexologists functioned as a small, international group of thinkers, constantly referencing each other's work. I focus on Ellis and, less centrally, Symonds as thinkers located specifically in turn-of-the-century England. Though this somewhat artificially separates their work from the international milieu of sexological textual production, Ellis's international citation practices reveal a logic informed by imperial and nationalist concerns.

Sexual Inversion was originally to be a collaboration between Ellis and Symonds, and, indeed, the volume was informed by the data of both and an initial dialogue between the two men; but, following Symonds's premature death in 1893, it was finalized and shaped by Ellis alone.[9] Both men envisioned *Sexual Inversion* as a response to the 1885 Labouchère Amendment and the changing perceptions of homosexuality in Britain in the 1890s. A homosexual as well as a poet and a classics scholar, Symonds in his work connects modern homosexual behaviors to the "heroic ideal of masculine love" in Dorian Greece. Sexologist and heterosexual Ellis distinguishes situational, temporary homosexual behaviors from inborn sexual inversion. Such distinctions among homosexual types, slippery and taxonomically difficult as they might be, form a basis for Ellis's argument against the criminalization of male homosexuality and the classifying logic of his analysis of the relation of gender to sexual deviance in women. Both men relied on distinctions between Occident and Orient to build their arguments against homosexuality as a decadent phenomenon, in favor of a model of homosexuality compatible with ideals of British citizenship.

Ellis begins *Sexual Inversion* with autobiography. In the opening sentences of his "general preface," he outlines his youthful grappling with "the problems of sex" and his "resolve" to make "one main part of [his] lifework . . . to make clear the problem of sex." Intertwined with the recitation of youthful resolve, he mentions time spent as a teacher in Australia, "living partly in an Australian city where the ways of life were plainly seen, [and] partly in the solitude of the bush." Invoking both the colonial city and the more "solitary" or exotic "bush," *Sexual Inversion* is framed not only by a universalized question of human development (a young man's questions of sex) but also by colonial topography.[10]

Ellis frames his study within the context of anthropology. He begins both the larger study of sexual inversion and his specific chapter on sexual inversion in women with an anthropological survey of world history, assuring his readers that "homosexuality has been observed in women from very early times, and in very wide-spread regions."[11] It is not until the end of the introductory chapter that "contemporary" British homosexuality is fully considered, well after sexual deviance is established as primitive and, employing the racially hierarchical theory of recapitulation, racially other.[12] Thus, one discourse critical to constructs of modern lesbian representations, sexology, finds its origins in the hierarchical separation of races, nations, and classes as well as the classifications of sexual activities, bodies, and genders.

Sexual Inversion draws on accounts of sexual deviance from nineteenth-century anthropology and travel literature as evidence of a universally existent sexual deviance. Havelock Ellis mobilized these ethnographies to construct theories of European and white North American sexual behaviors, identities, and classifications. Robin Hackett defines "modernist primitivism" as "the twentieth-century Euro-American self-representational mode in which images of people and cultures projected as other than the self or outside time and history are used as symbols of violence, energy, sensuality, regeneration, *de*generation, and freedom."[13] In Ellis and Symonds, we can see the basis of modernist primitivism in their uses of "the lower races" to both universalize and marginalize sexual behaviors beyond the norm of late Victorian ideologies of bourgeois domesticity.

The presence or absence of abnormal minority types of persons varies by race, culture, and history. The first chapter of *Sexual Inversion* provides a schematic progression of homosexual behaviors, from cultures and times most "distant" from the British ruling class to those closest. The opening summary for chapter 1 neatly demonstrates the hierarchy of racial evolution that frames Ellis's study:

> Prevalence of Homosexuality—Among Animals—Among the Lower Human Races—The Albanians—The Greeks—The Eskimo—The Tribes of the North-West United States—Homosexuality among Soldiers in Europe—Indifference frequently Manifested by European Lower Classes—Sexual Inversion at Rome—Homosexuality in Prisons—Among Men of Exceptional Intellect and Moral Leaders—Murat—Michelangelo—Winckelmann—Homosexuality in English History—Walt Whitman—Verlaine—Burton's Climatic Theory of Homosexuality—The Racial Factor.[14]

Moving from same-sex behavior found in animals to that of "the lower races," including primarily indigenous cultures, and on to that of the lower classes, the author presents homosexual behaviors in this introductory chapter in analytic tension with inborn sexual inversion: "lower" cultures and races seem to encourage or tolerate same-sex behaviors; whereas more "civilized" cultures and times more easily reveal a distinction between temporary behaviors and inborn inversion, given their social prohibitions against homosexual behaviors.

The contrast between modern British subjects and their others reveals Ellis's complex formulation of acquired and innate homosexualities. Hackett argues in her first chapter of *Sapphic Primitivism* that "the discrepancy between Ellis's claim that homosexuality is present everywhere and the examples he chooses to prove his point has largely to do with the fact that he differentiates between congenital and acquired homosexuality. *Congenital* homosexuality may be spread evenly around the globe and from era to era. *Acquired* homosexuality cannot be evenly spread around the globe . . . [because it] is a direct result of social acceptance . . . [which] is prevalent in the 'lower races' . . . and among the 'lower classes.'"[15] On the one hand, Ellis argues that homosexual behaviors are present across time, space, cultural circumstances, and even species. On the other hand, he distinguishes homosexual behaviors (whether culturally condoned or condemned) from "true inversion"—a physiologically and psychologically distinct type often hidden but always distinct from the majority of "normal" types: "On the whole the evidence shows that among lower races homosexual practices are regarded with considerable indifference, and the real invert, if he exists among them, as doubtless he does exist, passes unperceived or joins some sacred caste which sanctifies his exclusively homosexual inclinations."[16] Here, "homosexual practices" and "the real invert" both exist in the "lower races."[17] But without the properly scientific classification system (which Ellis elaborates in subsequent chapters), the key distinction between these two groups "passes unperceived" to observers such as anthropologists and travelers from the West.

In "civilized" times and places (Western Europe from the Renaissance forward, according to Ellis), "real inversion" is more readily detectable, because of the cultural aversion to homosexual behavior: "In modern Europe we find the strongest evidence of the presence of what may fairly be called true sexual inversion when we investigate the men of the Renaissance. The intellectual independence of those days and the influence of antiquity seem to have liberated and fully developed the impulses of those abnormal individuals who would otherwise have found no clear expression, and passed unnoticed."[18] In modern Europe, sexual inverts took on their own intellectual, as well as sexual and gendered, characteristics. These characteristics are positive for Ellis, aligning sexual inversion with creativity and artistic expression.

Ellis and Symonds approach the question of male homosexuality's genealogy through two very different, gendered strategies. Whereas Ellis takes great care to distinguish temporary homosexuality from true inversion in both men and women, Symonds, concerned only with male homosexuality, distinguishes vigorous, masculine comrade-love between men from debasing male effeminacy. Symonds makes this distinction by relying on a separation of noble, militaristic Greek men and men subject to "sensual" corruption, located primarily in "the Orient" and in "barbaric" nations. In his "A Problem in Greek Ethics," published as appendix A of *Sexual Inversion,* Symonds traces the development of "Greek love" from the Homeric era through fifth-century Athens.[19] He argues, "Greek love was, in its origin and essence, military. Fire and valour, rather than tenderness and tears, were the external outcome of this passion; nor had . . . effeminacy, a place in its vocabulary."[20] Much of his text is concerned with mapping the development of this comrade-love through myth, literature, history, and his own "speculation."[21] To distinguish Greek love from other, debasing homosexual acts (by the Greeks as well as others in the past and present), Symonds produces a nationalist homosexuality:

> The unisexual vices of barbarians follow, not the type of Greek paiderastia, but . . . [a] disease of effeminacy, described by Herodotus and Hippocrates *as something essentially foreign and non-Hellenic.* In all these cases, whether we regard that of the Scythian . . . impotent effeminates, the North American Bardashes, the Tsecats of Madagascar, the Cordaches of the Canadian Indians . . . natives of Venezuela, and so forth—the characteristic point is that effeminate males renounce their sex, assume female clothes, and live either in promiscuous concubinage with the men of the tribe or else in marriage with chosen persons. This abandonment of the masculine attributes and costume, would have been abhorrent to the Doric custom. (emphasis added)[22]

Greek love is masculine; homosexual behaviors among "lower races" are invariably effeminate and utterly different.[23] In support of his claims regarding the Bardashes and others, Symonds cites German anthropologist Adolf Bastian, British evolutionary philosopher Herbert Spenser, and unattributed "facts collected by travellers among the North American Indians."[24]

Thus, drawing on the literatures of ancient Greece and Victorian classical scholarship, Symonds, like Ellis, relies as well on nineteenth-century anthropology, evolutionary philosophy, and social Darwinism—discourses all deeply entrenched in the imperialist logic of late Victorian Britain—to produce his theory of homosexuality. Elazar Barkan remarks on the discursive congruence between classical and anthropological sources for sexology: "A frequent strategy for addressing 'the unspeakable' was through the Other— namely, ancient Europeans and contemporary savages—even though this meant invoking the most highly esteemed images (ancient Greeks) and the most denigrated ones (savages) within a single space. The attraction of the primitives was that they were viewed as closer to nature than Victorians. . . . In contrast, a high regard for the ancients codified sexuality as a respectable topic even in the idealized company of ethics and aesthetics."[25] Sexological measures of European, British, and Anglo-American behaviors were thus constructed from their onset through cultural distance as well as medical measure. When we consider the gendered location of these two sources (homosexuality in women was located only through medical or anthropological measure, reserving the "highly regarded" classical studies for the realm of men only), the distance between Symonds's Greek love and the evolutionary theories dependent on anthropology illustrate in bold relief the ideological stakes of the gendered and nationalist origins of British sexology.

The universalizing gestures in *Sexual Inversion*'s evidentiary frame can obscure the colonial project that underlies the classifications of deviant and normative bodies in the late nineteenth century. Recent work on colonial medicine, historical archaeology, and the history of anthropology illustrates the interdependence of colonial administrators, European military structures, and Western medical and social scientists in both the imperialist and intellectual developments of the eighteenth and nineteenth centuries.[26] The surveillance project of Victorian anthropologists and colonial administrators was twofold: they observed the indigenous peoples whom their governments sought to colonize and they recorded the activities of the lower classes of colonial settlers. Studying and controlling colonial subjects was both a classed and a raced project.

Reports from the colonies by administrators, officers, travelers, anthropologists, and doctors produced vast amounts of discourse that social scientists both in the colonies and in England sought to process and productively mobilize.[27] Sexology emerged as a discipline that promised to make order of the rapidly expanding fields of crainiometry, eugenics, anthropology, criminology, and others. Sexology's classifying logic aligned racial and classed deviance with gender roles and sexuality. Gendered and sexual deviance, then, could be mapped onto racial or classed otherness: "primitive" sexual urges could be located in their evolutionary place, and an often physiologically inflected order could be established between perversion, deviance, and normalcy. At the center of such narratives of national and individual development, European heterosexuality and gendered binaries provided normalizing stability.[28] Thus, by examining the data through which Ellis constructed his theories, and the recourse that the classicist Symonds also made to the anthropological and evolutionary work of his contemporaries, we can see how deeply the sexological theories of British homosexuality relied on narratives of colonial otherness, class differences, and imperial social sciences.

When discussing the "special case" of homosexuality in women, Ellis not only drew from the duality of Occident and Orient but also clung much more firmly than in his work on men to gendered binaries for his explanation of sexual deviance. Ellis's model of female homosexual deviance relies on the connection between masculinity and homosexuality in women. Just as his volume begins with an anthropological survey of world history, so too does the specific chapter on sexual inversion in women: "Homosexuality has been observed in women from very early times, and in very widespread regions." Citing women's homosexuality in indigenous women from Brazil to New Zealand to Egypt, Ellis accomplishes several tasks: he initially distances homosexual behaviors from his British, American, and European readers; he stakes out his study's global importance; and he locates his work beyond medicine alone. "As with male homosexuality," Ellis authoritatively states, "there are geographical, or rather, perhaps, racial peculiarities in the distribution of female homosexuality." In his move from a discussion of homosexual activities among women of "the lower races" to his work on European and white North American women, Ellis shifts his analysis. Whereas on the one hand, he discusses homosexuality in broad national strokes ("Among Arab women, according to Kocher, homosexual practices are rare [though in] Egypt, according to Godard, Kocher, and others, it is almost fashionable"), on the other hand, he classifies homosexuality as either situational or congenital for white women, rather than generalizing on the national or racial level. He describes, for example, homosexual activities in homosocial environments in British women's prisons and girls' schools. These activities should not be considered "true sexual inversion,"

Ellis concludes: "This is a spurious kind of homosexuality; it is merely the often precocious play of the normal instinct, and has no necessary relation to true sexual inversion." His anthropological tour, like his European case histories, demonstrates Ellis's critical, yet often incoherent, taxonomic separation of "true inverts" from other women who engage in homosexual practices. This taxonomy relies on racial distinctions and elides gender and sexuality.[29]

After noting the frequency of homosexual activities among women of "the lower races," Ellis proceeds to specific case histories of white European and North American women. He then concludes with a rearticulation of his central premise: that homosexual women are by definition masculine women, though the converse is not necessarily true. Ellis refers to congenital homosexuals as "inverts," thus obscuring the differences between female gender inversion (masculinity) and sexual inversion (homosexuality). This elision reveals the core of his theory—that gender deviance indicates sexual deviance. His chapter moves from the least to the most congenitally inverted women— from "normal," "feminine" schoolgirls and bourgeois married women to the masculine congenital "inverts." He then concludes abruptly with a consideration of "Lesbian love" among prostitutes, the most abject of all.[30]

Ellis's narrative structure implies a continuum of sexual deviance, yet he works conceptually against this narrative structure. Ellis strives to naturalize the congenital sexual invert as a biological and minoritized subject without simultaneously alarming the general population by universalizing a continuum of female sexual deviance. It is this tension, enacted narratively and thematically between his case histories, which indicate degrees of deviance, and his theory, which attempts to draw definite lines between "the normal" and "the inverted," a distinction with which Ellis struggles throughout his work. By calling upon bodily characteristics to distinguish between the truly inverted and the temporarily inverted, Ellis builds his theories on an unstable assumption: that gender inversion is qualitatively distinct from normative subjectivity, and that it is the equivalent of homosexuality.

At the onset of the study, Ellis argues that many women engage in sexual practices with other women because of a temporary unavailability of men. These situational inverts are far less likely in Ellis's descriptions to be marked as masculine. Just as their erotic relations with women give way to lasting bonds with men, so too do their bodies indicate a less permanent mark of sexual deviance through gender inversion. These women form a category of nonhomosexual, feminine women who nonetheless practice homosexual behaviors. This class includes women of the "lower races," British and American factory workers, women in convents, and girls at boarding schools. Ellis takes great care to assure his readers that sexual relations between girls at school are no cause for alarm: "With girls, as with boys, it is in the school at the evolution of puberty that homosexuality first shows itself. . . . In the girl who is congenitally predisposed to homosexuality it will continue and develop; in the majority it will be forgotten as quickly as possible, not without shame, in the presence of the normal object of sexual love." This configuration separates normal from deviant subjects, thus eliminating any possibility of acquired permanent homosexuality or a universalized potential for lifelong deviance. He buttresses this argument with testimony from "a lady who cannot be called inverted," who recounts experiences in school that arose from a combination of curiosity and coercion and, indeed, resulted in embarrassment and shame.[31]

In marked contrast to those more feminine women "who cannot be called inverted," Ellis defines the decidedly masculine "congenital invert," also called the "actively inverted woman," as a woman who has "a more or less distinct trace of masculinity. She may not be, and frequently is not, what would be called a 'mannish' woman, *for the latter may imitate men on the grounds of taste and habit unconnected with sexual perversion,* while in the inverted woman the masculine traits are part of an organic instinct which she by no means always wishes to accentuate" (emphasis added). The inverted woman has a masculine "organic instinct," not to be confused with the "taste and habit" of a mannish, though not inverted, woman. This passage sets up Ellis's definition of inversion in all of its glorious paradoxes. Women who are "organically" attracted to other women are so because of their own masculine physical traits. In the case histories that follow Ellis's theoretical section in this chapter (collected primarily from his wife's friends), he mentions physical traits of congenital inverts such as "a very decidedly masculine type of larynx" and "muscles [that] are everywhere firm with a comparative absence of soft connective tissue, so that an inverted woman may give an unfeminine impression to the sense of touch." Ellis refutes other supposed physical characteristics of congenial inverts, asserting, for example, "no connection, as was once supposed, between sexual inversion in women and an enlarged clitoris, which has very seldom been found in such cases." As Freud will do a few years later, Ellis provides detailed notes regarding his subjects' sexual organs, from their size and texture to their responsiveness to "titillation" by examining doctors,[32] as well as family histories of crime, neurosis, or other cultural abnormalities. Most case histories report some "neurotic temperament" either in the subject herself or in her family, implying a hereditary taint and invoking the specter of eugenic thinking. Thus, neurosis, as well as masculinity, became a marker of sexual inversion in women. Furthermore, only some masculine traits define sexual inversion: those unconnected to a more variable "taste or habit." Yet this line between the organic and the cultural blurs: homosexual women often dislike needlework and favor athletics. The markers of "inversion" (wherein homosexuality is equivalent to this congenital masculinity) vary from the cultural to the biological, but always, in the case of the congenital invert, without a sense of conscious volition. Indeed, Ellis defines what is "masculine" broadly enough so that taking a woman as a sexual object becomes a masculine characteristic: "The inverted woman's masculine element may, in the least degree, *consist only in the fact that she makes advances to the woman* to whom she is attracted and treats all men in a cool, direct manner" (emphasis added).[33] Here, object choice becomes a sign of masculinity and only, therefore, a symptom of congenital (gender) inversion. For Ellis, gender and sexuality collapse into one another, as gender identification appears inextricably linked to sexual identity. Object choice is a consequence, not a definition: homosexuality is a manifestation of gender inversion, not its source.[34]

For Ellis's model of female gender inversion to work, a congenital invert must be paired with a feminine counterpart. According to Ellis, every Western couple, whether same-sex or cross-sex, is fundamentally heterogendered, because the biologically female invert is gendered male. This may be where Ellis and Symonds differ most significantly: for Symonds, equality or "sameness" among "Greek" comrades produces a valorized British homosexuality in men; for Ellis, erotics between "the same" in women— European or "other"—are situational, not congenital. Congenital inversion described in his case studies of white women requires "difference" in the form of a masculine-feminine pairing. Ellis's attention to women breaks down any equation of homosocial and "true" homoerotic identities. His heterological theory makes same-sex pairings comprehensible in a cultural system that equates masculinity with sexual and social aggression, passion, and sex; whereas European females, almost by definition, must be asexual and disinterested in sex. Thus, whether cross-sex or same-sex, each Western couple comprises a so-called masculine aggressor and a passive, feminine partner.[35]

Havelock Ellis's account of the feminine partners of his white congenital inverts exposes a crack in the sexological logic of a gendered definition of inversion. The female sexual partner of the female congenital invert—the womanly or feminine homosexual—destroys the absolute minority position of the congenital invert, being neither masculine nor eventually heterosexual herself. To place this figure within his minority model of sexual inversion, Ellis must execute a series of tricky rhetorical gymnastics. "Womanly" inverts lack a specifically masculine character, yet they are not as feminine as "normal" women:

A class of women . . . in which homosexuality, while fairly distinct, is only slightly marked, is formed by the women to whom the actively inverted woman is most attracted. . . . They are not usually attractive to the average man, though to this rule there are many exceptions. Their faces may be plain or ill-made, but not seldom they possess good figures, a point which is apt to carry more weight with the inverted woman than beauty of face. Their sexual impulses are seldom well marked, but they are of strongly affectionate nature. . . . [They] are not well adopted for child-bearing, but who still possess many excellent qualities, and they are always womanly. . . . So far as they may be said to constitute a class, they seem to possess a genuine though not precisely sexual preference for women over men, and it is this coldness rather than a lack of charm which often renders men rather indifferent to them.[36]

Feminine inverts, then, are not masculine, but they lack necessary traits (beauty, childbearing capabilities, charm) to attract men and the force of a strong sexual drive to direct them toward men sexually. And although Ellis notes that such women possess a "genuine" preference for women, it is "not precisely sexual": "Their sexual impulses are seldom well marked." Feminine inverts are desexualized: they are distinguished from women who have sexual relations with women when men are not available to satisfy their normal sexual appetites; they are distinguished from congenital inverts by their passivity and unspecified sexual malaise, which, in a twist of logic, actually becomes a symptom of their deviance—itself a condition more often associated with a pathologically active female sex drive. Thus, the feminine invert, on the one hand, maintains the congenital invert's heterosexualized paradigm of desire, yet she points to the instability of medical classifications of women's desires, on the other hand. Although this cross-gender paradigm relies on a notion of women's naturally passive sexual position, the feminine sexual invert is distinguished from a "normal" woman almost solely on the basis of a diminished drive (her "sexual impulses are seldom well marked") and passive approach to sexual relations. In one sense, the feminine homosexual is both the epitome of white womanhood (passive) and the figure that disrupts that category entirely (homosexual).

Similarly, the feminine invert disrupts the clear equation of gender identity with sexual identity that Ellis constructs for the "true" inverts. An "absolute" or "congenital" invert retains a cross-gender desire even though she is coupled in a same-sex relation by virtue of her masculinity. The women who are attractive to these absolute inverts must, then, be "feminine." Yet, by Ellis's logic, such womanly women should "naturally" desire men. This presents a paradox for the sexologist, resolved by postulating that the sexual impulses of the congenital (masculine) invert's feminine sexual partner are necessarily dulled. This allows the feminine partner to retain erotics still grounded in a heterosexual scheme, which prevents her from sliding from the category of "deviant" into that of the completely fallen or hypersexual, feminine woman, exemplified by the prostitute. Ellis insistently differentiates between women who engage in homosexual activity and sexual inverts, arguing that because sexual inverts are congenitally disposed toward other women, they will not "become" normal. The class of Western European women to whom congenital, active inverts are attracted (and who respond to them sexually) threatens Ellis's core distinction: they appear normal, but do not behave normally, given the opportunity. This category of the feminine invert, the womanly woman who is sexually linked to the congenital invert, continued to plague medical attempts to represent female same-sex desire within a cross-sex paradigm in the twentieth century.

Ellis's distinction between situational and congenital homosexuality also mirrors the imperialist, racial hierarchy evident in his introductory sections. The "lower races" are fundamentally distinct from Western Europeans, just as the situational homosexual behaviors in which they engage are fundamentally different from the physiologically and psychologically distinct class of congenital inverts. Gay Wachman notes of the primitivism of early sexology that "the 'racial distance' of Polynesians and American Indians made speculation about their sexuality safe."[37] Distinguishing congenitally distanced homosexuals from the rest of the British population might have produced a similar sense of liberal "safety" in medial, as well as racial, distance. Yet these fundamental differences seem to undo themselves in Ellis's narrative and so must be actively maintained. Ellis's anthropological tour of homosexual behavior around the world must serve two functions: to universalize homosexual behaviors in men and women and also to distinguish situational from congenial homosexuality. Similarly, the feminine invert is a necessary component to Ellis's heterological classification of female sexual deviance (inversion) defined through gender inversion. In both cases, Ellis's structural distinctions are their own undoing only if culturally produced dualisms are allowed to be undone. Though the impulse of Ellis's work was reformist, socialist, and feminist, his founding text of British sexology rests not only in gender distinction but also in imperial taxonomies of racial difference.

Wilde's *Salomé*: "Daughter of Sodom"

Like Havelock Ellis's *Sexual Inversion,* Oscar Wilde's decadent play *Salomé* relies on a congruence of imperialist and sexological classifications.[38] Whereas Ellis produces sexual and gendered identities through detailed classifying systems and an enduring commitment to dualist erotic pairings, Wilde's play relies on decadent metaphor, tropes of the visual, and homoerotics produced through inference rather than classification. Like *Sexual Inversion,* however, *Salomé*'s sexual logic is produced through the representational politics of empire.

If Ellis wrote to bring British scholarship into dialogue with his German colleagues, Wilde wrote *Salomé* out of geopolitical, as well as cultural, antagonism. Written in France to be performed in England, *Salomé* was banned from the British stage in June 1892 because of its treatment of a biblical subject. Wilde responded by famously threatening to renounce his British citizenship if the play was not allowed in England.[39] The French version of *Salomé* was first published in France in 1893. Lord Alfred Douglas worked with Wilde on the English translation that was published, along with the original illustrations by Aubrey Beardsley, in England in 1894, though it would not be performed there for several more years, and was officially freed from British censure only in 1931. Even during its ban, however, *Salomé* remained a vital presence in elite discussions of women's sexuality, the rise of homosexual identities—both male and female—and the role of the person, play, or persona of Oscar Wilde in the British sexual modernity. As Regina Gagnier notes, "Had it been performed, a play like *Salomé* would have confronted Victorian audiences with a spectacle of purposelessness, 'unnatural,' unproductive, and uncensored art and desire."[40] In *Salomé,* Gagnier argues, Wilde intended to "confront Victorian audiences with their own sexuality. . . . Through the figure of Salome, he portrayed sex for sex's sake."[41] This discussion of Wilde's infamous play seeks not to recapitulate existing scholarship on the cultural and aesthetic implications of the erotics of the play but, rather, to point to the often-overlooked representational dependence of *Salomé* on a foundation of British empire in its presentation of sexual excesses, decadent subjectivity, and homoerotics.

Wilde's *Salomé* takes as its foundation the New Testament story (in Mark 6:14–29) of Herod's stepdaughter and the death of John the Baptist. Wilde's rendition of the story is set in King Herod's palace, in the shadow of the Roman Empire. Under a symbolist moon shining brightly over one evening's events, visitors to the court, as well as the king and queen's pages, observe the machinations of a lascivious Herod (also referred to as "the Tetrarch"), his tautly wound wife, Herodias, and Herodias's daughter, Salomé. Imprisoned at court is John the Baptist, called Jokanaan ("the Prophet,"), whose periodic ravings against the sexual and moral improprieties of the court worry Herod, offend Herodias, and entice Salomé. After Jokanaan repels Salomé's many advances toward him, Herod demands a dance from his stepdaughter. She dances on the condition that she receive a gift of whatever she requests from Herod, who readily promises her "even unto the half of my kingdom." Salomé then famously demands the death of Jokanaan so that she might obtain from his severed head the kiss that the prophet has denied her. After attempting to dissuade her by offering increasingly lavish gifts in exchange, Herod finally capitulates. Salomé receives her desired object on its silver charger and kisses its lips. The play ends with Herod's order to the executioner Naman, "a huge Negro," to kill Salomé herself.[42]

Wilde's play deals heavily in metaphor, and the plot serves primarily as a vehicle for the escalating relationships among the characters. Though Salome is unnamed in the New Testament itself,[43] her story was a common theme for European artists dating from the Middle Ages to the Renaissance and was, according to Jess Sully's detailed study of Wilde's predecessors, a favorite subject of other nineteenth-century decadent and symbolist writers contemporary to Wilde.[44] Already a story of family drama, religious maneuvering, murder, and women's power to manipulate men, Mark 6:14-29 in Wilde's treatment, alongside Beardsley's illustrations, is a representation of women's sensuality, erotic confusions, and perverse desires. These feminized powers intimidate kings and lead to the executions of both Salomé's love-object (Jokanaan) and Salomé herself.

The play takes place amid empire and political struggle. Herod is a puppet king, dependent on the support of Caesar; Jokanaan stands as a reminder of his moral and political volatility. Wilde alludes to the instability of Herod's throne late in the play but establishes early the context of empire and the fraught aggregation of various envoys, officials, and supplicants in Herod's palace. Salomé's second speech in the play, for example, describes the members of the feast within the palace, whom she has just left: "Within there are Jews from Jerusalem who are tearing each other in pieces over their foolish ceremonies, and barbarians who drink and drink, and spill their wine on the pavement, and Greeks from Smyrna with painted eyes and painted cheeks, and frizzed hair curled in columns, and Egyptians silent and subtle, with long nails of [jade] and russet cloaks, and Romans brutal and coarse, with their uncouth jargon. Ah! how I loathe the Romans!"[45] Listing Jews, Greeks, Egyptians, and Romans, this speech can be understood within its late nineteenth-century context as a litany of racialized national classifications. Salomé outlines physical and behavioral national characters of the political players within her country's (Roman) empire just as a nineteenth-century British anthropologist might recount the cultural and physical characteristics of various peoples under imperial rule. Indeed, the Roman Empire stood as a cautionary tale to late Victorians. Iveta Jusová reports that, "tending to compare their own imperial nation to the Roman Empire, nineteenth-century historians and writers warned ominously that the British Empire might follow its Roman predecessor and predicted its ultimate demise."[46] Wilde's *Salomé*, then, presents a compelling tableau of perverse desires within the context of decadence, symbolism, and the rise of male homosexual identities, all in a narrative setting predicated on anxieties about empire.

The play also opens with the scopophilic—with the erotics of the gaze in relation to Salomé and the visitors to Herod's court. Brad Bucknell remarks that "with . . . late nineteenth-century versions of the story, we witness the insertion of the gaze itself into the discourse, producing a kind of unconscious revelation of the power, and anxiety, of seeing Salome."[47] As soldiers, pages, and visiting Romans, Syrians, and Cappadocians stand outside the palace, they observe their hosts and speculate on the political situation as well as the fate of the bellowing prophet Jokanaan. The first line of the play belongs to the Young Syrian. "How beautiful is the Princess Salomé to-night," he comments. The Syrian's admiration not only establishes Salomé as a central erotic object but also sets in motion a jealous exchange with the Page of Herodias, who wants the Syrian's attentions for himself. "You look at her too much," the Page retorts. The Page then repeatedly warns against looking: "It is dangerous to look at people in such fashion. Something terrible may happen." The erotics between the Syrian and the Page come to a head after the Syrian kills himself as the Page cries out, "He has slain himself who was my friend! I gave him a little box of perfumes and ear-rings wrought with silver, and now he has killed himself!" Then a few lines later, the relation between the Syrian and the Page is refined beyond friendship: "He was my brother, and nearer to me than a brother." The Syrian is a gazer, but he is also simultaneously an object of homoerotic spectacle. Herod comments, "He was fair to look upon. He was even very fair. He had very languorous eyes. I remember that I saw that he looked languorously at Salomé. Truly, I thought he looked too much at her." Herodias's Page also remarks on the doubleness of the Syrian's sensual gaze: "He had much joy to gaze at himself in the river. I used to reproach him for that." The exchange between the Page and the Syrian establishes spectacle as a key element of the play, particularly a homoerotic gaze mediated through the force of Salomé's (initially absent) beauty. Once Salomé enters the stage, she is both the object of erotic gaze and an erotic spectator as well. Herod, as his wife repeatedly comments, gazes on Salomé "too much." Salomé's first speech similarly highlight's the Tetrarch's inappropriate gaze: "Why does the Tetrarch look at me all the while with his mole's eyes under his shaking eyelids? It is strange that the husband of my mother should look at me like that."[48] Herod's gaze is physically repulsive (he has "mole's eyes") as well as incestuous. Herod "looks too much," yet Salomé cannot staunch her own inappropriate gaze, just as she repeatedly cannot tear herself away from Jokanaan, another unwilling object of desire in the play. Sexual desire is forbidden, uncomfortable, and disastrous in this play, be it homoerotic, cross-generational, or heterosexual.

Wilde's Salomé expresses her erotic desire through metaphor and disavowal. When she first engages Jokanaan, the encounter is rhetorically produced through erotics. First Salomé demands, "I desire to speak with him," against the explicit orders of Herod. She circumvents Herod's orders through erotic manipulation of Narraboth, the Syrian—she smiles at him and promises to "let fall for thee a little flower, a little green flower." When Jokanaan appears onstage, he attempts to deflect her desiring gaze: "Who is this woman who is looking at me? I will not have her look at me. Wherefore doth she look at me with her golden eyes, under her gilded eyelids."

He then addresses her directly, connecting her gaze with sexual impropriety: "Daughter of Sodom, come not near me! But cover thy face with a veil." In retaliation, Salomé attempts to seduce Jokanaan through metaphors of the visual, insistently gazing at him despite his command to the contrary: "I am amorous of thy body, Jokanaan! Thy body is white like the lilies of a field that the mower hath never mowed. Thy body is white like the snows that lie on the mountains of Judaea. . . . The roses of the garden of the Queen of Arabia are not so white as thy body. Neither the roses of the garden of the Queen of Arabia, the garden of spices of the Queen of Arabia . . . There is nothing in the world so white as thy body. Suffer me to touch thy body." Here, using repetition and spatial metaphor, Salomé describes Jokanaan's body through registers of nature and empire: from her home in Judea to distant Arabia, from wild, untilled fields to cultured, planted gardens. Salomé describes her desire not just visually but through distinctive cartographical similes and metaphors of empire. Jokanaan's various body parts are "like the clusters of black grapes that hang from the vine-trees of Edom in the land of the Edomites, . . . like the cedars of Lebanon . . . a tower of ivory . . . a pomegranate cut in twain with a knife of ivory . . . the vermilion that the Moabites find in the mines of Moab, the vermilion that kings take from them . . . the bow of the King of the Persians, that is painted with vermilion, and it tipped with coral."[49] Salomé's desire is depicted as a map of areas within and adjacent to Judaea and the Roman Empire of the first century CE, and of the British Empire under Queen Victoria. The language of conquest and acquisition saturates Salomé's language here, a late Victorian reflection on an earlier empire. Thus, we see that the erotics of Wilde's *Salomé* depend, as does Ellis's sexology, on the cleavage of deviant sexuality to the rhetoric of empire.

Bourgeois Victorian culture "at home" is produced not only through rhetorical reliance on empire but also through the material trace of imperialism. Late Victorian "collections" are well-documented imperial projects, from the holdings of the British Museum to the drawing rooms of the ruling and middle classes. In *Salomé*, objects from the empire reflect the material trace of colonization at the heart of the empire. For example, note the importance of Salomé's request that the head of her beloved be brought to her "in a silver charger." This request for Jokanaan's head indicates not only the character's often-cited sadism but also the fetishization of the head as a collectible object to be displayed: Salomé wants not only to have Jokanaan killed but to possess him.[50] Jokanaan's head is just one of many possessions on display in *Salomé*. After Salomé's initial request, Herod attempts to dissuade her by offering her other, presumably more attractive or valuable rewards for her dance. His frantic attempts to bribe her reveal the spoils of empire as commodities amassed in the palace. Herod offers Salomé "the largest emerald in the whole world"; ". . . topazes, yellow as are the eyes of tigers . . . pink as the eyes of a wood-pigeon, and green topazes that are the eyes of cats"; and "onyxes like the eyeballs of a dead woman." When Salomé refuses these gems, Herod offers her tokens from the political reach of the Roman Empire: "The King of the Indies has but even now sent me four fans fashioned from the feathers of parrots, and the King of Numidia a garment of ostrich. . . . I have mantles that have been brought from the land of the Seres, and bracelets decked about with carbuncles and with jade that come from the city of Euphrates." Herod's Victorian collection indicates, on the one hand, his political power—kings from the Indies to Numidia want to ingratiate themselves at his court. On the other hand, these objects have no value to Salomé, who desires both revenge against Herod on behalf of her slandered mother and erotic authority over both Herod and Jokanaan. Herod's excesses of empire are both ubiquitous and futile in Wilde's narrative, but they are critical to the construction of Salomé as a desiring subject: in Salomé's refusing jewels, curiosities, and even the sacred "veil of the sanctuary" of the Temple in Jerusalem, her desires can be satisfied only by the suture of violence and erotics, when she kisses the lips of Jokanaan's severed head.[51]

At the conclusion of the play, the danger of the visual is repeated. After diagnosing Salomé as a "monstrous" being who has committed "a great crime," Herod declaims, "Put out the torches. I will not look at things, I will not suffer things to look at me. Put out the torches! Hide the moon! Hide the stars!" Salomé, like the head of Jokanaan, has become a thing that Herod no longer wants to see. The stage directions have Herod, before ordering Salomé's death (which ends the play), "turning round and seeing Salomé." In the course of the play, he has seen her too much, refuses to see her, and then finally reasserts his gaze and orders her death, seeing what he does not want to see. In her death, Salomé is positioned with the decadent East, the material trace of which she has rejected in favor of a pathologized sexual desire. Wilde's *Salomé* draws together the classifying gaze of the sexological and the scopophilic, the imperial collector and the curious object, the seer and the seen. Salomé's erotic subjectivity is predicated on empire as much as on erotics, and in this the play encompasses the tightly wound knot of self-styled radical sexual subjectivities in late nineteenth-century decadence.[52]

Victoria Cross: Daughter of Decadence?

The female New Woman writers of the 1890s and the male novelists associated with decadence are often paired together, either in sympathy or in opposition, both by their contemporary cultural critics and by literary scholars. Since Linda Dowling's 1979 watershed article on this topic, "The Decadent and the New Woman," feminist literary critics and historians of sexuality have struggled to pin down the elusive ideological relationships between New Woman writers such as Sarah Grand, Mona Craid, and George Egerton, and aesthetes and decadents such as Oscar Wilde. New Woman and male decadent writers were often published by the same presses,[53] satirized together in the pages of *Punch,* and attacked as a single unit by conservative cultural critics. As Ann Heilmann notes, "The New Woman writer and the [male] decadent artist seem perfectly complementary representations of the subversive politics of the *fin de siècle.* . . . Both provoked a fierce backlash from the conservative establishment; both became the target of satire. When Wilde was sentenced to two years hard labour, *Punch* celebrated the event as the death blow to Dandyism and New Womanism alike."[54]

But New Woman and decadent writers have also often been positioned against one another ideologically. Teresa Mangum suggests that Sarah Grand herself positioned New Woman writers in opposition to male decadents in her 1897 novel *The Beth Book,* countering "the 'art for art's sake' aesthetic of the 'stylists' . . . with the ethical aesthetics of the New Woman."[55] Ledger notes that, often explicitly or implicitly responding to charges of decadence, perversion, or degeneration, many New Woman writers were more aligned with a politics of social purity than sexual degeneration: "On the one hand she [the New Woman] was regarded as sexually transgressive, as heavily implicated in socialist politics, and as a force for change; on the other hand New Woman writers of the *fin de siècle* were usually (although not always) stalwart supporters of heterosexual marriage, they had little or no conception of female sexual desire (let alone lesbian sexual desire), and often had a considerable investment in eugenic and other imperialist discourses."[56] Whether through analogy, association, or antagonism, New Woman writers were bound to cultural fears regarding sexual perversion and moral decay. Like Wilde, they sought new rhetorical spaces beyond the confines of the Victorian novel's realist cultural plot. In her anthology of New Woman writings, *Daughters of Decadence,* Elaine Showalter argues that "women writers needed to rescue female sexuality from the decadents' images of romantically doomed prostitutes or devouring Venus flytraps, and represent female desire as a creative force of artistic imagination as well as in biological reproduction."[57] Rather than view New Woman writers in opposition to or as the "daughters" of their male compatriots, I hope to highlight the coinciding rhetoric between Wilde's *Salomé* and one example of New Woman writings to suggest a broader dependence on narratives of empire for the inscription of sexual liberties and libertines "at home."

The linkage between New Woman and decadent writers extends beyond either a dialectical relation or a shared status as agitators and instigators in late Victorian British culture. Common strategies of gender inversion and mutual engagements with the cultural politics of empire frame the terms through which these writers produce questions of sexuality, gender, and identity. In "Women in British Aestheticism and the Decadence," Regina Gagnier teases out the relations of decadent and New Woman authors to the questions of consumption and sexuality through an analysis of their gendered productive and reproductive frameworks.[58] She frames a New Woman eugenic project of racial motherhood in opposition to a male decadent, nonreproductive, sensual politics of sexuality: "The Decadent men wished to unravel and wear away their bodies in the pursuit of pleasure while the New Women shored up theirs as productive vessels."[59] This dichotomous reading is supported by the sexual and national politics of New Woman writers such as George Egerton and Sarah Grand.[60] Indeed, work on the imperialist politics of the New Woman writers reinforces not only the link between British women's liberation and the project of empire abroad but also the seemingly intractable link between reproduction and citizenship for bourgeois women of the 1890s. If we turn to the less-remembered New Woman writer Victoria Cross, however, her sexual and national politics appear to fall on the side of decadence rather than sexual purity or reproductive citizenship in Gagnier's formulation. No less dependent on the representational, economic, and political stakes of empire than, for example, Sarah Grand's *The Heavenly Twins,* Victoria Cross's story "Theodora: A Fragment" nonetheless illustrates the necessity of registers of imperialism for women's nonreproductive cosmopolitan nationalism as much as for a feminist subjectivity predicated on models of eugenic motherhood.[61]

Born Annie Sophie Cory in 1868, in Punjab, India, Victoria Cross (a pen name) was the Anglo-Indian daughter of a British military officer. Cross spent her childhood in India, passed at least a portion of her young adulthood in England, and, never marrying, traveled with her mother and uncle throughout Europe and the United States for much of her adult life. Cross wrote twenty-six novels, but "Theodora: A Fragment" was her first published story, and its controversial debut in the January 1895 issue of the avant-garde illustrated literary quarterly the *Yellow Book* secured her a place among notable New Woman writers. Unlike many of her colleagues, she was not apparently deeply enmeshed in the aesthetic scene in literary London, though "Theodora" did win her an epigram from Wilde, who speculated that "if one could only marry Thomas Hardy to Victoria Cross he might have gained some inkling of real passion."[62] The bulk of Cross's very briskly selling oeuvre consists of "erotic events in exotic settings";[63] specifically, several "Anglo-Indian romances, [in which] colonial India is reconfigured as a sexually liberating space for newly educated and adventurous English women seeking alternatives to traditional marriage and gender roles."[64] Even while challenging conventions of British literary realism and cultural conservatism, "Theodora" is as dependent on an imperialist logic for its sexual liberation as are more sexually conservative writings by other New Women writers occupied with maternity, rather than libertinism, as a route to female emancipation.[65]

Using gender inversion to signal a break from Victorian sexual and moral codes, "Theodora" relies on the language of medicine, decadent themes, and a colonial setting to produce a narrative ripe with sexual suggestions. When read in relation to Ellis's sexology and Wilde's *Salomé,* the story illustrates that both medical and literary productions of the fin de siècle rely on tropes of empire and structures of gender inversion through which to configure oppositional representations of female sexuality. Cross presents an important example of the stakes of empire for fin de siècle British feminism outside the realm of reproduction and maternity.

The plot of "Theodora" functions through the conditions of imperialism and is driven by thwarted erotic desires. The short story describes the erotic attraction between Cecil Ray, a male narrator, and the elusive Theodora Dudley. Framed by logistical impossibility, marriage between Theodora and Cecil is unlikely, given his financial limitations and a condition of her inheritance that discourages such a match. Like many sexological case histories, "Theodora" begins in the middle of its action, the morning after the two lovers meet. Cross's story is unlike most sexological case studies, however, in that gender deviance sparks a cross-sex, rather than same-sex, desire. The story spans two days: on the first day, Cecil calls on Theodora and, while exchanging sexually charged conversation, he invites her and her married sister (as chaperone) to his rooms to view his "curiosities" from his recent travels to "the East." The next day, at the second meeting, the display of the exotic objects culminates in a highly sexualized Theodora dressing in Cecil's "Eastern" clothes. The story ends with Theodora's exit after an impassioned kiss in the hallway, just a few days before Cecil departs (presumably alone) for Mesopotamia.[66]

Conditions of late nineteenth-century imperialism drive the story's plot. Cecil Ray, like other gentlemen of limited means, spends most of his time abroad in the empire, far from London. The action occurs just a few weeks before another departure, adding a sense of urgency and compression to his encounters with Theodora. Furthermore, Theodora elicits her invitation to Cecil's home by asking about his collections from his travels, after which he promises to show her "a good many idols and relics and curiosities of sorts." The erotic tension between the two builds as they play out their desire through a discussion of two foreign "idols" Cecil has collected: Theodora crowns with a ring from her own hand "a small, unutterably hideous, squat female figure," which Cecil describes as "the Hindu equivalent of the Greek Aphrodite." Cecil then places a statue of Shiva, "the god of self-denial," at Theodora's statue's feet in supplication. This exchange creates an erotic tension and intimacy between Cecil and Theodora, generated by the displacement of their forbidden desires for one another onto inanimate objects from the empire. Unlike Wilde's Salomé, whose desire is produced through her *renunciation* of certain spoils of empire, Theodora *leverages* empire to signal her desire. Erotics are produced, in "Theodora," through the material traces of imperialism.[67]

Cross reinforces Theodora's desirability through deviations from the conventional construction of the bourgeois Victorian "angel in the house." Theodora is quite unchastely a "hothouse gardenia" with "a dash of virility, a hint at dissipation, [and] a suggestion of a certain decorous looseness of morals and fastness of manners." In an exchange between Cecil and Theodora over the merits of sitting on either a couch or the floor—she prefers the floor, though it is "a trifle low," in order to avoid "the pain of falling"—Cecil remarks that "the ethics of the couch and the floor covered the ethics of life." Such banter reinforces Theodora's position as a woman of "loose" morals, yet this looseness does not compromise her position as a bourgeois "lady," in part because of her inherited wealth. This financial independence is predicated on sexual independence as well: Theodora will lose her inheritance if she marries, and so she must marry a wealthy man (Cecil is poor), remain chaste, or, as Cecil suggests, "forgo nothing but the ceremony."[68]

Cross also presents Theodora as a desiring subject by drawing her as a masculine woman in sexological terms. Theodora's features are continually described as beautiful yet masculine. Cecil observes, "I thought I had never seen such splendid shoulders combined with so slight a hip before." These masculine narrow hips and broad—though "splendid"—shoulders are written as far more erotic than a conventional women's physiognomy and echo Havelock Ellis's descriptions of female congenital inverts. Theodora's masculinity elicits Cecil's desire: he comments that he would not be nearly so interested in Theodora were she "the ordinary feminine type." Theodora's behavior is also inscribed as manlike: she insists on serving and mixing an alcoholic "peg" for Cecil rather than giving him the more decorous tea. Then, mixing the drink, "she looked . . . like a young fellow of nineteen . . . and there was a keen, subtle pleasure in this superficial familiarity with her that I had never felt with far prettier women."[69] Here, Cross inscribes heterosexual sexual desire through a suggestion of male homoerotics, as we also see in Wilde's *Salomé* through the erotic triangle of Herodias's Page, the Syrian, and Salomé.

Orientalism, as well as sexology, enables Theodora's erotics. Her heterosexual erotic masculinity escalates when she tries on Cecil's "Eastern" garments:

> She gave me the zouave and turned for me to put it on her. A glimpse of the back of her white neck, as she bent her head forward, a convulsion of her adorable shoulders as she drew on the jacket, and the zouave was fitted on. Two seconds perhaps, but my self-control wrapped round me had lost one of its skins. . . . She drew out a white fez . . . and then affecting an undulating gait, she walked over to the fire. "How do you like me in Eastern dress, Helen?" . . . Digby and I confessed afterwards to each other the impulse that moved us both to suggest it was not at all complete without the trousers. I did offer her a cigarette, to enhance the effect.[70]

Here, both the act of dressing Theodora in his own clothes and the visual effect of her cross-dressing causes Cecil to lose his thin veneer of self-control. The erotics of masculinity and the Orient create a powerful picture as Cross plays with female sexuality outside the parameters of nineteenth-century British, maternal citizenship. It is the potent combination of masculinity and the exotic that finally leads Cecil to lose control: the undifferentiated "East" produces both the conditions for desire and desire itself.

Whereas other New Woman writers rely on tropes of empire in opposition to their heroine's national identity and imperial, eugenic motherhood, Cross leverages the material traces and rhetorics of empire to write nonreproductive, heterosexual erotics for her English heroine. Theodora's eugenic unsuitability is philosophical and anatomical. Cecil muses that "Theodora was as unfitted, according to the philosopher's views, to become a co-worker with me in carrying out Nature's aim, as she was fitted to give me as an individual the strongest personal pleasure." For Cross's Cecil Ray, his eugenic "duty of the race" directly conflicts with his erotic desires. He comments several more times on Theodora's physical unsuitability for motherhood, alluding to her masculine frame and small breasts: "It was a breast with little suggestion of the duties or powers of Nature, but with infinite seduction for a lover." Like sexologist Ellis, Cross ties nervous tension to gender inversion—here a sign of desirability, not sexual deviance, and of passion, not procreation: "This passionate, sensitive frame, with its tensely-strung nerves and excitable pulses, promised the height of satisfaction to a lover. Surely to nature, [Theodora] promised a poor if possible mother, and a still poorer nurse." Cross produces the nonreproductive New Woman as erotic through her masculinity and her ties to empire, rather than through eugenic suitability or maternal instinct. Cecil's desire for Theodora is also distinctly "unnatural" because he feels a passion for her masculine body rather than a feminine maternal one. Marking his attraction as unnatural and transgressive, Cecil reflects: "My inclination towards Theodora could hardly be the simple, natural instinct, guided by natural selection, for then surely I would have been swayed towards some more womanly individual, some more vigorous and at the same time more feminine physique." Here, Cross diverges from sexologists like Ellis in the heterosexuality of the inverted woman. For Cross, a masculine woman can desire men; for Ellis, this is impossible—a masculine subject (male or female) should desire a feminine, not another masculine, object. Diverging from other New Woman writers who valorize maternity where Cross explicitly denounces it, Cross refuses to mitigate the erotics of her heroine through imperial motherhood, and instead produces an object of desire more in line with decadents such as Wilde.[71]

Like Wilde, Victoria Cross draws on the biblical story of Salome to produce nonnormative erotics in her narrative. When examining Cecil's collection, Theodora views his travel sketchbook, which contains pictures of his past lovers, including several beautiful male and female Sikhs and Persians. Not only are Cecil's portraits often ambiguously gendered, but also his relationships to his subjects are obscured, though always erotic. The first allusion to Salome appears when, looking through the sketchbook, Theodora asks Cecil, "Find me the head of a Persian, will you?" Like Salome in her request for the head of John the Baptist, Theodora demands an erotic object in the form of a disembodied head. Cross's allusions to Salome become explicit as Theodora and her sister prepare to leave Cecil's rooms near the end of the story. He offers each sister a curio from his collection, asking "if they thought there was anything worthy of their acceptance amongst these curiosities." When Theodora asks for Cecil's sketchbook and he demurs slightly, she replies with a faint smile, "Poor Herod with your daughter of Herodias. . . . Never mind, I will not take it." Cecil then insists that Theodora take this most prized possession, and, unlike Herod, he is rewarded not with the annihilation of his erotic object but with a passionate kiss. This Salome story ends with the "death" of Cecil's erotic ties to non-Western men and women and with an ignited passion between two orientalized British subjects.[72]

The fragment's final lines, however, foreclose a properly gendered and reproductive marriage plot. The story concludes not with the "moment of ecstasy" brought on by the couple's passionate embrace but in the quiet moment after Theodora leaves Cecil's quarters. Throughout the story, the heat of the tropics is favorably contrasted with the chill of London's winter. In the final lines of the story, Cross again contrasts cold and heat but replaces the heat of empire with Cecil's remembrance of the "kiss that burnt like the brand of hot iron on my lips." The empire becomes the erotic. Yet, this heat still on his lips, Cecil opens his doors "to [London's] snowy night" and, in the final line, "the white powder on the ledge crumbled and drifted in."[73]

Narratively a fragment that refuses to end in marriage, "Theodora" thus ends with the passion of empire cooled by the British winter. Cecil takes the feminized place in the domestic sphere as the masculine Theodora leaves in the night, though he himself will soon leave England for Mesopotamia. Departing from either Salome's end in death or an end of bourgeois marriage and eugenic motherhood, Cross's fiction can be read as subverting late

Victorian norms in its embrace of decadence and gender inversion. Such a celebratory reading runs the risk, however, of eliding the imperialist logic of Theodora's sexual freedoms or erasing the racial logic of narratives of inversion and decadence. It is crucial to read the story's dependence on orientalist tropes in the production of this sexually subversive, masculine New Woman.

Conclusion

Havelock Ellis's *Sexual Inversion,* Oscar Wilde's *Salomé,* and Victoria Cross's "Theodora: A Fragment" each generated strong critical reactions upon their publication. Both Ellis's and Wilde's works were banned in England; Cross's story was held as an example of "literary degeneration," and Wilde's connection to the *Yellow Book* (Cross's publisher) was in part responsible for the magazine's downfall after his arrest in 1895. Entwined by their interlocked receptions, these three texts also share rhetorical strategies in their production of female erotics and together mutually constitute emergent narratives of gender deviance in the service of sexual inversion. Scholarly work on these texts, following Foucault, often focuses on their use of medical or sexological categories to produce desire, but it is equally critical to read the structural and rhetorical force of British orientalism in their production of desiring bourgeois subjects.

Victoria Cross's story became a lightning rod for conservative critique of the overt sexuality of New Woman literature, and was held up as one of the most disgraceful examples of the "veritable plague of modern novels."[74] In "Sex and Modern Literature" (1895), B. A. Crackanthorpe decried the licentiousness of contemporary literature, specifically naming "Theodora." It is "revolting," he wrote, "that it should be possible for a girl to project herself into the mood of a man at one of his baser moments, faithfully identifying herself with the sequence of his sensations, as was done in a recent notable instance."[75] In addition to the erotic content of the story, the structural gender inversion in "Theodora"—the sexual ideas of a man (Cecil) inside the head of a woman (author Victoria Cross)—disturbed Crackanthorpe.

In another 1895 essay, "Literary Degenerates," Janet Hogarth decried the loss of morality to a worship of the science of psychology in contemporary literature by women. Citing "Theodora" as her primary example, Hogarth wrote, "If abnormal nerve excitement can be made to spell genius, what is to hinder every woman from obtaining the coveted distinction? . . . It is a little depressing that the ravings of lunacy should on the surface bear such a strong family likeness to what has hitherto been accepted as literature."[76] Hogarth critiqued cultural obsessions with sexological "abnormal nerve excitement" while simultaneously employing the language of psychology to dismiss the lunatics like Victoria Cross whose sexualized writings were the basis of their insanity. Evoking studies in female hysteria, Hogarth ended her piece with an appeal for Victorian morality to replace medical science as the social arbitrator: "Few people are without the germs of possible disease; but are the confused and morbid imaginings, which the sane hide in their breast, to be offered to the world at large as the discovery of a privileged few? To be silly and sinful is not necessarily singular. We commend this consideration to the authoress of *Theodora*."[77] Locating "Theodora" within the realm of pathology, Crackanthorpe and Hogarth participated in casting Victoria Cross as the infamous "woman whose novels were read behind locked doors; who [was] accused of poisoning the purity of British homes with her sordid writings."[78]

Perhaps akin to the widespread hand-wringing over New Woman writers in general, and Victoria Cross's promiscuous desiring subjects in particular, the ban on Oscar Wilde's *Salomé* can be said to have increased the play's purchase among English men and women seeking to transform the literary and cultural landscape of England in the 1890s. In *Oscar Wilde's Decorated Books,* Nicholas Frankel argues, "At a stroke . . . the 1892 censorship turned *Salomé* into what we would today call an avant-garde play, a negational play standing in opposition to the dominant cultural values of the day. Where prior to June 1892 there was at least a chance that *Salomé* would be read as continuous with certain strains in French literature and art, the censorship ensured that *Salomé* got reified into everything that opposed true 'Englishness.'"[79] From his hollow threat of exile over the production of *Salomé* to his role in the demise of the *Yellow Book*[80] to his soon-to-become-iconic status as the chief sodomite in England, Wilde's sexual and national politics were knitted tightly to the changing representational field of erotics at the turn of the century.

Standing apart as a disinterested scientific observer of emerging narratives of male homosexuality, female sexual "erotomania," and cultural degeneration, Havelock Ellis advocated for the decriminalization of male homosexuality and the classification of sexual inversion as psychological rather than moral or legal. His status as scientific expert did not, however, shield his own book from a difficult early publication history and censure in England. *Sexual Inversion* was first published in Germany in 1897, to generally positive reviews in the German medical press. Wilson and MacMillan published the first English edition shortly thereafter. As Jeffrey Weeks reports, however, "in the wake of the Wilde trial" the now-deceased Symonds's literary executor "bought up the whole edition and instructed that all references to Symonds be expunged from future editions." Thus, the second English edition was independently published and distributed by the Legitimation League, "a small society dedicated to sex reform," under Ellis's name alone. The secretary of the organization was charged, in October 1898, with selling "a certain lewd, wicked, bawdy, scandalous libel."[81] The Legitimation League settled the case and, as a result, all subsequent editions of Ellis's rapidly expanding *Studies in the Psychology of Sex* were published in the United States rather than in England. The first edition of *Sexual Inversion* discussed here had a quite limited circulation though a relatively wide impact, in part because of its censure. Lucy Bland reports that the volume "gave some publicity to homosexuality and lesbianism, not so much because of its circulation, which was minimal, but its prosecution the following year."[82]

On the one hand, *Sexual Inversion*'s censure generated welcome publicity for men and women seeking "expert" counsel to address their own erotic lives. Weeks reports that, following the text's censure, "hundreds of homosexual men and women wrote to Ellis, as they had earlier to Symonds, with their problems, their life-histories, information, and views."[83] On the other hand, historians of sexuality have been rather quick to read retroactively a widespread cultural acceptance and embrace of Ellis's models of sexual inversion: the mannish lesbian as congenital sexual invert, and the equation of gender deviance with sexual deviance.

Havelock Ellis wrote in 1897 that women's "modern movement of emancipation—the movement to obtain the same rights and duties, the same freedom and responsibility [as men] . . . carries with it certain disadvantages," including the "spurious imitation" of sexual inversion.[84] But the sexological equations of gender and sexual deviance were almost invisible in public debates over the status of women's citizenship. As the next chapter will illustrate, this sexological formulation did not impact in a widespread way popular debates about women's enfranchisement.

chapter 2

PUBLIC WOMEN, SOCIAL INVERSION: THE WOMEN'S SUFFRAGE DEBATES

These insurgent wild women . . . have not "bred true"—not according to the general lines on which the normal woman is constructed. There is in them a curious inversion of sex, which does not necessarily appear in the body, but is evident enough in the mind. Quite as disagreeable as the bearded chin, the bass voice, the flat chest, and lean hips of a woman who has physically failed in her rightful development, the unfeminine ways and works of the wild women of politics and morals are even worse for the world in which they live.

—ELIZA LYNN LINTON, "The Wild Women"

In 1891, Eliza Lynn Linton penned a vehemently antisuffrage article for the journal the *Nineteenth Century*. In this piece, she characterizes bourgeois women who leave the home and domestic sphere for the public sphere of politics as poor eugenic subjects. They have not "bred true" and they are "wild," masculine, and socially abnormal. Comparing the cultural masculinity of these public women with the physiological masculinity of "bearded" women and other sexological deviants, Linton defines suffragists, "the wild women of politics and morals," as not only unfeminine but also unnatural. Agitation for the vote indicates "a curious inversion of sex"—that is, gender inversion.[1] Such inversion may be the result of volitional deviance—that resulting from impure parental mixing—or of social Darwinist devolution. Yet, among all of her accusations of moral and developmental failure, Linton never accuses these inverted suffragists of homosexuality, nor does she explicitly discuss sexuality at all. Here gender inversion exists without sexual inversion, and the racial body politic will be preserved or destroyed through politics rather than procreation.[2]

The rhetoric of the women's suffrage debates demonstrates that turn-of-the-century female masculinity was not solely a sign of *sexual* deviance, as

31

sexologists would have us believe, but also a sign of *social* deviance and a challenge to the ideology of separate spheres. This chapter examines how debates over women's suffrage in Britain transformed turn-of-the-century notions of femininity and intersected in the production of modern sexuality for women by engaging with the terms of domestic, imperial, and national identities. I trace the fragmentation and partial dissolution of separate-spheres ideology as a dominant trope for bourgeois women by examining constructions of nation, gender, and sexuality within discursive battles over citizenship. The women's suffrage debates illustrate connections among nationalist and gendered ideologies of femininity. Furthermore, by the mid- and late twentieth century, readings of suffragist masculinity as female homosexuality misconstrued the role of masculinity in gender and sexual ideologies at the turn of the twentieth century. Geopolitics and sexuality were mutually produced in the British women's suffrage debates; and this mutual production set the stage for wartime and interwar reconfigurations of female sexuality through changing rhetorics of empire, nation, and identity.

The turn of the twentieth century saw cultural shifts over meanings of domesticity and the ideology of separate spheres. Women's agitation for full citizenship increased in several geopolitical locations while the British Empire first reached its zenith and then began to falter against anticolonial nationalist movements in the colonies. The politics of empire and gender equality came together under the sign of the "domestic." Amy Kaplan notes that "*domestic* has a double meaning that links the space of the familial household to that of the nation, by imagining both in opposition to everything outside the geographic and conceptual border of the home."[3] When suffragists and antisuffragists struggled over the proper roles of women and men in public life and the domestic sphere, they often engaged their debate through the terms of imperial power and proper racial and national, as well as familial, subject formations. Thus Linton characterizes the "wild women" of suffrage not only as sexologically inverted and culturally destructive women, but also as women who have not "bred true."

"Breeding"—that is, women's maternal functions—also figures prominently in discourses of separate spheres, suffrage, and empire. As Anna Davin and others have noted, bourgeois white women were seen as central to the population, defense, and ideological reproduction of the British Empire: "If the British population did not increase fast enough to fill the empty spaces of the empire, others would. . . . The birth rate then was a matter of national importance: population was power."[4] Not only was separate-spheres ideology critical to sustaining British gender ideologies, but also narratives of empire and nationalism positioned good British women as always mothers. Somewhat paradoxically, this model of imperial motherhood advocated for women's political duty as only domestic and (for the antisuffragists) resolutely "private."

In tension with emergent ideas of citizenship, nationhood, and identity were ideas of tradition and modernity. The rhetoric and activities of suffragists and their opponents shaped (in part) the change from "Victorian" to "modern" ideologies of sexuality and gender. Indeed, the rhetoric of the suffrage debates was much concerned with "the modern" (for those who advocated change) and "tradition" and "natural" roles (for those who opposed suffrage or tried to frame it within existing nineteenth-century ideologies). Suffrage women commandeered public space and the rhetoric of citizenship in their quest for the vote. In doing so, they redefined femininity, masculinity, and modernity, and created rhetorical spaces of emergent possibility for female sexual subjectivity divorced from domestic heterosexual monogamy.

This chapter analyzes the rhetoric of debates over women's suffrage from the 1890s through 1918, when some women were granted the parliamentary franchise in England.[5] Shifts in women's public roles corresponded to the changing representations of female sexuality and women's gender roles in the early twentieth century. The chapter focuses on various groups of suffrage agitators, and the ramifications of their rhetoric and actions on constructions of female gender or sexuality. Beginning with antisuffrage representations, I next examine moderate suffragists and then radical suffragettes, and conclude with a reading of Virginia Woolf's novel of Edwardian struggle, *Night and Day*.[6] I argue that debates over women's suffrage produced complexly feminine and masculine "public women"; that the "domestic" of the public/private dualism is always produced in reference or relation to that other dualism of domestic/imperial; and, finally, that such debates illustrate the historic and representational stakes of contests over citizenship, gender, and sexuality in the British public sphere.

Many historians of women's suffrage writing from the 1930s through the 1980s invoked lesbianism as a critical issue in turn-of-the-century debates over women's suffrage, often drawing analogies to the "lavender menace" of 1970s second-wave feminism. In 1935, for example, George Dangerfield's *The Strange Death of Liberal England* establishes the modern (prewar, militant) woman as one who, "through her new awareness of the possibilities of an abstract goal in life, was, in effect, suddenly aware of her long-neglected masculinity." He then describes the masculine militant suffragettes as comprising a movement of "pre-war lesbianism."[7] Like many other historians of suffrage writing from the 1930s through the 1990s, Dangerfield conflates the suffrage women's gender deviance with his own contemporary understanding of female homosexuality.[8] He illustrates that by the 1930s, a cultural linkage between gender and sexual deviance had solidified. Yet, as the rhetoric of the prewar women's suffrage debates themselves demonstrates, between 1890 and 1920 such a link, far from established, was in fact being forged in the charged arena of the public sphere.

This chapter challenges such anachronistic linkages between lesbianism and suffrage while still taking seriously the rhetoric that prompted historians to characterize suffrage women as homosexual. On the one hand, sexuality was of paramount importance in the rhetoric of suffrage debates, and deviant female sexuality, particularly, was a powerful force rhetorically harnessed by antisuffragists and responded to by suffrage advocates. On the other hand, I want to resist scholarly rewritings of gender transgressions as necessarily homosexual. Sexual deviance most often implied either excessive heterosexuality or frigidity. Lesbian readings of these texts reflect a mid- or late twentieth-century understanding of homosexuality but do not fully or necessarily characterize the relationship between gender and sexuality at the turn of the century. Concurrent discourses of sexology have been retroactively read as having a broad cultural purchase. Yet close readings of the entangled rhetorics of gender, sexuality, and nation in the suffrage debates indicate that the sexological formula of gender inversion as sexual inversion may have been more limited than historians of sexuality have sometimes assumed. Where sexologists lead us to expect lesbianism in masculine women in the prewar suffrage debates, we find citizenship instead. The representational space that the modern lesbian subject would occupy was being forged but was not clear or consistent during these years. It is the shaping of the representations of modern female sexuality, and, in particular in this chapter, the relationship of female sexuality both to the social functions of gender deviance and to the geopolitical consequences of nationalist rhetorics, that *Citizen, Invert, Queer* seeks to map.

Recent work on women's suffrage and the politics of empire highlights the conflicted and contradictory place of nationalism in the women's suffrage debates. Scholars illustrate the competing ideologies of imperialism and a liberal global feminism in the strategies, rhetorics, and alliances of the English suffragists with women in other parts of the British domain, from

Wales to India to Australia.[9] In the introduction to *Women's Suffrage in the British Empire,* editors Ian Christopher Fletcher, Laura E. Nym Mayhall, and Philippa Levine note that "the transnational forms of suffragism in the age of empire bear the marks of hierarchy as well as prefigure the future of what we have come to know as 'internationalism.'"[10] On the one hand, women's suffrage advocates promoted a liberal internationalism. On the other hand, suffrage women, seeking entry into the restricted realm of public citizenship, often tried to gain entrance through their disenfranchisement of other marginal classes: colonial men, black men, and working-class and immigrant women and men. In debates over enfranchisement, home rule, and party politics, imperialist ideologies underlay discourses of equity, liberalism, and domesticity. When we read these ideologies alongside of, rather than apart from, so-called domestic debates over sexuality, space, and femininity, the discursive and policy interconnections of imperial domesticity and a sexualized public emerge.

Gender Deviants and Sexual Deviance in Antisuffrage Rhetoric

Arguments opposing the vote for women mobilized sexual and gender difference to construct enfranchisement as a male domain. Antisuffrage women and men aligned women's positions as child bearers with social positions of child rearers. Citizenship was opposed to motherhood and equated with military and economic power. Women were deemed physically incapable of protecting the empire, giving rise to the "physical force" argument to render all women ineligible for citizenship and to reinscribe bourgeois women as mothers of the nation. Women's domain may extend from this biological reproductive imperative to a moral guardianship. For some antisuffragists, such a maternal role may extend to women a domain beyond their own children to include local social work or political involvement at a municipal level. In line with Victorian club work and social reform, antisuffragists argued that women's influence must remain cordoned off to social rather than political issues. From these premises came the broader, "positive" arguments of British antisuffrage that encouraged increased municipal voting and further education and social work for women.[11] The representational woman created in antisuffrage rhetoric embodied the contradictions of her creators and the changing conditions of her construction.

In 1889, "An Appeal against Female Suffrage" appeared in the British monthly the *Nineteenth Century.* Signed by 104 prominent women (including Virginia Woolf's mother, Mrs. Leslie Stephens), the appeal was drafted by Mrs. Humphry Ward, a popular writer of middlebrow Victorian novels and a well-known worker for women's education and social reforms. The appeal's opening salvo outlines the double terms of much antisuffrage rhetoric by coupling female participation in society with women's allegedly inherent limitations: "While desiring the fullest possible development of the powers, energies, and education of women, we believe that their work for the State, and their responsibilities towards it, must always differ essentially from those of men, and that therefore their share in the working of the State machinery should be different from that assigned to men." On the one hand, the appeal opens by asserting women's "powers, energies, and education," implying an active relationship of women to the state. On the other hand, the separate-spheres argument limits these powers by invoking "difference" as the fundamental characterization of the relationship between the roles of women and men. The figurative language in the section remains constant, as words such as *power, work, state,* and *machinery* resonate with images of industry and the public arena. This public rhetoric continues as the appeal outlines the "certain large departments of the national life [that] are of necessity worked exclusively by men." These departments include the "struggle of debate" in Parliament, the "hard and exhausting labor" of national administration, and the "heavy, laborious, fundamental industries of the State." In contrast, women "ought in some degree to have an influence on them all," but, the appeal regretfully reminds us, "in all of these spheres women's direct participation is made impossible either by the disabilities of sex, or by the strong formations of custom and habit resting ultimately upon physical difference, against which it is useless to contend."[12] This section highlights a tension between an essentialist politics of bodily difference through "disabilities of sex" and social constructions of "custom and habit." This dynamic tension resonates with concurrent social Darwinist ideologies that posited humans as active agents in the production of "natural" change. The use of the passive voice ("is made impossible," "against which it is useless to contend") reinforces an inevitability of a physical basis for separate spheres in an argument that would be expanded, refined, and repeated throughout the debates over women's suffrage.

Suffragists often seized upon the paradox that antisuffrage women argued for women's exclusively domestic position while actually doing a great deal of public work. The 1889 "Appeal" addresses this contradiction by drawing a firm line between "masculine" national politics and other, feminized forms of service to "the State." In a move that would be reasserted in 1908, at the formation of the Women's National Anti-suffrage League, female antisuffragists endorsed women's political participation on the municipal level by framing involvement in local governance as an extension of domestic duties, thus constituting local communities as autonomous social units divorced from the more athletic national government: "We are heartily in sympathy with all of the recent efforts which have been made to give women a more important part in those affairs of the community. . . . But we believe that the emancipating process has now reached the limits fixed by the physical constitution of women, and by the fundamental difference which must always exist between their main occupations and those of men."[13] In another context, Mrs. Ward dubs women's social work the "enlarged housekeeping of the nation."[14] Thus, elite women involved in cultural work outside their homes framed political involvement in such a way as to shore up "fundamental" differences between men and women based on physiognomy; to position their social work as acceptable feminine practice; and to further a conservative political and social agenda. Yet, in fact, these antisuffragists' public statements and activities transformed the very definition of femininity and domesticity that they hoped to shore up and protect.

Though public reaction to debates over women's suffrage ranged widely, images and arguments against it peppered the popular press, pamphlets, speeches, and cartoons in Britain. In London, the *Times* could be counted on to print letters from Mrs. Ward on the suffrage question, and *Punch* frequently weighed in on the apparent absurdities of the suffrage debates. The antisuffrage rhetoric and images in the popular press reflected cultural anxiety over the decline of separate spheres, a loss of femininity with gain of the vote, and the possible consequences of a coeducated electorate for Britain's position internationally and imperially. Arguments against women's suffrage coalesced around the "good," traditional woman, who did not need or want the vote, and a variety of frightening, "modern" apparitions who would abandon family, femininity, home, and nation to debase themselves at the ballot box or in the campaign for the vote. Representations depicted suffrage women as disrupters of normative gendered, sexual, and national identities predicated on often-hyperbolic idealizations of a coherent Victorian domesticity.

Many arguments against women's suffrage posited absolute divisions between men and women. Women who sought enfranchisement were decried as being masculine or as striving to be men. In her oft-quoted short book *Woman, or—Suffragette* (1907), antisuffragist Marie Corelli concisely stakes out this position: "With singular short-sightedness and obstinacy, the Suffragette seeks to be what Woman *naturally* is not" (emphasis in original). Violent militant suffragettes threaten not only their own femininity but the masculinity of men as well. Corelli describes the violent suffragette as "a nondescript creature who, while aping to be like a man, makes this attempted semblance of man ridiculous. No man cares to be libellously caricatured, and a masculine woman is nothing more than a libellous caricature of an effeminate man." For Corelli, gender deviance is the product of political and cultural displacement.[15]

The prosuffrage newspaper *Votes for Women* responded to such charges in November 1907:

> In the early days of the militant agitation opponents said that the leaders of our campaign were masculine women, and the cry was taken up by the public. . . . Pictures of women with short hair, billycock hats, and other articles of masculine attire were paraded as another argument against giving women the vote. . . . It is now known that this description was totally without foundation, in fact. The suffragette is essentially a feminine woman, with the full feminine grace and charm, and with the full feminine courtesy of manner. . . . But to the anti-suffragist, she is still masculine.[16]

To antisuffragists, suffragettes were masculine entirely because of their violent or advocative actions in the public sphere, not because of any sexual accusations or behaviors.

Behaviors or representations of men and women that threatened firm gendered roles and duties were said to destroy not only the women and men directly involved but British civilization itself, through corruption, sin, familial discord, or race suicide (the terms for destruction depended on the discourse being mobilized in any particular argument). Alluding to both a racial and a national threat from masculine women voters, Harold Owen's *Woman Adrift: A Statement of the Case against Suffragism* (1912) warned of a weakened England if women were given the vote:

> One ultimate consequence of this "liberation" would be the evolution of another type of woman than that of to-day. . . . Even to-day there is a new note of masculine strenuousness and assertiveness in woman as the result of her

freer movement in the world. . . . And side by side with this approximation to masculine characteristics there would be a corresponding decline of those traits which now we speak of as "womanly." . . . [Further,] a race of men born of several generations of mothers competing with men and each other in the struggle for life . . . and a race of men, moreover, who are no longer the protectors of women, but their rivals and "equals" is not likely to be a race of men that has altered for the better, judged by our standard of the qualities that constitute masculinity.

Owen links women's cultural masculinity with the racial weakening of English men and women of the future, a weakening resulting from "equality" in the "rough and tumble world of politics."[17]

Albert Venn Dicey made a related argument in 1909, in *Letters to a Friend on Votes for Women*. For Dicey, women's suffrage was disconnected from women's civic rights but was contingent on "whether the establishment of woman suffrage will be a benefit to England." He answers no to this question, on two central grounds. The first, more familiar terrain covers women's constitutional inaptness for politics. He then undertakes a lengthy exegesis of England's precarious international position:

In Ireland, we have resistance to the law which Ministers refuse to put down, and which may any day be transformed into organized sedition. The spirit of nationality is moving in Egypt. From India we hear of widespread conspiracy which might some day make armed revolt a possibility. Meanwhile grave questions are pending in Eastern Europe, whence an armed conflict may arise from which our honour and our interests may make it impossible for us to hold aloof. The very vastness of our Empire, and the envy with which it is regarded by other nations, provoke and expose us to attack. The necessary intricacy and entanglement of our foreign and colonial policy make it more than ever needful that the country should be guided by the cool head, the clear aim, and the tenacious purpose, which are to be found only in the strongest and most sagacious of men.

Dicey links the decline of the British Empire to the rise of modernity and gender equality. For Dicey, women are regretfully too "ignorant of statesmanship" and unschooled in "the most elementary principles of self-government or of loyal obedience to the laws of their native land" to be permitted the suffrage at such a politically precarious time.[18] We can read

Dicey's letter, further, as an indication of the necessary connection between the "domestic" and the "imperial" components of modernity, gender, and representation. Not only did the vote for women threaten women and men domestically (in the home and on the home front), but it also should not be permitted because of imperial unrest.

Thus, whether in reasoned statements or vehement tirades from men and from women opposing women's suffrage, rhetoric against masculine suffrage women cannot be read as diatribes against sexual deviance but must be understood as positions against deviation from gender codes aligned with broader nineteenth-century ideologies such as empire, racial purity, and separate spheres. The loss of domestic femininity of voting women lay at the root of several of the basic arguments of antisuffragists in Britain, yet the masculine female voter was but one of several figures in the rhetoric of opponents of women's suffrage.

Another prominent figure in antisuffrage rhetoric was the absent or bad mother. In a 1900 poster, titled "A Suffragette's Home," produced by the National League for Opposing Woman Suffrage, the votes-for-women campaign has literally stolen a wife and mother from her proper domain. The poster shows a man just home from "a hard day's work," as the caption indicates. But instead of being greeted with smiling children, supper on the table, and an appealing wife, he stands in the midst of crying children, a disordered room, and a note reading, "Back in an hour or so," attached to a "Votes for Women" poster on the wall. The absent mother-turned-suffragist has heartlessly disregarded the holes in her children's stockings, abandoned their care, and rejected the company of her husband. Suffrage, in other words, not only will inconvenience hapless husbands but will also destroy the domestic sphere.

Representations of suffragists as both undomestic and unfeminine, masculine women proved to be potent weapons. The twin specters of culturally masculine and domestically absent voting women symbolized the deterioration of gender norms and the dissolution of an enclosed domestic sphere.[19] These images are almost never sexualized in these representations, save for implicit anxiety about improper eugenic reproduction. Indeed, when a representative suffragist or voting woman *is* sexualized, she is most often either under- or over-*heterosexualized.*

Popular visual images of suffragists evoked failed or deviant heterosexuality as a way to both caricature and deride suffrage women. In England, "humorous" postcards depicting the arrests of militant suffragettes often

"A Suffragette's Home." Poster for the National League for Opposing Woman Suffrage, 1900. The Women's Library: London Metropolitan University.

"The Suffragettes." Postcard, Donald McGill. Reproduced in Lisa Tickner, *The Spectacle of Women*, 202.

portrayed suffragist women as oversexed and as receiving masochistic sexual satisfaction from being arrested. Two such cartoons, reproduced in Lisa Tickner's *The Spectacle of Women*, portray unattractive (though, it is critical to note, not masculine) suffragettes in the arms of robust, bemused constables. In one cartoon, titled "The Suffragettes," the large, round rump of a woman is seen on the shoulder of a struggling, oafish constable. One can see the back of the suffragette's hair and hat, her limbs sticking out all over, and one hand holding a "Votes for Women" sign. The caption reads, "Are we downhearted? NO!" The suffragette is out of control and, though rumpled, exuberantly exceeds parameters of traditional femininity.[20] The visual alone implies social deviance: the suffragette is not in her proper sphere, and the constable must remove her from the public arena. The postcard's caption, however, inserts a heterosexual narrative of erotic pleasure into her transgression, so that the figure now enjoys a forbidden sexuality of excess, rather than enduring the brutal violence of arrest.

A similar postcard depicts another robust, middle-aged suffragette in the arms of a more solemn constable who is clearly repelled by his load. In this cartoon, the physical position of the couple is sexual, suggesting that they could be walking over a marital threshold, but the background of a public square confirms that this is no scene of stable domesticity. This caption reads, "Slow march, constable, I'm having the time of my life!"[21] Here, both the visual and written texts sexualize and distort the physical violence that suffrage arrests actually entailed. The pose suggesting marriage both domesticates violence against suffrage protesters and sexualizes the suffragette.

Arrest was no joke for suffragettes: they were given long sentences and were often singled out for abuse by arresting officers as well as prison wardens. Arrested suffragettes refused food and were force-fed, a sadistic process that caused enormous pain and permanent physical harm. Tickner comments: "The more the militants took to violence, the more delighted was the Edwardian judiciary, its police force and prison officers to deliver the hiding they believed was deserved. But they could not do so without invoking the specter of female martyrdom. Humorous postcards defused the issue by domesticating it. The militant became the little girl in tantrum; the middle-class woman encountered the rough embrace of the law; and the harridan got—or sought—her just deserts."[22] These humorous postcards not only defused suffrage women's political actions in the public sphere, but they did so by constructing suffrage women as heterosexual deviants: undersexed, overexcited, or sexually bereft women.

Slow march, constable, I'm having the time of my life!

"Slow march, constable, I'm having the time of my life!" Postcard, Bamforth and Co., postmarked 1916. Reproduced in Lisa Tickner, *The Spectacle of Women*, 202.

The sexually bereft spinster also appeared in England's *Punch*. In a cartoon published on June 4, 1913, the satirist comments on the rash of arson attacks perpetrated by suffragettes. A bedraggled middle-aged woman sits before her hearth, unable to light a fire to warm the teakettle that sits to the side. The caption reads, "Militant Suffragist (after long and futile efforts to light a fire for her tea-kettle). 'And to think that only yesterday I burnt two pavilions and a church!'"[23] The joke is clear: the woman can fulfill her desires in the public sphere (where they are illegal and misplaced), yet she is not in control of woman's proper domain, the hearth. The cartoon's visual clues mark this suffragist as unmarried: in the room where she sits before the fireplace, tea things rest on an upended crate, and a faintly visible piece of furniture in the background appears to be a bed, not a couch—this suffragist lives in a studio, not a house. Furthermore, if this woman had a husband, the cartoon implies, she would not have to either literally or figuratively "light her own fire." As it is, the unattractive, soot-covered

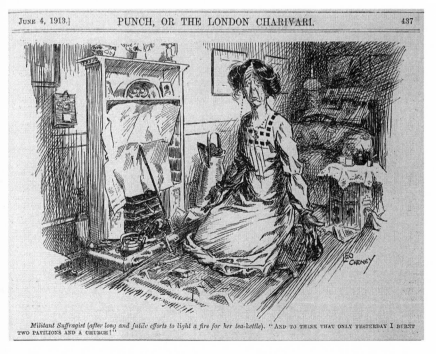

JUNE 4, 1913.]   PUNCH, OR THE LONDON CHARIVARI.   437

Militant Suffragist (after long and futile efforts to light a fire for her tea-kettle). "AND TO THINK THAT ONLY YESTERDAY I BURNT TWO PAVILIONS AND A CHURCH!"

"Militant Suffragist (after long and futile efforts to light a fire for her tea-kettle)." Cartoon in *Punch*, June 4, 1913, 437.

suffragist sitting before the cold fire in a modest nightgown lacks traditional feminine skills after having acquired socially unacceptable masculine
ones; she is an inept, frustrated spinster. Just as suffrage can yield an absent
wife and mother, so too, its detractors warn here, can it produce failed
heterosexuality.

Suffragist Evelyn Sharp's short sketch "Filling the War Chest" illustrates an
emergent possibility of same-sex erotics. This piece, originally published in
the suffrage press and then reprinted in Sharp's collection *Rebel Women*, twists
typical antisuffragist configurations of suffrage women's sexuality. It describes
a suffragist selling papers on the streets of London. When asked why she is
willing to stand "in the gutter" to sell her papers, the narrator reflects: "The
elderly gentleman who sold the penny Conservative paper knew why we
were doing it. . . . 'Doin' it to git theirselves 'usbands, that's what they're
doin' it for,' he would say conclusively, in denial of the usual contention of
the anti-suffragists, that we were doing it because of our distaste for husbands."[24] This vignette draws together the two earlier characterizations of
suffrage women's sexual desire: on the one hand, the postcards gathered by
Tickner suggest that suffragists presented themselves for public display and
(literal) manhandling because they had heterosexual desires that could not be
fulfilled by normative means of courtship and domesticity. Thus, as the "old
gentleman" in Sharp's sketch comments, suffragists must stand in the street
to "get 'usbands." On the other hand, Sharp herself presents the corollary
(and opposite) scenario: the "usual contention of the anti-suffragists" that
suffrage women, in their social and sexual deviance, *do not want* husbands,
do not desire men. This second scenario suggests three possible readings:
one alludes to the absent mother, who is in the street rather than at home
with a husband and children. A second reading presents the suffragist as
"man-hating" or frigid. The third possibility, legible only through inference,
is that if the paper seller does not desire men, she may desire women. This
suggestion points to emergent cultural possibilities for women's same-sex
sexuality as it begins to stand apart from domestic reproduction.

Representations of suffragists contained charges that all women who
wanted the vote must have oversexed, undersexed, or possibly same-sexed
desires. That suffrage activities prompted such diverse and contradictory
charges of deviant sexuality indicates both the disruption that such public
women produced culturally and the volatile and shifting representations
of female sexual possibilities. Pro- and antisuffrage links between political
agitation and sexuality constructed new representations of female desire

in the rapidly changing sexual culture of Britain in the first decades of the twentieth century. Residual configurations of bourgeois women as asexual mothers gave way to a dominant emphasis on women's domestic hetero-sexual desire. Antisuffragists twisted this desire by removing it from the domestic to the public sphere and by exaggerating or stifling it.

Womanly Women: Suffrage Reassertion of Traditional Gender and Sexual Roles

The "womanly woman" became one of the suffragists' strongest counters to popular depictions of masculine and over- or undersexed suffragists. Suffragists mobilized a continually renegotiated figure of the womanly woman to assure society that suffrage would not, in fact, destroy women's domestic desires. Militant and moderate suffragists alike insisted that all suffragist women should appear as physically feminine in dress as possible to mitigate or complicate the perceived masculinity of their claim for entry into politics and their unfeminine actions (be they lobbying, speaking in public, or committing arson) while pursuing such claims. The definition of "womanly" changed continually, however, in part because of the very same simultaneous insistence on femininity and public activism of the suffragists (and antisuffragists).

In the tradition of nineteenth-century women's organizations that positioned social reform as a domestic duty, many moderate suffrage organizations set out to equate suffrage advocacy with other domestic reforms, such as temperance, education, or hygiene. Alongside such advocacy came a caution from moderate suffragist leaders, in response to antisuffrage critics, not to neglect domestic duties while engaged in feminized reform movements outside the home. A common moderate rhetorical strategy argued for women's special position within the electorate as well as within the family. An editorial in the inaugural issue (April 15, 1909) of *Common Cause,* the organ of the moderate British National Union of Women's Suffrage Societies (NUWSS), sets out these terms: "It is this notion that women's suffrage means the breaking up of the home, the causing of domestic strife, the setting of woman against man that the very name of this paper is intended to deny. We hold that the liberation of women is the cause which good and intelligent men and . . . women have in common . . . and this because when you have freed women, you have given them scope to develop themselves and to protect their young, so that the cause of woman is also the cause of the man and of the child." This editorial develops the theme that political process is the concern of both men and women, but for different reasons: women need to vote to fully *protect* their children, not because they wish to abandon them. This piece repeatedly emphasizes women's maternity: "It is also the demand that the mother-half of humanity should be given its proper place."[25] Women generally, and suffragists specifically, are positioned as protective mothers who have a unique contribution to make to the nation, and who can do so most effectively with the vote. Historian Michelle Tusan summarizes: "*Common Cause* appropriated the ideology of motherhood and reform politics first articulated in the women's press during the New Woman debate in order to advance women's status as legitimate political subjects. The type of female activist cultivated in the pages of *Common Cause* remained the ultimate respectable radical: a public woman who claimed her place as a political actor on the basis of her private role as wife and mother."[26] Moderate suffragists sought, in the pages of their periodicals, on the streets, and in their meetings, to visually and textually reconcile motherhood and domesticity with citizenship. In doing so, they participated in their public resignification.

Maintaining a rhetoric committed to a domestic sphere proved a relatively successful strategy for moderate suffragists. The public sphere was not ideologically forbidden to them, as it was to antisuffragists. Suffragist domesticity encompassed the nation as well as the nursery. Moderates wrote numerous letters to newspapers, spoke in public, and amassed in elaborate parades designed to illustrate the existing support for "the Cause," as well as to draw more followers. In these public forums, the balance between suffragists' claims for equality and a continual emphasis on sanctioned feminine appearance, contained sexuality, and equitable rhetoric emphasized the tricky ideological and strategic lines of their arguments. In its most basic form, an argument for women's suffrage was an argument for gender equality. Yet, to diffuse the threat of radical equality in a culture that cherished notions of the "natural" distinctions between men and women, domestic femininity became one of the NUWSS's stock tropes.[27]

But this was not the only construction of femininity that the moderates advanced. Much of British moderates' publicity between 1906 and 1914 focused on distinguishing themselves from the militant Women's Social and Political Union (WSPU). Not only was the moderate "womanly woman" maternal and attentive to her family, but she also was a logical, rational creature who could engage in the existing political establishment rather than disrupt and destroy it (as the moderates argued militant tactics did).[28] Moderate suffragists argued that a modern femininity already existed, so that their work to gain the vote was the completion, not the beginning, of a metamorphosis for women. As Millicent Garrett Fawcett, president of the NUWSS, wrote to the *Times* on June 6, 1910, "We maintain that the changes which have already taken place in the social and industrial position of women in this country call for a corresponding change in their political *status*" (emphasis in original).[29] To that end, moderates emphasized the injustices to women who were already working and earning but could not vote as men could.

The NUWSS emphasized the conditions of womanly women as unenfranchised, feminine participants in the public sphere and affairs of state. As the January 5, 1911, cover of *Common Cause* depicts, some women had already been thrown against their will into the masculine public realm, yet they were denied a voice in the workings of the state. The image features a young working-class widow surrounded by three children and sheltering an infant in one arm. Labeled both a "bread-winner" and "tax-payer," she is not, in contrast to men in the same position, a voter. The cartoon implies that a masculine unity between the state and civil realms of the public sphere (the linkage of "bread-winner" and "tax-payer") cleaves apart, for women, where they have relative access (by necessity, here) to the civil sphere of labor and limited relation to the state via the payment of taxes, but not a democratically reciprocal relation with a vote. This argument is implicit rather than explicit in the image and is produced through the combination of a stark line drawing and bold type. The cover frames this call for equity as a correction, not as a transformation of existing roles for women, and visually serves as a rejoinder to the antisuffrage image of the absent suffragette. This widow is neither invisible nor masculine nor sexualized: she reminds readers of the failure of the state to either protect or enfranchise vulnerable, working women. That the woman is a widow presents an image of conservatism with a message of reform.

Furthering this mix of conservative social images and reformist politics, suffragists carefully presented a traditionally feminine face (and fashion) in public. In response to images of the unfeminine suffragist, suffrage periodicals frequently included notes about dress and sketches devoted to debunking the myth of the ugly suffragists. Here is a sketch titled "In the Tube," from *Votes for Women* on November 11, 1910:

VOL. II. No. 91. Registered as a Newspaper. JANUARY 5. 1911. ONE PENNY.

"Bread-Winner, Tax-Payer: Why Not Voter?" Cover illustration of *Common Cause,* January 5, 1911.

FIRST LADY. Yes I think she must be a Suffragette, or at least she looks like
one.

SECOND LADY. (smiling). But why?

FIRST LADY. Because she is so badly dressed!

Uncomfortable pause, while a rather smartly-dressed lady sitting opposite loosens her furs so as to show her "Votes for Women" button![30]

This dialogue simultaneously airs the stereotype of the badly dressed suffragette, refutes it, and provides an object lesson: be a smart dresser (and keep
your "Votes for Women" button handy) so that you, too, can educate the
public *without saying a word*. The "rather smartly-dressed lady" illustrates
successful navigation of changing definitions of public and private roles.
She does not put her good taste or proper behavior in jeopardy in the public realm (the subway, or "tube") or in "private" matters (loosening, but not
losing, her furs) by being a suffragist—merely being a lady and a suffragist
is activism, the sketch implies. Through a different medium but with similar intent, *Votes for Women* carried, for a few issues, a fashion column that
discussed how to dress smartly on a budget and where to buy good-quality
furs. Fashion, the paper told its readers, was a suffragist concern. Fashion,
we can discern, exemplified a successful suffrage navigation of the paradox
of women's transforming public identities.

The British Actresses' Franchise League (AFL) was a crucial part of the
English suffrage movement, not only because of the funds that its plays
and public appearances raised but also because its members represented a
familiar form of public femininity and even familiar faces to the theatergo-
ing public. By the early twentieth century, actresses were popular and relatively acceptable public women; their presence at suffrage events and parades
helped to neutralize anxiety produced by bourgeois women taking to the
streets.[31] Further, as Claire Hirshfield notes, "the beauty and popularity of
[AFL] members help[ed] to offset the widespread stereotype of the suffragette as mannish, unsexed, and physically unattractive. Ironically, the very
newspapers which regularly denounced suffragettes as 'cranks,' invariably
gushed over actresses as 'charming franchisettes.'"[32] The endearing "fran-
chisette" replaced the "crank," counterbalancing stereotypes of suffragists
as both "unsexed" and "mannish."

Because a "public woman" was, by Victorian standards, a prostitute by
definition, when suffragists took to the streets they took particular care
to project respectable—that is, invisible or asexual—bourgeois sexuality.

Suffragists used clothing in particular to signal simultaneously social defiance and adherence to conventions of respectable femininity. The leadership of suffrage organizations encouraged all of their members to dress in modest yet feminine clothing to present a visual image of conservative, safe feminine sexuality, particularly when marching or speaking in public. They would thereby violate one of the central tenets of separate-sphere ideology: that respectable (middle-class) women should remain in the private, not public, sphere. For example, the colors one wore on one's modest and feminine clothes signified the particular organization to which one belonged, and the white dresses worn in public marches and parades not only created a "clean" visual picture, which showed off the elaborate banners to their fullest, but also evoked images of purity and virginity. Clothing that signaled sexual purity asserted normative gender identification and sexual containment. By using their bodies and clothing as texts in public parades, suffragists hoped simultaneously to feminize and to publicize their desire for the franchise rather than let that desire further fears of female masculinity or excessive sexuality.

Moderate suffragists sought a redefinition of femininity that mandated the vote for women; they refuted charges of deviance by adhering to sexual conventions; and they strove to disengage sexual desire from suffrage while they reinforced traditional domestic femininity. Drawing on national as well as familial registers of "domestic policy," moderate suffragists sought to gain citizenship through transforming, rather than rejecting, gendered codes. The moderate argument for equity in the national body rested on their discursive adherence to gender difference. Such arguments transformed the "difference" of gender, while it reified racial and sexual norms.

"This New Day": Militant Reformulations

The actions of militant suffragettes radically reconfigured what "femininity" and "citizenship" meant for early twentieth-century culture. Yet, as we have seen, in the midst of this rebellion against the restrictions of old meanings of womanhood, there was an adherence to traditional definitions of female sexuality. In this section, I read and reconcile the apparent juxtaposition of the militants' use of conservative sexual codes and rhetoric, with their radical and transgressive actions. The militants consistently exceeded the boundaries of womanhood, first by appearing in the traditionally masculine public spaces at public meetings (just as moderates did), then by disrupting such meetings, and finally by taking up violent and destructive strategies expected less of female reformers than of male revolutionaries such as the contemporary Irish advocates of home rule or unionism. In juxtaposition with that of moderate suffragists, the militant suffragettes' platform advocated action over advocacy—as their slogan expressed it, "deeds, not words." This campaign of "deeds" included, over a span of ten years, the willful destruction of property through arson, rock throwing, golfcourse bleaching, mass window breaking, destruction of art in museums, smaller acts of sabotage (including dumping ink in public postboxes), personal bodily sacrifice through protest in the street, attempts to force their way into the House of Commons to see the prime minister, the sacrifice of individual lives following hunger and thirst strikes in prison, and the singular case of Emily Wilding Davison, who died after throwing herself in front of the king's horse at Derby Day on May 31, 1913.

Feminist scholars have analyzed the deeds of the militants by positioning their actions in opposition to separate-sphere ideology, arguing that the move to "masculine" action in the public sphere violated cultural norms of bourgeois femininity.[33] And indeed, the moderate suffragists objected to militant tactics precisely on the grounds that the militants gave women a bad name and simply proved to the male public that women were hysterical (hyperfeminine, hypersexual) creatures not rational enough for the responsibilities of full citizenship.[34]

The rhetoric (that is, the words, not the deeds) of the militant suffragettes complicates a reading of militant suffrage actions as divorced from nineteenth-century sexual and social conventions. Rhetoric found in militant speeches, tracts, and periodicals mediated suffragette violations of standards of feminine behavior through adherence to nationalist constructions of citizenship and through transformation of familiar registers (such as spirituality, medicine, and social purity) usually aligned *with* traditional Victorian gender and sexual ideologies. In the process, political reform wedded social revision through narratives of female sexuality. These representations transformed conservative discourses so that they worked against a reification of separate-spheres ideology and attendant female sexuality.

Similarly, militants sought to sustain a suffragist femininity by emphasizing femininity alongside the rhetoric of violence and war. Between 1906 and 1914, militant suffragettes declared war *against* the British government; from 1914 through 1918, they waged war *with* the British government. In both cases, they staked a claim to military tactics through feminized registers. Like the moderates, militant suffragettes had to navigate their exclusion from English citizenship strategically and discursively. Unlike the moderates, militants aligned themselves with a tradition of radical dissent rather than liberal reform. Laura E. Nym Mayhall notes of the militants, "They likened their fight to great emancipation struggles of the past, including the abolition of slavery, repeal of the Corn Laws, and Chartist agitation. . . . While suffragettes' protests challenged the authority of British institutions of government, they did not seek to restructure British society fundamentally."[35] The militants' representational challenge was to align themselves with histories of radical (male) British revolutionaries, and simultaneously to feminize their militancy as particular to "women's" struggle.

Militant suffragettes aligned their battle with those of radical men through strategic political coalitions and through discursive comparison and juxtaposition. Eschewing English "party politics" (thereby distinguishing themselves from the moderate suffragists, who were often in dialogue, if not in league, with the Liberals), militants vowed to target any and all British politicians who opposed women's enfranchisement and to support any and all in favor. This led, as historian Ian Christopher Fletcher reports, to many "doomed" alliances, particularly surrounding the question of Irish home rule.[36]

The militant suffragettes' relation to the Irish question was twofold: on the one hand, suffragettes insulted or courted Irish politicians, depending on their position on women's enfranchisement. On the other hand, the increasingly militant actions of both the radical Orangemen in the north and the agitators in favor of home rule in the south invited points of comparison with the actions and goals of militant suffragettes in England. In 1912, when the Ulster Unionists vowed to support enfranchisement of women in Northern Ireland, "the WSPU greeted the news that women's suffrage was included in the draft constitution for a provisional government in Ulster by taking all the credit and promising to support Unionists in return." This support for the inclusion of Ireland in Great Britain implicitly rested on discourses of race and nation in the suffrage rhetoric: "As if to underline Ulster's advanced position, *The Suffragette* made an invidious comparison between two decisions in British boroughs, one to deny the municipal vote to the English widow of a foreigner, and the other to register Peter Labengula, a son of the Ndebele king and a well-known black Edwardian."[37] The *Suffragette* positioned Ulster (Northern Ireland) as a site of advancement through its inclusion of women and its exclusion of blacks in their (still hypothetical) Ulster polity. Yet, a short two years later, the alliance between the British militant suffragettes and the Ulster Unionists shattered.

In May 1914, just a few months before the outbreak of the Great War, suffragettes raged at the inequitable treatment by the English government of violent protests by male Irish agitators and female suffrage militants. The May 1 cover of the *Suffragette* featured a bold headline, devoid of the usual cartoon or photograph: "ARREST Bonar Law and Carson!" Bonar Law and Edward Carson, leaders of the Ulster Unionists, were viewed as the instigators of recent violent Unionist protest against the debate over a home rule bill in the British House of Commons. The *Suffragette* editorial bitterly complained: "When women are militant, the cry is that the Government cannot do justice in response to such methods; but when Unionists commit 'grave and unprecedented' outrages, concession, and surrender are the Government's first—and, it would seem, their only answer. . . . If there is to be coercion for militant women, there must be coercion for militant men. If, on the other hand, there is to be concession for militant men, there must be concession for militant women."[38] Here, militant suffragettes drew a parallel between the actions of militant Unionist men and themselves, calling for the arrest of Law and Carson as equitable treatment to the arrest of their Mrs. Pankhurst. This rhetoric of gender equity demanded equal treatment of men and women and also placed the actions of the militant suffragettes in a context of political battle, rather than one of vandalism, hysteria, or other "domestic" unrest.

Alongside calls for gender equity, suffragettes continued to locate their violent actions within a framework of gender difference. Militant femininity invoked feminine spiritual registers to mediate public actions that resembled those of violent male revolutionaries. In this process, suffragists transformed the definitions of femininity and masculinity.

Between 1910 and 1914, the journals of the militant wing began to invoke frequently a "spiritual war" to be waged and won. Christabel Pankhurst was increasingly aligned with Joan of Arc as a symbol of female spiritual militancy. Pankhurst would appear in suffrage parades dressed as Joan of Arc, and her image was often superimposed over Joan's on the cover of the *Suffragette*.[39] Though Joan of Arc is now often considered a gender deviant or a cross-dresser, the Pankhursts chose her image as the sign of a sacred and independent feminine warrior in battle for the good against a gender-biased state. Through such imagery, suffragette leadership produced a visual connection to a history of radical women, they justified militant action as militarily necessary, they feminized the restructuring of gender codes, and they shored up their rebellion as a spiritual as well as a political matter.[40]

Militant suffragettes further reconfigured gender through attacks on male sexuality and valorizations of female chastity. By 1913, the rhetoric of sexual purity had joined that of spirituality in the English militant suffrage press.[41] An agitation for political enfranchisement may seem quite removed from a campaign for sexual purity, yet Christabel Pankhurst connected the two, both to demonstrate women's possible "special" or "different" contributions to the body politic and to reverse the typical conflation of women's bodies with sex and disease and men's with an asexual, disembodied "politics." First published as a series of articles in the *Suffragette,* Pankhurst's book *The Great Scourge and How to End It* argued that an epidemic of venereal disease in British men (she claimed that 75 to 80 percent of British men were infected with syphilis or gonorrhea) could be defeated only by enfranchised women. Here one of the most striking militant slogans, "Votes for Women, Chastity for Men," was born. For critics, this slogan signaled militant separatism and an argument for radical difference. It was cited by both Pankhurst's contemporaries and historians as an incitement to "sex war" and as a wholly outrageous tactic adopted by a man-hating spinster.

However, *The Great Scourge* is not, as Jane Marcus's introduction to the piece suggests, "a deliberate political choice to exacerbate *difference,* to conduct the suffragette movement as a sex-war against the enemy, men" (emphasis in original).[42] Rather, Pankhurst frames the piece as an appeal for equality: she defines chastity for men as "their observance of the same moral standard as is observed by women."[43] Through this appeal for equal standards of sexual behavior for men and women, Pankhurst inverted nineteenth-century medical discourse and posited a definition of modern womanhood predicated on "spiritual, political, and social" emancipation. Unlike her moderate colleagues, Christabel Pankhurst enthusiastically linked sexuality to political reform; *The Great Scourge* revises definitions of sexuality, masculinity, and femininity through a discussion of sexual, rather than political or social, behavior. She argues that female enfranchisement is vital to the sexual, as well as social, health of individual men and women and thus to the survival of England itself.

The Great Scourge appropriates two distinct discourses: social-purity writing and the medical discourse that "by the late 1910s . . . dominated the logic of much of the anti-suffrage sentiment that appeared in the editorials and letters of newspapers like the *Times.*"[44] Pankhurst seizes the narrative of social purity yet drops its "melodramatic narratives" in favor of the register of medicine.[45] She quotes medical "experts" to bolster her argument that venereal disease ran rampant through the male population of England, and she interweaves recitations of symptoms and proof of the inability to cure syphilis and gonorrhea with assertions that only the enfranchisement of women would force a moral and sexual change among English men: "The only people who dare face this evil of gonorrhoea and the only people who can overthrow it are women. When women acquire the necessary influence, political and social, they will have it in their power to convince men that to live cleanly or be cast out from the society of decent women are the alternatives open to them." A physical condition becomes a moral evil that cannot be cured medicinally but must be rectified by "influence, political and social." Women, Pankhurst argues, are not superior to men but, rather, have already achieved the state of moral (sexual) purity to which men must now subscribe. She rejects the argument for difference that positions women as a spiritually superior class; she argues that a suffragist position is one of radical equality:

According to man-made morality, a woman who is immoral is a "fallen" woman and is unfit for respectable society, while an immoral man is simply obeying the dictates of his human nature, and is not even to be regarded as immoral. . . . One is forced to the conclusion, if one accepts men's account of themselves, [that] women's human nature is something very much cleaner, stronger, and higher than the human nature of men. *But Suffragists, at any rate,* hope that this is not really true. They have more faith in men than men have in themselves, and they believe that a man can live as pure and moral a life as a woman can. The woman's ideal is to keep herself untouched until she finds her real mate. Let that be the man's ideal, too! (emphasis added)

Here Pankhurst ties sexuality to suffrage but does it through men's, not women's, sexual deviance. She first points to the inequality of sexual morality, yet, rather than defending women against charges of immorality, she inverts the Victorian configuration of woman as "the sex" and man as "human."[46] Thus, immoral women are no better or worse than immoral men in her mind, but the majority of "normal" men are expected to rise to the high moral standard of the majority of women.

In addition to indicting men's sexual "excess," *The Great Scourge* also defends (chaste) unmarried women. This argument refigures spinsterhood as a positive choice of healthy, normal women through the rhetoric of sexual purity. Pankhurst argues that until men are as chaste as women, women should not marry. She asserts that no woman is truly "safe" entering into marriage, because venereal disease can never really be cured, so even a man who claims that he is healthy could begin the marriage infected or could acquire syphilis or gonorrhea after marriage. She argues first for the naturalness and wisdom of unmarried women: "Marriage becomes increasingly distasteful to intelligent women—not motherhood, but marriage. There are numbers of women who long for children, but are not satisfied with the marriage laws nor with the men's standards of husbandhood and fatherhood." Pankhurst carefully separates marriage from maternity so that she can continue to invoke women's "natural" desire for children while maintaining that a *thinking* woman, acquainted with the reality of venereal disease that *The Great Scourge* exposes, can reject marriage on the basis of racial health yet maintain her womanhood. This is a "modern" rhetoric of female independence, but with a domestic frame. No sex-crazed spinster here! In fact, just as Pankhurst seizes medical registers for her argument, so too she lays claim to the socially conservative commentary of *Punch* for her militant polemic: "Mr Punch's 'advice to those about to marry—Don't!' has a true and terrible application to the facts of the case."[47]

Finally, Pankhurst invokes the language of social purity and eugenics to argue against procreative heterosexuality beyond strict monogamy. She argues that children born from parents with syphilis or gonorrhea weaken, not strengthen, "the race." Pankhurst again takes on a charge leveled against single women and uses the language of her detractors to bolster her argument: "The [English] birth-rate is declining. Bishops, men sociologists and others are bewailing the fact. Of course, they blame the women. That, men have done since Adam." Following this statement, Pankhurst transfers the blame for "race suicide" from single bourgeois women to "immoral" married men, noting that "gonorrhoea is a potent cause of sterility and miscarriage."[48] Cementing her argument that even unmarried women can be socially productive, she distinguishes modernity from the Victorian by rejecting the nineteenth-century call for women to sacrifice themselves for their families: "There can be no mating between *the spiritually developed women of this new day* and men who in thought or conduct with regard to sex matters are their inferiors. . . . 'Sacrifice yourself, sacrifice yourself,' is a cry that has lost its power over women. Why should women sacrifice themselves to no purpose save that of losing their health and happiness? Now that women have learnt to think for themselves, they discover that woman, in sacrificing herself, sacrifices the race" (emphases added).[49] Pankhurst combines a nineteenth-century narrative of social purity with suffrage narratives of women's spirituality and a call for the "modern woman" to claim her right to remain outside the institution of marriage while still "saving the race." Thus, for Pankhurst, new definitions of sexuality (both male and female) were just as closely linked to suffrage as more conventional readings of female sexuality were to antisuffragists. Because militant actions so clearly violated nineteenth-century conventions, Pankhurst reread such ideology; she, unlike her more moderate, "constitutional" colleagues, could not pretend that votes for women fit within a traditional domestic existence. She inverted such sexual ideology so that blame for its failure rested on British men, not on women.

In the second of two appendixes to *The Great Scourge,* Pankhurst tackles "the government and white slavery." This appendix establishes a logic of difference, unlike the body of the tract, which is produced through a politics of equality. The difference structuring this appendix is not gender difference, however. Rather, it is the difference of empire: white slavery is located outside of England, under the watch of the British military in India. For Pankhurst, English women voters stood as the moral guardians not only of their own race but of womanhood and sexual purity more generally: "The Government are themselves White Slave-mongers and upholders of vice. That is why they dare not meet the judgment of women voters." The "white slave" of this section is not white at all, but Indian. "The Government's abominable conduct where the womanhood of India is concerned has only to be known to make British women more determined than ever to win the vote. Under the rule of men, Indian women have been and are being enslaved, degraded, destroyed."[50] In her final section, Pankhurst revives old debates about the Contagious Diseases Acts in India and, following nineteenth-century British women reformers such as Josephine Butler, argues against the British medical surveillance of Indian sex workers.

Pankhurst produces a logic of difference neither between British and Indian citizens nor between "men" and "women" more broadly but, rather, between "pure" British recruits and their corrupted fellow soldiers. Quoting Dr. Louisa Martindale's 1908 book *Under the Surface,* Pankhurst juxtaposes the imperial British government with "pure and good" men and women: "Many a young boy or man comes out to India pure and good. It is the presence of the Government chaklas that first puts it into his head to lead a vicious life. Many resist for a time, but when they see their friends and their superior officers making use of these [zones of government-sanctioned prostitution], and when they are given to understand that the medical inspection makes it safe for them to go, sooner or later they give way."[51] The corruption of empire lay not with Indian or other colonized women but with British men and the residual medical regulation of "vice" in government-regulated cantonments.[52] Pankhurst ends her tract with the pressures of empire upon women and men in the "mother country" by constructing the consequences of empire as disease and race suicide.[53] British men responsible for the denigration of womanhood and the decline of the race were not those in England but those who had been corrupted by empire. Pankhurst thus neatly maintained a possibility of a pure domestic sphere in England itself, avoided dividing womanhood between the reproductive English woman and the contaminated Indian prostitute, constructed a narrative of essentially pure but corrupted British men, and ended her tract with a villain—British colonial officials—that was safely far from England and, as Philippa Levine notes, far from the concerns of most of the British public by 1913.[54]

Like her narrative of sexual purity and women's chastity at home, Pankhurst's call for the abolition of the containment system was "out of step with early twentieth-century sensibilities."[55] Yet, whether in or out of step, *The Great Scourge and How to End It* produced a suffragette rhetoric of purity and equality that radically challenged the imperialist, the sex-radical, the moderate, and the antisuffragist positions on women's sexual, gendered, and reproductive national roles. Adopting the rhetoric of nineteenth-century reformists amid a twentieth-century revolt allowed Christabel Pankhurst a level of discursive flexibility that in turn created representational space for a reinscription of gender and sexual possibilities.

Militant suffrage rhetoric appropriated nineteenth-century ideologies while violating traditional boundaries between feminine and masculine behavior. The shocking specter of violent women at war with their government violated traditional boundaries around bourgeois femininity. Yet, acutely aware of their transgressions, militants successfully mobilized strategies that placed them rhetorically inside, not outside, traditional parameters of womanhood, in part through rhetorics of English radicalism, spirituality, racial motherhood, and sexual purity. Domestic femininity was not upheld, yet traditional feminine sexuality was mobilized to maintain a militant femininity. Moderate suffragists refuted links between sexuality and suffrage, but militants sustained (and refigured) traditional definitions of female sexuality as their bedrock of respectability and moral superiority.

Virginia Woolf, Suffrage, and the Paradoxes of Edwardian Femininity

In early August 1916, Virginia Woolf began her second novel, *Night and Day*, which would be published in England in October 1919.[56] Written over the course of three years in the middle of the Great War and during the granting of partial women's suffrage in February 1918, *Night and Day* is often derided as an apolitical work with a seemingly Victorian worldview or Edwardian literary values.[57] However, such conventions in the novel actually reflect a debate over representations of women's sexuality and the rapidly changing position of British women in the public sphere at a historical moment that balanced pressures of imperial decline, world war, and encroaching women's enfranchisement. How are bourgeois English women, the novel asks, to negotiate their public occupations and private domestic duties at this moment of political and domestic transformation, and how will female sexuality be reshaped once the pedestal is knocked over in protest and the angel in the house leaves her drawing room to sell suffrage papers in the street? The novel uses a backdrop of Victorianism (defined through empire), realist narrative (a marriage plot gone awry), and modernist themes (alienation, sexual emancipation, fragmented consciousness) to produce a rhetorical disjunction reflective of its heroines' negotiation of the claims of traditional marriage and independent modernity.

Upon the book's publication, reviews of *Night and Day* either praised or damned it for its "realism . . . and spirit of Tennyson," its similarity to the tea parties in Jane Austen's novels, and its "deadly combination of literature and the drawing room."[58] An anonymous reviewer in the *Times Literary Supplement* was pleased to note that "*Night and Day* is only a love-story. It leaves politics, and war, and sociology and things like that, alone."[59] Katherine Mansfield's praise also critiqued: "We had thought that this world was vanished for ever, that it was impossible to find on the great ocean of literature a ship that was unaware of what has been happening. Yet here is *Night and Day* fresh, new, and exquisite, a novel in the tradition of the English novel. In the midst of our admiration it makes us feel old and chill: we had never thought to look upon its like again!"[60] Mansfield praised Woolf for the precision and beauty of her text, but she also implied that the novel was anachronistic and that Woolf herself was "unaware of what has been happening." To praise a young writer whose first work had been hailed as a part of the "new" modern literature as now a preserver of "the tradition of the English novel" was indeed damning. Such early reviews anticipate more recent criticism of *Night and Day*, wherein literary critics either chastise Woolf for a retrograde novel or defend the novel as a precursory or "stillborn" modernist endeavor.[61]

Whereas much criticism of *Night and Day* is primarily concerned with the text as an indicator of Woolf's stylistic development, I examine the novel's negotiation of modernity through the tension in the novel between "the drawing room" and women's role as citizens. In *Night and Day*, Woolf's representations of empire, suffrage, and education enact the difficulties of the prewar transition in British gender and sexual codes. Thus, although the book does indeed present elements of "a novel in the tradition of the English novel . . . [which] we had never thought to look upon . . . again!" it does so in the context of a debate over cultural representations of suffrage debates, the position of women in marriage, and the British public sphere. What some critics have understood as stylistic and thematic nostalgia constitutes only half of a representational contest within the novel and should be read more properly as an engagement with, not a break from, debates over aesthetics, modernity, and gender.

I do not attempt, as others have, to "recuperate" *Night and Day* as either an early modernist or a nascently "lesbian" text.[62] Rather, I am interested in its relationship to contemporaneous representations of the cultural and political transformations of early twentieth-century England. When one reads *Night and Day* as a suffrage piece, its contribution to debates over the relationship between women's suffrage and questions of modernity and sexuality becomes clear. Further, suffrage writings may emerge as not just vehicles for polemics but also texts imbricated in the aesthetics of modernity as well as its thematics. Alongside Sowon S. Park, I argue that "*Night and Day* is as much an exercise in undermining the conventional novel as constructing it."[63] Woolf redefines women, femininity, and sexuality by mapping the past onto the terrain of Victorian empire and highlighting the impasses for women under Edwardian cultural expectations.

In *Night and Day*, Woolf uses the cultural figure of the suffragist as a tool in the exploration of modern women's public, as well as private, needs and desires. The novel juxtaposes a modernity of cultural citizenship, paid labor, and women's sexual and social independence with an outdated model of Victorian intellectualism marked by faded curios of empire, conventional gender roles, literary inheritance, and the drawing room. Contemporary tropes of suffrage deviance are inverted and exposed through a comparison of the novel's sexually conventional female protagonist, the socially masculine Katharine Hilbery, to maternal suffragist Mary Datchet.

Woolf creates Katharine Hilbery as a woman with a conventional surface yet with modern desires beneath her dutiful facade and situation. The novel's opening line positions Katharine as an upper-class young woman in her family's Chelsea drawing room, presiding over the tradition of Sunday tea: "It was a Sunday evening in October, and in common with many other young ladies of her class, Katharine Hilbery was pouring out tea."[64] This properly classed and gendered function is situated among signs of English cultural (poetic) and political (imperial) dominance. Katharine's grandfather is a great Victorian poet, and her (as well as her mother's) unending daily occupation is the preservation and protection of his legacy. The Hilbery drawing room holds the legacy not only of a male poet but also of women's relations to empire. As Kathy J. Phillips notes, "The Hilberys themselves identify with the Empire so closely that they convert a tour of their house into a display of 'relics' from the conquest of India."[65] Mrs. Hilbery also creates a genealogy of feminine imperialists as she reminisces with her daughter: "'I can see them now, sweeping over the lawns at Melbury House in their flounces and furbelows, so calm and stately, and imperial (and the monkey and the little black dwarf following behind). . . . And that's Queenie Colquhoun,' she went on, turning the pages [of a family album], 'who took her coffin out with her to Jamaica . . . because you couldn't get coffins in Jamaica, and she had a horror of dying there (as she did), and being devoured by the white ants.'"[66] In her reading of this passage, Phillips notes, "Mrs. Hilbery accepts the lower status of both blacks and women," whereas Katharine "notices the contradiction between 'kind' and 'imperial' when she becomes 'angry' at the mention of an Indian servant."[67] Mrs. Hilbery reminds us that this Victorian drawing room is as surely the product and guardian of British Empire as it is of English literature. Katharine must navigate (and, Woolf implies, renounce) the legacy of both British imperialism and drawing-room domesticity in order to become a modern woman.

Katharine's love of mathematics and astronomy quickly complicates her position as the inheritor of British Empire and Victorian conventionality. She hides her passion for science from her very literary family, keeping a secret Woolf frames as a simultaneously modern and masculine one: "Perhaps the *unwomanly* nature of the science made her instinctively wish to conceal her love of it. But the more profound reason was that in her mind mathematics were directly opposed to literature. . . . There was something a little unseemly in thus opposing the *tradition* of her family" (emphasis added).[68] Femininity and tradition battle against Katharine's inner desires. She is aware of the transgressive and transformative nature of her desire to quantify the stars, and this desire lurks beneath the persona of the dutiful, tea-pouring daughter as the novel opens.

Katharine's masculinity is a continual, if subtle, motif throughout the novel. In addition to her "unwomanly" desire to study mathematics and astronomy, often outweighing her desire to marry, Katharine's physical gestures are frequently labeled masculine by her conventional fiancé, William Rodney. The two prepare to share tea before William proposes to Katharine: "He made the tea, and Katharine drew off her gloves, and crossed her legs *with a gesture that was rather masculine* in its ease" (emphasis added). Gender roles are inverted: William plays hostess and Katharine, far from a nervous bride-to-be, relaxes while she is served. Later, William notes that "the carelessness of her attitude seemed to him rather masculine than feminine." Katharine's masculine character distinguishes her from other women as well, including her younger cousin: "Where Katharine was simple, Cassandra was complex; where Katharine was solid and direct, Cassandra was vague and evasive. In short, they represented very well the manly and the womanly sides of the feminine nature."[69] Cassandra is the daughter of slightly impoverished Anglo-Indian parents; her poverty and imperial inheritance both amplify her femininity and malleability. Not incoincidentally, Cassandra ends the novel engaged to William.[70] Thus, the more feminine woman proves to be the more suitable match for socially conventional William.

Katharine's masculinity signals modernity—it is masculinity divorced from physical characteristics (for Katharine is consistently described as a beautiful woman in conventional feminine terms), and it implies no sexual deviance. Rather, her masculinity challenges traditional social expectations of marriage and women's acquiescence to their husbands. Ultimately, this masculinity extracts her from a "bad" engagement, and it gives her the self-determination to seek out relationships with women, as well as with Ralph Denham, the young man to whom she is engaged at novel's close. Far from being a detraction, in this novel's logic, Katharine's masculinity makes her far more interesting than either conventionally silly Cassandra or eternally earnest and pedantic William, both of whom play the feminine to Katharine's masculine.[71]

Katharine's masculine character is particularly striking when placed alongside the characterization of suffragist Mary Datchet. One might expect, were *Night and Day* as Edwardian and conventional as some critics would have us believe, that the beautiful young woman would be feminine to highlight the cultural masculinity of the suffragist. Yet the inversion of this expectation enables Woolf to challenge existing cultural perceptions of suffragists and working women, and also of the changing desires and positions of the majority of women "of a certain class," who ultimately choose marriage instead of work—women represented in this novel by Katharine Hilbery.

Whereas Katharine begins the novel by pouring tea within Chelsea's domestic realm, Mary enters the novel as her Bloomsbury rooms are about to be invaded by a literary club meeting.[72] Mary's private space is actually public, and her domestic quarters are designed for ready transformation into a meeting room. This publicly domestic space is also the space of the home country, the anchor of empire. As she darns a pair of stockings "at the end of a fairly hard day's work," Mary reflects: "Here she was at the very center of it all, that center which was constantly in the minds of people in remote Canadian forests and on the plains of India, when their thoughts turned to England."[73] Unlike Katharine's home, which is filled with the spoils of imperialism, Mary's rooms highlight a political and gendered domestic balance of citizenship and stockings. In *Night and Day,* empire is both invisible and ubiquitous. Katharine and Mary are positioned as opposite puzzles of modern femininity, each struggling with love, work, domesticity, citizenship, and femininity in surprising (and highly un-Edwardian) combinations.

Mary's and Katharine's physical selves also present contrasting pictures of embodied womanhood. Katharine's physical presentation is conventional, whereas Mary's is almost androgynously modern: Mary is "quite capable of lifting a kitchen table on her back, if need were, for although well proportioned and dressed becomingly, she had the appearance of unusual strength and determination."[74] Though perhaps better suited to carry a table than to pour tea, Mary echoes neither the harridan figure portrayed by antisuffrage activists nor the incompetent spinster drawn in *Punch.*

Furthermore, Woolf describes Mary as maternal, countering the antisuffrage charge of suffragists' lack of "natural" femininity: "A pleasanter and saner woman than Mary Datchet was never seen within a [suffrage] committee-room. She seemed a compound of autumn leaves and the winter sunshine; less poetically speaking, she showed both gentleness and strength, an indefinable promise of soft maternity blending with her evident fitness for honest labor."[75] Mary embodies the peaceful, fertile pastoral as Woolf aligns her with nature, labor, and maternity—a far cry from the "unnatural," violent suffragettes, who destroy property and starve themselves in prison. Further, metaphors of nature and maternity produce motherhood as an inherent quality in Mary that furthers her skills in the public workplace, countering the antisuffragist charge that women could not work for suffrage *and* maintain a desire and ability to have children. By positioning Mary's maternity within the committee room and making her the most "pleasant and sane" woman there, Woolf creates an alternative vision of suffrage women.

Like Christabel Pankhurst, Virginia Woolf distances marriage from maternity for modern women. Conventional Cassandra, engaged to William for only a few days, already exalts, "I hope we shall have a great many children. . . . He loves children." Yet the modern Katharine reflects, "She had known William for years, and she had never once guessed that he loved children." Katharine's relationship to marriage and maternity reflects cultural transitions in women's roles. Often viewed by older women as an ideal prospective wife—that is, as traditional, unlike other modern girls—Katharine is actually the opposite, as is exposed in her inner life as well as in her conflicts over the subservience that marriage seems to require for women.[76] Her engagement to William represents acquiescence to social and cultural conservatism, but her subsequent (and final) engagement, to Ralph, supposedly promises a model for spiritual companionship and a "modern" disregard for class lines and social hierarchy.

Mary's relationship to marriage, principally her internal battle over her own desire to marry Ralph, illustrates both Woolf's rendering of the modern in relation to the traditional in the novel and the position of women's public activities in relation to their domestic ones. Mary positions her suffrage work in opposition to her desire for marriage and calls upon her public work to ward off her desire for the more traditional work of being a wife: "To see Ralph appear unexpectedly in her room threw Mary for a second off her balance. . . . 'Now,' she thought to herself, as she screwed [the cold water tap] tight, 'I'm not going to let these silly ideas [of loving Ralph] come into my head. . . .' 'Don't you think Mr. Asquith deserves to be hanged?' she called back."[77] Mary uses suffragist politics as a shield against her own romantic inclinations for Ralph; suffragist talk is an antidote for romance.

Further, imperial citizenship both enables and forecloses romance for Mary. Just as Katharine's family aligns tradition with empire and great literary production, Mary's domestic desires emerge when she leaves her suffrage office at her lunch break to view art at the infamously imperialist British Museum. Whereas reproductive femininity is produced through the imperial genealogy of the drawing room for Katharine, the British Museum's spoils of empire (marked as universalist, classical "art") evoke similarly domestic thoughts in Mary. After staring at the Elgin Marbles, Mary "began to think of Ralph Denham. So secure did she feel with these silent shapes that she almost yielded to an impulse to say 'I am in love with you' aloud." Leaving the Elgin Gallery, Mary wanders among other objects from the empire and tries to imagine herself with Ralph "on a camel's back, in the desert, while Ralph commanded a whole tribe of natives."[78] These imaginings of imperial marriage fail her, and as Mary leaves the museum and approaches the suffrage office, her modern, suffragist, nonromantic, "impersonal" self takes over: "For, as she walked along the street to her office, the force of all her customary objections to being in love with any one overcame her. She did not want to marry at all. It seemed to her that there was something amateurish in bringing love into touch with a perfectly straightforward friendship, such as hers was with Ralph, which, for two years now, had based itself upon common interests in impersonal topics, such as the housing of the poor, or the taxation of land values."[79] Here, the representation of the suffragist is, first, one of a "normal" woman who, in proximity to an idealized classical world of aesthetic beauty (masking British imperialism), thinks of love and is swept away by emotions. At the same time, however, the suffragist qua suffragist does not want to marry and is concerned only with domestic (English) social and public issues. The unsubtle geography of Mary's desire works to reinforce the split between suffrage—or, more broadly, women's involvement in social issues—and the aesthetic world of classical art, which is dependent on empire, tradition, and the continuation of British culture through imperialism, marriage, and reproduction.

Not only does the juxtaposition of women's suffrage and marriage for women position Mary and Katharine in relation to the opposing "tradition" and "the modern," but it also participates in shifting definitions of womanhood. Katharine's desire to live alone, studying mathematics and astronomy, is initially presented as a greater barrier to romance than Mary Datchet's daily work for suffrage. Further, holding prosuffrage opinions in no way impedes even the traditional Cassandra from a successful courtship. After William expresses his indifference to politics, Cassandra rebukes him:

> "I don't think any man has a right to say that," said Cassandra, almost severely.
> "I agree. I mean that I detest politicians," he corrected himself quickly.
> "You see, I believe Cassandra is what they call a Feminist," Katharine went on.

Being a "Feminist"—at least for a few months—is no detraction for William. Nevertheless, ultimately, Mary continues her cultural work but cannot marry, and Katharine ends the novel with the belief that marriage to Ralph will not involve the "submission" that marriage to William would have. Feminist beliefs do not prevent marriage, but a commitment to public cultural work rather than private domestic duties might.[80]

As well as being positioned in relation to marriage, agitation for women's enfranchisement is positioned explicitly as work. When Katharine and Mary first meet, Katharine asks,

> "And you spend your life in getting us votes, don't you?"
> "I do," said Mary, stoutly. "From ten to six every day I'm at it."

For Mary, suffrage work parallels Ralph's job; she goes at it for eight hours each day—but she does not need to work for pay. Thus, Mary's suffrage work is not identical to other Londoners' work but in fact resembles a more Victorian mode of women's public service, in which bourgeois women value their tasks specifically because they can reach beyond the domestic sphere. Indeed, Mary offers up work as a solution for emotional, rather than financial, distress. After Ralph worries of Katharine's isolation and loneliness, Mary responds: "'There's always work,' she said, a little aggressively. . . . 'I was thinking of Katharine. She doesn't understand about work. She's never had to. She doesn't know what work is. I've only found out myself quite lately. But it's the thing that saves one—I'm sure of that.'" Directly afterward, Mary notes that work offers this emotional cure specifically for women: "'Where should I be now if I hadn't got to go to my office every day? Thousands of people would tell you the same thing—thousands of women. I tell you, work is the only thing that saved me, Ralph.'" Yet Mary also specifically defines engagement and marriage as work. As she remarks to a colleague of hers who attempts to recruit Katharine for a newly forming socialist organization, "'Marriage is her job at present.'"[81] Woolf's ironic juxtaposition of Katharine's engagements with Mary's cultural work again reflects the tension between traditional and modern work for bourgeois women.

Woolf depicts Mary as a member of a second generation of suffrage activists. The flighty and earnest Sally Seal represents an unbalanced, older suffragist who must continually be calmed down and reminded to work through organization and conversation, not action. In a swipe at militant suffragettes, the portrait of Seal falls in line with cultural stereotypes of the lonely and hysterical suffragette. Waging an internal war against the distraction of Ralph, "however teased by foolish fancies, [Mary] kept the surface of her brain *moderate* and vigilant, and subdued Mrs. Seal very tact-fully more than once when she demanded, 'Action!—everywhere—at once!'" (emphasis added). Mary is the moderate, whereas Mrs. Seal is in danger of succumbing to the militant slogan "Deeds, not words." For both Mrs. Seal and the domineering male suffragist Mr. Clacton, Mary's femininity poses a threat to successful attainment of their cause;[82] Mrs. Seal worries that "one of these days Mary, the young woman who typified so many rather sentimental and enthusiastic ideas, who had some sort of visionary exis-tence in white with a sheaf of lilies in her hand, would announce, in a jaunty way, that she was about to be married."[83] Because Mary represents sexual purity and visionary femininity to Mrs. Seal, she is "at risk" for mar-riage, a condition that, Woolf implies, the first generation of suffragists cannot reconcile with public-sphere activism. Like other moderate suffrag-ist writings, *Night and Day* positions the "good" suffragist as wholly femi-nine and sexually conservative.

Yet even as Woolf resists popular caricatures of suffrage and advocates a liberated social masculinity, this novel cannot reconcile marriage and pub-lic work. Although the juxtaposition of Katharine and Mary complicates ideas of the masculinized and unsexed suffragist and the uncomplicated, feminine woman bound for marriage (though it is Mrs. Seal who describes the former, and Cassandra the latter), ultimately, the novel ends with the promise of love and marriage for Katharine and a lonely and desexed—yet publicly productive—Mary. Woolf presents the multiple and conflicting desires of these young women, and offers a promise of a changed social rela-tion between men and women in Katharine's supposedly more "equal" and "modern" partnership with Ralph. Still, Woolf's modern young women must choose between embracing the public world of politics and work, or taking up a private life of love and (albeit a hopefully more equitable) marriage to a man.

The drive toward marriage structures *Night and Day* wherein its plot is driven by the question of who will marry whom and by a navigation of the transition to modernity through labor, empire, and gender. It is the dynamic navigation of seemingly incommensurate choices such as labor/love, domesticity/modernity, and empire/autonomy through which Woolf suggests possibilities for women's gendered subjectivity in modernity. Woolf's dualisms do not map neatly onto expected categories of Edwardian social life, yet she does not project an unfettered public identity for women—she plays with possibilities and foreclosures. For example, although Katharine's beauty and femininity predicate a conventional sexuality, her social desires for solitude and science transform the meaning of a "feminine" woman in the novel. Likewise, empire is a site of the past for the aristocracy but an encroaching presence in the cultural geography of London's middle class. And Mary's desires for Ralph negate the unnatural or unsexed suffragist, yet the marriage plot leaves her behind, because the novel can find no structure within which a working woman can also be a heterosexually desired subject. It is by reading carefully the suffrage sections of the novel that tensions and debates surrounding gender, sexuality, and nation in an emergent modernity are rendered visible. Suffrage signifies a move toward modernity within the novel, if a vexed one, as it also produces the debate among the female characters over how they will configure themselves as "modern women."

Conclusion

Just months after Christabel Pankhurst's row with the Ulster Unionists, Britain was at war. The outbreak of the Great War immediately transformed Pankhurst's war against the British government into a war against Germany. Within a year, all militant actions directed by the WSPU ceased, the *Suffragette* was renamed *Britannia,* and the energies and skills of both the WSPU militants and the moderate NUWSS faithful were focused primarily toward nationalist war efforts. Christabel's sister, Sylvia Pankhurst, was first marginalized and then profoundly isolated among the suffrage organizers in her oppositional stance toward the British government concerning suffrage and in her commitment to pacifism and internationalism. Her organ, the *Woman's Dreadnaught,* was also transformed by war. The

Dreadnaught agitated for living wages and war stipends for the working immigrant women of London's East End, and printed editorials and letters that opposed the war, voiced sympathies with the women suffering in Germany, and spoke out against the nationalism of other former suffragette leaders. All suffragist representations and energies, whether nationalist or internationalist, were transformed by war.

By the 1919 publication of *Night and Day,* women's suffrage was law in Britain. One of the myths of the British women's suffrage movement is that the vote was "given" to women over thirty-five years old in 1918 as a reward for their faithful service to the nation in wartime. (Women were enfranchised on equal terms to men in 1928.) Though there may be a grain of truth in this cultural myth, it denies the powerful work of both moderate and militant suffragists, as well as their allies in government, before and during the Great War. Though violent actions against the government ceased in 1914, lobbying efforts for the women's vote continued. By 1918, femininity had been successfully redefined to include women's participation in public life. Yet, as Woolf's novel illustrates, representation of bourgeois female sexuality remained a problem. Militant suffragettes' return to nineteenth-century registers of sexual purity, moderate suffragists' use of a politics of Victorian domesticity, and antisuffrage mediations of public agitation for private duty all reinforced a complex and changing relationship between sexual and gender representation.

If, as I have argued, the prewar women's suffrage debates transformed the representational politics of gender, engaged with ongoing debates about women's sexuality in modernity, struggled with the inheritance of a domestic ideology of both nation and home, and refigured women's relations to the state, then these transformations played out in equally complex ways throughout the war, to the point of limited suffrage in 1918, full enfranchisement in 1928, and beyond. Where this chapter has examined the very public debates that directly reshaped dominant ideologies of women's gender and sexuality, chapter 3 examines concurrent discourses of sex radicalism in more narrowly circulated journals, societies, and subcultural discussions. The thinkers and writers examined in chapter 3 produced work that illustrated the limits of prewar discourses of female gender and sexuality, rather than narratives seeking to redefine more mainstream discourses.

"A MORE SPLENDID CITIZENSHIP": PREWAR FEMINISM, EUGENICS, AND SEX RADICALS

I wanted to kiss him because it would have shocked him so much more than having to arrest me.

—LAURENCE HOUSMAN, in a letter to Sarah Clark, after his arrest by a "big beefy ugly policeman" at a suffrage demonstration (from Sandra Holton, *Suffrage Days*)

At the same time that moderate and militant suffrage leaders were promoting a conservative suffrage sexuality, renegade groups of British male and female advocates of women's liberation were meeting, writing, and producing very different versions of feminist sexual representations.[1] In the 1910s, birth control, free love, and male homosexuality appeared frequently as topics alongside women's suffrage in the pages of the *Freewoman*. Yet any significant discussion of female homosexuality is notably absent among these frank discussions. This chapter explores the paucity of representations of prewar female homosexuality in the face of frequent discussions of male homosexuality and female heterosexuality among prewar feminists. By reading debates over spinsters, male homosexuality, and sex reform by a group of self-styled sex radicals, I trace the emergence of female homosexuality as a representational possibility in the years leading up to the Great War, and I argue that the terms through which this category emerged reflect a struggle over the meaning of British sexual subjectivity and the nation's eugenic future.

The scarcity of a language for female homosexuality in contexts in which it might be retroactively expected suggests the impossibility of a coherent public category of female homosexuality in England prior to the Great War. In the representations of the sex radicals, the few pieces that do touch on female same-sex relations are most often framed through the language of sexology, eugenics, and/or national procreation. Indications of the emergence of such a public identity category can be detected, but most often only through inference, omission, and context, rather than directly or overtly as would be the case during the Great War (discussed more fully in chapter 4). When female homosexuality *is* rhetorically present in prewar writings, it is almost always in tandem with (and, I will argue, enabled by) references to male homosexuality.

The discursive visibility of female homosexuality during the Great War is predicated not only on sexological classification or through Victorian ideas of female homosociality but also on at least two additional representational fields: first, a complex (and often internally incoherent) dependence on ideas of the already well-established and -understood category of male homosexuality; and, second, on competing visions of the future of the British "race" or national character and the central role of women in the production of that future. This interconnection of national and sexual rhetorics in feminist, sex-radical cultural productions illustrates both the limits of emergent modern lesbian and gay male representations and their interdependence on racial and national ideologies. The emergence of lesbian representation in the public sphere cannot be read as a story of either liberal progress or the rise of collective consciousness of identity. As the writings of Edward Carpenter, Dora Marsden, Stella Browne, and others indicate, discourses of female homosexuality were born through representational struggles: political, gendered, sexological, and eugenic.

The discursive practices of sex radicals in organizations such as the British Society for the Study of Sex Psychology, the Eugenics Education Society, and Dora Marsden's renegade *Freewoman* journals generated an interlocking argument. While the efforts of suffrage leaders such as Millicent Garrett Fawcett and Christabel Pankhurst, and opponents such as Eliza Linton and Mrs. Humphry Ward, formed the dominant discourses of suffrage sexuality, their contentions were met with resistance by other, more marginal feminist and sex reformers. Representations of male homosexuality in the rhetorics of suffrage and sex radicalism point to the differing conditions of male and female homosexual representational possibilities at this moment in history. Early twentieth-century discussions of women's sexuality, spinsterhood, and feminism seem always to be entwined and implicated in debates over positive eugenics and the "British race," thus producing emergent discussions of female homosexuality through nationalist and racist conceptions of bodies, desire, and sexuality. The terms through which male homosexuality, feminism, and female sexuality were each represented by prewar feminist sex radicals set the stage for the emergent status of female homosexuality during the Great War.

Sexual Politics and the Future of the Nation: Eugenics and Neo-Malthusianism

The self-styled sex radicals discussed in this chapter participated in broad cultural debates over the transformations of ideologies of domesticity and citizenship, and the shape of twentieth-century British national identity. Women's sexuality, in these debates, was inextricable from national and individual reproduction, racial and imperial politics, and the roles of representation, governance, economics, and citizenship in modernity.

At the turn of the twentieth century, England experienced a drop in the birthrate, which was widely cited as "race suicide." Politicians, statisticians, economists, and scientists pored over records from the past century in attempts to trace the sources of the decline. This dip caused political concern for imperialists and nationalists, who either feared insufficient "people power" to sustain England's increasingly tenuous hold on its colonies or saw both the rise of university-educated (often single) British women and the increasing number of non-Anglo-Saxon (and often non-Protestant) residents of the "motherland" as evidence of the weakening of the "British race."[2] Thus, nationalist and racial concerns shaped population study in early twentieth-century England. Nineteenth-century discourses of social Darwinism and Malthusianism paved the way for neo-Malthusian and eugenic debates over the roles of sexuality, gender, and migration in England's future.

Because of widespread dismay over the nation's decline in population and cultural taboos regarding birth control, neo-Malthusians found themselves an embattled and suspect minority, whereas eugenicists were lauded for their prescient leadership on "the population question." Publicly advocating "family limitations" for all classes, turn-of-the-century neo-Malthusians advocated hereditary, economic, and cultural "quality" over mere "quantity" for family size. They argued that the British race was best served economically and culturally by limiting family size, particularly for classes unable or somehow unfit to raise the sons and daughters of the nation. Eugenicists (both female and male) urged educated middle- and upper-class women to marry early and increase their family size for the sake of the nation. Neo-Malthusians quietly advocated for "artificial means" of limiting family size, whereas eugenicists viewed birth control and deferred marriage as signs of individualistic selfishness at best, and national degeneration at worst.

England's experiences in the Boer War made neo-Malthusian arguments not only unpopular but also seemingly untenable. As historian Richard Allen Soloway reports, "Pointed questions about the physical quality of the race had been raised at the time of the Boer War both within parliament and without. The disproportionately large numbers of recruits from industrial towns who were unable to meet minimal physical requirements for military service fed earlier fears that urbanization was taking place at the expense of racial vigor."[3] One might make a neo-Malthusian argument from these recruiting difficulties, yet the responses to fears of "racial degeneration" in the face of industrialization and urbanization were decidedly eugenic: "A desire to protect the British empire, to resist the political aspirations of feminism and organized labour, and racist beliefs in the superiority of the British (usually 'English') race and hence the need to protect it from immigration and miscegenation, were all fundamental motivations [for eugenicists] as were less grandiose interests in public-health issues."[4] Eugenicists and imperialists took control of the population question, arguing for increased numbers of "fit" English sons and daughters.

In prewar England, eugenicists focused overtly on "positive" rather than "negative" eugenics. Unlike the "negative" American model of eugenics, which Nazi Germany took as its model a few decades later and which focused primarily on limiting the "unfit" from reproduction, British "positive" eugenicists publicly exhorted "fit" women to maximize their fertility through early, class-appropriate marriage and through an exclusive focus on maternity.[5] Yet it would be dangerous to minimize or dismiss the racial implications of British eugenics. Indeed, it is often those invested in separating British positive eugenics from American or German negative eugenics who tend to minimize the impact of both negative eugenics in general and the racial component of British positive eugenics.

On the one hand, Robert A. Peel, president of the Galton Institute, wrote in 1998, "It was not merely a distaste for birth control which prevented the Eugenics Education Society, in its early years, from developing a credible policy of negative eugenics; no theoretical basis for such a policy yet existed."[6] On the other hand, historian Dan Stone reminded us in 2001 that "although class concerns were a major factor behind the ideas and enquiries of the British eugenicists, no less important was a concern with race. . . . The centrality of race is shown in the way which (mainly Jewish) immigrants were discussed, and in the . . . racial hierarchy which saw the white European at the top and the black African at the bottom."[7] The program of positive eugenics in England had important distinctions from the eugenic campaigns in the United States and in Germany. Yet it would be a grave error to consider the positive eugenics of England less racially driven than the negative programs elsewhere.[8]

The Eugenics Education Society was founded in 1907 in England and took up questions of population, fitness, and national "racial health." This society, composed primarily of educated men and women from the middle and upper classes, maintained a clear distance from "radical" neo-Malthusian reformers, who advocated birth control and thus were seen to promote sexual excess: "Most eugenicists preferred to avoid any association with unsavory Neo-Malthusianism. Until the 1920s they were content to place their faith in the positive encouragement of increased reproduction among the fitter classes to offset the indiscriminate fertility of the less selective."[9]

Although neo-Malthusian and eugenic approaches to racial health generally stood in opposition to one another in their approaches ("positive" eugenicists emphasized the need to bear many "fit" children, whereas neo-Malthusians focused on smaller, "fit" families), many early twentieth-century feminists synthesized the two approaches through a focus on gaining control over reproduction by educated middle- and upper-class women in service of the nation: "When in 1904 Alice Vickery Drysdale, Lady Florence Dixie, and several other Neo-Malthusian feminists established a Woman's International Branch of the Malthusian League, they hoped to persuade the suffrage societies to endorse early marriage coupled with eugenic concepts of rational, selective motherhood."[10] These hopes were rarely realized, as birth control was widely viewed as shirking one's duty. In 1914, Mary Scharlieb accused married couples using birth control of selfishness, in "What It Means to Marry": "Worse even than this failure to marry is the determination too often found in married couples to enjoy the comfort and privileges of the married state without accepting its duties and responsibilities. . . . A Nemesis awaits such selfishness, and *not only is the country deprived of the sons and daughters who would make her strong, respected, and glorious,* but the childless household, or the home in which there is but one little one, is not in so good a position as those richer in children" (emphasis added).[11] Scharlieb encapsulates twin eugenic arguments against birth control: on an individual level, children would enhance the family in question and make them "richer" and in a better position; and, perhaps more significantly, on a national level, childlessness depleted and "deprived" the nation of strength, respect, and glory. It was against this backdrop of racial and nationalist arguments regarding married, heterosexual sexuality that the *Freewoman* entered into the discursive battle over women's liberation and sexual freedoms for men and women.

By 1911, the year of the *Freewoman*'s inception, the population question was deeply entrenched in moral, political, and scientific circles in Britain. That same year, the influential *Fertility of Marriage Census* was completed and the conservative National Council of Public Morals (NCPM) was formed. Soloway observes that "the NCPM . . . was particularly concerned with the collapse of domestic values, as its motto, taken from a 1911 speech of the new monarch, George V, indicated. 'The Foundations of National Glory are set in the homes of the people,' it proclaimed. 'They will only remain unshaken while the family life of our race is strong, simple, and pure.'"[12] Here, the language of racial strength indicates the widespread early twentieth-century understanding of race in England as the "eugenic sense of the 'better breeding' of the British themselves," as Lesley A. Hall concisely summarizes.[13] Dan Stone contests any benign reading of Edwardian racial politics when he reminds us that eugenic understandings of the "English nation" were intrinsically racist: "'Race' was not simply a synonym for 'nation' in Edwardian Britain, unless one accepts that the word 'nation' itself carried implicit racist assumptions."[14] The population debates of the early twentieth century exemplify Foucault's concept of bio-power: they illustrate the profoundly racial and national foundations and consequences of debates over female sexuality in prewar England.

While the biopolitical debates over population, race suicide, and married sexuality continued among clergy, politicians, and medical policy makers, and while suffrage agitations escalated, small groups of men and women began meeting, discussing, and publishing materials about sexual alternatives for men and women.[15] In November 1911, breaking from the Pankhursts' increasingly autocratic control over the militant British suffrage movement, Dora Marsden published the first issue of a new journal, titled the *Freewoman*. Marsden embraced an oppositional and provocative stance toward the Pankhursts, with whom she had previously worked, protested, and been jailed, thereby challenging the seamless equivalence of suffrage to early twentieth-century feminism. Although militant and moderate suffragists quarreled vehemently over the means by which the vote would be won (and which women would receive that vote), they had a common goal:

female enfranchisement. And, as demonstrated in chapter 2, both militant and moderate suffrage organizations worked hard to keep discussions of all but the most conservative and traditional sexuality out of their organizations. Marsden broke with that silent compact. In the pages of the *Freewoman* (November 1911–October 1912) and its successor, the *New Freewoman* (June–December 1913), discussions of birth control, free love, asexuality, abstinence, and male homosexuality flourished, both in articles and in the correspondence section.[16]

Concurrent with the rise of the *New Freewoman,* in June 1913, a new organization formed in August 1913: the British Society for the Study of Sex Psychology (BSSSP). Hall recounts that the organization formed "to advance a particularly radical agenda in the field of sex reform . . . [and] in the discussion of sexual matters [to aspire to] greater sexual freedom in society."[17] The BSSSP was first envisioned by a group of male homosexual reformers, including E. B. Lloyd and Edward Carpenter, both of whom also contributed to the *New Freewoman.* The society quickly sought out like-minded British women to broaden its scope and membership. Many feminists and sex radicals contributed to the *Freewoman* and its successor and also belonged to the BSSSP: Stella Browne and Kathlyn Oliver, as well as Lloyd, Carpenter, and Harriet Shaw Weaver, to name a few.[18] The *Freewoman* aimed to refocus the prewar feminist movement beyond suffrage and, in so doing, engaged with a variety of sexual, cultural, and political questions. Male homosexuality appeared in both the *Freewoman* and the *New Freewoman* in the context of feminism and women's and men's liberation from social conventions. The BSSSP initially was founded by male homosexuals with specific interests in sexological and/or anthropological perspectives on "the homosexual question" and then quickly broadened its mission to address eugenics, free love, and other pressing sexual and social issues.

The *Freewoman* and the BSSSP illustrate together the deep interconnections among a group of highly educated—and at times "eccentric"[19]—Edwardian reformers of feminism and sex reform. Both of these organizations sought profound social transformation through the transformation of gender and sexual roles. Dora Marsden sought to produce a space of active debate and dissent in the *Freewoman;* the BSSSP's mission was to disseminate knowledge through lectures and meetings about the importance of sex reform and sexual knowledge. Members of the BSSSP ranged from reformist to socialist; Marsden was unapologetically elitist and "individualist," seeing the "exceptional" and the "genius" as the road to cultural transformation. The debates and missions of these small but very significant organizations provided a counternarrative to the sexual conservatism of the mainline suffrage leaders and suggested alternative paths for the emergence of female and male sexuality in modernity.

Speaking of Sex and Inciting Debate in the *Freewoman*

The *Freewoman* encouraged lively discussions of female sexuality in its pages. Marsden's philosophy of individualism, combined with a commitment to debate and dissent within the pages of the periodical, led to the creation of a serial that was onerously abstract (in Marsden's pieces, principally) yet riveting (principally in the "Views and Comments" section, written by the editors about their mail, in combination with the Correspondence columns).[20] Yet the publication did not cover the whole of sexuality. Lucy Bland remarks, "In the early twentieth century, while male sexual abuse continued to concern most feminists, there also developed a more *explicit* engagement with questions of sexual pleasure, witnessed above all on the pages of a new journal called the *Freewoman*. Whatever its radicalism, however, the journal still implicitly assumed the norm of heterosexuality."[21] This organ, dedicated to open discussion of free love, chosen celibacy, and male homosexuality, among other topics, fell curiously silent on the topic of sexual love between women. This silence reflects not editorial timidity but, rather, a broader cultural difficulty with articulating female same-sex desire. This chapter explores the discursive lacunae surrounding female homosexuality among sex radicals. This is not to say, in any way, that women were not engaged in erotic behaviors or sexual relationships with one another. Indeed, as Bland remarks of this period, "certain feminists were beginning to identify as lesbian, adopting the labels provided by sexology."[22] It is precisely the implications of such disjunctions between identities and representation that this chapter explores. The absence of a narrative of female homosexuality independent from one on male homosexuality indicates, for me, its emergent status as a culturally legible category produced through discourses of nation, race, and citizenship.

The journal's inaugural issue, dated November 23, 1911, included several pieces that centered on debates about the relationships among women's enfranchisement, sexual freedoms, marriage, reproduction, and sexual psychology. Together, these articles laid the groundwork for months of debate within the articles, opinion essays, and correspondence of the journal, and they also indicated possible parameters of conceptualizations of female sexual autonomy in the prewar period. Both in Marsden's own "Notes of the Week" and in the article "The Psychology of Sex," by J. M. Kennedy, the *Freewoman* created a distance between its goals for women's liberation and the methods and goals of the Pankhursts, specifically, and the organized women's suffrage movement, more generally. Marsden boldly proclaimed, "We say that feminism is the whole issue, political enfranchisement a branch issue, and that methods, militant and otherwise, are merely accidentals. . . . We regret we have to differ so strongly from Miss [Christabel] Pankhurst . . . but we feel that, at this moment, she has lost her political balance."[23]

Following this denigration of suffrage as a "branch issue" of feminism, Kennedy laid out three classes of women: "the old fashioned housekeeper type . . . [who] is not distinguished for her intellect, but for her purely sexual side," the "advanced type—in which category we may reckon most of the Suffragists, the Fabian women, and so on—[who] are distinguished by their intellect only," and a third, "unnamed" type who "wish to bring about greater intellectual plus moral freedom for both sexes."[24] The members of this third, unnamed but "select" class were not sexual conservatives like the housewives, and they did not ignore sexual freedom in favor of the more limited goal of political enfranchisement. Here the *Freewoman* used the rhetoric of medical and scientific classification systems to produce a politics that most often promoted exceptionalism as a route to women's freedom.

Three other articles raised the question of women's sexuality in the inaugural issue; in each, the relation of women's responsibility or right to reproduce was intimately tied to her limitations or rights to free heterosexual expression. In "A Definition of Marriage," Edmund B. D'Auvergne draws on a comparison of Greek and Roman definitions of marriage to argue that marriage is necessary only when a couple procreates, and that all other (hetero)sexual unions need not require civil regulation; his essay argues that free love is a route to increased procreation: "Even the lawyers will grant that the continuance of the race is more important than the succession to property. The State, at any rate, [should have] no interest whatsoever in sterile alliances. It does not want husbands and wives, it wants parents and children. Yet so insane is our marriage law that it will not release the wife whose husband refuses to give her children, and will brand her as a criminal if she bears a child to another man."[25] In a discussion of contemporary polygamy, an author identified only as E. S. P. H. argues that a moral and civil insistence on the pretense of male monogamy harms the mistresses and wives of men who do not observe monogamy.[26] Both of these essays exhibit fundamental concerns with the relation of sexuality to state regulations of childbearing, and both engage the dominant eugenic thinking of the period. Finally, an anonymous essay entitled "The Spinster, by One" issues an opening salvo of what would become an extended debate on the physiological, psychological, political, and cultural characteristics of unmarried women.

Together, these articles in the first issue of the *Freewoman* indicate a commitment to debate and an exploration of the lives of women outside the conventional bonds of an idealized married, heterosexual, monogamous, reproductive sexuality. The terms of this discussion are framed by sexology, psychology, legal rights, eugenics, and transhistorical references to ancient Greece and Rome. Absent are concerns over conservative reception, immediate political consequence, and explicit discussion of female homosexuality. Debates over the role of suffrage, feminism, and intellect in the shaping of women's sexual subjectivities and "maternal functions" in relation to the nation are vigorously present.

The *Freewoman* and the *New Freewoman* focused primarily on British women and their struggles for sexual, political, and individualist emancipation. Like other suffrage journals, the *Freewoman* also included articles reporting on the conditions of women beyond England. International content in journals such as *Suffragette* and *Votes for Women* emphasized either the relative freedom of enfranchised women abroad (in New Zealand, for example) or the horrific conditions of "foreign" women, often in the British Empire, which might be corrected by enfranchised British women voters. The *Freewoman* followed this script as well, but with special attention to issues of sexual freedom, population, and the intellectual standing of women, either across national lines or in relation to men. As with all topics, the *Freewoman* provided a platform for a variety of dissenting views—here, on the relative "savagery" or "civility" of conditions for women around the world, in comparison to those in England. Yet the coverage of women and gender issues beyond England reveals one constant: all articles that highlighted foreignness or internationalism did so in order to situate the English women themselves in a particular sexual or cultural light. Unlike articles in *Votes for Women,* for example, which might seek to inspire English women with the success of suffrage in New Zealand or in a U.S. state, articles on the sexual and national positions of non-English women in the *Freewoman* were almost always implicitly articles about the future of the British race itself.

For example, in "The Persian Women," author R. H. Moreland used the familiar frame of European moral superiority to argue for the Persian woman as "the most degraded specimen of Moslem womanhood": "The Persian woman's capacity for agitation is small. There are few European women residents for them to come into contact with, and there are no girls' schools even. . . . Thus, although many of the women of Persia are dissatisfied, and have a vague feeling that something is wrong, they lack, and must inevitably lack for some time to come, the necessary intelligence without which their status cannot be improved."[27] Because Persian women had very limited contact with European women and thus lacked information or "intelligence" to revolt, this author argued, they were the most degraded of Muslim women. In contrast to this conventional view of British superiority, Cicely Fairfield used the occasion of a review of *The Position of Women in Indian Life,* by Chimnabai II, the maharani of Baroda, and S. M. Mitra, to critique English gender politics by suggesting that Indian women might in fact have more liberty than English women: "[The maharani] seems to regard the unseemly muddle into which women's affairs have fallen to-day in Europe as something for which Indian women should strive. In fact, she takes a step backward. . . . The authors have an immense enthusiasm for the cause of Feminism and see it as a coming force in the movement towards the unity of India. The pity is that they have not seen beneath the surface of English life."[28] Fairfield undercuts an idea of English egalitarianism, not through a direct attack on English gender inequality but through a critique of the developmental model of imperialist feminism that assumed British superiority in all things, including gender relations and women's freedom.

Comparison to women in Europe and in the empire furthered various authors' arguments regarding British nationalist motherhood, eugenics, and the role of women in nation building. Neo-Malthusians Bessie and Charles V. Drysdale compared England to European nations regarding birthrates and women's emancipation. In the second installment of his ongoing series of articles titled "Freewomen and the Birth-Rate," Malthusian League head Charles Drysdale asked his readers to "compare the status of the Frenchwoman, with her limited family, strong, capable, and healthy, looked up to as the head of the family and revered by her sons, with that of her German sister, toiling like a drudge for her numerous family, and despised by all mankind."[29] Did readers wish to be like the German "drudge" or the French mother of "strong, capable and healthy" sons? Bessie Drysdale condemned the French government's eugenic attempts to increase French fertility a few months later, in her "Foreign Notes." Condemning the "money prizes given to large families in France," she commented scathingly, "Four pounds seems a small compensation when one considers the trouble and expense of so many children, but it is at least satisfactory that the money was bestowed on the mothers and not the fathers!"[30]

Other advocates similarly used "foreign men" to shame British men and women. In an essay titled "The Unspeakable," Ellen Gaskell compared epidemics of cholera in India to venereal disease in England: "We are proud of our Imperial prestige, but reports in public newspapers are world-wide reading. Englishmen look with scorn on the men of the East for keeping their women secluded and safeguarded. What will India have a right to reply when reading of the effect of the non-seclusion of women? Cholera takes its toll heavily in India, but that kills only the body and is not passed on to another generation. The unspeakable may not kill the body but it does worse—it kills the soul."[31] Gaskell mobilizes imperialist assumptions of English superiority over Indians to strengthen her argument for cleansing England of the unnamed evil of venereal disease. Here, imperialist logic is used to build arguments on British sexuality; the empire produced the properly disciplined British sexual subject, both male and female. Articles in the *Freewoman* superficially "about" women outside of England functioned both to discipline English men and women and to bolster women's gendered, sexual, and cultural positions within England. Sexuality, reproduction, marriage, and education framed certain feminist positions and simultaneously served to construct and critique Englishness.

The reproductive future of the race appeared to be of paramount concern in the early issues of the *Freewoman*. Vigorous correspondence and subsequent articles followed the Drysdales' and D'Auvergne's articles, arguing both in favor of and against "artificial family limitations," race suicide, and overpopulation, and the valorization of motherhood as a key component of a freewoman's existence. Correspondent Margaret E. Hill (who added to her name "B.Sc.," indicating her bachelor of science degree) took up the issue "from a biological point of view." For her, females (of all species, apparently) are "entrusted the preservation of life, the conservation of type, and the purity of race" by nature. Yet "the human female has lost her great prerogative. As a bondwoman, she must perforce pander to the lusts of her lords and masters. . . . When women are spiritually free, we shall no longer know the prostitute or the atrophied spinster."[32] For Hill, women naturally controlled reproduction; feminism would end women's bondage to men and place them in their proper biological place of reproductive control. In contrast, I. D. Pearce wrote that "women should be giving birth to new thoughts, new aspirations, and new ideals [rather than] wasting their creative forces on merely increasing a very mediocre population."[33] In the first installment of "Freewomen and the Birth-Rate," Charles Drysdale made a related assertion that the rise of feminism, generally, and suffrage, specifically, correlated to a declining birthrate. This was a positive element for Drysdale, as he positioned himself against the "Imperialists and Eugenicists" who sought to increase, not decrease, the British birthrate and who argued against women's equality on reproductive grounds. A neo-Malthusian, Drysdale promised "a magnificent future [for] humanity when women demand their right as the mothers of the race to regulate their families in accordance with the possibilities of giving their children the best possible physical, mental, and moral inheritance and environments, and will refuse altogether to bring weakly and diseased children into unwholesome surroundings."[34] Arguing against dominant assertions of positive eugenic motherhood, this piece inverted arguments about race suicide to argue for a stronger British race through reproductive planning of smaller, more "fit" families. Together, these pieces debate the status of feminism through arguments for the best racial future of England: eugenic motherhood is positioned in opposition to neo-Malthusian reproductive limits; the empire is used to argue for women as mothers; and, throughout, each outcome for women is tied to the betterment of the race, be it the English race, the human race, or the female race across species. The language of selection and social Darwinism permeates these debates, as it does a concurrent debate about the status of unmarried women, the spinsters.

The *Freewoman*'s Correspondence column was also the site of a particularly lively debate during several months in 1911–1912, over the virtues of free love or celibacy for unmarried women. The many correspondents who wrote to the magazine on this subject included sex reformer Stella Browne, who argued in favor of free love, and Kathlyn Oliver, who defended the virtues of celibacy. Whereas these "spinster debates" have sometimes been read retroactively in the context of a hidden homosexuality,[35] I argue that at the time of their publication they were often entwined with debates over women's duties as mothers of the nation, set against women's sexual desires and women's increasing access to higher education and the public sphere.

Primarily at stake in this debate was the question of women's sexual activity: Was sexual activity necessary for, or deleterious to, women's health? Were sexual desires in women "natural," regardless of marital status? Was the "freewoman" a sexual woman? The anonymous screed in the *Freewoman*'s inaugural issue "The Spinster, by One" claimed that a spinster's unreleased "wild life-impulse" led to "all-pervasive unrest and sickness which changes all meanings, and queers all judgments, and which, appearing outwardly, we recognise as sentimentality."[36] This attack yielded many responses from contented spinsters, unhappily married women who envied unmarried friends, and others. From these responses, a debate emerged regarding the role of sexuality for women, physiologically, morally, and culturally. When Kathlyn Oliver wrote, "I am neither a prude nor a Puritan, but I am an apostle of the practice of self-restraint in sex matters," Stella Browne replied that "it will be an unspeakable catastrophe if our richly complex Feminist movement, with its possibilities of power and joy, falls under the domination of sexually deficient and disappointed women, impervious to facts and logic, and deeply ignorant of life."[37] For Browne, here writing anonymously as "A New Subscriber," sexual experience was a core element of cultural politics, power, and subjectivity. For Oliver, sexual practices were an element of marriage that was unnecessary or, at the least, unimportant for women who chose to remain single. If, on the one hand, sexual activity was necessary for the freewoman, as editor Dora Marsden seemed to argue, then questions of free love, serial monogamy, and childrearing outside of marriage became critical questions for the advancement of women. Sexuality, in other words, became a core tenet of feminism. If, on the other hand, sexual desire was easily ignored or suppressed, then the preoccupation with sexual matters in the *Freewoman* can be read as a distraction, rather than a constitutive issue, for freewomen.

The language of civilization, empire, and race permeated debates over the role of sexuality for modern women. For Oliver, "wide sexual experience" was aligned with animalism and against civilization and education. Her letter titled "More Plain Speaking" references her struggles for economic independence as well as weekly biology lectures she attended in which "we are told that the more advanced and the more civilised and intellectual we become, the less physical and the less dominated by animal instincts and appetites are we."[38] Though disagreeing with Oliver in substance, a correspondent who signed her name as "Tout Pouvoir" similarly mobilized tropes of animal/human distinction to argue against eugenic motherhood: "Is it so very important to continue the race at all costs? . . . Merely to breed healthy children in order to satisfy the demands of the State seems to me to put woman on a level with the brood mare!"[39] Directly following this letter, another advocate of selective motherhood made the racial metaphor explicit: "[Children] born from intense mutual passion . . . are always the best physically and mentally. . . . The child of intense passionate mutual love is as much in advance of the average child as the European child is in advance of the negro."[40] The following week, Oliver refuted Tout Pouvoir's call for eugenic passion and the possibility of passion as a civilizing influence. In a letter titled "On the Loose Principle," Oliver defines unrestrained sexuality as a primitive characteristic of men and women: "I cannot believe that we should be a happier and a nobler race if the primitive and animal instincts and passions in men and women were allowed and encouraged to run amok without any self-restraint or self-control."[41] Produced through registers of savagery or civilization, nationalist concerns such as eugenic motherhood and legally enforced monogamy framed debate over the status of freewomen's sexuality. So, like discussions in the journal and elsewhere in prewar England about birthrate and marriage, advocates of free love and female celibacy sought to stake out a claim to England's racial future.

The "spinster debates" were not a site of discussion of female homosexuality specifically. Though one could certainly retroactively speculate about the erotic lives of women such as the one who signed herself "Single, but Undismayed" and though Kathlyn Oliver herself claimed a homosexual orientation three years after this correspondence,[42] the spinster correspondence appears exclusively heterosexual; Stella Browne framed it as a discussion of "the 'normal' . . . hetero-sexual intercourse in contradistinction to auto-eroticism, and to the habits of those 'lower animals' of whom Miss Oliver disapproves so much, and knows so little."[43] Discussions of homosexuality in the *Freewoman,* whether overt or implied, remained almost exclusively about male homosexuality, where questions of the nation's racial future rested either on universalist parallels between male homosexuality in contemporary England and male homoerotic behaviors in classical Greece and Rome, or in discussions of sexological classification, rather than through debates over England's eugenic future.

Male Homosexuality in the *Freewoman*

Several early twentieth-century advocates called homosexuals "Urnings" or "Uranians," drawing on Karl Heinrich Ulrichs's use of the term. "Uranians," by Harry J. Birnstingl, was the first *Freewoman* article to explicitly take homosexuality as its topic. In the context of a discussion of "masculinity" and "effeminacy" in the suffrage movement, Birnstingl advocated a model of homosexual identity in men and women predicated on sexological classifications of sexual inversion as gender inversion. Appearing to follow Edward Carpenter's model of "the intermediate sex," Birnstingl drew sexology, gender roles, and suffrage together in an argument against criminalization and for the acceptance of a spectrum of gendered behaviors. This article, which began an ongoing debate between its author and Charles J. Whitby, MD,[44] illustrates the dependence of nascent representations of female homosexuality among the educated British elite on both sexological and male homosexual models; a connection between female homosexuality and women's liberation that was apparently absent in other cultural forums; and the idea of homosociality among women as a particularly twentieth-century phenomenon. Drawing on studies of male homosexuality, Birnstingl extrapolates female homosexuality as an emergent identity springing from feminism. This produces an alliance between gay men and female suffragists, some of whom Birnstingl assigns a sexological classification by drawing on gender deviance as sexual deviance.

Birnstingl begins by questioning the bifurcation of masculine and feminine "qualities and attributes of the two sexes" but moves quickly to a discussion of "a class of people who hover, as it were, midway between the sexes" and whose "position in society is as yet undefined." Drawing heavily on unnamed German sexologists as well as Carpenter, Birnstingl equates gender inversion with sexual inversion and implies both that combinations of masculine and feminine qualities are found in "the world's pioneers" and that such "inclinations" or "attractions" do not invariably "lead to any mechanical sexual act." Indeed, "probably in the majority of cases, certainly amongst women, they do not." Thus, Birnstingl argues that "Uranians" should be understood for "their weakness" rather than condemned by church or state as sinful or dangerous. Birnstingl concludes his essay with an indirect call not only to remove the stigma of Uranians but to decriminalize male homosexuality: "Criminal and sinful are by no means interchangeable terms."[45] Here, then, the criminalization of male homosexuality framed discussion of male and female homosexuality. Male homosexuality formed the model from which Birnstingl addresses homosexuality in general, presumably in both men and women.

Although men were more likely than women to engage in a "mechanical sexual act," Birnstingl indicates through his sexological references that many women working for gender emancipation might, unbeknownst to themselves, be Uranians. Moreover, sexological discussions of male homosexuality became models not only for an unknowing female homosexuality but also for feminism more broadly:

> An epithet that is often applied by those opposed to the Woman's Freedom movement in the shape of an argument is the word "sexless." They draw attention to the numbers of women in the ranks of agitators who are celibates and childless, and who seem insensible to the passion of love, thus, they declare, leaving unfulfilled the greatest mission in life. It apparently has never occurred to them that numbers of these women find their ultimate destiny, as it were, amongst members of their own sex, working for the good of each other, forming romantic—nay, sometimes, passionate—attachments with each other. It is splendid that these women, who hitherto have been unaware of their purpose, an enigma to themselves and to their relations, should suddenly find their destiny in thus working together for the freedom of their sex.

Birnstingl's statement indicates a few crucial points for a discussion of emergent female homosexual identities in the 1910s. First of all, Birnstingl is not accusing suffragists of homosexuality. Rather, he argues that the charges of the antisuffragists that suffrage women were "sexless," "celibate," and "childless" posited a lack of *any* sexual desire, not homosexuality specifically. Birnstingl suggests that such single suffragists themselves were unaware of their own membership in the class of Uranians, and that their homosocial, and perhaps sometimes homoerotic, relations with one another should be reinterpreted in light of sexological study. Lesbianism in this narrative is visible only through male homosexuality and is prompted by a homosocial feminist community. Birnstingl draws sexological work into conversation with debates about feminism, and the result, for him, is the assignment of homosexuality (Uranism) to women who "find their destiny in thus working together for the freedom of their sex." For Birnstingl, this is not a negative assignation; rather, "it is one of the most wonderful things of the twentieth century, a century which until now has been full

of wonderful things."[46] In other words, for Birnstingl, the convergence of
sexology, suffrage, and female homoerotic communities in an emergent
homosexuality heralded celebratory modernity. This performative utterance
became a rhetorical call for lesbianism to emerge. Birnstingl attempted to
attach lesbian identity to some suffrage women, yet I argue that his essay
summoned *lesbian representation itself* (not homosexual women) in a time
and in a periodical in which it had been all but absent.

In stark contrast to Birnstingl's celebratory summons of female same-
sex erotic possibilities, the April 18, 1912, edition of the *Freewoman* carried
a letter in the "Correspondence" section with a very different representation of women's erotic relations with other women. This letter, headlined
"The Human Complex," marks the only text I have found in the periodical
to deal with female same-sex erotics independent from male homosexuality. The correspondent (who signs herself only as "Marah") opens by linking her letter to earlier correspondence regarding the dangers to young girls
of prostitution. For Marah, female homosexuality paralleled prostitution
as something into which young girls could be "trapped" by predatory, "bi-
sexual" older women. She recounts her experience as a young girl alone in
London, lured into living with a "lady artist," to warn others: "For heaven's
sake, *Freewoman,* try and break down this shameful and dangerous ignorance which people allow their unfortunate girls to remain in."[47] In other
words, Marah supports free discussion of "bi-sexual" women as a way to
protect the innocence of young girls and to warn readers of an existing type
of women, the predatory "bi-sexual" or lesbian.[48]

This call for free discussion frames an unspeakable act by the lady artist.
Structured as a conventional tale of white slavery, the young woman, alone
in the world, naively accepts a generous offer of friendship and support:

> She was always envying me my youth, and praising me extravagantly, espe-
> cially the beauty of my hair. My head was quite turned by this admira-
> tion, and somehow it made me uncomfortable, too. . . . Knowing that I was
> now alone, my artist friend insisted on my coming to live with her at the
> studio. . . . It is very difficult for me to say now what I found out about this
> unhappy creature. I only understood it when I was older, and when it was
> all too late. This rich, clever—for she was brilliantly clever—artistic woman
> was bi-sexual. On the third day of my stay at the studio I ran away. I was
> thoroughly frightened—too frightened and ashamed to mention my awful
> experience to anyone.[49]

Marah positions forced contact with a homosexual (or "bi-sexual") woman as a peril of city life for a young woman. The discourse of excessive admiration and coercion leads up to the narrative of revelation and escape. Female homosexuality is a danger; experience of such danger comes to the young, but knowledge of it comes only with maturity and from a distance. Unlike the *Freewoman*'s other articles and letters that debate the virtues of male homosexuality, or a homosexuality in both men and women framed through sexological gender inversion, this wholly negative letter offers no cultural, medical, ethical, or literary explanation for the behavior it so sparingly describes. Indeed, given the letter's response to an essay about prostitution and its structure of seduction, betrayal, and flight, this text perhaps should be more properly grouped with the articles that debated white slavery, prostitution, and unwed motherhood, rather than those that explored the origins and cultural consequences of homosexuality in men.

Marah's letter remained relatively isolated amid an otherwise dynamic correspondence section. Only one follow-up letter, from "Northerner," was published in the journal, asking the editors for assistance in locating information about contraception and "books [that] have been written on this bi-sexuality which are sufficiently lucid and non-technical to be understood if put into the hands of a fairly well-educated boy or girl of eighteen or nineteen."[50] The editors replied only to the writer's query about "artificial limitations of families," with a referral to the Drysdales and their Malthusian League. Northerner was left in the dark regarding homosexuality. The editors of the *Freewoman* seem unwilling or unable to engage directly with female "bi-sexuality" apart from male homosexuality.

Marah's letter is the only piece in the *Freewoman* that explicitly, if still somewhat obliquely, took up female homosexuality on its own terms, apart from discussions of male homosexuality. The letter evokes the sexological narrative form of case histories through its physical descriptions, tale of entrapment, trauma, and tragic resolution: the bisexual woman dies two years after their encounter, and Marah reports that this "has been an experience which has embittered my whole life." The letter is grounded in "experience" but it is experience that can be understood only from a distance, after marriage and widowhood, and after a doctor ("the only living soul I breathed it to") informs Marah that "cases of this kind were *enormously on the increase.*"[51] Thus, although Marah's correspondence stands in stark contrast to Birnstingl's letter, on the one hand—he applauds female homoerotic relations, she regards such relations as unspeakable acts of trauma—on the other hand, both texts leverage sexology to provide an interpretive context to the acts that they describe so differently and an identity that lacks a rhetorical history or framework. Female same-sex practices may hold a long history, but, as the *Freewoman* illustrates, representations of these practices as the basis of an identity in modernity appear to be emergent at best.

Responses to the *Freewoman*

As its lively "Correspondence" section indicates, the *Freewoman* generated significant popular interest. The existence of a widely available weekly periodical that grappled explicitly with questions of sexual morality, free love, eugenics, and homosexuality had a significant impact, at least among members of its educated, urban readership: "The *Freewoman's* circulation was always small, but its influence upon feminists and sex radicals in Britain and the United States was far greater than its low print run might suggest."[52] In March 1912, at the suggestion and urging of correspondents to the journal, Marsden organized Freewoman Discussion Circles. A first organizational meeting for the clubs, held in April 1912, had an unexpectedly large turnout (fifteen or twenty people were expected, but one hundred came) and spawned several discussion groups in London and beyond.[53] The circles were anarchist and democratic in intent, so much so that Marsden herself was reluctant to attend the organizing meeting. Members of the central London discussion circle created a network for those "clever people" interested in "the question of women's suffrage and . . . sexual as well as economic issues."[54] The Freewoman Discussion Circles may be said to predate and predict the emergence of the BSSSP, with its interest in bringing scientific and political discussions of sexuality, feminism, and psychology to a nonspecialist audience. Yet the discussion circles differed critically from the soon-to-emerge BSSSP: the discussion circles were open to any interested parties, and their meetings were publicly advertised in the *Freewoman*.

The existence of the *Freewoman* drew critics as well as supporters, from both within the suffrage movement and outside it. The summer of 1912 saw a flurry of criticism in the correspondence section of the *Times,* among other locations. Mrs. Humphry Ward dubbed the paper "this dark and dangerous side of the 'women's movement.'"[55] In this letter to the editor of the *Times,* without explicitly naming the *Freewoman,* she railed against its "doctrine of the economic independence of women . . . motherhood outside marriage, by means of temporary unions for the purpose; its formal recognition by society, and the conditions on which the 'new maids' of the future will claim and enforce its arguments against the 'immoral' permanence of marriage; complete freedom of union, under the guidance of passion, between men and women; and other speculations and contentions . . . especially in the letters from correspondents."[56] In response to this letter, the NUWSS (England's leading moderate suffrage organization) sent in a letter from A. Maude Boyden distancing the moderates, and the suffrage movement more generally, from the *Freewoman.* Boyden's letter characterizes the *Freewoman* as "an obscure little periodical . . . this nauseous publication."[57] Lady Frances Balfour also replied to Mrs. Ward in the *Times* a few days later. In her letter, she obliquely defends the *Freewoman* by linking the "individualist" work of women's suffrage to the dissemination of knowledge about sexuality and to women's imperial project of "civilization." Directly refuting Ward, Balfour insists, "In a . . . misleading paragraph, [Ward] endeavors to make the suffrage movement responsible for the loosening of the ties of married life and for other signs of decadence in the morals of the race. . . . To us it seems otherwise. In our work for this cause we have learnt to believe in the doctrine of the worth and dignity of the individual. . . . We see this women's movement the whole world over. Civilization is raising the sex above the level of the inferior animal. Woman is no longer . . . goods and chattel."[58] Balfour links the *Freewoman*'s engagements with sexuality, free love, and marriage reform with the liberation of "our sisters in the East" through a doctrine of individualism and what we might now call a global feminism. Never directly defending the periodical's wide-ranging discussions of sexuality, Balfour instead turns her letter's argument on a feminism of empire and racial progress.

Another letter to the *Times* defended the *Freewoman* on scientific, not imperialist, grounds. Isabel Hampden Margesson wrote in response to another critique of the "nauseous publication": "Here come the same abuse, the same mud-throwing, which have ever been the weapons of those who would hinder the spread of knowledge of the laws of life, and the relationship of the sexes, amongst those who are defenseless without it." Invoking reformers from Florence Nightingale to Havelock Ellis to Josephine Butler, Margesson links free discussions of sexuality to nationalism through her claim that "knowledge" of sexuality "is vital" to the "health and morals of the nation." She presents an alternative to Ward's sanctimonious condemnation of the *Freewoman* as "dark and dangerous" by presenting it as the origin of a light of knowledge for England's future generations: "We are offered a remedy . . . that the youth of both sexes and in all classes shall be carefully instructed on the physiological and sociological aspect of the sex question by those who are competent to undertake such training in the interest of the State."[59] Margesson's letter to the *Times* defends the *Freewoman's* mission in the context not only of women's suffrage and religious morality but also of national health: both "the physiological and sociological aspect of the sex question." Homosexuality (female and male) disappears in this defense, as the procreation and socialization of future generations is marshaled as a defense against immorality.[60]

Such defenses of the *Freewoman's* mission proved ineffective by summer's end. In September 1912, the journal was unable to continue functioning economically following a boycott of the paper by its distributors, W. H. Smith, which was sparked by the controversial sexual materials published in the journal.[61] The journal's openness to a multitude of topics, sexual and otherwise, appears to have caused its initial demise.

"Literature" came to the rescue, to fill a financial gap and to provide a bridge in the paper's content so as to mark it more as a literary journal and less as a radical political sheet. With the encouragement of Mary Gawthorpe and Rebecca West, Marsden reimagined and refinanced the *Freewoman* as the *New Freewoman,* a still-political but now far more literary vehicle for discussions of feminism, freewomen, and sexuality.[62] Significantly, the masthead also changed, not only adding the word *New* before *Freewoman* but also modifying its subheading: "A Weekly Feminist Review" became "An Individualist Review." Marsden's commitment to controversy and expression of individualism continued, as did the publication of numerous articles connecting male homosexuality with women's emancipation. Yet, on the subject of homosexuality in women, the *New Freewoman* was as silent as its predecessor.

Feminist Women and Homosexual Men: Alliance and Exclusion

In two articles by male homosexuals in the *New Freewoman,* Uranism (male homosexuality) was linked to feminism thematically and rhetorically. This linkage provided a vital step in the rhetorical rendering of the sexual autonomy of "modern" women. Though the alliance of homosexual men with feminism, generally, and with the fight for women's suffrage, specifically, enabled an emergence of female homosexual representations later in the 1910s, this alliance excluded female homosexuality from the transhistorical chain connecting Uranian men and suffrage women from ancient Greece to early twentieth-century England.

In an article titled "The Status of Women in Early Greek Times," published in the *New Freewoman* on August 1, 1913, Edward Carpenter, the noted homosexual socialist whose writings are foundational to early twentieth-century progressive understandings of male homosexuality, argued against a history of ancient Greece wherein women were uniformly denigrated. The article begins thus: "It is well known that the Dorian Greeks, and those who were influenced by them, regarded a very close and personal attachment between men as part and parcel of their civic life; and it has sometimes been said that this kind of attachment was held in such high honour just because women at that time occupied such a low place and were so lightly esteemed." Carpenter's piece sets out both to prove that women were not actually "lightly esteemed" by the Doric Greeks and to cement a connection between male homosexuality and women's liberation. The essay reflects as much about contemporary 1913 Britain as it engages ancient Greece. Note that in his opening line, Carpenter calls his subjects "Dorian" rather than the equally commonly used "Doric," thereby calling attention, perhaps, to the "Wildean" argument within his broader topic. After thus framing his piece, the title of which indicates, after all, that it will be concerned with women, not with homosexual men, Carpenter cites various sources proving the respect for and equity of women in Sparta and Doric Athens. Particularly notable are his frequent references to the training of women as being "just like" that of the men: "They were taught to run and wrestle naked, like the youths. . . . They should go naked as well as the young men." Similarly, Carpenter highlights "a free intercourse, outside the limits of marriage, between healthy men and women," aligning himself with the contemporary advocates of free love while simultaneously making the familiar (and widely accepted) move highlighting Greek civilization as always more advanced than contemporary society and thus to be emulated.[63]

For Carpenter, the freedom, self-dependence, and political activity of women are linked to tolerance of male homosexuality in all cultures. After presenting both women's and Uranians' freedoms in Dorian Greece, Carpenter speculates "whether the Uranian temperament in the Dorian men— or such amount of it as existed among them—did not naturally favour rather than discourage this freedom and self-dependence and political activity of the women." He then argues that such a connection is already present in his contemporary culture: "In present-day life it pretty clearly is so. It is the Uranian classes of men, or those at least who are touched by the Uranian temperament, who chiefly support the modern's woman's movement."[64] Here, this article explicitly connects homosexual male liberation with women's suffrage and a more general fight for gender equality.

Carpenter makes this contemporary argument based on his "speculations" about the Doric Greeks; by asserting that male suffragists are homosexual or tend in that direction; and by arguing for a logical connection between male homosexuals and women: "The downright normal man . . . does not exactly want to see them [womankind] independent and self-determining of their fates." Such inverted men—those "in whom sex-polarity is not too pronounced"—view women more as equals and seek "comradeship" rather than sexual submission from them. Thus, like the Greeks who treated women on equal footing with their male comrades, Uranians decry the "enslavement" of women that later Greek societies and contemporary British society experienced. The article also implicitly appeals for male homosexual emancipation in order to encourage women's emancipation as well. As this piece was printed in a feminist periodical, it could be assumed that the readers desired the latter, and so, Carpenter's logic follows, they should tolerate, if not boldly advocate for, the former. He concludes the article by cementing the liberation of women with the freedom of Uranians: "Curious too to find that in our present-day civilisations where (till quite recently) the position of women had reached its lowest ebb, the Uranian attachment has similarly been disowned and its healing influences ignored."[65]

It is compelling how this article constructs both its female and male homosexual subjects. Carpenter depicts "women" transhistorically as a sexually unified class, attached to men yet desiring freedoms from their male counterparts. Women's legal and cultural status, not their desires, fluctuates across time. With his male subjects, Carpenter has a more difficult time: in this piece, men are at times divided into homosexual and heterosexual, but at other times this distinction breaks down. To use Eve Kosofsky Sedgwick's formulation, Carpenter both universalizes and minoritizes male homosexuality.[66] For the Dorian Greeks, male homoerotics were a universal condition, not an affliction of a certain class of men: quoting John Addington Symonds, Carpenter asserts, "This masculine love did not exclude marriage . . . the love of comrades became an institution."[67] The only fissure in Carpenter's narrative of the Doric Greeks is his curious side note, set off by dashes: "the Uranian temperament in the Dorian men—or such amount of it as existed among them— . . ."[68] This brief moment of uncertainty is ambiguous: Does Carpenter question how strong the Uranian impulse was in each man? Or was there only a segment of the Dorian male population that fully had the impulse individually? In other words, was Dorian Uranism the condition of a minority or a universalized one?

This unresolved side note is followed by another ambiguity with regard to men of the "present Day," that is, of 1913. Recall Carpenter's statement that "it is the Uranian classes of men, or those at least who are touched by the Uranian temperament, who chiefly support the modern's woman's movement." Within one sentence, Uranians move from a distinct "class of men"—a minority, clearly defined—to a group of men who contain, in differing degrees, a "temperament" that may or may not result in sexual desire for and activities with other men. This distinction illustrates the complexity with which Carpenter treats male sexual configurations. This complexity is striking both because it is symptomatic of the representations of male homosexuality at this time and because it contrasts with the lack of attention to female *sexuality* in this piece. Male sexual orientation is equated with women's gendered liberation: in other words, male sexuality is aligned with female engendering, thus erasing the complexities of female sexuality on its own. This would not be terribly remarkable were it not that in a feminist periodical that prided itself on the exploration of a variety of topics of interest to women (including female sexuality), references to male homosexuality frequently appeared, whereas references to female inversion were rare and considerably more muted. Male homosexuality appears in alliance with female heterosexual and political liberation; female homosexuality is either illegible, absent, or implied via its dominant representational "brother," male homosexuality.

Consider another example, an article titled "Intermediate Sexual Types," by E. B. Lloyd, published two months after Carpenter's piece, in the October 1, 1913, issue of the *New Freewoman*. This piece reviewed an "exhibit of intermediate human sexual types," arranged by Magnus Hirschfeld, on display at the International Medical Congress in London. Lloyd argued that gender was no longer an either/or proposition, and that just as society was moving toward a "growing sympathy and intellectual merging of the sexes to-day," society should accept the ambiguity represented by sexual, as well as gendered, indeterminacy and "intermediacy." Using gender-neutral language, the article weaves together discussions of social "androgyny" and "sexual intermediacy," which appears to imply homosexuality in men *and* women. The gender-neutral language is striking at first because Lloyd appears to refer to hermaphrodites as well as male *and female* homosexuals and therefore cannot assign a clear gender to the subjects of the article; unlike many of his contemporaries, this author considers male and female sexual subjects together. Toward the end of the piece, after Lloyd calls for a "drastic alteration" of the Criminal Law Amendment Act of 1885 (which criminalized *male* homosexual behavior), his list of "sexual inverts" affected by the law includes women *and* men: Sappho and Rosa Bonheur as well as Michelangelo, Walt Whitman, and Tchaikovsky.[69] Sexual inversion encompasses men and women for Lloyd, but, as with the sexologists discussed in chapter 1, inversion is predicated on a male model.

The relation between intermediate gendered behavior and intermediate sexual categories is also a complex issue here. Lloyd's article begins by stating its subject (in the title and opening sentence) to be "intermediate sexual types." This ambiguous phrase can mean hermaphrodites (a word used in the piece's second paragraph), people with a combination of bodily characteristics that are typically exclusive to one gender or the other. Yet an intermediate sexual type, as the title of Carpenter's 1908 book on homosexuality indicates, also implies members of the "third sex," or "sexual inverts": men who have sexual desires for men, and/or women who desire other women.[70] Hirschfeld's research focused particularly on male sexual inverts. Furthermore, Lloyd's subsequent mentions of Oscar Wilde and Havelock Ellis indicate that the piece considers *sexual,* rather than *gender,* indeterminacy. Finally, the author's appeal for a reform of the "injustices and brutality of our social and legal persecution of people of this type at the present day," particularly in comparison with the Greeks' "extraordinary freedom in these matters," furthers this interpretation. But sexual and gendered deviance are bound together in the piece, as they were increasingly bound culturally. The author's subject may be the oppression of male and female homosexuals, but the definition of a person of "intermediate sexual type" is wrapped around the language of *gender* inversion. In defining homosexuality sexologically, gender inversion becomes the overdetermined and dominant symptom of homosexuality, which translates into gendered and sexual ambiguity in this review of Hirschfeld's exhibit.

In Lloyd's essay, gender inversion is not simply a road to sexual inversion. In an extraordinary section, Lloyd links sexual inversion with an increasing emphasis on gender equity or androgyny. First, he describes an increasing androgyny in the culture at large: "But it must be remembered that to-day, in spite of all appearances to the contrary, the general stream of tendency is undoubtedly making for a very considerable fusion and blending of the so-called purely 'masculine' and purely 'feminine' intellect in the same person. . . . In a word, a steadily increasing number of normally constituted men and women are beginning to understand better the feelings and emotions of the opposite sex." Thus, social gender inversion is an increasing and inevitable result of intellectual progress that will yield better communications between "normally constituted" men and women and therefore, presumably, greater equality between the two genders. Lloyd then argues that a more open discussion of "sex questions," particularly of "sexual inversion," would further this project, and that sexual inverts themselves can facilitate this great cultural transformation. Sexual inverts (termed here "intermediates"), "sundered as they are from both sexes on the psychophysical side, may yet give very valuable help as a kind of mediators [sic] between them [the "normal"] on the intellectual and emotional side." In this manner (and following Edward Carpenter), a person who sexually desires a member of the same sex has a special cultural understanding of members of the opposite sex: sexual inversion reinforces gender inversion and social androgyny. Again, the merging of sexual and gender inversion is repeated and emphasized. And in this optimistic passage, gender divisions are relegated to an abstract, rather than lived, definition: "Generally speaking, nature abhors a hard and fast line just as it does a vacuum; and as we are now aware the chain of sexual continuity shows no break of any note, either on the physical or on the mental side, in its subtle gradations from the most womanly woman to the most manly man. Indeed, we have learned that, for thoughtful people at any rate, such antiquated abstractions as 'man' and 'woman' *per se,* will at no very distant date have to be relegated to realms of the philosopher's Absolute."[71] Here, the categories "woman," "man," "feminine," and "masculine" signify both sexual deviance and gender variations. Sexual inversion and gender inversion blend to connect the liberation of women to the liberation of male and female homosexuals. The social understandings and feelings of the opposite sex lead to an implied political, social, and psychic equality between the sexes in some imagined future. And in this future, in both this and Carpenter's articles, the specificity of women's sexuality disappears in a rush toward "equity" that pairs male homosexual liberation with women's gender equality. In short, female homosexuality is not a representational category in the pages of the *New Freewoman*; instead, female "sexual inverts" either appear primarily through the context of male homosexual representation or lose their sexual specificity under the general rubric of "women."

The *New Freewoman*'s discussions of homosexuality both mobilize sexology as an organizing framework and invoke transhistorical links from the ancient Greeks to the British moderns. Like Symonds, both Carpenter and Lloyd leverage certain implicit assumptions about the acceptance of homosexual acts in ancient Greece to bolster their claims for homosexual liberation in early twentieth-century England. By positioning themselves as the rightful inheritors of Greek cultural and sexual practices, these British sex radicals idealize an earlier representational model of a civically engaged male homosexuality, and they also produce a model of Englishness that ties male homoeroticism to citizenship, often to the exclusion of female homosexual representational possibilities.

We can see this exclusion through classical allusion reproduced in a second *Freewoman* article by Harry J. Birnstingl, "Interpretations of Life." As an illustration of the "ideal union" as a "complementary one . . . of *unlikes* rather than of *likes*" (emphases in original)—for example, of masculinity and femininity—Birnstingl offers up Aristophanes' speech in Plato's *Symposium*. "The male and female were originally one being," Birnstingl summarizes. "They were cut in twain by Zeus [and] afterwards, each part strived to find its complement; and . . . when they found each other, *whether they were likes or unlikes, that is, two males or a male and a female,* they remained henceforth inseparable" (emphasis added).[72] Birnstingl's summary critically omits Aristophanes' third dyad: that of female and female.[73] Birnstingl offers his summary to argue for an English marital partnership based on a classical model; yet even in the direct citation of a text that includes discussion of a female-female erotic bond, we can see the prewar lacuna regarding representation of a female homosexual possibility.

The engagement with sexology in the pages of the *Freewoman* and the *New Freewoman* signals the educational and cultural community surrounding the journals. The sex radicals sought to educate themselves and likeminded readers regarding sexual, cultural, and political issues, so it should not be surprising that they studied and circulated information available to a cultural elite: sexological, eugenic, and anthropological studies of sexuality often available only through private circulation or from foreign presses. This turn to sexology could be seen as the beginning of, or perhaps a broader shift in, British conceptualizations of sexuality and subjectivity. However,

Lucy Bland has warned not to overread the influence of sexology in Britain: "The power and influence of these sexological writings in the pre-war years must not be over-emphasized; their impact on ideas about sexuality did not come into full effect [in Britain] until the 1920s and 1930s."[74] Bland's caution is borne out in my readings of the suffrage debates, in chapter 2, as primarily devoid of sexological referents. As will be illustrated in chapter 4, sexological frameworks and linkages were becoming increasingly common in the late 1910s and early 1920s in discussions of male homosexuality specifically. Unlike absences of coherent representations of female homosexuality in the late nineteenth century or in the women's suffrage debates, by the late 1910s female homosexuality as an identity category began to take shape, if a nebulous and internally contradictory shape, in British public culture beyond the rhetorical realm of sexology.

Stella Browne and Edith Ellis:
Eugenics, Sexology, and Women's Sexual Variations

The community of *Freewoman* contributors, readers, and editors intersected both with political action organizations, such as those promoting suffrage, and also with societies established to transform British culture through medical and policy advocacy. Concurrent with the rise of the *Freewoman,* two other organizations also sought to influence the direction of British sexual ideologies: the Eugenics Education Society and the British Society for the Study of Sex Psychology. Both organizations were coeducational discussion forums, yet their membership and their approaches to their topics differed significantly. After its initial inception in 1913 by a small group of male homosexuals, the BSSSP quickly added as members a large number of both men and women interested in sex reforms, including Edith Ellis and Stella Browne. The Eugenics Education Society originated in 1907 at Francis Galton's quiet urging, and its founding membership consisted almost exclusively of medical and scientific men interested in legitimating and advancing the fledgling science of eugenics.[75] Though superficially disparate in membership and mission, both the radical BSSSP and the establishment Eugenics Education Society discussed British conceptions of sexual practices in the context of law, medicine, and culture, and each organization envisioned itself as investigating and perhaps influencing the gendered and sexual future of the nation.

This section discusses papers delivered to the BSSSP by Stella Browne and to the Eugenics Education Society by Edith Lees Ellis in the 1910s.

Each woman framed her discussion of women's sexuality through concern for England's racial future. Analyzed in tandem, Browne's and Ellis's works draw together feminist discussions of women's sexual practices, sexological classifications of homosexual behaviors in men and women, and the racial basis of sexual identities. The papers chart both the growing connections of the language of eugenics and sexology to emergent public representations of female homosexuality, and the discursive limits of such emergent representations in the 1910s.

Socialist feminist F. W. Stella Browne (1880–1955) was neither a medical doctor nor a scientist. Rather, she was an ardent advocate of free love and a birth control activist whose work consisted primarily of political speeches, correspondence, and agitation rather than studies, scientific or otherwise. Several of her essays from the mid-1910s elaborated on social and reformist themes initially developed earlier in her *Freewoman* correspondence. By 1915, her work drew together women's sexual liberation, racial health, and explicit engagements with female homosexuality in a sexological context.

In one 1915 paper delivered to the BSSSP, "The Sexual Variety and Variability among Women and Their Bearing upon Social Re-construction,"[76] Browne fine-tuned and developed themes introduced in her *Freewoman* correspondence: the importance of women's sexual autonomy; the psychological and physiological benefits for women of sexual intercourse inside and outside of marriage; and the relations of prostitution, frigidity, and enforced monogamy, on the one hand, and free love, sexual experiment, and sexual satisfaction, on the other, to women's social, physiological, and moral health. Her paper argues that "the variability of the sexual emotion in women is absolutely basic and primary." However, economic and political inequality suppress and "pervert" this variability, and social and religious prohibitions foreclose women's sexual expression or "normal [sexual] satisfaction." The constraints and perversions to which Browne initially refers include sadism or masochism, fetishism, and sexual-economic exchanges in marriage as well as in prostitution.

Browne argues forcefully for the liberation of women's sexual practices and cultural expectations so that women can experience the "variety and variability" that she claims are endemic to women's sexual fulfillment, their character, and their health. She emphasizes marriage reform, contraception, the lifting of taboos against premarital and extramarital sexual relations, and women's economic independence from men: "It is this variety and variability of the sexual impulse among women, which would mitigate against any real promiscuity, if women were all economically secure and free to follow their own instincts, and to control their maternal function by the knowledge of contraceptives (a most important part of women's real emancipation)."[77] Thus for the bulk of her talk, Browne universalized women's heterosexuality and connected their economic, moral, and physiological health to sexual freedoms.

Though she was a neo-Malthusian advocate of birth control, Browne also addressed positive eugenicists, arguing that women's free sexual expression, educated use of contraceptives, and increased sexual satisfaction with their male partners will result in more and healthier children, rather than fewer children. She claims that regular sexual pleasure can mitigate women's ill health during menstruation and forestall menopause. Furthermore, such decreases in "involuntary abstinence and repression" can potentially increase women's procreation. Finally, she ends this wartime essay with a call to remove the stigma of childbirth outside marriage, to alter the "Bastardy laws," and to unbar "a large percentage of young adult women . . . from legal motherhood"—a reference to the increased number of "war babies" and the scarcity of marriageable men during the Great War. In short, Browne marshals political, legal, medical, psychological, and sexological lines of argument in favor of free love. In a 1917 essay, "Women and the Race," published in the *Socialist Review,* Browne further developed this eugenic case for women's sexual liberation, marriage law reform, and women's education. "Only from 'intelligent and voluntary motherhood' can a finer and stronger race be developed; and that sort of motherhood remands respect and security," she wrote.[78] Eugenic motherhood appears intrinsic to 1910s discussions of women's sexuality, so Browne had to engage with this debate to make her case for women's sexual equality.

Browne also grappled with women's homosexual encounters in her BSSSP lectures, laying out an early version of what would next become a full talk and then finally an article a few years later.[79] In "Sexual Variety and Variability," Browne first attempts to normalize (universalize) the "sexual aberrations" already mentioned, adding to her list "artificial or substitute homosexuality" and "true sexual inversion." Citing Havelock Ellis, and calling on the BSSSP to research further this understudied realm of female sexuality, Browne asserts that "our maintenance of outworn traditions is manufacturing habitual auto-erotists and perverts, out of women who would instinctively prefer the love of a man, who would bring them sympathy and comprehension as well as desire." Cognizant, perhaps, of the many homosexual members of the BSSSP, Browne continues: "I repudiate all [who] wish to slight or deprecate the love-life of the real homosexual; but it cannot be advisable to force the growth of that habit in heterosexual people." When taking up the almost-unspoken topic of female homosexual behavior, Browne leaves the language of political or economic enfranchisement and takes recourse in the established rhetoric of sexology. It is only in this section of the piece that Browne cites another expert, the several-times-quoted sexologist Havelock Ellis: "[My] conclusions are based on life, not on books, though I have been confirmed in any personal opinions and conclusions by some of the greatest psychologists, especially Dr Havelock Ellis, whose immense research is fused and illuminated by an inspired intuition."[80] From a warning against socially directed, artificial homosexuality, Browne concludes the talk with her discussion of racial hygiene. "Absolute freedom of choice on the woman's part, and intense desire both for her mate and her child, are the magic forces that will vitalize and transfigure the race," she exhorts. Contraception, freedom, and economic emancipation would lead to healthier, happier wives and mothers of England. Such measures would also decrease autoerotic and homosexual behaviors among the women left on the home front in the early years of the Great War.

Edith Lees Ellis (1861–1916), eugenicist and wife of sexologist Havelock Ellis, was, like Stella Browne, deeply engaged with the issues of women's sexuality. Whereas in the first decades of the twentieth century Browne primarily located her work in culturally marginal enclaves of elitist sex radicals, Edith Ellis moved among a wider range of reformist communities: from her late nineteenth-century idealist, communitarian experiences with the Fellowship of the New Life (where she met Havelock Ellis and Edward Carpenter, among others) and her membership in the BSSSP to her work within the more widely regarded Eugenics Education Society. A novelist, essayist, lecturer, and reformer, "Edith Ellis *was* everywhere and *now* she is almost nowhere. She haunts as a footnote in biographies or histories of her period."[81] In 1911, for example, she addressed the Eugenics Education Society on the topic "Eugenics in Relation to the Abnormal," and in 1912 she addressed the Freewoman Discussion Circle in a speech titled "Eugenics and Ideals."[82] In these speeches, Ellis drew together concerns about eugenic citizenship, women's sexuality, and the place of homosexuality in England's racial future.

Edith Ellis's work provides an explicit bridge between sexological and other elite understandings of the relation of sexuality to culture and the racial future of the nation. Her own homosexuality also informs her writing, as well as her husband's case histories (she appears as "History XXXIV, Miss H" in Havelock Ellis's *Studies in Sexual Inversion*).[83] Her address to the Eugenics Education Society resulted in two published essays, "Eugenics and the Mystical Outlook" and "Eugenics and Spiritual Parenthood."[84] These essays highlight interconnections among eugenics, sexology, and radical sex reform in the 1910s; the intersections of communities formed around the *Freewoman,* the BSSSP, and the Eugenics Education Society; and a representation of female homosexuality that draws together sexological and feminist narratives.

Edith Ellis's two essays together produce an argument for medicalized identities and negative as well as positive eugenics. Like many other eugenicists, Ellis delineates groups of people who should and should not procreate and lays the responsibility of the eugenic future of the nation on women: "One of the chief points in the great circle of women's progress is for women to realise that, in them, lies the responsibility for the health and the sanity of the nation through their refusal to add to the misery of the world by bringing into it human beings who are badly handicapped even before birth. The consumptive, the epileptic, the feeble-minded, and the insane, under the code of the eugenicist, will not propagate their kind."[85] Ellis frames her eugenic perspective through women's liberation and progress: it is only through an embrace of eugenics, this passage suggests, that women will progress. Yet her model for eugenics moves beyond this familiar gesture of procreative regulation, encompassing cultural positions as well as more medicalized discussions of physical or mental "fitness" for paternity. Ellis adds children who are the result of rape (inside or outside marriage), prostitution, and loveless unions to her list of eugenically undesirable subjects. She argues that "a new vision of sex and an all-round education in the arts of both living and loving" will produce fit eugenic subjects: "When at last we realise that the uses of the flesh are not for destruction and folly, but *for the manifestation of a more splendid citizenship through the clean and ardent love* of those who are really mated in body and soul, we shall be beginning to understand sex in its finer sense" (emphasis added).[86] In the future of the nation, "a more splendid citizenship" will emerge through passionate, married, eugenically sound, heterosexual, procreative sex. Here, racial citizenship relies not only on mental and physical health but also on love.

This might seem a somewhat surprising conclusion from Edith Ellis, given her own homosexuality and open marriage. Yet one of her most significant contributions to the large early twentieth-century eugenic literature was her integration of subjects deemed unsuitable for biological reproduction into her schema of cultural reproduction:

> Consider the neurotic and the abnormal, for instance, and also the sane members of insane families. How can we secure that there shall be no waste or ruin for their special powers of work for the race? It is surely an accepted fact that many of the most capable people are neurotic or abnormal. . . . Is it not a part of Eugenics and a part of religion to indicate to these people how they can directly aid the improvement of the race? . . . It is our duty as advanced citizens to see to it that equality of opportunity for this end is given alike to the normal and abnormal men and women in our midst.[87]

Noting that "the neurotic and abnormal" are often particularly gifted members of society, Ellis decrees that those who should not procreate should choose "spiritual parenthood"—the production of art, music, or cultural advances—which she deems as important as actual parenthood.[88] Through this discussion of spiritual parenthood, Ellis takes up the particular issue of homosexuality or, as her husband coined it a generation earlier, "inversion." For Edith Ellis, inversion is a medical fact with which the eugenicist must grapple. Her discussion of inversion in "Eugenics and Spiritual Parenthood," along with the work of Edward Carpenter and Stella Browne, among others, signals one of the early integrations of sexological classifications of women as homosexuals into a slightly broader cultural conversation.

Like Stella Browne and Havelock Ellis, Edith Ellis distinguishes between congenital inversion and situational inversion, the latter of which, for her, falls under the category of "mock abnormality": "By mock abnormality, I mean an attitude towards passional experiments and episodes outside normal lines merely of self-gratification. Indulgence for the sake of indulgence, either in the ranks of the normal or the abnormal, is, in the light of modern ethics, a shame and a disgrace."[89] As a eugenicist, here signaled through a reference to "modern ethics," Ellis decries nonreproductive sexuality by eugenically fit subjects. For her, "mock abnormality" encompasses not only situational homosexuality but also other nonprocreative sexual acts by "the normal or the abnormal."

Congenital inversion presents another matter entirely for Edith Ellis. She draws on sexology and passion to argue for a dignified, if nonprocreative, place for homosexuals in England's eugenic future: "Science and love have proved that there are, and always have been, men who have the souls of women, and women who have the souls of men. This is the true abnormality." Here, Ellis defines homosexuality as gender inversion for both men and women. Unlike Carpenter, for whom homosexual women are an afterthought to his construction of Doric masculine homosexuality, and unlike Browne, for whom female homosexuality is often an unfortunate result of women's heterosexual repression, for Ellis, female and male homosexuality are considered on the same plane, though set apart, along with the insane, the syphilitic, and the neurotic, from the passionately reproducing heterosexual married couple: "There is surely a place in the great scheme of things even for the abnormal man and the abnormal woman, but it is not an easy place. . . . Under the highest laws of both Love and Eugenics I feel its place is one of spiritual parenthood. Neither bromides, loveless marriages, nor asylums will cure congenital inversion. The real invert is an invert from his birth to his death." Here Ellis advocates for the congenital invert, argues against institutionalization, and claims that forced heterosexual marriage is "against the aims of Eugenics." While congenital inverts generally should renounce sexual activities not predicated on "pure love," Ellis does argue for the eugenic acceptability of unions between congenital inverts: "The true invert, under Eugenics combined with ideals, has to face either total renunciation of the physical expression of love, or if Fate send him a true mate in the form of another alien, for in these things affinity has its own laws and pure love can be traced in strange hiding-places, then the bond shall be as binding, as holy, and as set for splendid social ends as the bond of normal marriage."[90] This fascinating passage recognizes legitimate homosexual relationships through a logic of eugenics. Having already established the importance of passionate, lasting unions between procreative husbands and wives, and then advocated for abnormals' "spiritual parenthood," Ellis here advocates for homosexual erotics through registers of cultural law ("as binding"), religion ("as holy"), and eugenics. Thus, Edith Ellis legitimizes homosexual subjectivity through narratives of cultural citizenship, sexology, law, and eugenic nationalism. This essay, given as a speech in 1911 and then posthumously published in 1921, quietly produced a legible female homosexual subject through a most unexpected language of eugenics and procreation.

Both Ellis and Browne grappled with questions of women's sexual autonomy, the racial health of the nation, and homosexuality. Whereas Browne advocated for heterosexual free love as critical to women's liberation, and argued that women's heterosexual freedoms would lessen cases of autoeroticism and "artificial homosexuality," Ellis integrated a discussion of male and female homosexuality into a theory of positive and negative eugenics predicated on individual restraint, procreative passion, and social Darwinist cultural hierarchies. Just as Browne derides "artificial homosexuality," Ellis eschews "mock abnormality" while carving out a special, nonprocreative role for inverts and other "abnormals" in the nation's racial future. If Browne looks toward free love and sexual variety to liberate women and to allow them to make good, procreative choices, Ellis turns to narratives of eugenic education and policy in her advocacy for enduring heterosexual love matches in order to produce the healthiest specimens for England's long-term racial health. In both women's polemics, female homosexuality is legible as an emergent cultural category. And, crucially, this emergent legibility is produced through racial narratives of reproductive sexuality as well as in relation to both the predominantly masculine narratives of male homosexuality established by other sexologists and the lacunae of other feminist discussions of women's marital and extramarital, procreative and nonreproductive heterosexual practices and desires.

Conclusion

The era of prewar feminism, suffrage, and sex radicalism ended with the appropriation by a small segment of British feminist reformers of the language and methods of late nineteenth-century sexology for their discussions of sexual politics and gendered identities. With the notable exceptions of Edith Ellis's 1911 lecture and Stella Browne's wartime pieces, this community of sex radicals, many of whom were homosexual themselves, left few traces of an emergent public lesbian identity.[91] Yet, as we see in the writings in the *Freewoman* and the *New Freewoman,* in papers delivered to the BSSSP and the Eugenics Education Society, and in the enthusiastic formation of Freewoman Discussion Circles, small groups of early twentieth-century British women and men were actively working to redefine the parameters of marriage, reproduction, birth control, and free love, as well as the legal structures and cultural sanctions surrounding female sexualities. My analysis of the discursive traces of these debates seeks to explore both the widespread public silence surrounding female same-sex sexual practices and their emergent possibilities, not only through the language of sexology but also through rhetorical associations with the debates over marriage, free love, and women's heterosexual autonomy. Whereas male homosexual suffragists and feminists such as Edward Carpenter forged strong political and discursive links between male homosexuality and (heterosexual) female emancipation, they did not, and perhaps could not, inscribe female homosexuality into this alliance. The hypervisibility and clear legibility of male homosexuality in the prewar period, from Oscar Wilde's trials in the 1890s to Laurence Housman's declared desire for a kiss from a policeman in the epigraph to this chapter, were not accompanied by similar language for female homosexuality. Yet, as chapter 4 will illustrate, the prewar cultural and rhetorical links between male homosexuality and feminism formed part of the foundation upon which representations of female homosexuality would be built a few years later.

AROUND 1918: GENDER DEVIANCE, WARTIME NATIONALISM, AND SEXUAL INVERSION ON THE HOME FRONT

In the spring of 1918, as Britain's military forces were in retreat and the country expected humiliating defeat at the hands of Germany, two judicial events raised rhetorical concern over female sexual representation. In one instance, a novel by pacifist Rose Allatini was quickly and relatively quietly banned under the Defense of the Realm Act (DORA). Written under the pseudonym A. T. Fitzroy, *Despised and Rejected* recounts the wartime trials of a female homosexual and a pacifist homosexual man. The other event was the far more notorious "trial of the century," in which well-known dancer Maud Allan sued the Independent member of Parliament Noel Pemberton Billing for libel. Allan's attorney claimed that a piece in Billing's newspaper headlined "The Cult of the Clitoris" implied that Allan was a lesbian. Spurred by wartime concerns over British masculinity, these two representational stories together mapped relations of gender to sexuality in early twentieth-century constructions of homosexuality.

By reading *Despised and Rejected* and Maud Allan's trial together and in the context of the Great War's home front, we see that emergent public lesbian identities were produced not only through medicalized discourses of sexology, female homosocial traditions, and eugenics, but also through discourses of xenophobic nationalism and ideological affiliations with homosexual male figures during the war. The potent combination of juridical scrutiny and nationalist attack enabled nascent representations of female homosexual identity that had previously been unarticulated or unimagined and challenges us to reconsider relations among nationalism, gender affinity, and sexuality in public culture. Critical attention to the intersections of xenophobia, nationalism, and home-front homophobia illustrates the intractable relation of the emergence of female homosexual identity to the politics of the British nation. It is not simply that discourses of wartime nationalism created the conditions for the interwar emergence of a coherent lesbian subject, but also that the cultural anxiety surrounding sexual deviance in turn shaped ideas of the nation itself through debates over women's citizenship, roles, and desires.[1]

Representations of female homosexuality in British public culture qualitatively changed during the war. In the prewar period, although female same-sex erotic relationships flourished, British culture lacked any coherent narrative of female homosexual identity. Indeed, such a public identity may be said not to yet exist.[2] This chapter illustrates that, through association with male homosexual representation and in opposition to discourses of home-front nationalism, distinct models of female homosexuality emerged in public discourse during the Great War. On the home front, dominant cultural discourses of nationalism aligned male homosexuality with both sedition and femininity at the same time that women were encouraged to illustrate their patriotism through both maternal femininity and cultural masculinity. Rose Allatini's novel illustrates how female homosexuality can emerge narratively through the negotiation of effeminate gay male pacifism and patriotic female masculinity. Similarly, the rhetoric in Maud Allan's trial over her performance in Oscar Wilde's *Salomé* unveils numerous connections between male homosexual identity, nationalist rejection of "decadent" and "foreign" art in the name of state security, and the multiple, contradictory meanings of female sexual deviance in the public sphere. Reading the representational politics of Allan's notorious trial through Allatini's banned novel reveals the critical role of wartime nationalism in producing the modern lesbian subject. Together, these cultural texts evince dynamic, interconnected narratives of nationalism, female sexuality, and homosexuality in Great War Britain.

"The German and the Sodomite"

During the Great War, rhetorical attacks on male homosexuality forged connections with charges of sedition on the home front. Discourses of national degeneration and elite effeminacy were projected not only onto men but onto marginalized women as well—both pacifist women and sexual or national outsiders. I argue here that narratives of homosexual male contagion and cultural anxieties over women's involvement in the masculine public sphere enabled a new rhetoric of female homosexuality to emerge on the British home front. Other scholars have taken the right-wing homophobic nationalist discourse as a dominant cultural fear, however, whereas I argue that readings of diverse cultural responses to Allan's trial challenge the ubiquity of this connection of sedition and male homosexuality in Great War Britain.

Cultural historian Samuel Hynes argues that English wartime stories were needed first to sever prewar ties between England and Germany and then to illustrate England's unequivocal superiority to Germany. This was accomplished, he indicates, through the perpetuation of a widespread wartime belief that male decadence was as much a cause of England's involvement in the war as a German incursion beyond its borders: "Two ideas were at work . . . the notion that the English upper-classes were corrupt, and the notion that public-school boys were effeminate aesthetes. Both relate to the idea of English decadence as a cause of the war, which had first appeared in the war's early months, and had been a commonplace of English war talk since then."[3] This notion of a morally corrupt and emasculated aristocracy aligned pacifists and male homosexuals with a decaying, decadent upper-class representation of British masculinity.

In contrast, a robust and strong working-class England could save the nation from itself (and its ruling class). According to Hynes, the war was supposed to counterbalance aristocratic decadence and cleanse England. Yet "that cleansing had not occurred." Instead, by the middle of the war, "the infection had burst out" in the form of increasing exposure of male homosexuality in all ranks of the military.[4] In other words, the sturdy masculinity of England's soldiers was no match for the artistic homosexual decadence growing in England since Oscar Wilde's 1895 trials. Here male gender deviance stood as the explanation for a war gone wrong.

A more extreme variation on the same theme postulated a German homosexual corruption of English soldiers. Newspaper accounts of Maud Allan's trial particularly perpetuated this notion. Michael Kettle documents "a growing belief, carefully fostered by the extremists and demagogues, that there was a German fifth column at work in England, sedulously spreading defeatism and vicious habits and openly obstructing the British war effort by corruption and blackmail."[5] These two trains of thought combined to produce a "homosexual panic": first (from Hynes), the belief that England had been corrupted and compromised by internal decadence before the war; and, second, the more appealing nationalist belief (illustrated by Kettle) that wartime British male homosexuality was an import, the result of decadent and tricky Germans.[6]

Implicit scapegoating of homosexual men became explicit in conservative writings that took aim at the Liberal Party and its leader, prime minister Herbert Asquith. A key proponent of this rhetoric was, ironically, Lord
Alfred Douglas, now a social and political conservative keen to renounce
all of his prior associations with Wilde and homosexuality. His June 1915
article "God's Lovely Lust" asserts, "It is just as important to civilization
that Literary England should be cleansed of sex-mongers and peddlers of
the perverse, as that Flanders should be cleared of Germans."[7] In January
1916, he published a satirical poem entitled "The Rossiad," which intended
to "cleanse" literary England of "sex-mongers" by associating them with
Germany:

> O England, in thine hour of need,
> When mounted Death on his pale steed . . .
> Two foes thou hast, one there one here,
> One far, one intimately near,
> Two filthy fogs blot out thy light:
> The German and the Sodomite.[8]

The poem's final line contrasts sharply with the nostalgia of the rest of the
poem. The poem's domestic threat is the male who is not in his proper place,
at the front, but instead is "near": the "Sodomite" embodies the threat to
England's "sons."

As Britain lost ground to Germany, right-wing associations of male
homosexuality with Germany increased. In the conservative *English Review*,
Arnold White's "Efficiency and Vice" claimed that the "efficiency" of Germans led them to a sustained effort to "undermine the stamina of British
youth" through a "moral invasion of England." This moral invasion consisted of "the systematic seduction of young British soldiers by the German
urnings [male homosexuals] and their agents. . . . Failure to intern all Germans is due to the invisible hand that protects urnings of enemy race. . . .
The tendency in Germany is to abolish civilization as we know it, to substitute Sodom or Gomorrah for the New Jerusalem, and to infect clean
nations with Hunnish erotomania."[9] Here, male homosexuality becomes a
German weapon. This rhetoric mitigates any prewar sympathies for Germany, for, as Kettle notes, Germany was seen as a civilized, prominent
neighbor of British businessmen before the war. The accusations of such a
homosexual insurrection could explain a recent admiration turned into a

current distaste. In addition, the rhetoric incites a patriotic fervor for both the war at home (to cleanse Britain of its foreign contaminants) and the one abroad (to protect England and its allies from further infection).

These narratives of male homosexual panic often elide the critical role of female sexuality in the construction of home-front sexualities. The position of women within the discourse of male homosexual infection is a curious one. At times, British women remain an undifferentiated class of mothers, wives, and sisters. In White's diatribe, for example, women are placed opposite male homosexual corruption as he argues that "the subjection of women is one of the foundation stones of the German creed, as their violation is a perquisite of their troops. The desirability of legalising unnatural offences is another of the broadstones of the German Empire." The rape of conquered women thus becomes associated with a German movement (much exaggerated in this literature) to revoke Clause 175, which criminalized male homosexuality in Germany in 1871.[10] Women were a class to be protected from heterosexual violation by the conquering army, a familiar rhetorical strategy from the war's early days.[11] But the rhetoric of the Allan/Billing trial and Allatini's novel *Despised and Rejected* illustrates that women's roles exceeded their positions as heterosexual victims or staunch British mothers. Women, some of whom evidenced a prewar capacity to disrupt the state in violent agitation for women's suffrage, were, in the last months of the Great War, also potential threats to simple nationalism and naturalized heterosexuality. The national threat, moreover, was almost always linked to the already well-established danger posed by the male homosexual.

This chapter places an analysis of the rhetoric of male homosexual panic in conversation with that of the over- and undersexed suffragists or feminists and the cultural anxieties surrounding female heterosexuality during wartime, to suggest a new rendering of female same-sex desire on England's home front. Public representations of female homosexuality in mid-twentieth-century Britain were made possible not solely by an increasing dissemination of sexological texts, as most historians of sexuality have assumed, but also by a combination of medical, legal, historical, and cultural factors. These factors included the increasing visibility of "passing" working-class women, widespread cultural discomfort with bourgeois romantic friendships, and the increased visibility of gay male representations after the Wilde trials of 1895 and in homophobic narratives of wartime patriotism. These cultural factors enabled new textual possibilities: female homosexuality's discursive disruptions of the narrative drive of marriage and heterosexuality, combined with the Great War's material, political, and economic agitations. Narratives of dislocation and displacement forged representations of female homosexuality through doubled rhetorical and cultural alienation of national outsider status. The Allan/Billing trial and Allatini's novel illustrate that although homophobic nationalist narratives enabled emergent narratives of female homosexuality, male and female homosexuality functioned quite differently in this rhetoric. By examining the Allan/Billing trial not only in the context of right-wing homophobic nationalism but also alongside Allatini's representations of female sexuality, this chapter seeks to complicate prior assertions by historians and cultural critics regarding the wartime ubiquity of a sexologically based, xenophobically produced public representation of lesbian identity. Nationalist homophobia may have created the conditions for public discussions of male homosexuality, but it was the congruence of this nationalist rhetoric with troubled sexual and gendered ideologies on the home front and the legacy of women's independence from the suffrage agitations that led to a legible—if not coherent—narrative of female homosexuality in Great War Britain.

Despised, Rejected, and Banned

Written by Rose Allatini in 1917, published under the pseudonym A. T. Fitzroy in May 1918, and banned under DORA in October 1918, *Despised and Rejected* illustrates complex relations among home-front nationalism, wartime sexual transformations, and pacifist resistance in Great War Britain. Though in circulation for only a few months, this pacifist novel of homosexual solidarity sold half its print run and was reviewed in the *Times Literary Supplement* before its censure.[12] The banning was covered by the *Times,* the *Daily News,* the *Herald* and the *New Statesman,* and was noticed by literati including Virginia Woolf.[13] The novel can be read as a cultural artifact as well as a curiosity: it both documents nascent lesbian representations and expands the pacifist literature of Great War Britain. In fact, these two domains—homosexual representation and pacifism—are mutually constituted in the world of the novel and in its censure. The prewar sections of the novel establish Allatini's sympathy with the sexological and cultural constructions of homosexuality established by Edward Carpenter, although the wartime sections complicate Carpenter's model of an exceptional "intermediate type" and reveal the historical specificities of male and female homosexual identity formations.[14] The novel's conclusion illustrates a more complicated relation of lesbian identity to male homosexual representations. The novel equates pacifism with feminized male homosexuality, and militarism with brutish heterosexual masculinity in both men and women. Women's gender presentations are mediated by their political, as well as their sexual, "type" in complex and often contradictory rhetorical moves. A reading of this novel's censure as well as the text's constructions of male and female masculinity, pacifism, and sexual identity reveal critical cleavages within British national identity, the role of gender and sexual conformity on the home front, and the interdependent yet distinct evolutions of male and female homosexuality in the public imagination in England in the early twentieth century. This reading constructs representative possibilities of female same-sex desire, rather than arguing for an excavation of already existent identities.

Despised and Rejected introduces its readers to its central characters, the young Dennis and Antoinette, in the years before the Great War. Young Dennis is a "square peg in a round hole" whose modern musical compositions alienate his family as much as his weak, "feminine" mouth and his childhood distaste for war toys, whereas the adolescent Antoinette reports that she "just [fits] in anywhere."[15] Dennis is depicted as a congenital sexual invert, marked as such from childhood, whereas Antoinette's homosexuality is inscribed first through her history of adolescent crushes on girls and women and then, in a surprising turn, through her love for Dennis. Thus, male homosexuality is represented through a paradigm of medical gender inversion and alienated modernity, but female homosexuality lacks the morbidity Dennis feels, and is produced in part through a queer sort of heterosexual desire. This critical gendered differentiation engages the gap in cultural representations of male and female sexuality in prewar Britain.

Difference has an organic basis in Dennis. As his mother comments apologetically to a new friend, "We could never get Dennis to play with soldiers or steamers or any of the usual toys. His father used to get quite angry. He always wanted his boys to be *manly* boys" (emphasis in original).[16] Here a nascent pacifism is aligned with effeminacy: even as a child, Dennis does not display appropriately masculine desires for war toys, and these desires, though coded as gender inversion, are also markers of Dennis's other deviance—his pacifism.

This gender inversion is not total: Allatini carefully establishes a continuum for all of her deviant characters. Dennis is handsome and masculine in some ways, yet his body reveals a "taint": "He was overwhelmed by the longing that always assailed him in a large gathering of strangers, namely to run away and hide . . . a longing that was absurd and incongruous in conjunction with his broad shoulders and length of limb. Perhaps his mouth alone, curved and sensitive above the firm chin, betrayed a nature in which such a longing, and others equally freakish, might hold their sway."[17] Dennis's desire to hide from crowds and other desires "equally freakish" are linked to physical gender inversions. Here, bodily inversion is tied to emotional alienation: cowardly feelings are "absurd" in an otherwise masculine-looking young man. This passage, which echoes the sexological narratives of Havelock Ellis and Edward Carpenter, establishes certain physical traits as masculine and others as feminine. Though Allatini does not construct Dennis as a parody of femininity, she marks his body as somehow feminine to convincingly inscribe his sexual inversion as inborn and unchangeable.

When Dennis recognizes his multiple alienations as symptoms of homosexual identity, the novel illustrates the cultural consequences of male homosexuality while providing an explanatory model for such desires. Dennis is

different, not only by reason of his music. It was not his music alone that he had striven to keep out. . . . He must be for ever an outcast amongst men, shunned by them, despised and mocked by them. He was maddened by fear and horror and loathing of himself.

Abnormal—perverted—against nature—he could hear the epithets that would be hurled against him, and that he would deserve. Yes, but what had nature been about, in giving him the soul of a woman in the body of a man?[18]

For Allatini, male homosexuality produces prolonged self-debasement and equals psychic gender inversion. Dennis links his sexual desire for his beloved Alan with a necessary "soul of a woman." Here, Allatini echoes Carpenter's formulation of homosexuality. Carpenter describes the "normal type of the Uranian man," who, "while possessing thoroughly masculine powers of mind and body, combines with them the tenderer and more emotional soul-nature of the woman." He may "have often a peculiar gift; . . . the artist-nature, with the artist's sensibility and perception. Such an one is often a dreamer, of brooding, reserved habits, often a musician."[19] Thus, Dennis's musical inclinations, his distaste for large groups, and his developmental and bodily effeminacy all lead inevitably toward male homosexual desire.

Like Dennis, Antoinette is homosexual, but her trajectory within the novel's plot and her psychic and physical composition differ radically from those of Dennis. Here Allatini diverges from Carpenter's model of the female intermediate type most clearly. The differences reflect the disjunction between cultural representations and conceptions of male and female sexuality generally, and specifically between the divergent ways that homosexuality could be conceived of for male and female subjects in 1918.

Unlike Dennis, Antoinette is neither a gender invert nor a social introvert.[20] Her youthful homosexual desires do not imprint innate feelings of isolation or difference, and she initially reflects none of the "special combination of qualities" or inner masculine nature that Carpenter says "homogenic women" have.[21] Rather, Antoinette views her erotic feelings toward other women either as unexceptional predecessors to her eventual love for men or as simply amusing diversions, experiences that she requires to keep herself entertained. Indeed, in stark contrast to Dennis, her desires for other women are not alienating feelings that precipitate fear, horror, and rejection, but "natural" emotions producing excitement and interest.

Antoinette's first homoerotic relations spell out the terms of female same-sex erotics in the novel and map her nascent homosexual characteristics. In the novel's first pages, Antoinette encounters Hester, an aloof woman with whom she is quickly enamored. Surrounded by families at a summer resort, the solitary Hester is often "armed with a masculine-looking walking stick."[22] Antoinette's fascination with Hester resembles nothing more than a nineteenth-century "schoolgirl crush": "She could have shouted aloud with the joy of being alive, and in love: if Hester would only allow herself to be loved, she would try to make up to her for all of the bitterness and disappointment that might have been in her life. Antoinette was young enough and mad enough at the moment to believe that anything was possible."[23] Antoinette's love resembles a schoolgirl crush rather than either a mature heterosexual passion or Dennis's masochistic agonies over Alan. As Martha Vicinus notes, the language of love, romance, and denial frequently imbued the late nineteenth-century discourse of adolescent girls' attachments to older women. Like many of the girls discussed by Vicinus (and by early twentieth-century educators and sexologists, including Havelock Ellis), Antoinette prefers to love from afar, and finds, with Hester, that intimacy destroys rather than strengthens her love. Vicinus argues that these schoolgirl "raves" were not necessarily (nor necessarily not) "precursors" or "veils" for more modern homosexual attachments. By the mid-1920s, when female homosexual representations circulated more widely, such schoolgirl relationships were more heavily monitored and censored.[24]

In *Despised and Rejected,* Antoinette's schoolgirl crushes become symptoms of her eventual homosexuality. This narrative runs counter to Havelock Ellis's sexological diagnosis of such "raves" or "flames" as transitory and nonpathological. Ellis acknowledged the "sexual element" in these raves yet distinguished them from "true" homosexuality, which, to him, comprised the combination of gender inversion and same-sex desire that he labeled "congenital."[25]

Unlike Ellis, who did not view schoolgirl crushes as a sign or symptom of homosexuality, Allatini establishes both Antoinette's love for Hester and her multiple girlhood crushes as symptoms of her lesbianism. Antoinette first views her schoolgirl "flames" as indications of an eventual heterosexual fire: "If already this world of women and girls, narrow though it was, could contain for her such a wealth of thrills and excitement, how much more wonderful must be that other world, the world beyond school, the world of men." Yet, where Ellis would predict greater cross-sex things to come, Antoinette is sadly disappointed after her adolescence and boarding school years. Despite her anticipation, men cannot satisfy her as women and girls do. It is not until Hester appears that Antoinette's desires are rekindled: "It was a long time since she had been as happy and excited as she was now. Her schooldays had held occasional periods of a similar excitement, but the three years since she had left boarding-school had been conspicuously barren, compared with what had gone before."[26] Antoinette views her relationships with girls and women in school much in the same transitional light by which Ellis viewed them, yet Allatini constructs them as indicators of Antoinette's emerging sexual inversion. Like her cropped hair, Antoinette's relations with women could be seen as something other than symptoms of homosexuality, but in Allatini's narrative they must function as its predictors.

Antoinette's schoolgirl crushes serve two functions. First, they place her in the context of same-sex erotics. Yet, because such crushes were so common, they also establish Antoinette's desires for women outside the realm of perversion into which discussions of male homosexuality seem inevitably to fall. Delighted that her crush on Hester relieves the boredom of "her fruitless search in the world of masculinity," Antoinette is unaware of any possible stigma such a relationship might hold: *"Antoinette was free from the least taint of morbidity*; unaware that there was aught unusual about her attitude—Hester herself had perceived this—she merely felt that she was coming into her own again, and was healthy-minded and joyous in her unquestioning obedience to the dictates of her inmost nature" (emphasis added).[27] Like that of Dennis, Antoinette's homosexuality is innate or "inmost." On the one hand, Antoinette is unaware of any "morbidity." On the other hand, the narrator is painfully attuned to the morbid possibility of her feelings. As Laura Doan notes in her discussion of this passage, "In Antoinette Allatini thus creates a well-adjusted female Uranian who is more capable than her fellow Uranian Dennis in coping with a life on the margins of so-called normal society."[28] Taking this point a bit further, it seems to me that although female homosexuality, because of its integration into Antoinette's adolescence, is less troubling than Dennis's physical and psychic inversion, it is also more difficult to represent textually. Thus, for example, Antoinette's schoolgirl crush is necessary to establish her homosexual subjectivity, but it is imbued with narrative tension; it can be read as both sexual and asexual, innocent and morbid.

Antoinette's homosexuality must be verbally revealed to her by the novel's other central homosexual character: Dennis inadvertently informs her of her identity, incorrectly assuming that she already has this self-knowledge. She cannot "know" her own homosexuality without assistance. As she traces her homosexual development through her schoolgirl crushes, she wonders why they seem so innocent and natural to her. At her request, Dennis explains "how he knew" of her taint:

> "My child, the way you looked at that woman [Hester] was quite enough." . . . Rapidly she cast her mind over those school-girl passions of her early youth. . . . *This, then, was the taint of which he spoke; the taint that they shared, he and she. Only whereas he had always striven against these tendencies in himself, in herself she had never regarded them as abnormal.* It had seemed disappointing, but not in the least unnatural, that all her passionate longings should have been awakened by women, instead of members of the opposite sex. (emphasis added)

This passage illustrates key differences between constructions of male and female homosexuality while it also demonstrates the continuum or slide from "innocent" romantic schoolgirl crushes to homosexuality. Antoinette's internal monologue that reveals her love for Dennis immediately follows, producing a cross-sex desire for Dennis, a homosexual man, that mediates her identification as a lesbian: "A wave of burning tenderness and longing came over her. It was a shame that he should have to suffer so horribly from the consciousness of his abnormality, while her own had never caused her the slightest uneasiness."[29] Antoinette's cross-sex "burning tenderness" both tempers her own homosexual revelation and highlights narratively the difference between a female homosexual identity and a male homosexual identity. Female same-sex attraction causes no "uneasiness," but male homosexuality produces a "despised and rejected" subject.

Antoinette's romantic relationship with Dennis increases in intensity through the novel. Paradoxically, however, her growing heterosexual (queer) desire for Dennis functions in the novel as a symptom of her true homosexuality. Gay Wachman explains this cross-sex construction: "Since she and Dennis believe that inversion is innate and permanent, it is possible for Antoinette to suffer simultaneously from her unrequited heterosexual love for Dennis and from her 'terror and loneliness of the Ishmaelite, outcast among men and women.' It is hard not to become impatient at this point in the novel; Allatini permits no glimmer of opposition, or even common sense, to penetrate this fog of ideology."[30]

Wachman appears to retreat from her own formulation of lesbian "crosswriting" here, refusing to read Antoinette's love for Dennis as a cross-sex, homosexual affiliation.[31] Instead, Wachman turns to the biographical, dismissing the construction of Antoinette's sexuality in a historical trajectory: "I am inclined to identify aspects of Antoinette's situation with Rose Allatini's."[32] This biographical elision, however, forecloses a more nuanced reading of Antoinette's subjectivity in an otherwise seminal reading of this underanalyzed novel; for the novel itself produces an emergent lesbian identity through Antoinette's affiliation with male homosexuality. After Dennis reveals himself as a homosexual, Antoinette first doubts her own homosexuality but then finds it again via cross-sex affiliation with Dennis:

> She said, "Will you tell me what it means, Dennis, that I should care for you like this?" She really meant: "Doesn't it prove me perfectly normal after all?"
>
> And he understood and answered the unspoken part of her question. "It's only another proof of your abnormality, my poor child. No normal woman could care for me, I'm sure. You only do, because you are what you are, and I am what I am. It's 'like to like,' as I said."

Allatini's "like to like" serves up Antoinette as a full-fledged homosexual woman, no matter how strong her passion for Dennis may appear. We see this narrative structure again when Antoinette is attracted to a fellow pacifist woman, Pegeen. Antoinette's love for Dennis tempers this passion but does not extinguish her homosexual desire: "Antoinette was fully alive to Pegeen's attraction, and realised that she might have had one of her swift burning passions for her, had she not been so entirely absorbed in Dennis, the greater love blotting out all possibility of a lesser."[33] Pegeen is figured as predominantly heterosexual, but, like Antoinette's earlier loves, she also flirts with women. This brief flirtation illustrates Allatini's depiction of women's sexuality as far less rigid than that of men.

The configuration of Antoinette's desire for Dennis alongside her desire for women is critical to understanding Allatini's representational model of emerging female homosexuality. First, her "like to like" attraction to Dennis establishes a gender-integrative identity category that connects male and female subjects, constructing homosexuality as an identity for both men and women based primarily on sexual deviance. This further enables Allatini to construct a homosexual woman without having to create a same-sex erotic desire outside previous literary models. The novel's early homo-erotic sections echo "smashing" novels, wherein girls experience crushes on one another and their teacher. Later, with Pegeen, Antoinette can *be* a homosexual without Allatini's having to script the culturally difficult subject of female homosexual desire. Same-sex desire is the subtext of Antoinette's lesbian identity, but is never as explicit as Dennis's male same-sex desire.

Allatini's representation of male and female homosexuals combines, but does not merge, sexual and gendered inversions. For men, feminine characteristics present an incontrovertible symptom of homosexuality. For example, in her jealousy of Dennis's lover Alan, Antoinette realizes her gendered disadvantage: "She could quite well imagine how he would appeal to Dennis . . . this terrible boy against whom she was utterly powerless, for he seemed to possess all of the fascination of her own sex as well as of his." Feminine "fascination" is a powerful element in same-sex attractions between men. Yet male homosexuality is not produced as *only* gender inversion. Dennis explicitly rejects any wholly feminized male lover: "'Damn you, don't talk and look like that!' Dennis blazed out [at Alan] in a sudden rage, 'you might be a woman, intolerant of all favourites but yourself!'" Such gender inversion is present in a lesser degree in women's sexual inversion; but it is not the primary symptom in women, for Allatini, that it is for men. Cross-sex attachment—"crosswriting" for Wachman, or "like to like" according to Allatini—can produce a female homosexual as readily as cross-gender identification in this novel.[34]

Like gender inversion, sexual inversion (homosexuality) comes in degrees. Following Carpenter, Alan explains to Dennis, "We're both right over the border-line of the normal—I more than you because no woman could ever attract me in the least."[35] Unlike Ellis and Freud, who aligned homosexual women more strongly with gender inversion than with homosexual men, Allatini renders Antoinette closer to the "borderline of normal" than Alan and Dennis, as her great passion is for a man. Yet the fact that Dennis, too, is an invert places Antoinette across that line, adding to her numerous attractions to women, both as a girl and a young woman. For men, then, homosexuality is more clearly wedded to gender inversion. For women, representations of an identity predicated on same-sex desire are more complicated: gender inversion can, but need not, lead to sexual inversion; romantic friendships are often, but not always, symptoms of mature homosexuality; and the perversion and deviance associated with male homosexuality come only through an identification of female same-sex desire with the more-established identity of male sexual inversion. These conditional symptoms within the novel reflect the broader context in which Allatini wrote: a society wherein male homosexuality had a legally defined position, but where the concept of female homosexuality was far less formed and thus both more mutable and more challenging to represent.

Yet Dennis's homosexuality also surpasses prewar representational models. His sexual deviance both elaborates on prewar medical and legal articulations of male homosexuality and is also produced by the Great War's associations with pacifism and modernity.[36] Structurally, male homosexuality equals pacifism, and these two identities reinforce each other in the novel. As the novel concludes, Dennis is imprisoned and rejected by most of his family for refusing to join the army, not for gross indecencies. Pacifists, like homosexuals, have a "natural bent" that will not be corrected or erased by imprisonment. From the start of the novel, when Dennis's refusal to play with war toys marks him as unmanly, pacifism stands for and alongside male homosexual identity.

The novel's enmeshed relationships between gender, nationalism, and sexual identity are further entwined by men's and women's relations to war. Both pacifism and male homosexuality are aligned with modern "progress" rather than a premodern "instinct" advocated by the pro-war characters in the novel. Dennis's patriotic father declares that "if a man's got no fight in him, he's unnatural, that's what I say, unnatural." Dennis, then, is unnatural as much because of his pacifism as because of his other innate and "unnatural" identity as a male homosexual. Dennis links pacifism (and, implicitly, male homosexuality) to modernity and strength, rather than to more familiar registers of weakness and degeneration. Just as "man" has "conquer[ed] nature with his ships and his railways," so too should the "war-instinct" be conquered: "You want progress and the conquest of natural difficulties in every possible direction, and yet you won't admit that a man can conquer *himself.* You're shouted down as 'unnatural,' if you as much as speak of overcoming an instinct that is nothing but a hindrance to civilisation and progress" (emphasis in original).[37] Allatini reverses the logic of "instincts" to associate heterosexual aggression with the premodern and the conquering of "man" by "*himself*" with enlightened modernity. Dennis's father cannot counter his son's logic, so he dismisses it as the "twaddle" of "you and your artistic friends." Noting Allatini's debt to Edward Carpenter in this matter, Claire Tylee observes that "Allatini links her analysis of 'manliness' to the current cultural debate about the degeneracy of the British race and the decadence of English culture."[38] Lines are firmly drawn in this novel: modern pacifists, artists, and homosexuals stand on one side; premodern (also characterized as "Victorian") middle-class heterosexual men are on the other.

War produces masculinity in both women and men; rather than uniformly reinforcing conformity to gender codes, war highlights the masculine in all warmongers and the feminine in all pacifists. Dennis and Alan, as well as their male heterosexual pacifist compatriots, are feminized. In contrast, militaristic women are "khaki-clad females who say they wish they were men, so they could kill a few Huns themselves." Not only do such women "wish they were men," but several take on masculine attitudes and clothing: "Lily Hallard, very military indeed in her V.A.D. uniform, openly confessed that she didn't like the prospect of having a shirker for a brother-in-law; and in her loud-voiced aggressive manner tried to convert Dennis to a proper frame of mind."[39] This "conversion," of course, inevitably fails, as Lily is the wrong ideological and sexual stripe to sway Dennis.

The novel's publishing history replicates this analogy between homosexuality and pacifism. Released in May 1918, the novel was banned in October of the same year.[40] As Virginia Woolf noted in her diary, it was "burnt by the hangman."[41] Yet, unlike D. H. Lawrence's *The Rainbow, Despised and Rejected* was not censured for its immoral sexual content.[42] Rather, the novel was prosecuted under the wartime "Defense of the Realm" regulations and was found "likely to prejudice the recruiting, training, and discipline of persons in his Majesty's forces." Thus, although its homosexual content would undoubtedly warrant moral, if not also legal, censure, this novel was removed from circulation not because of its homosexual theme but because of its twin—its pacifist content. As alderman Sir Charles Wakefield noted in his ruling, "the question whether the book was obscene was not before him, but he did not hesitate to describe it as morally unhealthy and most pernicious."[43] While Wakefield considered whether or not he should (or could) send the publishers to prison, he satisfied himself by imposing the maximum fine permissible—one hundred pounds plus costs to each defendant.

The defense in the case argued against the novel's seditious effects by claiming that even though Dennis is a pacifist, the novel itself presents both sides of the issue. In fact, homosexuality was invoked as a defense against pacifism: Mr. Whitely, for the defense, argued that "the title . . . referred to the abnormal sexual tendencies of the hero, and not to his pacifist views." This unsuccessful strategy failed in part because, rhetorically, pacifism and homosexuality appear intractably connected to each other and to Dennis. On the home front, or at least in Wakefield's courtroom, homosexuality could not be extracted from pacifism: they were entwined not only in the text of Allatini's novel but also in its censure.

But what of Antoinette? The legal censure of the novel made no mention of the textual female homosexuality, nor any of the novel's connections between suffrage women and pacifist men. Was the figure of Antoinette irrelevant in the legal proceeding because women were exempt from required military service or because female homosexuality was not against the law? The relationship of Antoinette's gender identification to feminized pacifism is ambiguous. Decidedly *not* the "mannish lesbian" who would proliferate in British letters by the late 1920s, Antoinette is neither a mannish patriot like Lily Hallard nor an abjectly feminized male pacifist such as Dennis or Alan.

The key to the novel's representational innovations lies, in fact, with Antoinette. Allatini uses familiar tropes of schoolgirl romance and heterosexual desire to establish Antoinette's homosexuality thematically. Yet the novel's conclusion reinforces this figure structurally and establishes a necessary connection between Antoinette's emergent homosexual representation and the Great War. Novels written in the midst of the conflict posed a problem for conventional narrative: Who would win? Would a given story end in victory or defeat, tragedy or celebration? Narrative indeterminacy reigned, troubling narrative closure, reflecting the national indecidability in which the texts were written, and, indeed, contributing to modernity's embrace of alienation and disruption.

Despised and Rejected demonstrates how this ideological indecidability constructed narratives of female homosexuality in the 1910s: no "happy ending" could be conceived for Antoinette in which her homosexual orientation remains intact. Laura Doan argues that Antoinette is included in Allatini's illustration of Carpenter's vision of a "new race" of sexual intermediates, through her reproductive capabilities: "The female Uranian is crucial for she alone can reproduce a race of the highest caliber in her unique capacity to love her male counterpart and in her potential to create pure-bred intermediates. Allatini literally fleshes out Carpenter's idealized vision of the future and positions Antoinette in the forefront of 'the advance-guard of a more enlightened civilization.'"[44] Yet Allatini does not include Antoinette in Alan and Dennis's homogenic future: she remains instead on the margins, unsure of her role. The novel ends with Dennis in prison for resisting conscription and Antoinette alone, rejected by her family for her pacifism yet unable to "stand by her man" because, of course, Dennis *has* a "man," his lover Alan, also in prison. It is this lack of love from Dennis, not a cross-gender reproductive utopia, that concludes the novel: "Not that she minded being on the unpopular side. She could have enjoyed . . . the rebel-sense of her unofficial right to stand by him, if only he had loved her. But—by his lack of love, he debarred her from this right, just as she had been debarred from official congratulation and condolence. She was an outcast in a double sense."[45]

Although Antoinette's homosexual *desire* has faded by novel's end (we hear no more of Hester or Pegeen), her homosexual *identity* has not. Just as Dennis is a "double outsider" as a pacifist and homosexual, so too is Antoinette. Here Allatini critiques and supplements Carpenter's utopian vision of a Uranian future, because this vision (and the prewar culture in which it was conceived) does not yet hold a clear place for the female homosexual. The novel ends in narrative indeterminacy and ideological indecidability—about the war and about Antoinette's future. Yet, as unstable as her position is, the figure of Antoinette demonstrates the possibilities that dominant discourses of male homosexual contagion and destruction could produce. Though thematically a clearly defined lesbian subject was still evasive, the narrative structure of the novel's end places Antoinette beside Dennis in the camp of pacifism, homosexuality, and difference.

What remains certain, then, is a narrative and thematic possibility of a future emergent lesbian identity.

"An Unprecedented Orgy of Scandal and Disorder": ## Rex v. Pemberton Billing

Like *Despised and Rejected,* the rhetoric of female homosexuality in the Allan/Billing libel trial depended for its articulation on wartime discourses of nationalism. In contrast to the textual strategies of Allatini's novel, the discourse of lesbianism in the trial drew its ideological and rhetorical force from linking excessive female sexuality generally to lesbianism specifically.[46] In the rhetoric surrounding the trial, for example, Maud Allan's alleged lesbianism was linked to her sexually provocative dancing career and knowledge of sexual anatomy, whereas Allatini's novel produces female homosexuality through Antoinette's intimacies with women and her close association with Dennis. Laura Doan notes that the Allan/Billing trial marks "the beginning of an important shift in the visibility of lesbianism in English legal discourse and in the public arena."[47] In her analysis of the case, Jodie Medd also argues that "the very *suggestibility* of lesbianism . . . rendered it a particularly powerful vehicle for figuring the wartime problematic of uncertainty, illegibility, and (mis)representation. Not only are sexual secrets considered commensurate with national ones, but the wartime dilemma of unknowability and uncertainty finds an analogy in the highly suggestive but ultimately unknowable notion of female homosexuality." Yet when read in conjunction with *Despised and Rejected* and its banning, Allan's libel trial does in fact help us to "know" what Medd calls the "ultimately unknowable notion of female homosexuality."[48] The rhetoric of female sexual desire, deviance, and representation mobilized in this trial by the prosecution (Allan) and the defense (Billing) leverages medical diagnoses beyond the hospital, highlights the increasingly direct relationship of lesbian erotics to the law, illustrates the interdependence of male and female homosexual representation, and cements the bond between an expanding rhetorical power of female homosexuality and British nationalism during World War I.

The details of *Rex v. Pemberton Billing* make for salacious gossip—a middlebrow dancer entangled in matters of sedition, possibly with the former prime minister's wife!—and compelling cultural study: How did the players each discursively render female homosexuality? What do the daily newspaper reports contribute to our understanding of a trial for which no official record exists?[49] What was the role of sexology in this "trial of the century"?

Rather than duplicate existing excellent studies on the trial, this section builds on that existing work to bring critical attention to the role of nationalist and orientalist discourses in the trial.[50] Read in conjunction with *Despised and Rejected,* the trial confirms the relationship between modern lesbian representation and racialized wartime nationalism. Daily newspaper reports, as well as private correspondence and collateral cultural texts, invite not an analysis of a single (and now missing) legal record but a moment of multitextual cultural production. As the Great War appeared ever more bloody and endless, the trial's position in British public culture illustrates how the gendered and sexual politics of the war played out through homefront nationalist rhetoric. Discourses of national belonging and betrayal produced new representational possibilities for female sexuality in general, and homosexuality specifically.

In the first months of 1918, Noel Pemberton Billing drew women into the web of homosexual intrigue that other conservative pundits had previously limited to men. A self-described patriot sprung from England's middle class, Billing was elected to the House of Commons on a platform that combined military strength through aviation with xenophobic patriotism.[51] Billing attempted, for example, to popularize such notions as "Jewish ghettos and yellow star badges; anti-German and anti-alien strictures."[52] His anti-German sentiments sat awkwardly with his admiration for German "efficiency" and fascist politics. Beyond his activities in Parliament, he advocated for these extremist views through the Vigilante Society, which he founded in June 1917, and its organ, first named the *Imperialist* and then renamed the *Vigilante* in February 1918.[53] Billing's encounters with Maud Allan and the London production of *Salomé* began with two articles published in these newspapers in early 1918.

On January 26, 1918, an article appeared in the *Imperialist* that would prove to be the opening volley in Billing's most public battle with the liberal establishment in England, which he accused of corrupting the nation and bungling the war. Headlined "The First 47,000," the article announces the existence of "a book compiled by the Secret Service from reports of German agents who have infested this country for the past 20 years, agents so vile and spreading such debauchery and such lasciviousness as only German minds can conceive and only German bodies execute." Billing claims, "The officer who discovered this book while on special service briefly outlined for me its stupefying contents which all decent men thought had perished in Sodom and Lesbia." The "Black Book" allegedly contained a list of 47,000 corrupted British subjects, men and women from all professional, social, political, and military ranks: "Wives of men in supreme position were entangled. In lesbian ecstasy the most sacred secrets of State were betrayed. The sexual peculiarities of members of the Peerage were used as a leverage to open fruitful fields for espionage."[54] The sensationalized language of degeneracy and the explicit challenge to the ruling class reinforced fears that an effete British elite would be unable to defeat Germany. Notably, lesbianism appears as a national threat alongside male homosexuality (the reference to "wives of men in supreme position" attacked specifically Margot Asquith, the wife of the recently unseated Liberal prime minister). As Medd notes, "The Billing trial signals the first time the discussion of *female* homosexuality obsessed the British popular press" (emphasis in original).[55] Not only did lesbianism emerge in public discourse, but female homosexuality also appears as a correlation to sedition, as had male homosexuality previously.

Billing hoped this article would elicit a libel trial and thus create a forum, beyond the House of Commons, in which to air his wild accusations of sedition in the Liberal Party and corruption throughout England's ruling classes. When the general public failed to rise to the bait of his Black Book report, he soon seized an opportunity to reignite this spark of controversy. The occasion was the private performance of Oscar Wilde's long-banned play *Salomé,* starring Maud Allan in the title role. On February 16, 1918, Billing published a short paragraph in the *Vigilante* headlined "The Cult of the Clitoris." The notice's entire text reads thus: "To be a member of Maud Allan's private performances on [*sic*] Oscar Wilde's *Salome* one has to apply to a Miss Caletta of 9, Duke Street, Adelphi, W.C. If Scotland Yard were to seize the list of these members I have no doubt they would secure the names of several of the first 47,000."[56]

This headline finally yielded the publicity Billing had been courting. On March 8, 1918, Maud Allan and the play's producer, Jack Grein, began proceedings to charge Billing with criminal libel. These two plaintiffs fit perfectly with Billing's paranoid fantasies of a compromised and corrupted Britain. Grein was a "foreigner"—a naturalized English citizen, born in Amsterdam—and his foreign birth clearly concerned his lawyer, Travers Humphreys. Humphreys made a point of describing Grein in the pretrial hearing as "a gentleman who has been a British subject by naturalization for some twenty-three years."[57] Grein was, according to Hoare, "an ardent suffragist who dressed like a dandy, [so that] his whole demeanour would have shrieked decadence to Billing." Maud Allan also "shrieked decadence" in her own way: she can be likened to Isadora Duncan and Mata Hari in her "[challenge of] Victorian concepts of femininity." Allan was born in Canada and raised in San Francisco, and she had studied and performed in Germany and throughout Europe before moving to England and finding some success onstage.[58] When Billing targeted Grein and Allan, he choose two subjects who were already suspect to his rightist companions.

Thus began "the trial of the century" and the war's most public interrogation of female sexuality. Running from May 29 through June 4, 1918, the trial generated a media circus covered by dozens of British and European newspapers. Covered by papers from the highbrow *Times* to the popular-press *News of the World,* this trial engaged and enraged the British public. Whereas members of the ruling elite might worry about their own reputations or associations with the case as they read daily reports in the *Times,* the working-class readers of the *News of the World* or British *People* may have viewed the trial coverage as "another story about the titillating sexual misdemeanors of the elite."[59]

In the trial's course, witnesses, lawyers, and the presiding judge debated the relationships of nationalist identities, medical terminology, and popular representations of female sexuality. Throughout the trial, the importance of the "German origins" of sexology played directly into nationalist hysteria; and the status of female homosexuality was challenged, questioned, refined, and brought into a public light in a simultaneously shrouded and yet also incessantly repeated fashion. Female homosexuality was variously defined as hyperfemininity, masculinity, a perversion such as sadism, and a symptom of sedition. Throughout the trial, Billing, who chose to represent himself without legal counsel, argued all sides of this issue, illuminating the dramatic flexibility of the emergent category of "the lesbian" in 1918. Allan's lawyer defended her against charges of sexual impropriety and inferences of female homosexuality by similarly mobilizing multiple models of homosexuality, nationalism, and femininity. The rhetoric of the trial illustrates the wartime relationships among medical definitions and legal uses of female homosexuality, cultural understandings of deviant female sexuality and gender construction, the imbrication of Wilde's play with such understandings, and, finally, the implications of rhetorics of lesbianism that emerged in increasingly public capacities in the final years of the Great War.

The Black Book was the material object around which the trial revolved—and it was missing. This mysterious tome carried within it—or so Billing and his supporters claimed[60]—the confirmation of a German plot to weaken England by homosexual contamination. The reported Black Book and its 47,000 traitors yoke the rhetoric of patriotism and anti-German sentiment to a homophobic discourse of infiltration and contagion. Jean Bobby Noble comments, "The entire existence of the Black Book is predicated on the hysterical and panicked spectre of racial and sexual passing."[61] Billing brought together powerful fears of a well-established male homosexual subjectivity with fear of a more nebulous and far less familiar specter of female homosexuality. Male homosexuality was already easily grasped, and its "degenerative" qualities well documented. But what of female homosexuality? Billing linked the two together through his rhetoric of "Sodom and Lesbia."

The ubiquity and mystery of the 47,000 names allegedly listed in the Black Book enabled Billing to accuse any man or woman who opposed or irritated him of being on the list. As the court proceeding was turning against him, Billing called his lover, Mrs. Eileen Villiers-Stuart, to the witness box to verify the existence of the Black Book. Scholars diverge on her role: she was originally sent to Billing by Liberal Parliament members to blackmail him, but she later apparently crossed over to his side. After the trial's conclusion, in July 1918, however, she recanted her testimony supporting Billing and signed a statement claiming that much of Billing's evidence regarding the Black Book had been concocted.[62] In court, she testified that she had seen what is most likely a nonexistent Black Book. When, in Kettle's words, "Billing . . . lost his temper—mainly with himself, because of his inability to use his star witness properly," and the judge, Justice Darling, attempted to remove Villiers-Stuart from the witness box, Billing began shouting questions at his own witness:

BILLING: Is Justice Darling's name in that book?

MRS. V.-S.: It is, and that book can be produced. . . . It can be produced; if it can be produced in Germany, it can be produced here. Mr. Justice Darling, we have got to win this war, and while you sit there, we will never win it. My men are fighting, other people's men are fighting—[63]

Here, patriotism mingled with wild accusations of homosexuality and sedition. After accusing Judge Darling of homosexuality, Mrs. Villiers-Stuart proceeded seamlessly into her justification for what she later confessed was false testimony: "We have got to win this war, and while you sit there, we will never win it. My men are fighting." She then quickly named former prime minister Asquith and his wife as members of the 47,000 as the judge ordered her from the witness box. Accusations of homosexuality were equivalent to accusations of sedition, and any trite expression of patriotism seemed justification enough for otherwise grossly libelous speeches.

This general accusation of homosexuality was located most specifically in the allegedly libelous headline, "The Cult of the Clitoris." The origin of the headline points to the anatomical term's popular obscurity and was central to Maud Allan's claims of libel. Noel Pemberton Billing did not actually author the infamous paragraph and its headline, but, as the publisher of the newspaper, he took responsibility for the piece, which was actually written by Harold Sherwood Spencer, an American who had been dismissed from both the U.S. and British armies for mental instability.[64] Spencer was also the source of the Black Book story, and it was shortly after he met Billing that the first article about the "47,000" appeared in the *Imperialist.* Spencer's testimony about the Black Book exposed his belief that German soldiers were deliberately corrupting English men and women by means of homosexual acts:

BILLING: Have you received information as to the kind of vices catered for by German agents, say yes or no?

SPENCER: Yes.

BILLING: Is sodomy one of them?

SPENCER: Yes.

BILLING: Is Lesbianism another?

SPENCER: Yes.

BILLING: Have you read the play "Salome"?

SPENCER: Yes.

Billing connected Wilde's *Salomé* to lesbianism and German vice by association, as he led Spencer through an exposition of the contents of the Black Book. Spencer later complicated any clear meaning of "Lesbianism" by noting, "I think the Germans were very clever in advocating this as a means of corrupting people by means of Sadism as they have."

Spencer conflated lesbianism with hypersexuality in general as he described how he came up with the phrase "Cult of the Clitoris," testifying that he telephoned his village doctor and asked for "an anatomical term":

ıs it?

ris. . . . In consulting with a physician I had been informed
superficial organ that, when unduly excited or over-developed,
ıe most dreadful influence on any woman, that she would do
the most extraordinary things if she was over-developed in a superficial
sense.

BILLING: Did you subsequently satisfy me that the title in question was the
best title that could have been employed to explain what we wished to
explain?

SPENCER: Yes . . . it was the most decent and technical way in which a disagreeable thing could be expressed.

Here, Spencer first appealed to medical science to provide an exclusive
language that would not corrupt innocents and would minimize the danger
of disseminating information about female sexuality too broadly. Spencer
produced a meaning for *clitoris* that alluded to *all* women's potentially dangerous sexuality as much as it accused or libeled a specific woman, Maud
Allan: "When unduly excited or over-developed, [the clitoris] possessed the
most dreadful influence on *any* woman" (emphasis added).[65]

Whereas Spencer testified to the universal threat of the clitoris, another
one of Billing's witnesses explicitly linked the term *clitoris* with a more specific deviant female sexuality: lesbianism. During the trial, Billing asked
Dr. J. H. Clarke, a medical doctor and Billing's close friend, if any term
other than *clitoris* could have been used in the headline, "having regard to
the fact that it was necessary to arrest the attention of the sophisticated and
to avoid affronting the unsophisticated":

CLARKE: I cannot think of another title except the term "Lesbianism," and
that word would be equally well known to the initiated, and equally unintelligible to the uninitiated. . . .

BILLING: Is "clitoris" an uncommon word?

CLARKE: It is a Greek term. It is an anatomical term. The only obscenity is
what is unnatural. There is no obscenity in an anatomical term.[66]

Clarke poses *clitoris* and *Lesbianism* as synonyms, both representing an
unnatural obscenity that could be known only by "the initiated"—a nebulous group that might include anyone from medical students to perverts.
The "anatomical" clitoris functions metonymically as an equivalent to

lesbianism. This equivalence was also prevalent in much of the discourse throughout the trial, but it conflicted with other mass-cultural understandings of the clitoris. For example, also in 1918, Marie Stopes published a popular sex manual, *Married Love,* in which she outlined in explicit, normalizing detail the physiological functions of the clitoris.[67] Yet in the Allan/Billing suit, "clitoris" became code for perversion generally, and female homosexuality specifically.

At a pretrial hearing, magistrate Sir John Dickson implied a widespread understanding of "clitoris" as lesbianism. He first censured Billing for immaterial discussions of various perversities in the courtroom, including sadism and necrophilia, and then reined him in by restricting the case to only one sort of perverse behavior, lesbianism: "I really do not want, for the sake of myself or those here, to go into all forms of unnatural vice. Everybody knows the thing exists, but we do not want the details of it." Further cementing the equivalence of "clitoris" and female homosexuality, Allan's attorney, Mr. Hume-Williams, appealed to the jury in his closing argument as to the severity of the libel: "Do you think that you would not have . . . taken immediate steps to clear your character . . . [if you were libeled with a] heading so repulsive as 'The Cult of the Penis'? Yes, but 'The Cult of the Clitoris' is worse. . . . It means lesbianism."[68] Again, anatomy becomes perversity, and "lesbianism" is a clearly defined category to which jurors can refer. But "clitoris" was also considered a "technical" word known only to perverts and experts. Both of these terms were available for technical and popular use, yet not so firmly defined beyond medical circles as to hold static meanings. Both sides (and, by the conclusion of the case, the judge as well) used the two terms as best suited them, often changing their definitions from day to day as well as from witness to witness. Clearly female homosexuality was an intellectually available category, but one that had not yet jelled in public discourse. The Allan/Billing trial rendered lesbian identity as explicitly sexual in a way that Allatini's novel did not: by associating lesbianism with the clitoris and with sexual perversion, female homosexuality could articulate female erotics as well as associations between women. Yet, as in *Despised and Rejected,* these erotics need not be only between two women.

Further complicating any relationship among anatomy, identity, and perversity, mere *knowledge* of sexual perversion was proof of perversity. At the trial, Billing questioned Allan about the headline and her understanding of Wilde's *Salomé.* On both topics, Billing attempted to implicate her through her knowledge of perversion. In his Plea of Justification, Billing argued that if Allan was in fact a "lewd, unchaste, and immoral woman," performing material "so designed as to foster and encourage obscene and unnatural practices among women," then he—Billing—must be found not guilty of libel.[69] To prove both Allan's and *Salomé*'s obscenity, Billing attempted to link Allan in his cross-examination with all sorts of perversions and knowledge of perversion. In doing so, he used several strategies, the first of which was to associate her with criminal perversion by association.

When Maud Allan was twenty-two years old, her brother Theo Durrant hacked two young women to death. He was executed after being declared a "moral monster" by the popular press and diagnosed as suffering from "*psycho mania sexualis*" by medical witnesses.[70] Billing raised this event at the onset of his questioning of Allan, and when she asked "if this has anything to do with the case," Billing replied that "the vices referred to . . . are hereditary. . . . In this case, Salome . . . over the bleeding head of John the Baptist . . . [with his] raised lips, is a clear case of sadism." Thus, Billing implied that Allan shared a "hereditary taint"—sadism—with her brother, and then revealed it in her theatrical persona. Billing attempted to establish perversion as hereditary so that Allan's sexual immorality could be inferred from her brother's alleged sadism.

Billing also implicated Allan in perversion through her knowledge of the defamatory headline:

BILLING: Did you understand the title [to the paragraph] at first sight?
MISS ALLAN: Yes.
BILLING: Are you a medical student?
MISS ALLAN: I am not an actual medical student, but I have read many medical books.

Billing attempted to incriminate Allan again through association, by asking if her friends knew what the headline meant, whether they were medical students, and so on. He then tied Allan's perversion to her prewar travels to Germany and her minimal costuming in the German performances. Having established Allan as a indecent, hypersexual, German-loving woman, Billing questioned her about *Salomé*, hoping to force her to admit the erotic nature of the play, which she steadily avoided doing by describing it as "Art" and as depicting "spiritual longing" rather than sexual excitement or perversion. Billing attempted to elicit an admission that the play depicted sadism, drawing upon the German associations of such sexological classifications. She refused, though she confessed to knowing the meaning of the word *sadism*. Billing then asked if she had read the works of Richard von Krafft-Ebing and Iwan Bloch, two pioneering sexologists, to which she replied, "I do not know the names."[71] Billing's questions equated knowledge of perversion to perversity itself, and associations with things German to sedition.

Allan attempted to defend her chastity by neutralizing the erotics of *Salomé* through a register of orientalism. When Billing associated her performance with sadism, hypersexuality, and indecency, she responded by reclassifying the text of the play as an Eastern curio: "That is Oriental thought, is it not?" She also asserted her cosmopolitan fluency in contrast to the provincial ignorance of her inquisitor: "It is quite uncustomary for a Westerner to understand the imagery of the Oriental people."[72] Orientalist fetishism both elevated Allan's cosmopolitan knowledge and protected her against homosexual and seditious accusations. Yet Allan's orientalist projections failed rhetorically: attempting to distance herself from German sexology and homosexual knowledge, she instead was distanced from British patriotism and heterosexual propriety.

Billing continued to exploit the relation among the play, its author, and deviant sexuality in his examination of Lord Alfred Douglas. Countering Allan's interpretation of the play, Douglas testified that Wilde "intended the play to be an exhibition of perverted sexual passion excited in a young girl . . . [and that] there is one passage which is sodomitic." At Billing's prompting, Douglas testified that Wilde was reading Krafft-Ebing's *Psychopathia Sexualis* as he wrote *Salomé*: "I know of my own knowledge that this book was written after a study of Krafft-Ebing. . . . Normal healthy-minded people would be disgusted and revolted by [*Salomé*] . . . and [sexual perverts] would revel in it. That is just what they like." In direct contradiction to Allan's interpretation of the play's "soulful" meanings, Douglas testified, "It is nothing to do with her soul at all," though he said Wilde would call the play's perversion and sadism "spiritual. That was part of the jargon":

JUDGE: He would call spiritual what you would call sadism?

LORD ALFRED: Yes. With those sorts of people evil is their good; everything is topsy turvy; physical is spiritual; spiritual is physical, and so on; it is a perversion, an inversion, of everything. Wilde was a man who made evil his good all through his life. That was the gospel he preached.

Renouncing Wilde and the play that he himself originally translated,[73] Douglas called into question Allan's interpretation of *Salomé* and successfully (if vitriolically) handled his cross-examination, wherein Wilde's infamous letters to him were brought into the courtroom.[74] The repetition of earlier courtroom moments involving Douglas and Wilde's estate further linked *Salomé* not only with the sexual perversion of sadism but also with homosexuality, whether it be lesbianism directly attached to Maud Allan or male homosexuality, aligned with her through the association with Wilde.

Like Allan, Douglas sought to clear his own name by linking *Salomé*, and his youthful involvements with Wilde, to the East. Douglas couched his testimony not only in the language of sexology but also in that of sedition: he consistently vilified Wilde, the play, and Allan as German, German-influenced, or, at the very least, un-English. When Judge Darling asked Douglas about Wilde's language, he replied that decadents such as Wilde described the language in *Salomé* (language Douglas himself had translated from French to English) as "beautiful, classic, and so on. They will not speak of it by the outspoken English name; they disguise it." Further, these "disguises" hid seditious influences. When Billing asked Douglas, "Is the idea in this book rather more German *kultur* than British ideal?" the latter replied, "Yes, decidedly." Not only were Wilde's language un-English and his sexologically influenced ideas German, but Douglas defined Salomé herself, as played by Allan, in orientalist terms: as a "girl in the East [who] matures much earlier than an English girl would."[75] Douglas distanced himself from Wilde through sexological and nationalist terms, he reinforced the connection between homosexual association (female and male) and Germanness, and he effectively linked anything German with literary, sexual, and political decadence.

Thus, homosexuality simultaneously occupied several different positions within this judicial spectacle. On the one hand, Billing's witnesses described homosexuality as a German disease that had contaminated Britain, and Allan's witnesses defended themselves against such charges. On the other hand, homosexuality was the result of a weakened Britain, of decadence, and of the British legacy of the "evil" Oscar Wilde. Yet this male homosexuality was also associated with a representation of sadism by a female character in a play, and by the alleged female homosexuality of the actress herself. Female homosexuality was understood as much by association (with Wilde or Krafft-Ebing, with Germany or the Far East) as by means of anatomy (the clitoris). Allan's perversion, in particular, was both contagious (she caught it from Wilde, crossing gender, death, and the written word) and congenital (she shared the taint with her murderous brother). Finally, female homosexuality was known by an anatomical sign (the clitoris); a piece of anatomy found on all women, it became dangerous and "excited" only on the bodies of perverts, and paradoxically it always indicated homosexuality.

The conclusion of the trial proved as messy as the various definitions of perversion elicited during its course. After calling witness upon witness linking Allan with German homosexual contagion, sexological knowledge, and indecency, Billing denied that his speech ever contained an implication of homosexuality. Interrupting defense attorney Hume-Williams's closing statement, Billing jumped in:

BILLING: He says that I have accused Miss Maud Allan of being a Lesbianist. The accusation that I made was that she was pandering to those who practiced unnatural vice by this performance.

DARLING: Do I understand you then that you withdraw any suggestion that she is a Lesbian?

BILLING: I have never made that statement.

DARLING: If you have been understood to have done so, will you absolutely withdraw any such suggestion?

BILLING: Certainly, my Lord; I have never suggested it.

Hume-Williams vehemently objected: "This was not an accidental libel. . . . Miss Allan in her indictment says: You have said I am addicted to lesbianism and I am a lewd and improper woman; and you get the answer of Mr. Pemberton Billing: What I said in this alleged defamatory libel is true. That is his attitude."[76] Judge Justice Darling rejected this assertion and instructed the jury to define *clitoris* solely as "sadism" and to disregard any mention of lesbianism in the proceedings.[77] Like the indeterminate status of lesbian identity at the conclusion of *Despised and Rejected,* the discursive status of lesbianism was thrown into confusion at the trial's end. This indicates the incoherent nature of female homosexual subjectivity in the British public sphere during the Great War. The cleavage of the clitoris to lesbianism broke down at the conclusion of the trial, and, as a result of Darling's instructions, after only eighty-five minutes of deliberation the jury returned a verdict of not guilty, exonerating Billing.

This "trial of the century" and its attendant cultural meanings drew together British fears of losing the war to Germany, losing the nation's men to carnage, and losing the nation's morals to perversion. That a crisis prompted by such "political" and traditionally masculine concerns was played out on the body of a woman through a play by the dead Oscar Wilde cannot surprise. In fact, it seems almost necessary that, as England struggled against what seemed to be a certain military defeat, a woman should appear to carry the weight of her only recently conferred citizenship. The discourse surrounding Maud Allan established female homosexuality as a concept for public consumption, and one that stood in relation to, yet independent from, male homosexuality. The verdict in this trial did not determine that Allan herself was a lesbian or the priestess of a perverse cult; rather, it found that female homosexuality, twisted and confused as it was in the public mind, had a place in that mind. Just as *Despised and Rejected* ends in a necessarily oblique and indecidable state, so too does this judicial story: the war remained unresolved, and the mysterious Black Book with its 47,000 names never appeared. The threat of female sexuality was too potent when combined with a threat of German infiltration. We can see now that Maud Allan *had* to lose her case.

"No One Here Speaks or Thinks of Anything but the Billing Case"

The impact of this trial beyond the courtroom walls was complicated and contradictory. On the one hand, the trial had an enormous impact: even leaving aside all of the many parties who were slandered in the proceedings (those named as members of the 47,000 or as friends and lovers of others), newspapers, including the *Times,* carried daily reports on the proceedings. On the other hand, if we examine the trial's impact from historical distance, we can see that recent scholarship on it has, at times, overestimated the ubiquity of Noel Pemberton Billing's conceptions of German homosexual corruption and vice in wartime England. A brief comparison of contemporaneous reports of the Billing trial with other wartime journalistic discussions of sedition, vice, and pacifism demonstrates that the trial produces just one critical perspective on Great War Britain among many. This does not diminish the discursive power of the "Sapphic sedition" but, rather, allows us to situate this cultural moment within a broader context of emergent lesbian representations. Here I will consider the impact of the Billing trial in contemporaneous British media and more recent scholarship, and then offer a brief counterexample of wartime feminist pacifism that pointedly ignored the Billing case, thus indicating the existence of different narratives of gendered opposition to the Great War. Like the representational possibilities that emerge in Allatini's novel, it is the presence of a language of Sapphic sedition in those narratives that indicates an important cultural shift. The rhetoric within the trial and the media frenzy surrounding it indicate the power of Billing's accusation—whether widely accepted, debated, or dismissed—in the early summer of 1918.

During the trial, British newspapers ranging from the *Times* of London to the *Manchester Guardian* to the *Daily Telegraph* carried daily, detailed coverage of the proceedings, often quoting long sections of testimony and debate verbatim.[78] Printed alongside reports from the front, the "trial of the century" both distracted readers from the reports of increasing casualties on the front lines and participated in the "battle" on the home front. The case's notoriety was also not limited to a home-front audience: officers on the front in France received news of *Rex v. Pemberton Billing* with varying degrees of alarm and amusement. Homosexual poet and, by 1918, war resister Siegfried Sassoon wrote in his wartime diary, "The papers are full of this foul 'Billing Case.' Makes one glad to be away from 'normal conditions.' And the Germans are on the Marne and claim 4500 more prisoners. The world is stark staring mad."[79] Duff Cooper wrote to his fiancée, Diana, from the front that "no one here speaks or thinks of anything but the Billing case." She responded by reporting on conversations about female homosexuality: first that a mutual friend "mentioned incidentally—and true to her school—that she did not believe in vice among women"; and then a story about "Lord Albermarle [who] is said to have walked into the Turf [Club] and said, 'I've never heard of this Greek chap *Clitoris* they are all talking of.'" The Billing case generated discussions of female homosexuality on both the home front and the front lines, at least among members of the upper class. Duff Cooper illustrated a belief among some officers of a conflation of homosexuality and sedition in another letter to Diana: "We argued about Asquith and Lloyd George. One of my brother-officers maintained that Asquith was 'all in with the Huns' and he believed that Mrs. Asquith was a 'female bugger' that being as near as his limited vocabulary allowed him to get to Sapphist."[80] At least one homosexual officer worried about the impact of the case on himself and his brothers, whereas many heterosexual officers and civilians thought it something of a joke. These anecdotes, combined with the coverage in the *Times* (which never actually mentioned the word *clitoris*), demonstrate that the Billing case generated talk about female homosexuality generally; that "Sapphism" was a very much-discussed, if not widely accepted, part of British culture; and

that, at the same time, lesbianism was such an unformed concept as to have
no consistent, clear, or acceptable terminology with which to describe it.

Scholars have assumed a widespread concurrence in British mass culture
with the fears and ideas Billing and his cohort expressed. Samuel Hynes
draws a powerful picture of rampant hysteria on the home front by citing
Arnold White's and Lord Alfred Douglas's claims to "Hunnish erotomania,"
described earlier in this chapter. Yet archival research calls into question
scholarly assumptions about the cultural ubiquity of Billing's conflation of
homosexuality and German-sponsored espionage. Almost all of the wartime pieces cited by Hynes, Medd, and others were either published or
republished in Billing's own journal. Indeed, with few exceptions, all the
authors of these texts also gave testimony, or were supposed to have given
testimony, in Billing's defense at trial.[81] Thus, although the mobilization of
lesbianism in the service of nationalism marks a clear discursive shift in the
history of sexual representation, one must be cautious in overreading the
widespread influence of Billing's, Spencer's, and Douglas's views of German
homosexual contagion on a broad English public.

Following the trial, for example, a report appeared in a British newspaper condemning the verdict and bemoaning its interpretation abroad:
"Some idea of the regrettable effects produced abroad by the recent Old
Bailey trial may be gathered from the fact that so reputable and influential
a newspaper as the 'Corriere della Sera' of Milan, is apparently prepared to
accept as well-founded all the unsavoury 'revelations' made during the hearing of the case, and fails to appreciate the light in which they are regarded
by responsible people in this country."[82] The writer of this note, published
in the *Daily News* on June 15, 1918, regretted that the Italian press read
Billing's accusations as true facts, implying that "no one" in Britain did.

Similarly, there is no mention of the Billing trial where one might expect extensive coverage. Sylvia Pankhurst's staunchly pacifist *Worker's Dreadnought*, for example, studiously ignored the trial, even though it covered
many public debates regarding sedition.[83] The first issue of the *Dreadnought* printed Siegfried Sassoon's statement against the war.[84] Subsequently,
the paper printed letters regarding Sassoon's case, including one that made
critical mention of the "effete" House of Commons.[85] Given the journal's
extensive coverage of related issues, one would expect to see at least some
discussion—whether as a news report, editorial, or letter—of the apparently much-discussed Billing trial, which evoked similar themes of the
"effete" leadership of the nation, sedition, and legal censure on the grounds

of nationalism.[86] Thus, we must be careful, as we consider the importance of emergent discourses of female homosexuality brought forward in the Billing case, not to globalize the trial's ideological impact or to overstate the prevalence of British fears of German homosexual contagion on the home front. The emergence of this homophobic nationalist rhetoric is in itself significant, however widespread or local its political impact at the time.

Postwar Postscripts: Lesbianism and the Lords

On March 9, 1921, the bishop of London introduced to the House of Lords an amendment to the 1885 Criminal Law to address "a most unnatural sin" between women.[87] This Criminal Law Amendment Bill, the result of a joint committee between the two houses of Parliament, would, if passed, raise the age of consent (for sexual relations) for girls to sixteen years old, and would prevent men from claiming that they "believed" a girl younger than that actually to be of legal age. After passing the House of Lords, the bill went on to the House of Commons, where a new clause was introduced that would add female homosexual acts to the 1885 Labouchère Amendment, which had criminalized male homosexuality.[88] This revised bill was returned to the House of Lords, where this new clause was rejected. As a result, no bill was passed that year, and female homosexuality remained outside the criminal code.[89] Women's sexual activities were viewed as predicated on knowledge, not desire; a deliberate suppression of information about women's possible homosexual activities was deemed a more effective damper than their criminalization.

Though the law was not altered, the debates over this proposed amendment indicate enormous changes in English conceptions of female homosexuality, most broadly since the 1890s and specifically since the Great War.[90] "Lesbian love" was now a concern for the nation's governing body, and much as the MPs decried the necessity of tackling such a "beastly subject,"[91] this vice was now (thanks in no small part to the tremendous publicity of the Billing/Allan affair) clearly of grave nationalist, moral, medical, and legal concern. The rhetoric of the MPs in both houses indicates that, although by 1921 female same-sex erotics were clearly a more widely discussed topic than in prewar Britain, there was no clear idea as to why, how, and when such desires overcame women. MPs invoked moral arguments as well as medical ones, and "solutions" included criminalization, eugenic "self-extermination," and the eventual decision to maintain a pointed legal silence around the subject.

Discussions of female homosexuality first arose in the House of Commons, on August 4, 1921. In his introduction of the lesbian clause to the Commons, Mr. Macquisten asserted that the clause was a "long overdue" addition to the criminal code. He described homosexual acts between women as universal and always culturally disastrous: "These moral weaknesses date back to the very origin of history, and when they grow and become prevalent in any nation or in any country, it is the beginning of the nation's downfall." Evoking the Roman Empire's collapse, as well as the more current issue of British divorce law, he asserted that homes were ruined by "the wiles of . . . abandoned female[s] who had pursued" married women, who in turn had "forgotten the dictates of Nature and morality." Thus, national identity became a victim of perversions of nature. Macquisten regretted having to speak on such a matter and knew that for some of his colleagues "the mere idea of the suggestion of such a thing is entirely novel; they have never heard of it." Yet he was confident that ministers of Parliament who "engage either in medical or in legal practice know . . . these horrors." He concluded with a call to "stamp out an evil which is capable of sapping the highest and the best in civilisation."[92] Discourses of "the natural" and the national here blended with arguments that placed female homosexuality within the purview of moral, medical, and legal provinces.[93]

This opening speech lays out many of the internal contradictions and assertions that would characterize both sides of the debate, in both houses. The construction of the "abandoned female" in relation to the unsuspecting wife whom she corrupts establishes female homosexuality as a universal condition. Both women turn to homosexuality after experiences with men: the first woman has been abandoned by a man, and the second sexually abandons her own husband. Homosexuality is not contained within congenitally homosexual bodies but can dangerously spread to women previously categorized as "normal" wives who forget or lose their natural place.

Another sponsor of the clause, Sir E. Wild, made a similar point as he recounted the experience of a prominent nerve specialist "who has told me with his own lips that no week passes that some unfortunate girl does not confess to him that she owes the breakdown of her nerves to the fact that she has been tampered with by a member of her own sex." Here one woman "tampers" with an innocent "unfortunate" and thus causes neurological (medical, bodily, psychic) harm to her victim. In this scenario, the aggressor appears to be definitively (congenitally) homosexual, and the "unfortunate girl" a victim of an unwanted assault. Yet still, as in Macquisten's example, the status of homosexual behavior is unstable. This scenario (and Wild's comprehension of it) reflects the divisions among homosexual or inverted women that Havelock Ellis draws. Indeed, Wild reported that the medical expert referred the House to the works of Ellis and Richard von Krafft-Ebing, should they require a list of "the various forms of malpractices between women. . . . [However,] my own feeling is simply to refer to the Lesbian love practices between women, which are common knowledge."[94]

Yet, contradicting the doctor's assertion that "Lesbian love practices . . . are common knowledge," in the first speech opposing the clause Col. Wedgwood began by promising to define "lesbian vice" for "any members of the Labour party" who did not know "in the least what is intended by the Clause." In what could be a partisan assault on the whole Labour Party, Wedgewood assumed that most Labour MPs did not attend public school, where "the ordinary public school boy studies the classics in which he reads about what is known as Lesbian vice. He finds all about Sappho, and when he goes to college he reads Swinburne, and that is the only way decent people in this country ever get to hear of this sort of thing."[95] Public school education is the only comprehensible location for "decent people" to learn of such practices. Yet what might be a slight against uneducated members of another party was actually the opposite: Col. Wedgwood himself was a member of the Labour Party.[96] Thus, this speech should be read more properly as a criticism of aristocratic knowledge of "Lesbian vice" in contrast to a purer (uninformed) working-class (or middle-class) masculinity. Much like antiaristocratic narratives of masculinity promulgated in wartime homophobic discourse, Wedgwood's lesson on Swinburne and Sappho simultaneously allowed him to speak of female homosexuality and to condemn others (as well as himself) for their knowledge of it. As in the Billing trial, knowledge of sexual deviance was dangerous and could implicate one in the very perversion of which one speaks.

Significantly, there was no way in this logic for decent *women* to learn of such practices. Women did not go to all-male public schools and read Sappho and Swinburne, so any woman who had knowledge of such practices became immediately suspect. Further, the homosocial environments of girls' schools necessitated enforced silence against homosexual incursions. Opponents of the clause argued that decent women would learn about such unnatural vice only if it was criminalized and thus culturally as well as criminally coded. Wedgwood continued to outline the key objections to the clause: first, it would dramatically increase blackmail; and, further, evidence would be so difficult to obtain and/or so unreliable that convictions under such a clause would be nearly impossible. Thus, "for one conviction that could be got in ten years, you may have, on the other hand, endless blackmail."[97]

Sir Wild rejected these arguments by stating that difficulties of proof and blackmail should not deter lawmakers from their duties: "This vice does exist, and it saps the fundamental institutions of society. In the first place it stops child-birth, because it is a well-known fact that any woman who indulges in this vice will have nothing whatever to do with the other sex. It debauches young girls, and it produces neurasthenia and insanity."[98] In postwar England, bourgeois procreation was an area of great concern, given that many men in the procreative generation had been killed in the war. Laura Doan notes that in the debate allusions to postwar "race suicide" produced powerful arguments for the criminalization of lesbian sex acts: "[A] concern for the welfare of young girls pales in comparison with a lesbian threat that strikes out at a vulnerable society, indeed the survival of the race itself."[99] And indeed, England's obsession with race suicide continued through the 1920s. Thus, eugenic fears of race suicide had a newly tilled ground in which to grow: that of lesbian contagion. Such an argument suggests that after the Great War *women* were somehow in danger of losing their procreative powers to the homosexual contagion that British men had successfully defeated during the war. Thus, we can see how the wartime nationalist homophobia discussed earlier could be transformed into a discourse of eugenic and sexological contagion after the war, in parliamentary debate.

Lt. Col. Moore-Brabazon attacked Wild's discussion of vice to argue that "we are not dealing with a crime at all. We are dealing with abnormalities of the brain." This "vice," he argued, should not be criminalized, because it was not within the woman's control to prevent her mental illness. To further prove his point, Moore-Brabazon provided a most interesting possibility: if the House decided "to deal with mental cases in the law courts . . . to go on logical lines, we should soon be introducing Measures into this House to give penal servitude for life to the hermaphrodite." Moore-Brabazon believed that the hermaphrodite and the lesbian, unlike the male homosexual, were products of their bodies, not of their volition. Female homosexual sex was as bodily determined as the anatomy of a hermaphrodite. Moore-Brabazon went on to assert, "In this case we are not trying to inculcate a fear of punishment. That already exists in society to-day, because the pervert is undoubtedly despised and shunned by all grades of society." Unlike his colleagues who worried about influence and contagion, Moore-Brabazon wished to "leave them entirely alone . . . because these cases are self-exterminating. They are examples of ultra-civilisation."[100] This configuration of "ultra-civilisation" harks back to Carpenter and Allatini, who both advocated for the rights of homosexuals from just this position. Yet, unlike Allatini's view, "ultra-civilisation" was "unnatural" to this minister of Parliament, and because it lacked sufficient "nature," it would, if let alone, disappear. This argument was not persuasive. Despite an appeal not to "introduce into the minds of perfectly innocent people the most revolting thoughts," at 11:41 p.m., with only 201 members of the 707-member House present, the Commons passed the clause by a 148–53 vote.[101] The clause was then sent to the House of Lords for approval.

The members of the House of Lords concurred with Moore-Brabazon's strategy of leaving female homosexuality uncriminalized. Yet they themselves could not resist the temptation to speak about this horrible vice, much as they supposedly regretted doing so. Unlike in the House of Commons, no one in the House of Lords who advocated passing the clause actually favored its principles. Rather, those few who spoke in favor of it (its sponsor himself eventually asked that the clause be withdrawn from consideration) did so only to pass the whole bill.

Each speaker in the House of Lords (like several in the Commons) prefaced his remarks with a regret that he must speak about female homosexuality at all. The Earl of Malmesbury began, "My Lords, I am extremely sorry to raise a discussion upon what must be, to all of us, a most disgusting and polluting subject." The Earl of Desart mitigated his distress with the hope that few people would read the debate: "I much regret that such a question has even been discussed. I may perhaps draw cold comfort from the realisation that there are not many people who read the debates of either House."[102] This speaking of the unspeakable reinforced the cultural status of female homosexuality: it was still outside the realm of acceptable topics (such as male homosexuality, the existence of which, as negatively as it was viewed, was not questioned, nor was the necessity of occasionally speaking about it), yet it was also making incursions into a cultural discussion beyond medicine and the circle of friends of or participants in female homosexual communities.

The bulk of the arguments in the House of Lords revolved around the issue of disseminating information about female homosexuality. The lord chancellor asserted that "the overwhelming majority of the women in this country have not heard of this thing at all. If you except a sophisticated society in a sophisticated city, I would be bold enough to say that of every thousand women, 999 have never even heard a whisper of these practices." The Earl of Desart condemned the disseminating of such information because of the damage it would cause: "I am strongly of opinion that the mere discussion of subjects of this sort tends, in the minds of unbalanced people, of whom there are many, to create the idea of an offence of which the enormous majority of them have never even heard." Further, he worried that, should young women learn that female homosexuality was an identifiable phenomenon, the "occasional manifestations" of the frequent "romantic, almost hysterical, friendships that are made between young women at certain periods of their lives" would become blackmailable offenses. Thus, Desart drew the connection between female homosexuality and the familiar (if increasingly stigmatized) phenomenon in the homes of the upper-class: the romantic schoolgirl crush. He simultaneously linked the crush to and tried to sever it from the new and "unspeakable" vice of homosexuality. He extended this point by noting that women would submit to blackmail rather than risk exposure in the courts: "We know the sort of publicity that sort of thing gets, and it cannot be stopped." This was a not-so-oblique reference to the out-of-control publicity that the Billing trial had received only three years earlier. Desart finished his speech by noting that cases of female homosexuality comprised an "extremely small minority, and you are going to tell the whole world that there is such an offence, to bring it to the notice of women who have never heard of it, never thought of it, never dreamed of it. I think that is a very great mischief."[103] The House of Lords rejected the lesbian clause and thus defeated the entire Criminal Law Amendment Bill for that session. They hoped to preserve the alleged ignorance of British women of this "very great mischief."[104]

But the mischief had already been done. By the time of this debate, in 1921, female homosexuality was established in British public discourse as well as in the practices and speech of a minority of British subjects. Whereas prior to the Great War, narratives of female homosexuality were largely illegible if not affixed to those of male sexual deviance, the public trial of Maud Allan and wartime novels such as *Despised and Rejected* produced an emergent rhetoric of female homosexuality. Though the "Sapphist," "lesbian," or "invert" of this rhetoric was not associated with a defined social position or sexual practice, the subject position was nevertheless emerging in public discourse.

Through these associations with gay male identity and in dynamic tension with gendered home-front nationalism, female homosexuality "went public." Female homosexual representation appeared first as an indefinable subset of male sexual inversion in a prewar periodical, then through cross-sex homosexual identification in *Despised and Rejected*. Male and female homosexual identities could not be theorized identically, but they had to be theorized in relation to one another if a comprehensive picture of their historical emergence was to be drawn. Without Dennis's internal awareness of his perversion, he would not have articulated his taint to Antoinette, and her homosocial relations would not have become representable as homoerotic. Likewise, male and female homosexual identities were linked in the Billing trial. Without the public outrage and discursive explosion of the Wilde trials of 1895, a generation earlier, Noel Pemberton Billing would have been far harder pressed to define Allan's performances of Wilde's Salomé as homosexual. Furthermore, it was the perceived difference between male and female sexuality on which the House of Lords relied when they defeated the Criminal Law Amendment in 1921. Assuming that female sexual expression could be curtailed by a suppression of their descriptions, they distinguished female and male homosexuality legally, ignoring the cultural evidence of their interconnections.

Finally, without the rhetorical need to construct national outsiders through discursive sexual abjection, mid-twentieth-century public culture may not have seen the rapid increase and consolidation of coherent lesbian identities. Rhetorics of orientalism and homophobic patriotism shaped emergent lesbian representations. The "domestic" spaces of the bourgeois bedroom and the home front together produced ideas of normativity, modernity, and identity. We cannot understand sexual politics apart from geopolitics and biopolitics; we must read the ideological and material consequences of citizenship for modern queer identities.

chapter 5

BOY-GIRLS AND GIRL-BOYS: POSTWAR LESBIAN LITERARY REPRESENTATIONS

This book begins with a 1928 review of Compton Mackenzie's novel *Extraordinary Women*, entitled "The Vulgarity of Lesbianism." In the introduction, I pair the review with Leslie Feinberg's 2001 antiwar polemic to illustrate two twentieth-century instances in which gender and sexual variation are linked to the Great War. Yet the 1928 review does other work as well: it draws discourses of nationalism, gender, and sexuality together with those of sexology, literary value, and women's suffrage in the production of representations of female homosexuality. The anonymous reviewer complains,

> Twenty years ago such a theme [lesbianism] would have seemed *outré* and altogether unsuitable for treatment in a novel; but it is impossible to dismiss it quite so confidently in these post-war days of boy-girls and girl-boys. Then it was merely a problem for the psychopath—and the less said about it the better. Now it is a comparatively widespread social phenomenon, having its original roots no doubt in the professional man-hating of the Pankhurst Suffragette movement, but owing very much to wider causes arising out of the war and its *sequelae*.[1]

This review charts a dramatic shift in lesbian representation from pre– to post–Great War England, rewrites preceding histories of suffrage and sexuality, and signals the multiple cultural vectors that produced that shift. Aligning gender inversions ("boy-girls and girl-boys") with postwar homosexuality, the review also offers female homosexuality as a distinct category apart from female masculinity. Homosexuality's relation to sexology is also explored: it should be a problem for the "psychopath," but it cannot now be only that, because of its dissemination, via postwar gender inversions, into the general population. This passage also illustrates how postwar reflections on the Great War and the prewar suffrage movement shaped not only 1920s perspectives on the recent past but later conceptions of the early twentieth century as well. Here, for example, female homosexuality emerges as a corollary to the radical suffragette movement. Mrs. Pankhurst's contemporaries did not link the militant suffrage leader's activities to lesbian representation, but by 1928 critics did. Further, the reviewer blames the Great War for the spread of lesbianism as a "comparatively widespread social phenomenon," a charge borne out by chapter 4 of this book, which demonstrates the rhetorical adhesion of homosexuality to wartime nationalist anxieties.

Something, this review signals, had changed in public discourse from the moment in 1921 when the House of Lords voted to keep female homosexuality out of the criminal code for fear that lesbianism's articulation under the law would result in its rampant dissemination throughout England. Ten years after the war's end, the headline of the 1928 review, "The Vulgarity of Lesbianism," appeared in a respectable weekly—marking a significant leap from 1918, when the London *Times* felt unable to print the word *clitoris* in conjunction with Maud Allan's libel trial.

By 1928, female homosexuality was a comprehensible category in the British cultural lexicon. This legibility not only resulted from wartime transformations of sexual and gendered representations of British women ("these post-war days of boy-girls and girl-boys"), but also was produced through England's relations to the domestic rise of women in the public sphere and the interwar international challenges to the British Empire. In reading the rhetorical, ideological, and cultural foundations of female homosexual representations in three British novels and their receptions in the final months of 1928, this chapter illustrates the centrality of a rapidly transforming British national culture to the emergence of modern lesbian sexual representations.

All published in the second half of 1928, Radclyffe Hall's *The Well of Loneliness,* Compton Mackenzie's *Extraordinary Women,* and Virginia Woolf's *Orlando* represent female same-sex erotic relations through various literary strategies and toward different ends. Through a close reading of the three texts and their receptions, 1928 emerges as a moment that crystallized a critical transition for lesbian representation. These texts present different models of female homosexuality, yet they all rely on both normative and deviant configurations of nationalist subjectivity to structurally and thematically produce a lesbian subject.

Other scholars have discussed the importance of Hall's *The Well of Loneliness* and Woolf's *Orlando* as watershed texts in the development of "lesbian literature" in the history of sexuality, or, more recently, as part of an emergent literature of transgender and transsexual subjectivity.[2] When read with *Extraordinary Women*, these texts help us understand the necessary connections of sexual identities to nationalism. *Orlando*, perhaps the most slippery of the three, produces a nationalist subject as a site of critique, but it also relies on the stability of England and Englishness to produce a chimerical protagonist. Hall and Mackenzie similarly construct stable British subjects for their diverging, multiple constructions of female same-sex erotics. *The Well of Loneliness* and *Extraordinary Women* refashion wartime representations of women and female sexuality and then represent the domestic emergence of a female homosexual subject through the terms of imperialism. Through comparing these two explicit representations of the Great War's role in changing sexual cultures, with *Orlando's* more oblique commentary of England's imperial powers and decline, we can parse the ideological effects of wartime conflations of gender, sexuality, and nationalism in relation to emergent interwar lesbian representations.

In *The Well of Loneliness*, Hall uses the patriotic ideal of a masculine England to construct a sympathetic nationalist lesbian protagonist. In the farcical *Extraordinary Women*, Mackenzie pokes fun at England's postwar obsessions with sex while also maintaining British masculinity as the normative standard against which his lampoon is grounded. In *Orlando*, Woolf genders and sexes Orlando through subject-object relations of England and its European and colonial others. All these novels struggle to represent a relatively new cultural phenomenon—homosexuality in women—through an oblique, direct, or metaphoric leverage of Britain's decreasing global dominance as referents for their representations of female homosexuality. "England" becomes the almost invisible signifier of sexual and cultural normativity. For Mackenzie, England is the absent center; for Woolf, a site of gender and sexual conformity; and for Hall, the pastoral ideal, always already centered, yet, like a vanishing horizon line, always deferred.

The three authors not only produced radically different texts but also inhabited differing positions in relation to the emergence of female homosexuality as a clearly delineated identity in British public culture. Virginia Woolf famously occupied the center of the sexually ambiguous and modernist literary community of Bloomsbury. Her marriage to Leonard Woolf precluded neither textual work on female same-sex sexuality nor her own intimacies with women, most famously with Vita Sackville-West. Radclyffe Hall, in contrast, classified herself as a sexual invert following sexological tradition, echoing aspects of nineteenth-century realism that produced, in part, her representations of sexual inversion. Compton Mackenzie's personal stakes in emergent lesbian representations are less obvious. Married three times, and to all appearances heterosexual, Mackenzie traveled in social circles that included many homosexual men and women. The subject of *Extraordinary Women* arose from his friendships with homosexual women such as Romaine Brooks, who vacationed with him on Capri in the prewar years. As Allison Wee remarks of Mackenzie, "Though he obviously did not write about women involved with other women from an 'insider' perspective as did Hall, Mackenzie was not a complete 'outsider' either."[3] Each of these authors' biographies contributes to, but does not determine, the representational choices each makes regarding female same-sex desire. The intratextual contradictions and intertextual dialogues between the production, circulation, and contents of the three texts reflect the multiple models of female homosexuality emergent in the interwar period.

In 1928, the multiple literary representations of lesbianism presented a historical moment in which that identity was no longer the incoherent nexus of the cultural anxiety of wartime Britain, but nonetheless remained under formation. Representational strategies drawn from eighteenth-and nineteenth-century narratives of cross-gender passing and bourgeois women's romantic friendships combined with legal and sexological explanations of male homosexuality. New in the 1928 novels was an additional emphasis on excavating origins of female homosexuality itself. As soon as lesbianism was formed as a cultural identity, it required an origin story and a reconfiguration or consolidation of normative subjectivity. The novels of 1928 inscribe genealogies relying on these cultural discourses, with special attention to (either in the form of divergence from or allegiance to) the two competing medical discourses of sexology and psychoanalysis and through narratives of national otherness or allegiance. The sexological origin stories are most often produced in the context of a stable and universal heterosexual British subject. This unified subject is lampooned in some of the textual and extratextual productions of the novels of 1928, and it is reconsolidated in others, but throughout, Britishness, cross-gendered love, and a reinforced cultural masculinity function together to stabilize nationalist subjectivities that female homosexual representations threaten to queer.

Postwar Boyish Girls: Mannish Dress and Masculine Votes

In 1928 England, questions of gender deviance dominated debates over the status of femininity, feminism, and female sexuality. From the debates over the 1928 enfranchisement of women, termed the "flapper vote," to England's "boyette" high fashions, interwar British women continually negotiated changing standards of femininity, masculinity, and female subjectivity. My readings of the novels and their attendant cultural markers establish both the necessary presence of gender inversion in representations of lesbianism by 1928 and its perpetually unsteady relationship to homosexuality. Gender inversion is linked rhetorically to female homosexuality but can never be only its origin, symptom, or equivalent: gender deviance forms a *contested* relationship to same-sex desire. It points to narrative choices and rhetorical inversions that enabled the competing models of lesbianism and national identification in play in 1928. Gender inversion at that time was in conversation with representations of female homosexuality and women's negotiations of their roles as feminine citizens and/or national and sexual outlaws. The forms these negotiations took, as well as the ideological positions they constructed, determine the direction of the conversation in any particular text and in others influenced by it.

Gender inversion's rhetorical and thematic force did not necessarily imply homosexuality. In *Fashioning Sapphism*, Laura Doan persuasively argues, for example, that the interwar masculine fashions embraced by upper-class British women did not always signal cultural deviance or homosexual behaviors. Doan's extensive research into British fashion illustrates that masculine attire was not consistently a sign of lesbianism in the 1920s, just as I have argued that textual representations of masculinity were not universally signs for homosexuality during and before the war: "The meaning of clothing in the decade after the first world war, a time of unprecedented cultural confusion over gender and sexual identities, was a good deal more fluid than fixed."[4] Masculine clothing indicated (and, some would argue, superseded) the masculine privileges of public occupation and citizenship that wartime England allowed women. This background created a context for female masculinity beyond the register of medicine and beyond the temporarily accepted masculinity of women in wartime, which now in the 1920s was being actively suppressed. In particular, masculine clothes "did not always signify 'lesbianism' . . . [but] in a culture where cross-dressing was not the exception but the norm, these [cross-dressing] women would have been positioned by observers at different points along a wide spectrum of female masculinity." Doan argues for a double reading of masculine attire: masculinity was an opportunity for lesbian women to both communicate their erotic identities to one another and also "pass" as ladies of high fashion in the broader culture.[5]

Female masculinity played out not only in the British fashions of the mid-1920s but also in England's political environment of the decade, mapping debates over masculinity and femininity in women onto questions of citizenship and nationalism. On July 2, 1928, the Equal Franchise Act granted British women the parliamentary franchise on the same terms as men. This equalization was generally regarded as an inevitable corollary to the first enfranchisement of women, in 1918,[6] yet this act was not passed without "patient, low-key lobbying"[7] and consistent pressure on the Conservative government by those recently enfranchised female voters. Opponents termed this second act "the flapper vote," as it would enfranchise women under thirty years old on the same terms as men of their age group. The anxieties raised in the pages of such weeklies as the *Daily Mail* indicate increased trepidation over women's political and sexual power: opponents of the bill focused not on the economic or regional dynamics of the groups to be enfranchised but on their perceived material and cultural status. In contrast to prewar opponents of women's suffrage, who worried over the vote's impact on domesticity and child rearing, by 1928 opponents feared the political power that young, sexually sophisticated and boyish girls could wield if enfranchised.[8] As Martin Pugh reports, the proposed enfranchisement "provided the opportunity for an unusually bitter and relentless attack upon women in general and 'Votes for Flappers' in particular. . . . Scaremongering tactics built upon [the "sex war" concept of the prewar period] by highlighting the large number of women voters in various constituencies: 'Men Outnumbered Everywhere.'" Such propaganda highlighted cultural fears about young women, describing them as "incorrigibly irresponsible and ignorant."[9] Although the 1928 legislation is often overlooked in histories of women's suffrage, this "quietly bestowed" vote, which "was widely taken for granted" before its passage, had a crucial social and political impact.[10]

The 1928 vote assured women's standing as political agents equal to men, but the debates leading up to its eventual passage highlight the increasing anxiety over young women, public women, and female masculinity circulating in the mid-1920s. Much has been written about the flapper of the 1920s, her new social and sexual freedoms, and the possible implications of such unbridled heterosexuality in British culture following the annihilation of so many of the nation's young men. Such analyses are often disarticulated, however, from Britain's rapidly changing international position in the decade following the Great War. It is my contention that "domestic" debates over the rapidly changing status of English women must be read through the rapid challenges to British political and cultural imperialism in the 1920s and 1930s. Reading the shifting global political geography in conjunction with domestic and cultural politics opens up new interpretive possibilities for the three British novels under discussion. These novels of 1928 responded to anxieties about women's wartime sexual, economic, and social freedoms and reacted to the colonial threats to Britain's global political power by linking domestic sexual deviance with foreignness and exoticism: in other words, with national otherness as well as sexual otherness.

Unruly Empires, Rowdy Women, and Interwar Nationalist Anxieties

The treaties that ended the Great War were intended to weaken Germany politically and to restructure the balance of power in Europe in favor of France, England, and the United States. Yet this proved to be a mixed victory for England's imperial reach. Donald McKale notes, "Britain, forced by its triumph to focus much of its postwar attention and resources on preserving its position in the Middle East and elsewhere in its empire, had been weakened more in victory than Germany in defeat."[11] The reshuffling of former German colonies in Africa and Asia at Versailles led not to western European and British stability in their expanding colonial empires but, rather, to an increase in anticolonial nationalist agitation for independence in India, Africa, East Asia, and the Middle East. Germany's holdings in eastern Europe were assimilated into existing nation-states or constituted as "new" nations, and Germany's colonies in Africa and Asia, technically awarded to the League of Nations, were primarily administered and controlled by France and Great Britain. This chasm between the treatment of Germany's African and Asian colonies and their European ones generated tremendous interwar hostility against the British and French and spurred nationalist movements for independence in their non-European holdings. To name only a few examples: Gandhi and the Indian National Congress continued to agitate for Indian independence; African nationalist, anticolonial political movements grew in conjunction with the rise of pan-African nationalism in Germany's former colonies; and in the British holdings in the Middle East, both Jews and Palestinians tried to pressure the English into honoring their wartime promises of independence. Thus, in the 1920s, England found itself fighting to maintain political and social control over its colonies and protectorates abroad as well as to rein in English women fresh from their wartime freedoms and political enfranchisement. "The moment of English modernism," Simon Gikandi has written, "in spite of a certain canonical insistence on its ahistorical and hermetical character, was generated by a crisis of belief in the efficacy of colonialism, its culture, and its dominant terms."[12] What historians of English gender relations have seen as purely domestic struggles in the 1920s must be understood as representational struggles over England's position internationally. The interwar preoccupations with the Great War as a source of domestic turmoil and with the transformations of gender and sexual roles also reflect a postwar anxiety about England's ability to control the spoils of war—its unruly empire as well as its unruly women.[13]

This is the historical and cultural context of women's interwar position in England: the nineteenth-century anthropological and eugenic origins of sexology; a recent history of homophobic patriotism on the home front; the renegotiation of women's political and cultural roles at home in both suffrage and war work; and the violent destabilization of colonial power. Not only was political culture transformed, but so too was British popular culture. "The interwar period saw a range of anxieties about nation and empire explored in popular culture," Alison Oram reports. This anxiety manifested itself through representations of sexual and racial degeneration in the popular press.[14] Modern lesbian subjectivity emerged in the midst of this cauldron of assaults on traditional ideas of Englishness. By reading emerging female homosexual representations through the nationalist anxieties surrounding their production, we can understand that modern lesbian identity was predicated on such anxieties, and sexual deviance was inextricably linked to both home-front nationalism and the failing British struggle for global ascendancy.

By 1928, a combination of British women's masculine high fashion, mass-cultural representations of "female husbands," political enfranchisement (or the assumption of it, following the home secretary's April 1927 announcement that the act would appear in the next legislative session), and postwar political and economic emancipation created fertile ground for the literary transformations of female sexuality: not just glorifications of reproductive postwar heterosexuality, but representations of female homosexuality as well. The "flapper vote" and the masculine fashions of the 1920s produced representational spaces for women to occupy beyond sexological categorization such as the mannish woman or cultural representations of female homosexuality as a decadent corollary to Wilde-ism. As Doan reminds us, "Lesbians might be mistaken for flappers and flappers might be lesbians. . . . The playfulness worked in all directions, and any woman who embraced the trend could revel in sexual ambiguity."[15] This ambiguity could serve women well materially; it would be celebrated by artists such as Woolf, lampooned by others like Mackenzie, and vehemently resisted by more polemically political novelists such as Hall.

As women claimed "masculine" political power and appropriated men's clothes and cultural spaces on the home front, representational room was created for a broad spectrum of female sexual and social identities.[16] Women's political emancipation also shifted its relation to England's role as a fading imperial power. Women not only symbolized the nation's domestic fecundity, purity, and morality, but also embraced their British citizenship and advocated for their faltering empire. In each novel examined here, British citizenship becomes wholly or partially incommensurate with women's homosexual practices. Each author structurally and thematically engages questions of masculinity, citizenship, and same-sex erotics, illustrating the conflicted and cacophonous relations that gender inversion, sexual practices, and national identity forged in the interwar period. Political, aesthetic, and institutional analyses demonstrate that literary production does not merely reflect or record existent cultural patterns or historical shifts but produces new representational possibilities, which in turn shape culture.

Hall's Inverted Englishwoman

Radclyffe Hall's now infamous novel *The Well of Loneliness* is most often read through the lens of sexology. And indeed, Hall cultivated this reading by prefacing the novel with a commentary by Havelock Ellis. However, rather than adopting Ellis's sexological model of female masculinity wholesale, Hall relies on the inclusion of the "gentleman invert"—the aristocratic, mannish homosexual woman—within a transhistorically constant construction of British masculine identity to argue for her protagonist's humanity, British citizenship, and "right to . . . existence" expressed in the novel's closing lines.[17] The construction of the female gentleman invert as Enlightenment male citizen not only draws on sexological mobilizations of female masculinity in service of female homosexuality but also relies on the denigration of the novel's many national and racial others: non-English women, African Americans, homosexual Frenchmen, and Jews. Moreover, Hall rewrites the Great War: she retroactively reinscribes the war not as a moment of nationalist moral panic but as an opportunity for sexual inverts such as Stephen Gordon to participate fully in a nationalist project as important, if not unqualified, national subjects.

The Well of Loneliness follows its heroine, Stephen Gordon, from childhood through maturity. Born to the wealthy, landowning Sir Phillip and Lady Anna, who anticipate the birth of a son, the aristocratic Stephen is a gender invert from her birth: physically, psychologically, and sexually she resembles an English man more than a woman, yet she is female. After a childhood of gendered alienation, Stephen leaves the English countryside for London. During the Great War, she serves in a women's ambulance-driving unit, where she meets the feminine woman of her masculine dreams, Mary Llewellyn. The two eventually settle down in Paris, where they meet other lesbians and gay men. At the conclusion of the novel, Stephen drives Mary away, into the arms of a man, tragically sacrificing her own happiness so that Mary will have security and love with a heterosexual family unit of her own. Had Stephen access to her "rightful" place at the center of British culture, the novel implies, Stephen and Mary would have been able to return to England and marry. Yet the novel's own structural as well as thematic construction of England as an island of stable heterosexual national identity forecloses this possibility of happier resolution. From the novel's opening lines, England is irrevocably heterosexual, so much so that Stephen's many attempts to step into the role of masculine British citizen-subject appear bound to fail.

The Well of Loneliness begins by describing Stephen's family home, Morton, an idealized pastoral manor house, and her mother, Lady Anna, the mistress of that manor. Citing Margot Gayle Backus, Sarah E. Chinn notes that "Morton is . . . *the* signifier for an impossible but uncomplicated, heterosexualized, aristocratic Englishness" (emphasis in original).[18] We see that Morton "is indeed like certain lovely women who in youth were passionate but seemly; difficult to win but when won all-fulfilling." One such perfect woman is "Lady Anna Gordon . . . as lovely as only an Irish woman can be . . . the archetype of the very perfect woman, whom creating God has found good."[19] Note that the embodiment of ideal femininity is not England but its colony Ireland. The other near-perfect woman in the novel is Stephen's lover, Mary Llewellyn, an orphan from Wales. Idealized femininity, then, is embodied by women from England's "Celtic periphery."[20]

"Backus argues that the Celticness of Anna Gordon (Irish) and Mary Llewellyn (Welsh) is constructed as the sensual feminized 'other' to Stephen's insistent English erectness."[21] Racialized Anglo-Saxon masculinity lies at the heart of Britain, but it is produced through feminine, peripheral, Celtic territories.

In contrast to England's feminine acquisitions, England itself is masculine and enduring. Morton's master, Sir Phillip—"a tall man and exceedingly well favoured"—is both intellectual and virile. Before his marriage to Lady Anna, "he had sown no few wild oats, yet Anna's true instinct made her trust him completely."[22] This landowning aristocrat is no wartime effeminate aesthete but represents all that Hall finds most noble about England. It is this nobility that "longed for a son" and sired instead the masculine but female Stephen.

Hall strives to make Stephen also embody a landed British gentry of strength, intelligence, and courage. Monied, handsome, and manly, Stephen rides the hounds, courts the neighboring women, and loves Morton.[23] The gender invert, the novel argues, should hold the respect and power she was born to. Yet she cannot. Stephen calls English masculinity into question through her female embodiment. Hall cries for equality, but the gendered logic of national identity is overwhelming: the unjust social stigma of cultural and sexual inversion deprives Stephen of her rightful position as lord of her manor. She fails to secure the affections of the crass yet beautiful American neighbor (another woman who is not English), Angela Crossby. After professing the purity of her love, Stephen is stymied by Angela's question, "Could you marry me, Stephen?" When Lady Anna discovers her daughter's homosexuality (after the selfish Angela betrays her), Stephen first tries to defend her desires by positioning them within the respectable discourse of chivalrous, protective love: "As a man loves a woman, that was how I loved—protectively, like my father. I wanted to give all I had in me to give. It made me feel terribly strong . . . and gentle. It was good, good, *good*—I'd have laid down my life a thousand times over for Angela Crossby. If I could have, I'd have married her and brought her home—I wanted to bring her home here to Morton. . . . If I loved her the way a man loves a woman, it's because I can't feel that I am a woman. All my life I've never felt like a woman." Stephen's sexual and gender deviance—her inversion— precludes her from taking her rightful place in masculine England's social order. She cannot bring Angela home to Morton and, in fact, after this confrontation she is exiled. Lady Anna demands that she leave Morton:

"'The same roof mustn't shelter us both any more; one of us must go.' . . . Morton! They could not both live at Morton. Something seemed to catch hold of the girl's heart and twist it. She stared at her mother, aghast for a moment, while Anna stared back. . . . But quite suddenly Stephen found her manhood and she said, 'I understand. I'll leave Morton.'"[24]

Homosexuality will taint Morton, and by extension England, so Stephen must leave. In rhetorical double reversal, Stephen's masculine love for women forces her into exile, yet her chivalrous masculinity, her "manhood," ennobles the exile and reinforces her subjectivity as an aristocratic (masculine) British subject. The exile of the homosexual from "home"—from the English countryside, and from her ancestral home in this case—is a trope repeated in *Extraordinary Women* and evident in much twentieth-century lesbian and gay literature and culture.[25]

Stephen retreats first from Morton to London but she soon moves from London to Paris in search of a community of writers. Once there, she finds not other writers but other homosexuals. Thus, within the novel's nationalist logic, Stephen must move farther from England and its heterosexual masculinity to meet other homosexual women. Homosexuality means that home ceases to be home. Here it is both a familial and a national alienation. If England is a masculine protector of its feminine colonies, then there is no space for a masculine woman: Stephen disrupts representations of imperial power relations as well as sexual ones.

Hall's depiction of the Great War complicates the strict gendered binary of England and its others. Just as war can literally redraw national boundaries, so too can it resignify cultural ones. In "*The Well of Loneliness* as War Novel," Susan Kingsley Kent writes that "the anxieties produced by the Great War were often articulated through an idiom of gendered and sexualized language that stressed the blurring of boundaries between men and women, warrior and civilian, heterosexuality and homosexuality."[26] Yet this is an articulation born of historical distance, reflection, and revision. Ten years after Armistice Day, Hall reread the Great War as a moment for cultural transition and temporary acceptance of inverted women: in wartime, England overlooks Stephen's female body and embraces her into the masculine nation. Yet even in a fictional interwar revision, this embrace is provisional and holds only on the front lines of the war outside England, in France.[27]

The novel's wartime section draws together a diverse group of women, each seizing an opportunity to "serve the nation" in more of a masculine than a feminine capacity. For Hall, the Great War provides an opportunity to bring homosexual women into the national community. This stands in direct opposition to the wartime representations in which male homosexuals were further ostracized by wartime homophobia. Hall connects homosexuality to war when she writes, "England was fighting for her right to existence," prefiguring the novel's final lines, in which Stephen calls out for God to "give us [homosexuals] the right to our existence!"[28] Rhetorically Hall linked England to the homosexual in direct opposition to dominant representations of homosexuality, which positioned sexual deviants as England's others.

Initially in *The Well of Loneliness,* the war appears to be yet another source of alienation for female gender inverts: even the most effete men, such as the homosexual Jonathan Brockett, "with the soft white hands, and the foolish gestures, and the high little laugh—even he could justify his existence" by enlisting, while Stephen stands, as always, midway between men and women: "She, Stephen, might well be crushed out of existence—of less use to her country, she was, than Brockett. She stared at her bony masculine hands, they had never been skilful when it came to illness; strong they might be, but rather inept; not hands wherewith to succour the wounded." She has no place as a feminine caretaker on the domestic front and initially cannot reach a battlefield. Yet eventually Stephen joins a women's ambulance corps and gets to the front lines. In the ambulance corps Stephen and other homosexuals like her discover one another and find a way to serve England: "And England had taken her, asking no questions—she was strong and efficient, she could fill a man's place, she could organize too, given scope for her talent. England had said 'Thank you very much. You're just what we happen to want . . . at the moment.'"

If the war's start appears to polarize men and women, England's increasing scarcity of men quickly bridges the gap. In the war section of the novel, Hall deliberately rewrites wartime homophobia a decade later to serve the interwar lesbian. Though the narrative qualifies England's acceptance of deviance as provisional, at best, Hall seizes the opportunity to demonstrate the national allegiance that inverts generally, and Stephen particularly, hold. In addition to Stephen, other sexual inverts willingly step forward to do their duty to England: "Miss Smith who had been breeding dogs . . . ; or Miss Oliphant who had been breeding nothing since birth but a litter of hefty complexes; or Miss Tring who lived with a very dear friend"—all came to the aid of their country, along with "even really nice women with hairpins [who] often found their less orthodox sisters quite useful." Unlike her prewar efforts to win Angela Crossby's love, Stephen leverages the wartime crisis of masculine scarcity to shore up her own chivalrous national subjectivity. Masculine lesbians like Stephen find a place of service during the war, both to England and to the feminine women whom their "courtly" natures seek to please. In Hall's narrative, inverted women willingly replace men socially. Thus, in the ambulance unit, Stephen meets Mary Llewellyn, her true love. Stephen's growing love for Mary is carefully guarded so as not to besmirch the reputation of the many "purely feminine" women who served with "no stigma to live down in the war, [with] no need to defend their right to respect."[29] British womanhood remains protected and idealized in the novel—through both the heterosexual women who go to war with nothing to prove, and Mary herself.

After the war, Mary and Stephen must find a home, for, despite their wartime service, England (embodied now by Lady Anna, the mistress of Morton) still exiles them. The two travel from France to Orotava (a popular nineteenth-century resort in the Canary Islands) before they can make their love verbally or physically explicit. It is in Orotava where Mary initiates their sexual relationship[30] and where both "Stephen and Mary can imagine themselves beyond the confines of binaried gender."[31] Chinn's close reading of the Orotava section of the novel reminds us that lesbian desire can be consummated only outside—not only away from England, but outside Europe as well: "Stephen is part colonial aristocrat, part eager tourist, seeking to immerse herself in the 'authentic' natural world of the island that provides the template for an unfettered sexuality. This is the world that gives permission to lesbian sexuality."[32] That permission is granted because the "exotic" geocultural space of Orotava not only resonates with imperialist discourses of native sexuality but simultaneously reinforces the stable, hegemonic heterosexuality of its absent master, England.

After their island honeymoon, Mary and Stephen settle down together in permissive Paris among other expatriate homosexuals who are poor, dying, or decadent.[33] England remains Stephen's longed-for center of heterosexual and national stability in the novel, with homosexuality always written outside its borders. The novel's narrative voice critiques this national ostracism, but it remains structurally intact. The Great War allows Stephen a temporary acceptance into the national family, but it is not sustained in the postwar period.[34] Even after serving her country and receiving a medal for her bravery, Stephen cannot go home.

For Hall, Paris signifies not only a space of homosexual possibility but also a location of degeneration, decadence, and poverty in contrast to the traditions, stature, and wealth of pastoral England. This disjunction further reinforces England as a longed-for space of heteronormative masculinity, where Englishness equals whiteness, aristocracy, and dignity. Cosmopolitan Paris is home to artists and homosexual women and men from Poland, Boston, the Scottish Highlands, and Germany, all characterized as the members of a "miserable army" living in exile. Yet various characters respond to this exile quite differently. Whereas Stephen regards Paris wholly as a poor substitute for the "social intercourse" found at Morton, Mary reacts to their English exile by attempting to build a homosexual community in Paris: "That spring, Mary seemed fanatically eager to proclaim her allegiance to Pat's miserable army. Deprived of the social intercourse which to her would have been both natural and welcome, she now strove to stand up to a hostile world by proving she could get on without it." This representation of interwar Paris contrasts sharply with its more widespread image of cosmopolitan expatriate vibrancy, and indeed contrasts with Mary's own engagement with Parisian homosexual nightlife. Paris tries to contaminate Stephen and Mary. And indeed, it is Mary's "emotional, hot-headed nature of the Celt" that allows her to embrace Paris on more comfortable terms than Stephen can .[35] Aristocratic, English Stephen must remain above the gaiety and temptations of Paris, whereas the Celtic Mary engages with them.

This cosmopolitan contamination is represented through racially as well as sexually and economically marginal figures in Paris, such as the homosexual Jew Adolphe Blanc, "a quiet, tawny man with the eyes of the Hebrew," and an anonymous youth whose "gray, drug-marred face [had] a mouth that trembled incessantly."[36] Moreover, racialized otherness exacerbates Stephen's national alienation. In what Jean Walton has called the critical "transitional scene, a kind of early introduction to later episodes in the novel that take place in what is construed as a depraved, public atmosphere,"[37] sexual and racial outcasts initially find solidarity, but ultimately they are narratively distinguished, and English racial and national superiority is maintained. The scene is an evening when two black brothers entertain Stephen and her homosexual friends in a Paris studio. Like the exotic island geography of Orotava, adopted for Stephen and Mary's sexual adventure and national consolidation, the oppression and alienation of Negro spirituals are appropriated by the community of white inverts. Walton reminds us that this is "a familiar appropriation. . . , where an African

American musical tradition is incorporated into a white European context so as to procure an emotional response . . . that, it is presumed, could not be produced in any other way."[38]

Henry and Lincoln, the two brothers—one "pale" and "patient," the other darker and more "primitive"[39]—elicit a double movement of identification and then distance from their inverted audience. When they first sing, "Lord, I want to cross over into camp ground," the listening white homosexuals identify with and connect to the "terrible, aching homesick hope that is born of the infinite pain of the spirit." Even the hardened Valérie Seymour "forgot to be pagan" as she listens to the music. Yet this moment of solidarity between black and white subjects, intensified as the black men sing a plea for liberation, "Didn't my Lord deliver Daniel / Then why not every man?" quickly ends. Lincoln's "small bow which seemed strangely foolish" breaks the spell of solidarity, and the brothers "were just two men with black skins and foreheads beaded with perspiration." The bond between African Americans and English homosexuals must be broken if the logic of Stephen's claim to power, her cherished masculine British aristocracy, holds any narrative or ideological strength. As the brothers depart, Henry reasserts his primitive sexual impulse, "bawl[ing]" in a "high falsetto: 'Oh, my, what a shame, I ain't nobody's baby.'"[40] Henry, both feminized and infantilized, falls back into his properly primitive eugenic place, and the narrative reasserts Stephen's superior national, gendered, and class position.

The novel ends with a plea for acceptance. If British culture would only accept Stephen as part of the masculine national body, then Stephen and Mary would be able to come "home" to England. Yet such a happy ending of romantic closure and national security is impossible, both narratively and culturally. Because Stephen is a gender invert, she cannot be head of an English household, cannot provide for her feminine partner, and cannot return to the national family. The novel ends in Stephen's betrayal of Mary and Mary's subsequent flight into the arms of the (real) man Martin, who will marry her and thus rescue her from the decadent expatriate world of interwar Paris. Stephen's betrayal becomes heroic martyrdom. After tricking Mary into abandoning her, Stephen stands alone in her house in Paris (still exiled from Morton) and, arms outstretched with "burning rockets of pain . . . all welded together into one great consuming agony," she cries, "Acknowledge us, oh God, before the whole world. Give us also the right to our existence!"[41]

This end serves several functions. First, it constructs the congenital invert as a tragic hero denied her rightful love and happiness as well as her proper place in her ancestral home. Additionally, this end maintains a heterosexual marriage plot: for Mary and Martin, the story ends with the promise of a wedding and the possibility (from the point of view of martyred Stephen) of a "happily ever after" for Mary.[42] Finally, the narrative ambiguity about Mary's homosexual status appears to be superficially diffused: she was just waiting for the right man to come along. Yet, like Stephen, Mary remains on the outskirts of the British Empire. Martin will marry her, but he will not take her to England. Instead, he will take her to his home in the Canadian wilderness. If the narrative appears to reassert Mary's heterosexuality as well as her femininity, and if the logic of heterosexual England and the sexually as well as nationally marginalized colonies is to hold, then Mary's presumed end in Canada signals her continuing position as a sexual, as well as a national, outsider.[43]

Extraordinary and Extranational Women

In contrast to Radclyffe Hall's tragic polemic of national alienation, Compton Mackenzie writes an extremely funny satire of wartime and interwar female homosexuality. Yet, despite this difference, *Extraordinary Women,* like *The Well of Loneliness,* locates its lesbian loves outside of England and constructs female homosexuality in opposition to British masculinity. Both novels shore up British political and cultural capital by equating England with masculine stability and by mapping sexual deviance onto England's feminized geopolitical others.

Published only weeks after *The Well of Loneliness, Extraordinary Women* recounts the trials and tribulations of a Sapphic tribe vacationing on a fictional island, Sirene (modeled on Capri) in the final months of the Great War and the early interwar years. The plot centers on the masculine, English homosexual Rory and her pursuit of the nationally and sexually ambiguous Rosalba. Each of the novel's dozen characters provides her own model of female homosexual identity and desire, and each character takes a turn pontificating on the "true" nature of lesbian erotics or presenting her own homosexual origin story. The resulting cacophony of conflicting lesbian representations produces a satire of both the women themselves and the culture obsessed with cataloging and containing them.

Whereas *The Well of Loneliness* promotes one version of female homosexual representation, that of gentleman invert and feminine partner, in

Extraordinary Women it is extraordinarily clear that in 1928 lesbian representation had not fully solidified in the British imagination, that multiple models of homoerotics were in play, and that no one origin story for female homosexuality dominated this discourse. All of the characterizations of the extraordinary women in the novel, however, share a concern with national identity, gender inversion, and the Great War.[44] This constant is all the more striking, given the novel's otherwise multivocal, almost chaotic, representations of female homosexuality. Drawing on this common concern, we see that female homosexual subjectivity is predicated on establishing sexual deviance through and in opposition (be it playful or earnest) to Britishness, citizenship, and the modern nation-state.

Extraordinary Women, like *The Well of Loneliness,* conforms to an emerging interwar convention wherein England cannot be the site of sexual perversion and sexual deviance is always foreign, or can be practiced only in exile. A summer resort, Sirene provides both seasonal and national escape from the dampers of English sexual and social conventions. However, Mackenzie positions Sirene as an island getaway that is inevitably touched by the gendered and sexual effects of the Great War as well as its economic and national impact, which its visitors hope to flee. On Sirene, the desire to geographically and metaphorically escape the war highlights the war's many cultural and political effects. The local Sirensi link the female tourists' homosexuality to a shortage of men resulting from the war: if men are scarce because of the war, then women must take on masculine duties. Not only will women fill the breach (or breeches) left by soldiers gone off to war, but they will satisfy each other sexually for the same reason: "[The local Sirensi] ascribed the phenomenon of Rosalba and her friends to the war. 'Poor women,' they said, 'there is a scarcity of men.' . . . They were genuinely sorry for Rosalba. When they saw Rory hanging affectionately on to her arm, they remembered what they had suffered during the war themselves from substitutes for bread."[45] The relationship between mannish Rory and her more feminine paramour Rosalba is read by the Sirensi as a poor substitution predicated on gender inversion as a copy of male masculinity. The citizens of Sirene (not to be confused with the summer visitors who make up the female homosexual population of the island) attribute the women's romances with one another to scarcity: Rosalba must make do with Rory, as a substitute male, just as they had to endure food rationing. Homosexuality signals not only national instability but also, obliquely, patriotic self-sacrifice.

Rosalba's grandmother, her wealthy Swiss guardian, also attributes Rosalba's social transgressions to the war, yet she is concerned primarily with Rosalba's masculinity rather than her sexual-object choice. Rosalba is a fashionable "New Girl": masculine yet not mannish, sexually adventurous yet not a sexological invert. Visiting her grandmother in Switzerland, Rosalba's wartime masculinity presents a problem that it does not on Sirene. The Swiss "did not recognize in Rosalba a purely decorative expression of the instinct that led other young women to drive lorries in France. They merely stared at her because they thought it odd that such a pretty young woman should be trying to dress and behave as much like a handsome young man as she could." Note that Rosalba remains fundamentally feminine—"pretty"—underneath her masculine clothing. Here, the Great War produces a temporally specific female masculinity: some women drove ambulances at the front, Rosalba dresses as a man. And unlike the French or Sirensi, the Swiss are troubled by gender expression. The narrative attributes this difference to the Swiss's preoccupation "with a prosperous neutrality": because the Swiss did not fight in the war, they are unable to interpret correctly the wartime origin of Rosalba's masculinity.[46]

Throughout the novel, both the narrator and the characters consistently attribute female masculinity to the war. Female *homosexuality*, however, is more complex and contradictory. Some characters do ascribe female homosexuality to the war, but the narrative structure and the opinions voiced by the homosexual characters also give homosexuality an alternative, longer history. The Greek quotations from Sappho's fragments of poetry that begin each chapter of the novel, for example, produce a transhistorical female homosexuality, refuting lesbianism as a purely modern invention produced by the war. Furthermore, the relations among national identity, female masculinity, and homosexuality are never fixed; the novel continually reinvents and redirects their entanglements.

Almost all of Mackenzie's Sapphic tourists have ambiguous sexual and national identities, reflecting the contemporary fluidity or unsettledness of both sexuality and nationalism. Rosalba reeks of European decadence, echoing wartime fears about the downfall of the British Empire. And, indeed, Rosalba almost engineers the financial, cultural, and sexual downfall of Rory, one of *Extraordinary Women*'s very few British characters. The flighty Rosalba is a sexual and national hybrid: just as her gender presentation varies with her audience, so too can her nationality. Her mother marries five men, from France, Austria, Spain, Sicily (Rosalba's father), and then

Switzerland. This cosmopolitan sexual debauchery is passed down to her daughter, who wanders among several nations, genders, and lovers. She is, in fact, a woman without a country. Similarly, Zoe Mitchell, one of Rosalba's rivals, is Minoan, but her marriage to a wealthy American jeweler complicates her nationality and finances her sexual adventures and international travels.

In the interwar period, British law stated that a woman's citizenship changed upon marriage to that of her husband.[47] Thus, heterosexuality and national identity were directly related for women. If married women lost and gained citizenship as a result of their sexual partners, homosexual women could face the prospect of being nationless or could renounce national affiliation altogether as they renounced or rejected institutionalized heterosexuality. If *The Well of Loneliness* seeks to gain admission for sexual inverts into the national family, *Extraordinary Women* revels in the connection of sexual deviance to geopolitical transgression. Yet this celebratory outsiderness also continues to position England as a stable, heterosexual center. In *Extraordinary Women,* England is off the hook: all this fun debauchery and transgression makes for a great summer escapade but it leaves England's sexual, gendered, and colonial power relations wholly intact. Whereas Hall attempts to transform or challenge England's masculine national body, Mackenzie reinforces it by insisting on the foreignness of women's gendered and sexual transgressions.

Several characters of ambiguous nationality but clear homosexuality are described as "Greek"; like the Sapphic epigraphs to each chapter, characters associated with Greekness establish transhistorical lesbian identity as well as an ancient distance from the modern British state. A tension exists here between sexual and gendered deviance predicated on citizenship (women without nations) or national crisis (the Great War and its aftermath), on the one hand, and more universalized identities constructed through rhetorical and cultural identifications with "Greek love," on the other.

Mackenzie creates the character of Cléo Gazay to contrast with Rosalba, both nationally and sexually. The authorial voice assures his readers that "if he [the narrator] has conveyed to the reader an impression that Rosalba had anything of the age of Pericles about her. She had not." In other words, Rosalba should be associated not with the essential, "Greek" formulations of homosexuality but with more contingent cultural and historical ones. By way of contrast, our narrator then introduces Cléo: "She really did resemble, not merely convey an impression of numerous statues of antiquity. . . . Cléo came from the Midi, and the fancy that she inherited her outward form from far-off Greek ancestors who had settled on its seaboard was not too extravagant." This character embodies a homosexuality predicated on Greekness and masculine artistic genius: "She was masculine enough to play [the piano] well, yet not masculine enough to be one of the world's genuinely great pianists. Her playing was never judged as a woman's, but as the performance of a man of undisciplined genius. . . . Her femininity dragged her back just as her petticoats always seemed to drag her back."[48] Cléo's homosexuality is indicated by her masculine genius but cemented through her association with Greek love.

Similarly, the other artist in the novel, composer Olimpia Leigh, is trans-historically Greek and essentially homosexual. Olimpia embodies Sappho in modern form, as both her appearance and her sexual prowess attest. Her national identity is, like that of so many of the other Sapphic tourists, mixed: "Olimpia was the daughter of an American financier [her father] and of a Swedish mathematician who had also been a musician and a scholar of Greek [her mother]." Yet her essence is Greek: "From her mother, too, Olimpia inherited her Greek scholarship. She claimed to think in ancient Greek, and she was fond of . . . quot[ing] Dionysius of Halicarnassus on her side and end of the argument by murmuring in that low thrilling voice of hers, 'But you only know Greek from the outside, do you?'"[49] Olimpia refutes any necessary connection between masculinity and homosexuality by disavowing wartime masculinity and instead embodying Sappho through androgyny and artistic genius.

Olimpia's principal rival and ontological opposite is Rory, the British sexual invert who pursues the ephemeral Rosalba. Where Olimpia's nationality is hybrid, Rory's is singular; Olimpia rejects gender inversion and masculinity, whereas Rory embodies the mannish lesbian. Rory "was so masculine as almost to convey the uncomfortable impression that she really was a man dressed up in female attire. But she was without doubt an Englishwoman who had lived for over twenty-five years in Paris."[50] Like Hall's Stephen Gordon, Rory lives in Paris before moving to Sirene. Yet she is "without doubt an Englishwoman." Ultimately, Englishness remains in narrative opposition to homosexuality; like Stephen Gordon, Rory must remain in exile from either her sexuality or her country.

Rory is not the only exile who finds a permanent home on Sirene. Mackenzie draws two male homosexual characters in *Extraordinary Women*: one is a sexological sissy whose function I will discuss later, and the other a brooding, aging count who functions as Rory's foil in the novel. Like many of the novel's characters, Count Marsac's homosexuality is signaled by his "Greekness." Marsac functions in the novel both to draw out the similarities and alliances possible between male and female homosexuals and to highlight the differences with which men and women are treated under the law. Marsac surrounds his villa with a wilderness of protective landscaping, so as to avoid possible surveillance and persecution of his sexual activities. Even on Sirene, gay men have more to lose legally and culturally than lesbians. Yet their similarities also emerge: "'We must certainly be allies,' the Count proclaimed. 'For I think we are both believers in the Greek ideal of love.' . . . 'It is an extreme pleasure for me, *mesdemoiselles*,' the Count vapoured, 'to think of you propagating the Greek ideal in Anasirene. I can assure you that when I sit dreaming on my terrace the music of the Lesbian flutes will steal across the air to my ears with very great ravishment.'" Attempting to establish a solidarity of sorts across the gender divide, the count nevertheless fails: his overattachment to the Greek ideal exceeds any commonality the women might share with him. He is excessive and odd, even to Rory and Rosalba. And although they feel great sympathy for him (past public embarrassments are alluded to), even Rory views him with some distaste and a sense of superiority. She "could not help congratulating herself on possessing in Rosalba somebody who was far nearer to the Hellenic ideal than anybody the Count had succeeded in finding."[51] Male and female homosexuality share a proximity to things Greek, which in this text is always a euphemism for homosexual behavior or desire.

The other homosexual man in the text functions quite differently. Whereas Count Marsac signals the male homosexual link to classical Greece and is not physically described as overly masculine or feminine, Daffodil epitomizes male femininity and gender inversion. This young Norwegian is described as an "old-fashioned" womanly man: "He had nothing of the modern girl about him; *he was as delicately feminine as a keepsake of fifty years ago. He was indeed a real womanly man,* with his wide forget-me-not blue eyes, his silky yellow hair, and exquisite rose-leaf complexion, of which he took the greatest care, never going out without a parasol and always wearing a mask when he was bathing. He was a friendly happy creature who danced, and danced very well, with all the girls; and he was never rude or boisterous" (emphasis added).[52] Daffodil is physically totally feminine, and Mackenzie's description of him playfully takes up a Victorian language of romantic excess, just as the text insists on his "old-fashioned" feminine appeal. Daffodil is not a modern deviant or a perversion of nature; rather, he is described just as a conservative Edwardian woman might have been. However, he still maintains his place as a man in social hierarchies: he dances with the girls, and although his manner is never rudely masculine, he is not totally feminine in his activities. He can play both the boy's and the girl's roles.

An intermediary, Daffodil occupies a privileged position in the novel and in the lives of Mackenzie's extraordinary women. It is assumed that he is not sexually interested in women, but his sexuality is subsumed under his alliance with women through their mutual femininity. Rory calls on Daffodil to assist her when Rosalba deserts her before a party: "Rory was glad to welcome Daffodil as her first guest that night. Woman or man would have embarrassed her for different reasons, but this exquisite epicene with his benevolent neutrality soothed her anxiety." Zoe relies on Daffodil to rescue her after a drunken fall and remarks, "Give me a Cissie [*sic*] when a poor girl's in trouble."⁵³ Thus, as a sexual and gendered intermediary, Daffodil can accomplish what "women" and "men" cannot—he can dance with the girls and show men where to put their coats (the province of males), but he can also soothe Rory's nerves and perform his tasks without intruding, both of which are feminine characteristics in this novel.

At the novel's end, Daffodil provides a resolution and helps Rory to reestablish her identity after Rosalba (and the rest of the summer visitors) deserts her. The novel concludes as Rory watches the last boatload of visitors depart the island, and with it her remaining hopes of winning Rosalba's love. While she is desolate and alone, a comforting Daffodil suddenly appears, calling out to Rory his need for a cup of tea: "A cup of tea! How clever of Daffodil to divine the real need of her being! That was what she wanted. . . . There was no escaping it. She *was* longing for a cup of tea as ardently as thousands and thousands of ordinary women at home in England were at this very moment longing for their cups of tea."⁵⁴ The cup of tea functions to remind Rory of an essential gendered and national identity underneath her sexual escapades and pursuit of Rosalba. She is, fundamentally, British, and she is also here reinscribed as a woman. Like "thousands and thousands of ordinary women at home in England," her "ardent" love, "the real need of her being," is now fixed on a proper object: a cup of tea.⁵⁵ The wholesome tea brings Rory back to a sensible, normative moment with Daffodil. Indeed, this ending presents a cross-sex coupling, that of Daffodil and Rory. It is, of course, a queer tea party: one might also read it as a homosocial coupling, where the feminine Daffodil shares a cup with his newly (re)feminized friend Rory. In both readings, Rory finds her place as a British woman in properly national and gendered subjectivity. Still, Englishness can recuperate Rory, but not in a homosexual frame: she has either Rosalba with wine or Englishness with tea but, just as Hall's Stephen cannot have Mary, Rory cannot have Rosalba and Englishness both. Moreover, unlike all the other tourists, Rory has purchased a villa on the island and elects to remain on Sirene. Rory cannot go home. She may drink her tea and long for nationalist normalcy, but she can never attain it. Mackenzie leaves Rory on her island, and in so doing assures his readers that England remains untainted by the amusing, yet disturbing, specter of female homosexuality.

Woolf's Imperial Androgyny

Virginia Woolf's fantastical novel *Orlando* is the third British novel published in 1928 that grapples with the representations of female same-sex desire. Like *The Well of Loneliness* and *Extraordinary Women, Orlando*'s representations of lesbian erotics are dependent on tropes of national otherness and inscribed through the politics of empire: "For Love, to which we may now return, has two faces; one white, the other black; two bodies; one smooth, the other hairy. It has two hands, two feet, two tails, two, indeed, of every member and each one is the exact opposite of the other. Yet, so strictly are they joined together that you cannot separate them."[56] Woolf's representational politics appear initially to privilege questions of androgyny and sameness over difference in the production of a desiring subject. However, when one reads the racial and national politics of *Orlando*'s transhistorical and androgynous desires, we can see familiar rhetorical foundations of a "white" and "smooth" British heterosexual propriety produced through racialized "black" and "hairy" differences.

In *Orlando,* Woolf simultaneously plays with realist narrative form and the genre of the biography, rewrites a literary history of England, and produces a novel that violates cultural gender and sex boundaries through her doubly gendered character. This "biography" charts the extended life of Orlando, a character who is born an Elizabethan nobleman, travels to Turkey, becomes a woman, lives with "gipsies," returns to England, writes, marries, bears a son, and is alive in 1928, the present day of the novel. Woolf dedicated the biography to "V. Sackville-West" and included photographs of Vita Sackville-West in the text, which she labels "Orlando." Sackville-West's son Nigel Nicolson has described this book, in a now oft-quoted phrase, as "the longest and most charming love letter in literature."[57] Unquestionably, the lover is Virginia Woolf, and she writes to Sackville-West. Yet this novel, which discusses same-gender love textually and stands as a same-sex love token materially, does not produce a narratively coherent portrait of Sapphic love or lesbian identity. Instead, female same-sex erotics are inscribed through gender transgression and imperial sexual adventure. Beside Mackenzie's playfully explicit Sapphic tourists and Hall's medicalized invert, Woolf produces a female same-sex desiring subject in *Orlando* by calling rigid gender categories into question, by leveraging sexualized imperialist histories of otherness, and by interrogating a transhistorically stable category of English nationalist identity.

Much feminist critical ink has been spilled either decrying or defending *The Well of Loneliness*'s "old fashioned" style and its "conservative" (sexological) formulations of lesbian subjectivity in contrast to Woolf's more "clever" (modernist, experimental) style and her ("coded") constructions of female same-sex erotics. Rather than debating the merits of each text's formulations of desire, however, my reading of *Orlando* centers on the role that nationalism plays in the constructions of Orlando as a desiring subject. *The Well of Loneliness, Extraordinary Women,* and *Orlando* all inscribe same-sex desires through nationalism, though through very different textual strategies and with various resulting representational possibilities and limitations. In *Orlando,* Woolf both challenges and ultimately reinscribes a heterosexual British nation-state as Orlando travels across time, space, and gender. Through numerous geocultural and national locations, Woolf creates textual possibilities of gendered transformation that is dependent on (though it often simultaneously critiques) British imperialist cultural and nationalist productions.

Orlando opens with a declaration that, through an act of colonial violence, both establishes and calls into question Orlando's gender. "He—for there could be no doubt of his sex, though the fashion of the times did something to disguise it—was in the act of slicing at the head of a Moor which swung from the rafters."[58] The novel's first word, the pronoun *He,* normally innocuous enough, is destabilized by the parenthetic comment that follows it. Orlando is a "he," the biographer reassures the reader, even though he may look like a "she." From the beginning, Orlando's sex is not essential but predicated on visual clues. If, as Judith Butler notes, "the materiality of sex is constructed through a ritualized repetition of norms,"[59] Woolf sets out to challenge these norms from the very start of her text. Sex is destabilized in *Orlando* through repetitions that denaturalize and render visible the cultural production of sexual and gender norms.

Even as Orlando's gender position is called into question in this opening passage, the section simultaneously shapes Orlando's masculinity through a history of British imperial violence and collection. Jaime Hovey notes of this passage, "From the first page of *Orlando,* the narrator stabilizes Orlando's indeterminate gender by articulating his masculinity within the racialized terms of national identity."[60] Kathy Phillips similarly remarks that "to be a 'man' as expected of Orlando [in the Renaissance sections of the novel] means murderous racism or suicidal sacrifice."[61] The indeterminacy of gender is shored up through geography (Orlando's ancestral home), imperial violence (the murder of the Moor), and empire (the Moor's head located in Orlando's home).

If gender identity is produced through colonial violence in the novel's opening pages, sexual desire is similarly predicated on the dynamic tension between home and empire in *Orlando.* One of Orlando's first erotic encounters is with none other than Queen Elizabeth, binding sexuality to nation at the outset: "He had been kissed by a queen without knowing it," the "biographer" writes. This unknown sexual protection keeps Orlando from the dangers of the warfare and nation building of Elizabethan England: "For how could [Queen Elizabeth] bear to think of that tender flesh torn and that curly head rolled in the dust? She kept him with her. At the height of her triumph when the guns were booming at the Tower and the air was thick enough with gunpowder . . . she pulled him down among the cushions where her women had laid her (she was so worn and old) and made him bury his face in that astonishing composition. . . . 'This,' she breathed, 'is my victory!'"[62] The young male Orlando's erotic contact with the aging queen both substitutes for and supplements his nationalist duty: here he is feminized as the consort of an aging queen as his beauty surpasses her military victory. For the young Orlando, sexuality supplants national identity as it becomes a different kind of nationalist "service."

This early feminized nationalist concubinage contrasts with Orlando's freewheeling adolescent sexual explorations on the ships coming into port from foreign lands. On the docks, empire provides the space of sexual exploration on the fringes of England—at her shores. "Every day sailed to sea some fine ship bound for the Indies; now and again another blackened and ragged [ship] with hairy unknown men on board crept painfully to anchor. No one missed a boy or a girl if they dallied a little on the water after sunset; or raised an eyebrow if gossip had seen them, sleeping soundly among the treasure sacks safe in each other's arms."[63] Here empire enables Orlando's nonmarital, cross-class (hetero)sexuality: imperialism produces the permissive, working-class sunset space away from the restrictions of the English court.

Orlando again ventures beyond the propriety of the English court in his love affair with Sasha. Here gender indeterminacy is coupled with a national difference. When Orlando first sees Sasha, his desire for this un-known person is clear, as is Sasha's national identity. Sasha's gender remains unclear for several moments: "He beheld, coming from the Muscovite Embassy, a figure, which, whether boy's or woman's, for the loose tunic and trousers of the Russian fashion served to disguise the sex, filled him with the highest curiosity. . . . These details were obscured by the extraordinary seductiveness that issued from the whole person."[64] Gender indeterminacy thwarts sexual desire in the moment when Orlando cannot discern Sasha's sex, and thus does not know initially whether or not he can approach her sexually.

Once assured of Sasha's femaleness, Orlando must escape the court to romance her. Woolf's necessarily oppositional "two faces of Love" are not male and female in this case, but Muscovite and English: the lovers con-verse in French and romance one another away from the physical proximity of the English court. If Sasha's gender is initially indeterminate, desire is produced through national difference (English/Muscovite) rather than the more conventional gender difference (masculine/feminine): "Sasha . . . after all had not English blood in her but was from Russia where the sunsets are longer, the dawns less sudden, and sentences often left un-finished from doubt as to how best to end them." Sasha's foreign splendor produces a crisis of language that supplants the crisis of gender indetermi-nacy. And similarly, these crises are mediated by national difference that constructs desire outside of England: Sasha is "nothing like he had seen or known in England. . . . He wanted another landscape, and another tongue. English was too frank, too candid, too honeyed a speech for Sasha. . . . She never shone with the steady beam of an Englishwoman."[65] On the one hand, the international romance is valorized. On the other hand, we see it ultimately shattered by the potential violence of empire and of national difference.

Sasha's betrayal is prefigured by a puppet show of Shakespeare's *Othello* enacted on the ice. Orlando identifies with Othello's intercultural violence:

"The frenzy of the Moor seemed to him his own frenzy, and when the Moor suffocated the woman in her bed it was Sasha he killed with his own hands." Yet it is not Orlando, but Sasha who betrays her paramour after Orlando has agreed to renounce his place in the English court. Sasha ignores his coded signal for escape and instead returns to the Muscovite ship as it departs London. Sasha does not, as planned, cross-dress in a romantic homoerotic elopement. What is supposed to be a homoerotic escape from England becomes a reassertion of gendered and national boundaries. Woolf plays with transgressions of citizenship as well as gender in the Sasha section, yet at its conclusion, gendered and national norms reassert themselves over Orlando's transgressive desires: Sasha is refeminized and naturalized by her sexual indiscretion with a large, Russian, "hairy sea brute,"[66] and Orlando (briefly) returns to his proper national place—first at court, and then at his ancestral home.

Orlando's sex transformation occurs when he is serving the English court as a diplomat in Constantinople, a city that often represents geopolitical indeterminacy and change. Both European and Asian, Constantinople has been conquered by the Roman, Byzantine, and Ottoman empires. Constantinople can be read as a site of ideological and cultural transformation but also, and more importantly, as a location of imperial conflict.[67] On the relation between Constantinople and Orlando's sex change, Phillips remarks that "the moment when Orlando turns from a man into a woman illuminates a crucial element in the ideology of empire building. Just as the Turks in Constantinople rise up against the Sultan, Orlando falls into a trance from which he awakens transformed into a woman."[68] Sex transformation and the gender of imperialism are linked in *Orlando*'s trajectory. Yet even though Constantinople can be read as critical to the moment of Orlando's sexed transformation, the narrative of the novel erases any specificity to Orlando's role as a colonial official in the city. "The dearth of information about Orlando's sojourn in Constantinople suggests that the queering of Orlando's identity obfuscates his official role as governor," Hovey suggests.[69] Indeed, Orlando's moment of sex transformation is written as mythic rather than historical, universalized rather than political:

> Orlando woke.
> He stretched himself. He rose. He stood upright in complete nakedness before us, and while the trumpets pealed Truth! Truth! Truth! we have no choice but to confess—he was a woman. . . . No human being, since the

world began, has ever looked more ravishing. His form combined in one the strength of a man and a woman's grace.[70]

Trumpets of truth and a ravishing form that cannot be exceeded by anyone "since the world began" mark Orlando's transformation from male to female or, perhaps more properly, from ambiguously male to androgynously female. Orlando's androgyny embodies a utopian perfection of male and female much like the androgynous vision at the close of *Despised and Rejected* and the "androgynous mind" for which Woolf advocates in *A Room of One's Own*. Yet it is distance from England that enables this androgyny. Just as Mackenzie's playful, Sapphic tourists are able to cavort easily away from England, Orlando's transformation of sex is smoothed by her distance from home and nation.

When Orlando becomes a woman, her sexual "preferences" do not significantly change: "And as all of Orlando's loves had been women, . . . though she herself was a woman, it was still a woman she loved; and if the consciousness of being the same sex had any effect at all, it was to quicken and deepen those feelings which she had had as a man."[71] Here, the heterosexual imperative is apparently destroyed. Orlando preferred women as a man, and now she prefers women as a woman. Her desired objects do not change, though her own sex has changed. Object choice is divorced from gender except insofar as her new gender "quickens and deepens" her prior feelings. Of course, Orlando's same-sex desires are not simple or stable, nor are the genders of her lovers consistent or unchanging. Proximity to England appears to determine, at least in part, how Orlando navigates her sexual desires as well as the parameters of her gendered performances.

Once Orlando becomes a woman and leaves Constantinople (whether she is prompted by her gendered transformation or by the political revolt remains ambiguous), she lives with a group of gypsies, free from gender roles, sexual encounters, and, at least for a time, Orlando's other obsession, writing. Yet when Orlando's desire to write and to render experiences into aesthetic form resurfaces, she must leave the gypsies: "Instead of prohibiting love in writing, as the English Home Office did in the [Radclyffe] Hall obscenity case, the Gypsies prohibit love of writing, especially when the object choice reflects a foreign pathology: the 'English disease,' a love of Nature."[72] Orlando's aesthetic desires can thus be linked to homosexual desire and bring with them complications of "civilization," capital, gender difference, and sexual identity.

Whereas Woolf describes Turkey as a locus of gendered indeterminacy, Victorian and Edwardian England becomes a site of gendered deception and sexual navigation. Orlando does not think about the implications of her female body until she departs the gypsies and leaves Turkey aboard an English trading ship. As she prepares to return to England, she is first confronted by gender convention, in the shape of an English sea captain: "It is a strange fact, but a true one that up to this moment, she had scarcely given her sex a thought. Perhaps the Turkish trousers, which she had hitherto worn had done something to distract her thoughts; and the gipsy women, except in one or two important particulars, differ very little from the gipsy men. At any rate, it was not until she felt the coil of skirts about her legs and the Captain offered, with the greatest politeness, to have an awning spread for her on deck that she realized, with a start the penalties and the privileges of her position." In this passage, as elsewhere, the gypsies are constructed atavistically: following the logic of turn-of-the-century sexual science, "primitives" may be read as less gender-differentiated, in contrast to the bifurcated, "civilized" gender differentiation of bourgeois British culture.

Aboard ship, as she moves from a "primitive" and gender-neutral representational space to a "civilized," gender-polarized British national culture, Orlando contemplates and experiments with the boundaries of womanhood and female erotic power. Her sexual and cultural autonomy become more and more restricted as the ship reaches, first, Europe, and then England itself. When she first boards the ship in Constantinople, Orlando does not concern herself with chastity: directly following her revelation—or "start"— we learn that the hesitation "was not caused . . . by the thought of her chastity and how she could preserve it. In normal circumstances, a lovely young woman would have thought of nothing else. . . . But if one has been a man for thirty years or so, and an Ambassador into the bargain, if one has held a Queen in one's arms and one or two other ladies . . . one does not perhaps give such a very great start about that." In contrast, once the cliffs of Dover are within sight of the ship, Orlando becomes much concerned with sexual proprieties and restrictions: "As the chalky cliffs loomed nearer, she felt culpable; dishonoured; unchaste; which, for one who had never given the matter a thought, was strange." Orlando cries out in alarm when she first sees England. Her cry is interpreted as a patriotic exclamation by the ship's crew, but in fact it is a cry of dismay and fear that for a woman, England "meant conventionality, meant slavery, meant deceit, meant denying her love, fettering her limbs, pursing her lips, and restraining her tongue."[73] For Woolf, then, as for Hall and Mackenzie, proximity to England signals both a valorized national cultural identity and restrictive gender and sexual roles for women.

Yet unlike Mackenzie and Hall, however, Woolf does inscribe same-gender erotics onto Britain in her text. She does so through gendered indeterminacy and class transgressions that mediate relations to the nation. As Erica Johnson argues, "Orlando's elemental relationship to national space ensures that his/her national identity remains both constant and English. By substantiating the continuity in Orlando's transhistorical, transgender character through national identity, though, Woolf shows Englishness to be composed of exclusions as well as inclusions, revealing the extent to which national identity is haunted by what she might have called 'invisible presences.'"[74] Orlando leverages classes that are excluded from the gendered and sexual restrictions of the upper class to indicate same-gender erotics and same-sex intimacies within, as well as outside of, England.

In the eighteenth century, Orlando utilizes masquerade to escape some of the restrictions of aristocratic British femininity. By cross-dressing Orlando, Woolf can inscribe lesbian erotics of transgression and evade both the sexological model that Hall draws on and the distance from England necessitated in Mackenzie's satire: "Her sex changed far more frequently than those who have worn only one set of clothing can conceive; nor can there be any doubt that she reaped a twofold harvest by this device: the pleasures of life were increased and its experiences multiplied. From the probity of breeches she turned to the seductiveness of petticoats and enjoyed the love of both sexes equally." Female Orlando's cross-dressing becomes a vehicle through which Woolf communicates female same-sex desire in the context of a progressive gender transgression rather than through medicalized sexual deviance. In the eighteenth-century section, as Orlando "enjoys the company of women"—sometimes as a man, other times as a woman—she does so with "public women": working-class women and prostitutes who, like Orlando, function in relation to sexual constructs of British nationalism yet outside codes of bourgeois sexual respectability: "Several were the natural daughters of earls and one was a good deal nearer than she should have been to the King's person."[75] Products of extramarital sexual relations, Orlando's female compatriots are separated from the upper-crust ideal of British masculinity not only through gender but also through class and "legitimacy." In this way, Woolf's female same-sex erotic relations remain predicated on a representational politics of difference, even as they appear superficially to consolidate women of different social statuses together in gender solidarity.

This epoch of erotic gender solidarity ends with the advent of the nineteenth century. Through Orlando's relationship with Shelmerdine, Woolf illustrates the power of nineteenth-century gender conventions and the limits of Orlando's transgression of gender, class, and sexual codes. Orlando and Shel's marriage can be read as either a same-gender or an androgynous union that triumphs over the very conventions to which it appears to succumb. Yet a close reading of the role of empire in the construction of this partnership may reveal the limits of Woolf's critique of nationalism and the imperialist power of discourses of sexuality in the novel.

As Orlando enters the nineteenth century, she must obtain a husband. The company of other women is now inadequate: "The Nells and the Kits of Drury Lane, much though she favoured them, scarcely did to lean upon." This involuntary compulsion to marry invokes nineteenth-century social Darwinism and eugenic heterosexuality: "Orlando could only suppose that some new discovery had been made about the race; they were somehow stuck together, couple after couple, but who had made it, and when, she could not guess. It did not seem to be Nature." This unnatural yet compulsory coupling imposes itself upon her: "Though the seat of her trouble seemed to be the left finger, she could feel herself poisoned through and through, and was forced at length to consider the most desperate of remedies, which was to yield completely and submissively to the spirit of the age, and take a husband."[76] Hovey notes that "Woolf critiques Orlando's acquiescence in compulsory English heterosexuality by humorously casting Orlando's longing for a husband as unhealthy, as the cause of neurasthenic bouts of mania and lethargy."[77] Sexual science asserts itself in a drive toward eugenic reproductive heteronormativity, rather than through sexological classifications of homosexual deviance.

Marriage results pathologically from cultural pressure, yet the husband whom Orlando eventually locates disrupts a narrative of naturalized heterosexuality rather than solidifies it. This disruption is produced through the parodic excesses of overblown romance and questionable gender identities:

"Madam," the man cried, leaping to the ground, "you're hurt!"

"I'm dead, Sir!" she replied.

A few minutes later, they became engaged. . . .

An awful suspicion rushed into both their minds simultaneously.

"You're a woman, Shel!" she cried.

"You're a man, Orlando!" he cried.

Never was there such a scene of protestation and demonstration as then took place since the world began.[78]

The textual ambiguity of these passages derails any scheme for desire predicated on gender or on the binary logic of heterosexuality. Does Orlando wish Shel a woman because she (Orlando) desires only women sexually? Is the same true for Shel with men? (Is he, like Vita Sackville-West's husband, Harold Nicolson, a homosexual man?) Or is Orlando seeking a similarly androgynous partner? The location of Orlando's desire for Shel is obscured, first by the ironically brief courtship, and then by the instability of both the genders and sexual-object choices of Shel and Orlando.

This marriage, compelled by the force of nineteenth-century conventions, is called into question not only by gender indeterminacy but also by the demands of empire: "She was married, true; but if one's husband was always sailing round Cape Horn, was it marriage? If one liked him, was it marriage? If one liked other people, was it marriage?" Here, Shel's absence calls the marriage into question, but this challenge is also critically linked to "liking other people." Empire is a threat to a definition of marriage, rather than its support. That distance from Shel, however, may actually enable Orlando to sustain her marriage. As Hovey astutely highlights, "Both Orlando and Shelmerdine understand that sexual sustenance may lie outside a bourgeois and heterosexually monogamous English respectability." Critically, Hovey asserts that these transgressions of British propriety "displace desire onto the exotic other."[79] Hovey points us to the section of *Orlando* in which Shel and Orlando agree that "negresses are seductive, aren't they?" without undue marital, sexual, or gendered strain. Here, "negresses" signal not only interracial erotics but also homosexual desire for the female, married Orlando. Thus, whereas empire might weaken a conventional marriage—"It would no doubt have been different had she lived all the year round with him, as Queen Victoria recommended," Orlando muses[80]—following Hovey, we might argue that empire actually enables Orlando and Shel's union.

Throughout this "biography," Woolf evokes female same-sex erotics through textual coding, allusions, substitutions, and gender transformations. Markedly more elusive than either Hall's polemic or Mackenzie's satire, she nonetheless similarly mobilizes ideas of nation, empire, and normativity to construct her desiring subject. For Hall and Mackenzie, England is ground upon which their either playfully Sapphic or tragically inverted characters cannot stand. Woolf, in contrast, manages to repatriate Orlando, but she does so through allusion and suggestion, in a character who "enjoyed the love of both sexes equally" and who rejoices in her transgression of sexological and ontological classificatory models. Woolf may critique imperial power and the force of empire in *Orlando,* but the novel also relies on the structural, ideological, and discursive distance between England and its colonial others to inscribe desire.

Orlando appears to conclude with married, reproductive heterosexuality: the ideal of bourgeois British national culture. Sexual and national otherness enables domestic stability at empire's center: Orlando's exploits with the gypsies, her sexual explorations of England's docks, and Shelmerdine's kisses in the dark with negresses appear to be in the past, or at least outside the frame of the novel's conclusion. Yet Woolf, in her elliptical narrative, does not rest here: she slips into this picture of national domesticity the suggestion that Orlando loves many people, including, but not exclusively, her husband. Here Woolf differs most sharply from Hall and Mackenzie in her relation to nationalist formations of sexuality. Like *Extraordinary Women* and *The Well of Loneliness, Orlando* absolutely relies on the structure of the British Empire to inscribe transgressive female same-sex erotics. Yet, unlike the other texts, *Orlando* retains the suggestion of female same-sex erotic life in England at the novel's conclusion. Because these relations are suggested rather than explicit; because, as feminist critics have suggested, Woolf's experimental narrative choices defy expected sexological configurations of female same-sex desire; and, I believe, because such desires are produced through cultural as well as rhetorical marginalization, Woolf succeeds where Mackenzie does not attempt and Hall fails, to produce a representation of female same-sex desire within Britain that can remain intact, if implicit, at the narrative's conclusion.

Immediate Receptions: The Stakes of Representation

In August 1928, the *Sunday Express* published a call to arms: "I know that the battle has been lost in France and Germany, but it has not yet been lost in England, and I do not believe that it will be lost. The English people are slow to rise in their wrath and strike down the armies of evil, but when they are aroused they show no mercy and they give no quarter to those who exploit their tolerance and their indulgence."[81] This war call was not an appeal to defend England against a military invasion. Rather, this was the first assault on Radclyffe Hall's novel *The Well of Loneliness*. James Douglas's diatribe more famously closes with the declaration that he "would rather give a healthy boy or a healthy girl a phial of prussic acid than this novel."[82] In the less-discussed passage, Douglas marks female homosexuality as an evil supported by its own army, positions England within an ongoing battle that has not "yet" been lost, and constructs a patriotic imperative to foreclose public discussions of lesbianism. By establishing female homosexuality as the next great threat after the Great War, Douglas deftly mobilizes England against female homosexuality—much as Hall's novel itself does through Stephen Gordon's martyrdom and exile from England. Douglas's rhetoric demonstrates not only a "culture war" over the status of literary productions but also, and perhaps more significantly, a nationalist stake in the circulation and reception of certain texts that inscribe female same-sex desires.

Interwar lesbian representational possibilities engaged with questions of national identity, empire, and geopolitical, as well as gendered and sexual, otherness. The receptions of the three novels discussed in this chapter also demonstrate that, as in *Rex v. Pemberton Billing* and in the censorship of *Despised and Rejected*, there was a strong state interest in the regulation and containment of discourses of female homosexuality. The radically different treatments by publishers, reviewers, and readers of the three novels allow us to read the national, cultural, and political, as well as aesthetic, stakes of each of these novels, as well as to measure the representational shifts that their publications represent for interwar nationalist positions and sexual possibilities.

Just as the political and cultural shifts outlined at the start of this chapter indicate how textual representations of female homosexuality could be conceptualized in the postwar period, the politics of publishing also indicates how and to whom the novels were marketed. Release dates and pricing can significantly affect our understanding of how the books were publicly received. Knowing, for example, that many people had read and reviewed *The Well of Loneliness* and *Extraordinary Women* prior to reviewing *Orlando* makes certain absences and presences in reviews of Woolf's book all the more notable. Furthermore, the care with which Hall's publishers distributed her novel and the relative abandon with which *Orlando* and *Extraordinary Women* were published demonstrate what types of works were considered dangerous by their authors and publishers.[83]

Other material conditions of the novels' publications situate their immediate reception and the institutional reception of homosexual themes in British novels. The price at which books were sold indicated as much about their content as their production. Books viewed as "dangerous" or in some way unsuitable for children and/or uneducated classes of readers were priced higher than their production and demand would warrant, to limit the book's circulation. At publication, *Orlando* was the least expensive of the three novels. Its price, nine shillings, was only slightly higher than the typical price of seven shillings and sixpence for most novels. Here the slightly elevated price marks the book as "literary fiction" but not pornographic: still well within normal price ranges.[84]

Extraordinary Women was sold initially at the extraordinarily high price of twenty-one shillings. This price can be explained by two factors. First, as a few reviewers noted, only two thousand copies were printed and the "type has been distributed," so no new editions seemed likely to be printed. Thus, scarcity provides one reason for the initially high price.[85] Yet pricing the novel so steeply also would signal that it was in some way dangerous or salacious. Raymond Mortimer refuted this implicit assumption in his review of the novel in *Nation and Athenaeum*: "I should add, in case anyone is misled by the high price at which the novel is published, that it is in no way pornographic."[86] Indeed, reviewers steadfastly refuted this connection when discussing *Extraordinary Women*'s price. The *New Statesman* even advocated another printing with an outrageously low price: "The edition is limited to two thousand copies; the price is one guinea; the 'type has been distributed.' We do not understand why this should have been done, or what magic should seem to Mr. Mackenzie or his publishers to reside in the figure 2,000. If a book is worthy of reading why should not as many people as possible be able to buy a copy and read it? We suggest a new edition at 3s. 6d. [three shillings and sixpence]. It seems unlikely that Sir Archibald Bodkin will, in this case, venture to interfere."[87] This review of *Extraordinary Women* was published on August 25, six days after the storm broke over *The Well of Loneliness* in the *Sunday Express*. The editors of the *New Statesman* were clearly differentiating *Extraordinary Women* from the legal flurry gathering around *The Well of Loneliness*. Here, they evoke the possibility of censorship by mentioning Sir Archibald Bodkin, the director of public prosecutions. They then refute any possibility of obscenity by suggesting both a lower price and a larger printing. No objection could or should be made to this book, they argue, so it deserves a lower price.[88]

In contrast to *Extraordinary Women,* the initial price of *The Well of Loneliness* seems remarkably low, particularly considering the trouble that the novel's publication caused only weeks after it appeared.[89] Priced at fifteen shillings, Hall's book was double the normal price of novels but still significantly cheaper than *Extraordinary Women.* After Hall's publisher, Jonathan Cape, ceased production in England and moved its printing and distribution to Paris, however, the price of her novel soared.[90] Before the scandal, copies cost five dollars in the United States, for example, whereas a bookseller in New York City was selling copies for ten dollars after the novel was banned in England and under court challenge in the United States.[91] The various prices of the novels indicated, then, their expected positions in their respective markets. Price appears to have determined how booksellers and readerships would view the work: as a serious novel, an inexpensive romp, or something with a promise of forbidden erotics. Price, furthermore, suggested the publisher's estimation of a book's moral or cultural content. Hall's relatively inexpensive novel could indicate her publisher's desire to locate *The Well of Loneliness* within the ranks of noninflammatory literary fiction—a desire that failed to deflect the scrutiny Douglas reserved for Hall alone, ignoring Mackenzie.

Even before their novels' publications, Hall herself fumed over her book's comparison to Mackenzie's satire and sought to preempt any publicity she might share with those whom she termed "her enemies."[92] *The Well of Loneliness* was first published in England on July 27, 1928, shortly before Mackenzie's *Extraordinary Women* appeared, in early August. Hall's English publication date was, in fact, moved forward from the autumn in a successful bid to precede Mackenzie's.[93] Hall's concerns about the possible scoop of her novel by *Extraordinary Women* were not entirely unfounded: some reviewers paired the two novels. Mackenzie's novel went to a second British edition, whereas Hall's was banned after a protracted court battle.[94]

Immediately after its release, *The Well of Loneliness* became embroiled in a public debate over the status of lesbian representation. Douglas's editorial in the *Sunday Express* prompted Hall's publisher to submit the novel to the Home Office for review, which eventually led to a British ban predicated on charges of obscenity. The British seizure of the book and subsequent trial has been compared to the trials of Oscar Wilde in its importance for public representational politics of female homosexuality. Jean Bobby Noble notes of the British trial that "inversion, already medicalized, is now 'nationalized' as well. Coming ten years after the Pemberton Billing trial,

The Well obscenity trial remains caught in a panicked epistemological contradiction where Englishness is whiteness is heterosexuality, with perversion and inversion being its necessary national Other."[95]

The trial's terrain has been well covered by others,[96] so here I will note only that the trial garnered tremendous publicity in literary weeklies such as *Nation and Athenaeum* and the *New Statesman,* as well as dailies such as the *Times.* Members of the Bloomsbury literary elite such as Leonard and Virginia Woolf and E. M. Forster rallied (sometimes reluctantly) around Hall to support her right to publish and sell the book.[97] Public opinion appeared split over issues of literary freedom, censorship, and the prevalence of sexological as opposed to psychoanalytic models of homosexual identity. Finally, Sir Chartres Biron ruled the book obscene because of its sympathetic portrayals of female homosexuality, rather than the female homosexual representation itself. Rejecting arguments in favor of an inborn inversion (as opposed to volitional perversion), he ruled the novel "an offence against public decency, an obscene libel," and he ordered all copies destroyed.[98] Prior to this decision, however, Jonathan Cape had shipped the typeset plates of the novel to Paris, where the novel continued to be printed and from where it sold briskly, if covertly.

A few months later, *The Well of Loneliness* was similarly tried in New York, but with a different outcome. The New York court ruled the novel not obscene after defense attorney Morris Ernst favorably compared *The Well of Loneliness* to a late nineteenth-century French novel that had previously been brought up on charges of obscenity in New York but had been subsequently cleared of those charges.[99] Ernst contended that *Mademoiselle de Maupin,* by Théophile Gautier, contained material far more shocking and dangerous than *The Well of Loneliness.* Thus, he successfully argued, Radclyffe Hall's work could not be obscene.

In each of these cases, state interests were defined through how female homosexuality was represented in the novel, not by debates over whether female homosexuality could be excised from the literary canon outright. Editorialist James Douglas appears to have "won" his "war" in England but lost a similar battle in the United States. Notably, neither of these skirmishes involved Mackenzie's *Extraordinary Women,* though that text contained similarly descriptive accounts of lesbian relationships. Adam Parkes notes, of the British decision, "In Hall's case, the aggravating factor seems to have been not the subject but the treatment. Whereas Woolf's fictional biography, [*Orlando,*] like Mackenzie's satire, sets out to make readers laugh, *The*

Well of Loneliness pleads the cause of sexual inversion by taking up an aggressively polemical stance."[100]

Hall's competitive anger at *Extraordinary Women* exploded in April 1929. As her novel stood on trial in the United States, she learned that "*Extraordinary Women* was to be published in a cheap popular edition [in England] and without interference by the Home Office." Hall's biographer Michael Baker reports that Hall was infuriated by this decision and wrote, "Here and now I renounce my country for ever, nor will I ever lift a hand to help England in the future."[101] Here Hall constructed the unfettered circulation of Mackenzie's text as a personal and national betrayal, much as Wilde had done at *Salomé's* ban, thirty years before. Just as her protagonist Stephen Gordon is exiled from Morton and England, Hall viewed the legal disinterest in *Extraordinary Women*, in the face of the trial of *The Well of Loneliness*, as her own rhetorical, if not geographic, exile.

Published two months after *The Well of Loneliness* and *Extraordinary Women*, *Orlando* achieved success attributed at least in part to the cultural interest in lesbianism generated by Mackenzie's and Hall's novels. Discussing *Orlando* in relation to the British obscenity trial of *The Well of Loneliness*, Sherron Knopp notes, "The publication of *Orlando* in the midst of this scandal gave Virginia her first public triumph. Leonard Woolf, noting that the book sold twice as many copies in six months as *To The Lighthouse* had in a year, calls it the turning point of her career, and [Quentin] Bell matter-of-factly attributes its success to the sudden 'topicality' of 'the sexual theme.'"[102] Certainly the publicity surrounding the trial of *The Well of Loneliness* could well have increased public appetite for literature on similar topics. Discussing the impact of Hall's book on public discourses of lesbianism, Sonja Ruehl asserts, "Although she stepped into the space that [Havelock] Ellis had created and defined for lesbianism, Hall made the space more public. This was to mean that others, feminists for instance, could engage with and challenge that definition in a more publicly accessible way."[103] Just as Hall made a medical discourse more accessible to popular audiences, she also may have enabled more coded, less didactic discussions of lesbianism—such as those in *Orlando*—possible.[104] Adam Parkes has similarly drawn on the stylistic differences among the novels in his suggestion that Mackenzie's satire and Woolf's use of fantasy and modernist, rather than realist, narrative codes in *Orlando* saved these two novels from the censoring and legal proceedings that *The Well of Loneliness* endured.[105]

Contemporary literary reviews of the three novels draw similar distinctions between Hall's realist literary and politically polemical style and the more satiric and light-handed treatments of the cultural role of lesbian desire in Mackenzie. In reviews of *Extraordinary Women* and *The Well of Loneliness,* almost all critics create a split between style and theme. In reviews of *Orlando,* in comparison, the text's subject—the life of Orlando over three hundred years, several commitments, and two genders—appears inextricable from Woolf's style, her modernist experimentation, and her much-heralded subtlety and humor. The early reception of all three texts produced a modernist tension between form and content. Lines between the "old" forms—sexology, realism, sentimentality—and the "new"—psychoanalysis, narrative experiment, modernity—were reinforced and rearticulated even in the reviews of three texts that refute such divisions and produce more complicated relationships among medical and literary forms, conservative and modern subjectivity.

The reviews explicitly engage three interconnected debates in these novels: debates over the status of psychology and medical definitions of homosexuality; contests over changing definitions of literary quality, which we may now read as a struggle over the terms of modernity; and engagements with the relation of formal artistic experiment to cultural change. But a fourth reading is absent. If we also read the novels' productions of lesbian subjectivity through a frame of contemporary geopolitics, we can see that the contemporary reviews of each novel reinforce the invisibility of its nationalist foundations. Debates framed in terms of progress and modernity render Englishness invisible and thus universal, yet the debates in the reviews over cultural change and over the effects of the Great War on literature and women's roles may indicate, when read through the novels themselves, an anxiety regarding, rather than an assumption of, a universalized British subject.

Almost without exception, the early reviews of *The Well of Loneliness* attempted to separate an evaluation of the novel's artistic merit from its controversial, "modern" subject. Leonard Woolf's review in *Nation and Athenaeum* provides the most explicit example: "Her [Hall's] present book invites consideration from two points of view: as a work of art and because of its subject." About Hall's treatment of homosexuality, described via allusions to Sappho then termed "the abnormal," Leonard Woolf has only praise and support: "As a study of a psychology which is neither as uncommon nor as abnormal as many people imagine, the book is extremely interesting.

It is written with understanding and frankness, with sympathy and feeling. The chief of those 'unsolved problems,' to which Mr. Havelock Ellis refers [in his commentary on the novel] is, of course, caused by the instinctive and barbarous attitude of society, and particularly of British society, towards the abnormal."[106] Here Leonard Woolf constructs England as "barbarous" for its homophobic attitudes, in opposition to his review's normalized discussion of "the abnormal." Yet, although he expresses clear support for the rights of homosexuals, he cites sexologist Ellis, not novelist Hall, to support his position, and frames this as an issue of psychology, not literature. This enables him to support homosexual emancipation while still severely criticizing the book as a piece of literature: ultimately, he determines that "the book is a failure." Woolf, it seems, agreed with L. P. Hartley from the *Saturday Review,* who speculated that "the few beautiful lines . . . would do more than do Miss Hall's five-hundred fiery pages."[107]

Vera Brittain's review of *The Well of Loneliness* for the English feminist weekly *Time and Tide* neither entirely condemns nor condones the novel. Initially echoing Leonard Woolf's review, Brittain articulates the "doubleness" of Hall's novel, its subject, and its success as a piece of fiction: "Miss Radclyffe Hall's important, sincere, and very moving study demands consideration from two different standpoints. In the first place, it is presented as a novel, and is therefore open to criticism as a work of imagination. . . . In the second place, it is a plea, passionate yet admirably restrained and never offensive, for the extension of social toleration, compassion and recognition to the biologically abnormal woman."[108] Brittain finds fault in the work's literary merits, because "it is unduly long and overburdened with detail. . . . Its shape is indefinite, and it leaves behind a sense of lost links which might have fastened its various parts more connectedly together." Moreover, her text is "old-fashioned." Yet, unlike Leonard Woolf, she believes that Hall intended the piece to stand on its theme rather than its style, so this is where Brittain focuses her critical attention. She emphasizes that, like all "problem[s] . . . better frankly stated than concealed," female homosexuality should be openly debated.

Brittain's critique of the novel centers on Hall's use of gender inversion to define female homosexuality. This leads to what Brittain calls "the exaggeration of sex differences . . . to which the English middle classes of the eighteenth and nineteenth centuries were particularly prone."[109] Brittain argues that Hall perpetuates "old" standards of masculinity and femininity at the expense of British feminist women: "This confusion between what is 'male' or 'female' and what is merely human in our complex make up persists throughout the book." Here Brittain rejects Hall's implications in the early chapters that Stephen's "tomboyishness" and then her masculinity determine her homosexuality. Brittain articulates a concern that *The Well of Loneliness* would cause all independent women to be suspected of perversion. She concludes her piece with a strongly worded statement to prevent such inferences: "If one of the results of women's education in the eighteen-nineties really was to attach the ugly label 'pervert' to a human being whose chief desire was for a wider expression of her humanity than contemporary convention permitted, then that education was an evil thing indeed."[110] Brittain simultaneously places Hall's novel within a national conversation regarding the roles of British women and universalizes her own position within that debate: rather than naturalizing a hierarchy of gender differences, as Hall does in her novel, Brittain advocates the acceptance of women's broader public roles in British culture as an expression of their "humanity." Brittain's review implicitly critiques Hall's nationalist nostalgia for "tradition" at the expense of gender equity.

Like reviews of *The Well of Loneliness,* reviews of Mackenzie's *Extraordinary Women* distinguish subject from style. Yet, because Mackenzie's novel is a satire, some who find the subject of female homosexuality offensive are more likely to applaud its form and generally approve of the novel. A very brief review of the novel in the *Nation* by "C. P. F." describes its topics as "single-track ladies . . . seen by a humorous and civilized eye." This reviewer enjoys the satiric style of the novel and concludes, "This seems to be the one right method for treating fictionally what are called perversions. Perhaps eventually some of our over-serious young Americans, taking courage from Mr. Mackenzie, will see fit to handle normal love-making with the same entrancing absurdity. The world do move."[111] C. P. F. valorizes satire as a tool of modernity and disparages "variations on the theme of Lesbianism." In contrast, the *Times Literary Supplement* disapproves of Mackenzie's approach to his subject. As in the *TLS* review of *The Well of Loneliness,* artistic merit and topic are considered separately.[112] Its review of Mackenzie's novel notes that "its subject is outside the interest of the ordinary novel-reader" but that "Mr. Mackenzie's treatment of the abnormality is devoid of offence." Still, although the review has only praise for the novelist's creative abilities, the piece's unpopular subject seals the fate of the novel: "It is strange that so experienced a novelist could not see the want of variety in his subject, which all his knowledge, all his skill in improvisation, and all his quotations from Sappho cannot conceal." Here neither Mackenzie's skill nor his claim to a transhistorical connection to the Greeks is of any use, given the form and topic he selected: "We question . . . whether this novel does not prove that the theme of abnormality, treated with light humour, is extremely unfruitful."[113] Unlike Hall, whose serious polemical purpose undermines her art, Mackenzie uses a light touch that undermines his skill. For the *Times Literary Supplement,* it seems, form and content are always incompatible when the topic is "abnormalities." In all of Mackenzie's reviews, he is distanced from his subject in a way that the mannish invert Hall cannot be from hers. And it is somewhere between this praise of Mackenzie's biographical distance and a distaste for Hall's closeness that the reviews of *Orlando* place Woolf.

In reviews of Woolf's *Orlando,* which almost uniformly hail the book enthusiastically, aesthetic concerns dominate cultural commentaries. This is hardly surprising, given the innovative uses of language and genre that make up *Orlando.* Yet the interweaving discussion of Woolf's sexual subject with her novel's form is particularly striking. Woolf's "fantastical" (this word is repeated in several reviews) premise, that a person can live across several centuries and two genders, becomes assimilated into discussions of her formalist project. When gender or sexual variation is mentioned at all in the reviews, it is either hinted at in the context of formal experiment or dismissed as unimportant. The form that Woolf chose successfully diverts critics hostile to "abnormalities" or "perversions," leaving most readings of her novel to sympathetic reviewers. The review of *Orlando* in the *Times Literary Supplement* provides a startling contrast to reviews of Mackenzie and Hall: "Some such thoughts [about gender instability] may hover within call as we read 'Orlando,' but they need scarcely press into sight. For nothing could be much less like a treatise on psychology or heredity than this. It is a fantasy, impossible but delicious: existing in its own right by the colour of imagination and an exuberance of life and wit."[114] This praise of Woolf's novel directly refers to the negative review the *TLS* gave only two months before to *The Well of Loneliness* for being too much a thesis on psychology. *Orlando*'s modernist "fantasy" and "prose so swift and sparkling that it leaves us almost breathless and sated with good things" nullify any unpleasant, "psychological" content that the novel contains. In short, the form in which the content is delivered in Woolf's novel apparently renders such content harmless to the *TLS*.

The dedication to and photographs of Vita Sackville-West as "Orlando" in the "biography" provided the occasion for a few veiled references to the homoerotic implications of the text. The *Saturday Review* commented that "if Mrs. Woolf, out of compliments to the friend to whom the book is dedicated, paints a recognizable picture of the vastest of historic English country houses there is no cause for protest."[115] Orlando's estate is, as Bonnie Kime Scott notes, "Knole, the family home denied Vita by male primogeniture in 1928."[116] Thus, through an allusion to Knole, Woolf's relationship with Sackville-West is given an implicit nod. Such a comment need not interfere, however, with "passages of extreme brilliance" and "spasmodic ingenuity" in *Orlando*. Similarly, Barrington Gates, in *Nation and Athenaeum,* a rave review that praises "the greatness of [Woolf's] tricks," her "genius," and her "poetic truth," made a more sophisticated wink at the relationship of Sackville-West to the novel: "The question 'Who is Orlando?' has a particular meaning, which is challenged by the photographs which illustrate her career. Mrs. Woolf is quite capable of making her up out of her own head. But if, as seems probable, she took a contemporary original and worked backwards, I am going to plump, as one of the uninstructed public, for a Sackville of Knole."[117] *Orlando* here becomes a roman à clef to be decoded: the reference to Vita Sackville-West could not be more clear in this periodical which was edited by Leonard Woolf and for which Sackville-West herself wrote. More important in this quotation, however, is the subtle relationship between Woolf's creative genius and her choice to model Orlando after Sackville-West. Her talent is great enough, the reviewer states, to create her own Orlando. By noting that Woolf drew on a real-life model, however, the reviewer inserts Woolf's relationship with Sackville-West into a discussion of both "literary skill" and the novel's "passionate flesh and blood" character.

These reviews of all three novels indicate two critical points. First, debates over the status of modernism were played out as debates over literary value and the role of psychology (and, more broadly, science) in literature. By reading each reviewer's negotiations of these controversial formations, we see the necessary structural interdependence between critiques of form and content, between aesthetics and ideology. Sexual and gender deviance within the pages of a more fantastical and experimental text appears to have been more acceptable than a conventional novel. This is not, as some later critics have guessed, because the culture at large was unaware of female homosexual representations and any indicators in Woolf's texts would thus go unnoticed. Contemporaneous reviewers' multiple references to "Mrs. Woolf's friends" seem to refute that supposition. Rather, I think, it was more comfortable to place representations of female homosexuality and gender ambiguity within the realm of the fantastic or impossible in a novel than to import models of such deviance from medicine. Many objections to Hall and Mackenzie arose when the reviewer noted the psychological aspect of the novel or its overly predominant "thesis." These are critiques of realism and psychology as much as critiques of homosexual representation. The role of British cultural formations in the production of each text remains almost entirely unarticulated in all the reviews. The reviewer of Mackenzie's novel in the *New Statesman* comes closest when he asserts that by 1928 lesbianism was "a comparatively widespread social phenomenon . . . owing very much to wider causes arising out of the war and its *sequelae.*" In direct contrast to wartime representations, by 1928 female homosexuality had indeed become a clear category in the public imagination. No longer equated with sadism, as it was in the Maud Allan trial, or so unspoken culturally that the Parliament shuddered to hear of it, words like *Sapphist, lesbian,* and *abnormal* now had clear meanings. Perhaps the reviewers from the *New Statesman* and the *Nation* were both correct: "It is impossible to dismiss [lesbianism] quite so confidently in these post-war days of boy-girls and girl-boys" as it was in the prewar period, but it is also undeniable that "the world do move."

The three novels discussed in this chapter illustrate broad debates over ideology and cultural change in the interwar period. In the midst of British women's legal emancipation and cultural retrenchments, surrounded by the disintegration of Britain's global imperial power, each of these texts and its reception indicate the mutual dependence of constructions of sexual subjectivity and the politics of nationhood and citizenship. By reading these novels through their cultural, geopolitical, economic, and literary moment of production, I argue for the imbrication of constructions of citizenship with emergent discourses of lesbian identity. Like Hall's Stephen Gordon, Mackenzie's Rory cannot "go home" to England to enjoy her cup of tea. And although Woolf's Orlando hints at female same-sex relations within her marriage, these teases are as predicated on the politics of national distancing as are the exiles in Hall's earnest and Mackenzie's parodic pictures of the masculine British gentleman invert. Though Hall, Mackenzie, and Woolf played with many different representations of female same-sex desire, it was the convergence of masculinity with female same-sex desire in the gentleman invert that, following the discursive explosion of 1928, would remain the dominant representational possibility of lesbian identity for British culture for much of the twentieth century.

afterword

DRAG KING DREAMS DEFERRED

Citizen, Invert, Queer traces the emergence of coherent public representations of female homosexuality in early twentieth-century British public
culture. I argue that discourses of imperialism, eugenics, and gendered citizenship profoundly shaped the emergent representations of female sexuality in general, and homosexuality in specific. Contrary to prior histories of
British lesbian subjectivity that privilege medical models of homosexuality,
Citizen, Invert, Queer situates the sexological model of "congenital inversion"
as one vector among many cultural narratives through which masculinity
in women was understood, and was only one of several representations of
female homosexual erotics in play in the 1910s and 1920s. Radclyffe Hall's
"mythic mannish lesbian" emerged as the dominant model of female
homosexual identity by the mid-twentieth century through discourses not
only of sexological inversion but also of masculine citizenship, racial subjectivity, and women's shifting wartime roles.[1]

The moral sex panics of Great War Britain simultaneously transformed
gendered and sexual ideologies and produced women as nationalist subjects
in opposition to sexually and racially abject others.[2] These early twentieth-
century rhetorical moves in Britain have informed my thinking about the
domestic and transnational politics of gender and sexuality at the turn of
the twenty-first century. When, in the mid-1990s, I began thinking about
the emergence of lesbian identity in the early twentieth century, the incoherent and competing discourses of lesbian identities in that period seemed
to resonate with a similarly cacophonous and confusing moment in the
emergence of a common language for transsexual and transgender identities in the United States in the 1990s. During the Great War, words like
Sapphist, invert, lesbian, and *homosexual* were making forays into public

discourse, yet it was unclear what exactly these terms meant (as illustrated, for example, in *Rex v Pemberton Billing*). Members of various same-sex erotic communities often preferred one term over another, and those preferences indicated profound cultural, economic, and political differences. Similarly, in the 1990s in the United States, members of what was coming to be called the "transgender community" (or simply the "gender community") were working to define and distinguish terms such as *transsexual, transgender,* and, later in that decade, *genderqueer*. Again, preferences or community standards indicated not only a varying understanding of what these terms stood for but also different political, cultural, embodied, economic, and racial positions.

As I conclude this project, I write amid further iterations of home-front nationalism and renegotiations of racial, sexual, and gendered citizenship in the United States. The United States has now been waging war in Iraq and Afghanistan for longer than it was involved in either World War I or World War II. The renegotiations of citizenship and identity on my own home front neither simply echo earlier conflicts nor reflect a progression or progress narrative in some fantasy of cultural evolution, a century later and an ocean away from Great War Britain. Rather, in each time and place, vectors of power have transformed cultural identities and subject positions both through deliberate strategies and as the result of resistance, dissonance, or cultural momentum. The position of U.S. women in relation to military service, for example, has radically shifted in the past decade through a struggle among military policies, ideologies of motherhood and gender, and an unstable relationship between "combat" and "support." Similarly, racial and religious categories in American popular imaginations have continually transformed, as post-9/11 shifts in cultural narratives of racial profiling from "driving while black" to "flying while brown," for example, can indicate.[3] Here I will suggest an application of the method developed in this book for the intersecting fields of queer theory and transnational feminist cultural studies—a method that foregrounds questions of nationalism in the production of sexual subjectivities.

To illustrate this application, I now turn my analysis from Great War Britain to post–September 11 America. In her concluding chapter of *Queering the Color Line,* Siobhan Somerville makes a similar historical leap. I travel across time and space not to undo the historical or national specificity of this book's argument, but rather, in Somerville's words, "as a gesture toward the kinds of readings and analyses that my guiding questions make possible."[4] By way of conclusion, I read Leslie Feinberg's 2006 antiwar novel of gendered and sexual resistance, *Drag King Dreams,* both in the context of ongoing definitional debates about transsexual and transgender identities and through the lens of home-front nationalist culture. In Feinberg's novel, deviant as well as normative gendered and sexual identities are produced through state power and the ideologies of citizenship and national belonging. By considering cultural productions in circulation almost a century after my book's center of analysis, I hope to suggest a theoretical framework integrating queer studies and transnational feminist theory. I will conclude by suggesting the ongoing importance of cultural and political ramifications of discourses of citizenship in queer cultural formations, and the importance of interrogating the sexual, gendered, and racial underpinnings of representations of the nation, particularly in periods of great national crisis, conflict, and transformation.

The 1990s in the United States saw a proliferation of transsexual and transgender politics, culture, and academic studies. One can trace increasing public visibility and legibility of communities formed through affiliations and coalitions of transmen, females-to-males (FTMs), and drag kings, from the formation of FTM International, in 1986, through community and mass media responses to the 1993 murder of the young person known widely as Brandon Teena, to the plethora of emergent identity terms such as "tomboi" and ongoing debates within lesbian and trans communities about the permeable or divisive relations of butch female identities to FTM trans identities.[5] The "border wars" documented by C. Jacob Hale, Judith Halberstam, and others between butch lesbians and FTMs highlight the multivalent cultural category of transgender and its still-uncertain relationship to the more widely culturally legible categories of lesbian and transsexual.[6] The novels and community histories of Leslie Feinberg stand alongside monographs by Jay Prosser, Judith Halberstam, and Jean Bobby Noble, each contributing to public dialogues surrounding emergent transgender and transsexual identities. Together, these discursive, mass-cultural, and subcultural representations stage debates over queer subjectivity, gendered embodiment, cultural production, and community history.

Particularly notable are the frequent appearances of Radclyffe Hall's novel *The Well of Loneliness* and Havelock Ellis's sexological classifications in discourses of transgender and FTM transsexual identities at the turn of the twenty-first century. As early as 1994, Feinberg drew on *The Well of Loneliness* to discuss the difficulties of representing gender variance and transgender subjectivity in literature.[7] In 1998, both Prosser and Halberstam positioned Hall's novel within histories of emergent transsexual or transgender identities. Prosser claims *The Well of Loneliness* as a transsexual rather than a lesbian text. In contrast, Halberstam produces a reading of Stephen Gordon's female masculinity as transgender, rather than transsexual, arguing for masculine inversion as a distinct form of masculine female identity not to be conflated with either lesbian or transsexual identity. Noble suggests that the figure of Stephen Gordon as an exemplar of the sexological invert "represents a productive contradiction" in the construction of a "representational history"[8] claimed in both lesbian and trans communities. These are but a few examples of the ways in which the early twentieth-century representations of inversion were revisited and reinterpreted at the turn of the twenty-first century in service of emergent gender identities rather than as origins of homosexual identities.[9] The complex interplay of gender inversion, sexual inversion, and subjectivity is reformulated to construct a trans genealogy in lieu of earlier productions of lesbian history and identity. The production of trans identities in the context of queer, wartime culture in the post-9/11 United States, similar to the production of homosexual identities through the earlier moment of home-front cultural transformation in Great War Britain, is as dependent on structures of national belonging or abjection as it is on debates over gender and sexuality. Leslie Feinberg's 2006 novel of post-9/11 struggle, *Drag King Dreams,* presents solidarity among gendered, sexual, and national outsiders as both the consequence of and the antidote to neoliberal formations of citizenship in the United States in the early twenty-first century.

Drag King Dreams opens with its first-person narrator and gender-indeterminate protagonist, Max, attempting to differentiate hirself from hir cross-dressing friend and courageous civil rights lawyer Victor/Vickie.[10] "She's an activist, not a street fighter," Max thinks to hirself. When Vickie is murdered by street thugs, the difference between Max's always-visible gender difference and Vickie's ability to "change . . . clothes and go back to the day world and be a lawyer" is dissipated by the narrative: both Max and Vickie are at risk in the novel.[11] Here, Feinberg intervenes in the so-called border wars by rejecting hierarchies of oppression among differently gendered characters, instead modeling a community composed of butch lesbians, FTMs, males-to-females (MTFs), drag kings and queens, and others. Max learns hir lesson of genderqueer solidarity after Vickie's death: ze transforms from individual defensive "street fighter" to participant in collective struggle. Max's journey through the novel is one of increasing political and social action, as well as increasing solidarity with hir Muslim neighbors. *Drag King Dreams* weaves together street violence and state violence against queers, transpeople, Muslims, undocumented residents, and war resisters. Feinberg invites hir readers to understand violence against queers as parallel to yet also intersecting with American histories of racial violence and post–9/11 iterations of state-sponsored and home-front hostilities, detainment, and discipline.

Feinberg refashions the meaning of Manhattan as a post–9/11 "ground zero": for *Drag King Dreams,* September 11, 2001, marks both rupture and continuity for sexual, gendered, and racial outsiders in the United States.[12] One the one hand, the repeated arrests of transgender and queer characters in the novel reference the police brutality and arrests of butches and femmes in the 1950s and 1960s, as described in painful, realist detail in Feinberg's first novel, *Stone Butch Blues.* On the other hand, *Drag King Dreams* broadens the dragnet to include the arrests and disappearances of Muslim and South Asian men in the post–9/11 moment of counterterrorist state violence. *Drag King Dreams* explicitly links these two forms of state violence, arguing for solidarity and alliance. As hir characters with oppositional identities sustain and resist their multiracial and multigendered communities and engage with the consequences of 9/11, Feinberg argues for oppositional subjectivity predicated on solidarity and struggle against both gender and sexual norms and against capitalist and imperialist state power. By drawing transgender and queer characters through explicit plots of resistance and abjection, not only does this home-front novel make explicit connections between national, sexual, and gendered representations, but in so doing it also produces gendered and sexual subjectivity in relation to narratives of nationalism and state power.

In the character Thor, an FTM bartender and antiwar activist, Feinberg produces a transgender subject through the dynamic relation of gender-queer identity and communitarian responses to state repression. Thor's arrest at a protest against the detention of Muslim men following 9/11 illustrates Feinberg's insistence on solidarity: "He left the protest at the detention center alone to go to the bathroom. The cops followed him and busted him in the john." What is crucial here is not only the vivid reminder of the continual cultural and state violence against trans people but also the fact that Thor's arrest for gender transgression occurs at a protest in support of disappeared Muslim men. As Thor's supporters from a rainbow of political and cultural communities amass outside the police station where he is held, the chant comes from the crowd, "Stop the war! Free Thor!"[13] In Feinberg's novel, the freedom of transmen to function in civil society is one and the same with the same right for Muslim men after 9/11. *Drag King Dreams* insists that queer rights are immigrant rights are worker's rights are the rights for safety from racial, sexual, and gendered violence. Thor is released from jail because of both the savvy negotiations of his civil rights lawyer and the massive crowd of supporters who wait, chant, and demand his freedom outside the police station. The novel constructs a binary system of oppressed and oppressor: resistance must come through collective struggle, despite the violence (such as Thor's beating at the hands of the police) that resistance brings. Thor's arrest demonstrates his threat to the state both as an antiwar activist and as a genderqueer. "Stop the war! Free Thor!" produces Thor's trans subjectivity as much through home-front conditions of cultural injustice as through his individual gender transition.

Thor also represents the limits of collective action for individuals under a neoliberal state. In a scene of intimacy and domesticity (in contrast to most of the novel's depictions of Thor in public spaces of work, protest, or prison), Feinberg presents the incommensurability of Thor's gender identity with U.S. family law. Sitting in his apartment, Thor explains his male name to Max: "'[Thor] was the most popular god of the people.' He speaks quickly, 'They would call on him to bring them fertility.'" After establishing his own subjectivity through a lineage of fertility, strength, and power, Thor tells Max, "This Thursday [the day named for Thor] is the day the courts gave my ex full custody of my child. . . . When the judge said he was granting custody to the father, I almost shouted with joy. And then I realized he didn't mean me; . . . there was my child who is of my flesh . . . and they ripped us apart like we were a piece of paper." Here Feinberg articulates both a limit of self-fashioning and a politics of resistance. Thor comes to court "with my piercings and my tattoos, and all my fatness" as a transman and as a father to stake claim to the child he birthed as a mother.[14] Yet Thor's subjectivity as a man, a genderqueer, and a parent lies outside the parameters of the neoliberal state. The court not only denies custody to Thor as his child's father but also denies him custody as a failed mother. Nationalist motherhood, in this novel, has no space for a mother-turned-father.

Though a native-born, white citizen, Thor is disenfranchised because of his gender. In contrast, Hindu immigrant Netaji first appears to have successfully adopted survival strategies for safely earning his living driving a New York City taxicab after 9/11. When Max asks Netaji if he is being "hassled" by cops or passengers, "Netaji leans inside the open window of his cab and pulls out a Mets baseball cap. 'Hello, boss,' he says in a new low voice. He lifts the brim and winks at me." Netaji fashions a gendered and national identity of "Mets fan" to insure his safety. Netaji does not add an American flag to his taxicab, a common protective move by some South Asians and Muslims in the United States following 9/11; he takes up a consumerist symbol of the "national pastime" rather than one of the nation itself. Yet this shield proves insufficient, and midway through the novel, Netaji is disappeared. Max thinks to hirself, "I don't understand what is happening." Ze then protests aloud, "Netaji's not Muslim," and the more politically savvy Thor replies, "It's a big dragnet. Lots of people are getting caught in it."[15] To be working-class, to be a person of color, to fall outside gender or sexual norms, and/or to refuse the politics of imperialist nationalism is to be at risk in this novel.

Feinberg draws Max's chosen family as a multiethnic, multigendered group. From hir long-standing comrade the HIV-positive African American MTF Ruby; to white transman Thor; to Deacon, an African American gay man; and Jasmine, a Chinese American woman with a shrouded gendered past; to Netaji, whose sexual and gender orientations remain unexplored but whose taxicab frequently appears to whisk members of the group away from danger, Max's intimate circle illustrates multicultural American genderqueers and sexual outlaws functioning as an unorthodox family. Feinberg develops Jewish Max's connections to hir Middle Eastern male neighbors through geographic proximity, narratives of history, and shared experiences of outsiderness. Max struggles to establish relationships with hir neighbors Palestinian Hatem and Egyptian Mohammad, but ze forges connections with these two men through mutual kindness and through their mutual histories of resistance.

After a fire in their apartment building, Hatem invites Max into his friend Mohammad's nearby grocery store. Max initially tenses for an anti-Semitic response when Hatem confirms hir last name: "Rabinowitz, yes?" Watching television coverage of the impending U.S. military strikes in Iraq with Hatem and Mohammad, Max stakes out hir political position by naming "the sliver of land on the map" Palestine rather than Israel. As Max leaves the grocery store, ze thanks Mohammad with an awkwardly stylized "Thank you for welcoming a stranger." The narrative continues: "Mohammad claps one hand to his chest as he continues to hold my grip firmly, 'Ah, my friend, we are cousins.'" Feinberg privileges one historical narrative (that of Semitic relationships) over another (that of a Jewish-Muslim conflict). On the one hand, Egyptian Mohammad and Jewish Max are cousins because of a shared biblical genealogy. On the other hand, Max's Jewish resistance to the imperialist state of Israel is produced not only through hir politics but also through hir identity as a Jew—through "properly" read histories of Jewish resistance. For Feinberg, the solution to the seemingly intractable problem of Israel for progressive American Jews is not to reject a politics of identity (which might more conventionally align all Jews with Israeli state policies) but to choose the *correct* lineage of identity: secular, socialist, and oppositional. This lineage also constructs Max's gendered relation to Mohammad: later in the novel, when Mohammad is rearticulating his friendship with Max and Max's childhood (Jewish) friend Heshie, he stumbles over pronouns:

> Mohammad leans forward and says to Heshie, "You are always welcome at my store. Anytime. Your friend here, she . . . he is like my own family."
> Mohammad looks chagrined at having stumbled on my pronoun. I am taken aback. What am I surprised about? That he knows I'm queer? Who doesn't? Of course Hatem knew, too.
> Mohammad places his hand on my elbow. . . . "We are cousins."
> . . . I will never be a stranger in Egypt.[16]

Mohammad's verbal stumble produces Max as a transman, and Max's response links hir gender to queerness. Mohammad's final gesture of touch and reassertion of kinship also rewrites history: Jews were biblically "strangers in Egypt," but Max and Mohammad write a new history. Together they stand in opposition to American and Israeli imperialist aggression, and together these two "cousins" bridge ethnic, gender, and sexual divides.

This utopian vision of Jewish and Muslim cousins is disrupted by increasing state violence, the dismantling of outsider communities through police violence, and the disappearances of men of color and queers. In contrast to Netaji's mysterious disappearance, Max's Palestinian neighbor Hatem is arrested in front of witnesses, but then he is similarly detained and disappeared. Hatem's arrest follows his protest of police brutality: he witnessed a white police officer sexually threatening a Latino child on the street and intervened on the child's behalf.[17] The arrest and subsequent disappearance of hir neighbor incites Max to action; first ze creates flyers on hir own and then ze joins Thor's People's Fightback Network to oppose the disappearances of Muslim men. Feinberg's novel models solidarity as Max's individual goodwill and acts of friendship transform into collective action and public protest. The arrests of heterosexual Middle Eastern and South Asian men both signal a new tactic of state repression following 9/11 in the United States and also depict a continuity of disenfranchisement: Hatem is arrested for speaking against police brutality and sexual abuse—hardly a post–9/11 invention—in solidarity with and in defense of youths of color, yet the consequences of his arrest and then assumed deportation are heightened under the policies of attorney general John Ashcroft.[18]

Cultural difference not only functions as a site of solidarity and connection in the novel but also flags the novel's possible limits of identification. Max not only forges alliances with hir Middle Eastern neighbors and genderqueer comrades but also seeks connections among differently gendered people across history and culture. In an early section of the novel framed by hir desire to travel away from New York City and "the house arrest that the world has sentenced me to," Max finds national and cultural diversity in Manhattan through its Italian restaurants, Irish bakeries, and a Philippine parcel service. Ze recalls the previous year when ze stumbled into a Navratri celebration in "Little India":

> The music electrified my sinews and muscles. I wanted so much to step into this circle, to become part of it, but this was not my dance.
>
> I watched women dancing differently than men; some old women dancing differently than some young. . . .
>
> And then I noticed one person who did not dance like the women or the men. . . . I saw another person, dressed in a flowing sari not unlike those worn by women standing nearby, who I would have guessed was born male-bodied.
>
> I wanted to create a path across the street to talk to both of them, but what would I say? In what language? What made me feel connected to them? . . . There's so much I don't know. Are they sacred in their culture, while I am profane in mine? . . . Once, long ago, we were all honored. Perhaps now what we share is the almost forgotten memory of ancient songs.[19]

Feinberg's text presents both sensitivity to cultural difference and desire for transcultural and transhistorical connection among differently gendered people. On the one hand, Max is aware that "this was not my dance" and that ze does not have any unmediated claim to kinship with the hijra whom ze sees at the celebration. On the other hand, the narrative forges a connection between genderqueer Max and the hijras: they share a "memory of ancient songs" that link them as others within their respective cultures. Unlike Mohammad's historical assertion that he and Max are "cousins," Max's unspoken affinity with the unnamed hijra serves not to forge a history of resistance but to produce a mythic common origin for differently gendered people across history and culture. In this passage, transcultural desire and ahistorical identification are in tension with calls for cultural specificity and coalition.

Any desired identification among all genderqueers is also undercut by a minor character, Weasel, who functions as an example of class warfare within the ranks of transmen and queers. When Max refuses to listen to Weasel's racist joke, Weasel counters, "I don't know why you have it in for me, bro. What'd I ever do to you? We're all in this together. We're all up against The Man." Feinberg rejects a politics of identification based solely on gender or sexual orientation, as Max replies, "You're a trust fund baby from Connecticut. Your family owns half this island. You *are* The Man. . . . I'm not your brother. . . . Get the hell out of my sight." Weasel's class privilege and bigotry—as he leaves the bar, he shouts, "You'll be sorry, you Jew bastard!"[20]—place him outside the sphere of solidarity and opposition. Though Feinberg's narrative relies on narratives of transcultural and transhistorical connections among differently gendered people, and though the text explicitly calls for coalition and solidarity, the figure of Weasel illustrates the limits of what can sometimes appear to be an all-inclusive politics: characters who work to understand cultural difference are embraced; racism and elitism exclude others from the circle of mutual support and cross-community connection.

Drag King Dreams argues for the stakes that nonimmigrant queers have in fighting for the liberties of immigrants and in struggling against imperialist and capitalist oppression (mainstream U.S. politics). Feinberg's novel urges its readers to choose paths of solidarity and resistance rather than those of isolation or complicity. Links between sexuality and citizenship are made explicit at Victor/Vickie's memorial service. A Latino farmworker eulogizes his friend through the words of Estelle, Victor's wife: "They killed [my] brother for crossing a border that shouldn't be there. And they killed Victor for crossing a border that shouldn't be there." Later in the service,

Ruby describes Vickie: "She was always there for all the people who don't have papers, don't have passbooks. People who can't pull out their ID when cops demand to see it."[21] In *Drag King Dreams,* genderqueers and immigrants (not to mention queer immigrants) share an embattled relation to a state against which they must struggle as activist and street-fighting revolutionaries.

The novel concludes in a jail cell: Max, Deacon, Ruby, Thor, and Jasmine have been arrested following a massive antiwar, antidetention protest organized in Vickie's memory. As they plot collective struggle in their jail cell, each is called out by prison guards—perhaps for release, but more likely for a brutal beating. The guards hail the characters by their given names, committing acts of discursive gendered violence that will either usher in or stand in for physical assault. Yet the novel ends with a tone of hope and triumph: though Hatem is still incarcerated, Netaji has probably been deported, and Max's chosen family faces continual state violence, Max has found hir way back to collective struggle and away from individual alienation.

Transgender identity is produced in direct opposition to the repressive state apparatus in this final scene. The reader knows that Thor both is and is not Carol Finster, Ruby both is and is not Tyrone Lanier, and Max both is and is not Maxine Rabinowitz. *Drag King Dreams* produces trans identities in explicit opposition to the state (as Thor's proud performance of his masculinity both in the prison cell and in family court demonstrates), but the novel just as surely produces trans identities through engagement with state power and home-front nationalism. Max's gender identity is produced not only through hir erotic communications with the "old school femme" ze meets online but just as forcefully through hir jailer's power, hir desire for transcultural connection to the hijras in Little India, and masculine bonding with hir "cousins" Mohammad and Hatem. Home-front nationalism—both its repressive effects and its representational politics—delineates Feinberg's response to the border wars, which for Feinberg represent not a struggle between lesbians and transsexuals for claims to history or community but, rather, a struggle of the abject against the powerful; the work of "the people who don't have papers, don't have passbooks" to reside in national and gendered safety, against the police, the government, and the "trust-fund [babies] from Connecticut."[22]

Feinberg's novel works to produce collective struggle as the necessary, if not the natural, response to oppressive state and ideological violence. I suggest that we read Feinberg's model both as a product of post–9/11 culture, as it tries to shape that historical moment into one of heightened conflict and thus heightened possibilities for widespread solidarity, and also as Feinberg's own commentary on the border wars not only among queer and transgender communities but also between American LGBT communities and others "who can't pull out their ID when cops demand to see it." Max must negotiate hir gender and sexual identity in *Drag King Dreams*, but this negotiation is conducted not only through Max's relation to a national culture and a state apparatus hostile to gender and sexual transgression but also in the midst of nationalist, racial, and geopolitical violence. Max comes into hir own subjectivity through solidarity and through revisions of history that align Jews with Muslims, transmen with drag queens and gay men, and activists with street fighters. Gender identity is distinct from sexual identity in this home-front novel, but both are produced through solidarity and resistance to state power. Without the backdrop of war and the omnipresence of state repression, Max would remain in sexual and gendered isolation, in "no man's land," rather than in struggle and solidarity.

The home front is a battlefront for the disenfranchised in *Drag King Dreams*. When read through discourses of gendered and sexual citizenship as well as through narratives of solidarity, resistance, and opposition to state power, *Drag King Dreams* illustrates the importance of a critical reading practice for queer studies that highlights the ideological power of citizenship and the nation in the formation of discourses of sexual and gendered subjectivity. By reading emergent gender and sexual communities through their relationships to nationalism and citizenship, we can better understand the ideological and discursive interdependences among dominant and oppositional communities and representations. Specifically, *Drag King Dreams* both participates in and charts the emergent production of trans identities in U.S. public culture. These emergent identities are produced through discourses of citizenship and the nation in a moment of political and culture home-front violence. By reading *Drag King Dreams* as the coda to *Citizen, Invert, Queer*, I hope I have illustrated the ways in which citizenship remains a powerful vehicle through which early twentieth-century homosexuals and early twenty-first century genderqueers are defined, whether through attempts at association such as those enacted in Radclyffe Hall's *The Well of Loneliness* or in explicit opposition in Leslie Feinberg's *Drag King Dreams*. Both Hall and Feinberg constitute their sexual and gendered outsiders through their relations to the state and mythologies of the nation. By highlighting the constitutive nature of discourses of the nation for sexual and gendered subjectivity in Feinberg's novel, we can understand queer and genderqueer subjects as both implicated in and also produced through narratives of nationalist identities as well as in opposition or exclusion to them.

ACKNOWLEDGMENTS

I could not have completed this book without the support of numerous colleagues, comrades, and institutions. First, warm thanks to Richard Morrison at the University of Minnesota Press, an ardent advocate for this project from very early stages. With Adam Brunner, Tammy Zambo, Alicia Sellheim, and Laura Westlund, he shepherded the manuscript through the publication process with care, intelligence, and good humor.

San Francisco State University provided me not only with the time and resources necessary to complete this project but also with a vibrant intellectual community in which to work. I gratefully acknowledge a 2003 summer stipend award, a 2004 assigned-time grant, a 2006 faculty minigrant that supported research in London, and a 2006 Presidential Award for Professional Development, which gave me a semester of uninterrupted writing time. Librarians at San Francisco State University and the University of California, Berkeley; and excellent special collections in the Bancroft Library at the University of California, Berkeley, in the Harry Ransom Center for the Humanities at the University of Texas at Austin, and at Stanford University, the British Library, the Women's Library in London, and the British Public Records Office made this project richer.

This project can be traced back to an undergraduate honors thesis on Radclyffe Hall's *The Well of Loneliness* for women's studies and English at Wesleyan University. At Wesleyan, I was mentored by an outstanding faculty, particularly Gertrude Hughes, Henry Abelove, Christina Crosby, Ann Cvetkovich, Ann duCille, and Richard Ohmann. In the English department at Brown University, David Savran, Tamar Katz, and Ellen Rooney supervised my doctoral dissertation and taught me a great deal. Nancy Armstrong, Carolyn Dean, and Elizabeth Weed also helped me to become a better scholar, teacher, and colleague. My fellow graduate students at Brown, especially Elisa Glick, Faye Halpern, Meegan Kennedy, Gautam Premnath, Kasturi Ray, and Annette Van, created a crucial intellectual community.

While completing my dissertation, I worked with two other graduate students in a feminist dissertation group that Tom Metcalf once infamously called the "ladies knitting circle." I am the third "lady" to publish her book from our "circle": Michelle Elizabeth Tusan's *Women Making News: Gender and Journalism in Modern Britain* and Durba Ghosh's *Sex and the Family in Colonial India: The Making of Empire* form the first two parts of our trilogy. Durba and Michelle are outstanding readers and critics, and they taught this literary scholar to think historically. I am continually grateful to them for their friendship and intellectual generosity.

I have had the incredible good fortune to work with Inderpal Grewal and Caren Kaplan. Caren's and Inderpal's groundbreaking work in transnational feminism challenged me to reconceptualize my work on early twentieth-century British culture in a transnational frame. Their mentorship, collegiality, support, and intellectual challenges provided me with the critical tools to center questions of nationalism and citizenship in my work on queer subjectivity. I thank them for their friendship and for the models of their teaching and scholarship.

At San Francisco State University I have colleagues and students who care passionately about intellectual work and who have supported the writing of this book in many ways. This project would not be complete without the encouragement of my colleagues in the Department of Women and Gender Studies and especially without the support from my former chair, Minoo Moallem, and from dean Paul Sherwin. Within and beyond my home department, many colleagues read my work and provided crucial feedback and essential deadlines. Jillian Sandell and James Martel read every page of this manuscript: I cannot thank them enough for their incisive engagements. Thank you also to Nan Alamilla Boyd, Jessica Fields, Julietta Hua, Kasturi Ray, Loretta Stec, Amy Sueyoshi, and Gust Yep. My meticulous graduate research assistant, Sharon Miller, helped pull it all together. Invitations from the Sexuality Studies Department and the Women's History Month committee to present early versions of this work on campus created important opportunities for the development of the project. I also acknowledge my students at San Francisco State University, whose passion for social justice helps me to think about the stakes of academic work on sexuality, war, and identity.

Conversations with many colleagues sharpened my work on sexuality, nationalism, gender, and cultural studies. By reading portions of this manuscript, offering advice about publication, sharing their expertise, and encouraging my research, Lucy Bland, Melissa Bradshaw, Laura Doan, Leslie Feinberg, Linda Garber, Jane Garrity, Inderpal Grewal, Judith Halberstam, Caren Kaplan, Jodie Medd, Minoo Moallem, Parama Roy, Gayle Rubin, Siobhan Somerville, and Jennifer Terry contributed to this project; this book is better for their dialogue with me.

This multidisciplinary work has been made easier through the generous help from colleagues, family members, and friends. I have specific debts of thanks to pay here: to my mother, Ellen Cohler, whose language skills I did not inherit, for assistance with French and Italian translations; to my father, Tim Cohler, for his advice about the law in the United States, and to Edward Kling for the same in Britain; to Cashman Kerr Prince for invaluable assistance with all things Latin and Greek; and to Suzanne Fox for her expert editorial eye.

I cannot thank my parents enough for their support of my education. I also acknowledge the legacies of my grandmother Rose Axenfield and my uncle William Cohler. My grandmother taught me to read (at the tender age of three) and set me off on a life of learning. Uncle Billy died when I was very young: his memory reminds me of the importance of queer history and subjectivity.

Many friends and family members have seen less of me—and more of the book—than they may have preferred over the past years. For their loving support, heartfelt thanks to Karen Boyd, Izumi Cabrera, Jana Cerny, Ellen Cohler, Tim and Anne Cohler, Rick Cohler, Mary Doyno, Sharon Gregory, Hershey Hirschkop, Kim Howerton, Michael Howerton, Jeanette Hsu, Judith Klau, Melinda and Norman Peacock, Cashman Prince, Linda Rodriguey, Alisa Rosen, Tacy Trowbridge, Ray and Lois Voss, and Angela Zaragoza. Masha Raskolnikov is my buddy in the academic trenches: our shared loves for queer theory and decadent desserts have fueled this project. Eva Pendleton has been my women's studies comrade from the beginning: her intelligence, love, and humor are invaluable. John Magee has been more involved in this project than any high school science teacher ought to be: his faith has kept me on track, his intellectual curiosity profoundly shaped chapter 4, and he has been my companion on many Wildean adventures.

I dedicate this book to Barb Voss: my best critic, my staunchest supporter, and my loving spouse. When we met, Barb was an underemployed archaeologist and I was a high school math teacher. We now both teach and write about gender, sexuality, and culture. She keeps me intellectually honest: her archaeological research reminds me of the relationship between representation and materiality. Her work makes mine smarter, and her love makes my work possible. There are not enough words to enumerate all she does for me or all she has contributed to this project, so here I will simply say thank you.

NOTES

INTRODUCTION

1. Feinberg, "Anti-war Message to Pride Marchers."

2. "The Vulgarity of Lesbianism: *Extraordinary Women* by Compton Mackenzie," 614.

3. In *Citizen, Invert, Queer,* I primarily use the term *homosexual* to describe erotic relations between members of the same gender when referring to the late nineteenth and early twentieth centuries. Although terms such as *invert* and *Sapphist* were also used at that time (and will be used here, as appropriate, to indicate debates about specific terms), the inconstancy and incoherence of representations of same-sex erotics (the very subject of this book) make any unified historical accuracy impossible. *Homosexual* has the grammatical benefit of implying acts *or* identities, depending on context, and is sufficiently out of use today (unlike the term *lesbian,* which was also in some use in the early twentieth century) to remind readers of the historically contingent nature of the language of sexual classification.

4. On the transformation of lesbian and gay communities in the United States during and after World War II, see Berubé, *Coming Out under Fire.* Boyd, in *Wide Open Town,* and Chauncey, in *Gay New York,* both complicate Berubé's thesis by elaborating the continuities, as well as ruptures, produced by World War II in urban gay subcultures in the United States.

5. See Benstock's *Women of the Left Bank,* as well as her "Expatriate Sapphic Modernism," 183–203; and Scott, *Refiguring Modernism.*

6. In her study of interwar British "Sapphic modernity," Laura Doan similarly warns against an overreading of modernist cosmopolitan lesbian communities: "It is a mistake to presume too great an interconnectedness of national cultures in relation to a lesbian subcultural style. . . . Such attempts to 'internationalize' lesbianism often result in misunderstandings and in the development of myths, such as the myth that situates Radclyffe Hall in the [interwar] Parisian lesbian scene" (*Fashioning Sapphism,* xix–xx).

7. For foundational work on "imperialism and motherhood," see Anna Davin's essay of that title. See also McClintock, Mufti, and Shohat, *Dangerous Liaisons*; and Kaplan, Alarcón, and Moallem, *Between Woman and Nation*, on questions of nation, gender, and modernity.

8. Garrity, *Step-daughters of England*, 3.

9. My use of the phrase and thinking about "female masculinity" is deeply indebted to Judith Halberstam's groundbreaking 1998 monograph of that title.

10. Some key histories of lesbian and gay identity that explore a sexological foundation (for better or for worse) include Weeks's *Coming Out*; Faderman's *Surpassing the Love of Men*; Hart's *Fatal Women*; and Bland and Doan's *Sexology in Culture*, in which an essay by Jay Prosser also considers the relation of transsexual identities in sexology. On sexological inversion in relation to transsexual or transgender identities, Halberstam writes, "The history of homosexuality and transsexuality was a shared history at the beginning of the [twentieth] century and only diverged in the 1940s, when surgery and hormonal treatments became available to, and demanded by, some cross-identifying subjects" (ibid., 85).

11. Noble, *Masculinities without Men?* xxix.

12. Stoler, *Race and the Education of Desire*, 9.

13. Foucault, *History of Sexuality*, 43.

14. Foucault describes bio-power as "an explosion of numerous and diverse techniques for achieving the subjugations of bodies and the control of populations" (ibid., 140).

15. Stoler, *Race and the Education of Desire*, 6–7.

16. Foucault, *History of Sexuality*, 105.

17. Sedgwick, *Epistemology of the Closet*, 36.

18. Allatini, *Despised and Rejected*, 220.

1. IMPERIALIST CLASSIFICATIONS

1. In 1894, Grand and Ouida both published essays naming the "New Woman" in the *North American Review*. For accounts of the term's genesis, see Ledger, *New Woman*, 8; and Katz, *Impressionist Subjects*, 43.

2. Boehmer, *Empire, the National, and the Postcolonial, 1890–1920*, 4.

3. Spivak, "Globalicities," 75.

4. See Soloway, *Demography and Degeneration*; and Davin, "Imperialism and Motherhood."

5. Ledger, *New Woman*, 64. See also Jusová's *New Woman and the Empire*. In her introduction, Jusová writes, "As present-day feminist scholars have begun to acknowledge, many British *fin-de-siècle* women were actually deeply invested in the maintenance of the British empire, and their work was often steeped in their imperial culture's racial bias" (5).

6. See Said, *Orientalism*.

7. See, to name but a few examples, Spivak, "Three Women's Texts and a Critique of Imperialism"; Burton, *Burdens of History*; and Grewal, *Home and Harem*.

8. Weeks, *Coming Out*, 58.

9. Symonds contacted Ellis in 1891, proposing a collaborative project on sexual inversion that would be "scientifically, historically, [and] impartially investigated, instead of being left to Labby's inexpansible legislation," referring to the 1885 Labouchère Amendment (Symonds to Ellis, quoted in Koestenbaum, *Double Talk*, 44). In "Symonds's History, Ellis's Heredity," Joseph Bristow argues that the collaboration was a vexed one from the start, with two competing visions of the volume's intervention in studies of sexual inversion. Wayne Koestenbaum similarly argues that Ellis excised and erased Symonds's voice from the text, removing the contributions of a gay poet and scholar in favor of a heterosexual, medical authorial voice (*Double Talk*, 43–67). In the preface of *Sexual Inversion*, Ellis outlines Symonds's contributions as primarily the supply of "about half" of the case studies of male inverts, "a very excellent and pointed series of questions" Symonds posed to them (xiii), and his previously (privately) published "A Problem in Greek Ethics," which appears in the book as appendix A. In subsequent editions, much of Symonds's contribution is reshuffled, and Ellis is listed as the sole author, at least in part because of the pressures put on his publisher by Symonds's family to remove Symonds's name from its prominent place on the title page (Bristow, "Symonds's History, Ellis's Heredity," 82).

10. Ellis and Symonds, *Sexual Inversion*, v.

11. Ibid., 77.

12. Siobhan B. Somerville analyzes the "powerful analogies that structured the theory of recapitulation" in far greater detail. See *Queering the Color Line*, 24–27.

13. Hackett, *Sapphic Primitivism*, 3.

14. Ellis and Symonds, *Sexual Inversion*, 1.

15. Hackett, *Sapphic Primitivism*, 26.

16. Ellis and Symonds, *Sexual Inversion*, 9.

17. Leela Gandhi argues that in Ellis's own text, "the tenuous homology of the 'savage' and the 'homosexual' . . . gave way to a symbiosis, as the functions and identifications of these two excluded figures began imperceptibly to collapse into each other"(*Affective Communities*, 50).

18. Ellis and Symonds, *Sexual Inversion*, 14–15.

19. Ibid., 163–251.

20. Ibid., 174. In her study of twentieth-century militarism, Kathy J. Phillips remarks of the distinctions between Ellis and Symonds, "By contrast, Symonds, himself homosexual, clearly resents both the residual aspersion of abnormality and the demeaning label feminine. He therefore insists that male pairs are *more* manly than other men, yet when he does so, he locates this masculinity precisely where his peers found it, in the warrior model. The disagreements between Ellis and

Symonds neatly sum up and focus larger cultural tensions within the dominant, imperial push for war" (*Manipulating Masculinity,* 20).

21. Ellis and Symonds, *Sexual Inversion,* 187.

22. Ibid., 186.

23. Symonds tempers this radical difference in his discussion of the possible origins of Greek love: "We might be led to conjecture that paiderastia was a remnant of savage habits, ignored by Homer, but preserved by tradition in the race. . . . We ought to resist the temptation to seek a high and noble origin of all Greek institutions. But there remains the fact that, however they acquired the habit, . . . the Greeks gave it a dignity and an emotional superiority which is absent in the annals of barbarian institutions" (ibid., 188).

24. Ibid.

25. Barkan, "Victorian Promiscuity," 59.

26. See, for example, Ernst and Harris, *Race, Science, and Medicine, 1700–1960;* and Bell, *Frontiers of Medicine in the Anglo-Egyptian Sudan, 1899–1940.*

27. In colonial Australia, for example, the sexual practices of British convict laborers were surveyed, recorded, and classified by prison managers and colonial administrators. Historical archaeologist Eleanor Casella traces correspondence between Australian prison superintendents and their supervisors in Australia and England regarding the punishment of "female inmates for their 'unnatural vices'": "Pioneers such as Krafft-Ebing, Sigmund Freud, Havelock Ellis, Iwan Bloch and Magnus Hirschfeld debated their medical theories of biological transsexualism and homosexual inversions over forty years after Superintendent Irvine pondered the elongated clitorises of his convict inmates" ("Bulldaggers and Gentle Ladies," 143, 148). Not only did Superintendent Irvine's musings predate the development of European sexology, but the reports from him and his colonial criminologist, biologist, and anthropologist colleagues actually generated the data often called upon in the production of the emergent field of sexology in the late nineteenth century.

28. For more on the interconnections of sexology and race, see chapter 1 of Somerville, *Queering the Color Line;* and Burdett, "Hidden Romance of Sexual Science."

29. Ellis and Symonds, *Sexual Inversion,* 77, 80–82.

30. Prostitutes represented extreme sexual deviance, though not the most extreme embodiment of masculinity. Here, the taboo against prostitution supersedes Ellis's general rule that the more masculine a female subject, the more deviant she is.

31. Ellis and Symonds, *Sexual Inversion,* 82–83, 85.

32. See, for example, ibid., 90. Unlike Freud, Ellis relies on notes of other practitioners and does not claim for himself, as Freud did with Dora, the "rights of the gynaecologist" (Freud, *Dora,* 3).

33. Ellis and Symonds, *Sexual Inversion,* 87–88, 97–98.

34. Yet, within this framework, Ellis maintains a space for the sexually normal woman who covets the signs of masculinity culturally. As we shall see in the case of the suffragists explored in chapter 2, this appears to be a necessary caveat.

35. Ironically, it is this very definition of women as constitutionally asexual against which Ellis argues in much of his other work.

36. Ellis and Symonds, *Sexual Inversion,* 87.

37. Wachman, *Lesbian Empire,* 65.

38. Bristow clearly outlines two issues regarding the publication history of Wilde's *Salomé*—its original publication date and the question of the final accented *e* in the title: "In the case of *Salomé,* the date appears as 1893, since the original French text was published in that year by the Librairie de l'Art Indépendent in Paris and by Elkin Mathews at John Lane in London. The play went into two weeks of rehearsals in June 1892, only to be refused permission for public performance by Edward F. Smyth-Pigott, Examiner of Plays for the Lord Chamberlain. The first English edition, translated by Lord Alfred Douglas and illustrated by Aubrey Beardsley, was published as *Salome* (without the final accent) in 1894 by Elkin Mathews and John Lane in London and by Copeland and Day in Boston. Throughout this [Bristow's] volume, both *Salomé* and Salomé have been presented with the accent, since this is how both the title and the proper name appear in Wilde's original French text" (Bristow, *Wilde Writings,* x). I follow Bristow and use the accent; though my focus is specifically on the text in the context of British literary and cultural history, the text's origins in French (and the author's Irish identity) form part of the cosmopolitan and imperial composition of the text.

39. See Downey, *Perverse Midrash,* 2; and Lewsadder, "Removing the Veils," 520, for more on Wilde's hollow threat to remain in Paris.

40. Gagnier, *Idylls of the Marketplace,* 140.

41. Ibid., 165.

42. Wilde, *Salomé,* 26, 4.

43. Salome is first named in the historical record by Flavius Josephus, in *Antiquities of the Jews* (bk. 18, chapter 5, no. 4). See Downey, *Perverse Midrash,* 96–98.

44. Sully, "Narcissistic Princess, Rejected Lover, Veiled Priestess, Virtuous Virgin."

45. Wilde, *Salomé,* 5.

46. Jusová, *New Woman and the Empire,* 3. Linda Dowling concurs, noting this as "the central metaphor employed by enemies of the avant-garde to express their urgent dismay: late-Victorian England, as involved in problems of Empire as Imperial Rome in its decline, had entered its Silver Age—English culture, on the analogy with Rome, was threatened from without, betrayed from within. And though—or perhaps because—they were attempting to overthrow the cultural assumptions of their critics, the decadent and the New Woman both assented to the truth of this metaphor" ("Decadent and the New Woman," 447–48).

47. Bucknell, "On 'Seeing' Salome," 503. Edward Burns remarks, in a similar vein, that Salomé "exists in the domain of the look, and [her] narrative is plotted by the hazards of looking and being looked at. Salome works out her fate within the domain of the visual" (Burns, "*Salome*," 33).

48. Wilde, *Salomé*, 1, 2, 5, 13, 14, 16.

49. Ibid., 7, 8, 10, 11, 12.

50. Chapter 4 addresses the early twentieth-century readings of Salomé's sadism and their connections to sexological pathologies.

51. Wilde, *Salomé*, 29–35.

52. Ibid., 36.

53. Publisher John Lane and editor Henry Harland provided much of the institutional connective tissue between the New Woman and the decadent writers, and their willingness to publish women writers in the *Yellow Book* deserves much credit. See Chan, "Morbidity, Masculinity, and the Misadventures of the New Woman in the *Yellow Book*'s Short Stories"; and Heilmann, *New Woman Fiction*, 44–46.

54. Heilmann, *New Woman Fiction*, 47.

55. Mangum, "Style Wars and the 1890s," 49.

56. Ledger, *New Woman*, 6.

57. Showalter, *Daughters of Decadence*, xi.

58. Gagnier argues, on the one hand, that "the women of Aestheticism were consistently sensitive to the manifold politics of aesthetic production and consumption. If they sometimes reinforced gender and heterosexual stereotypes of production and reproduction while countering the excess of male Decadents, they also confronted their implication in commodity culture more directly than some of the male aesthetes" ("Women in British Aestheticism and the Decadence," 240). On the other hand, "the male Decadents also resisted stylistic reproduction, or realism, by an anti-realist decadent style that self-consciously performed its femininity in relation to the more masculine realism of mid-Victorian fiction" (243).

59. Ibid., 248.

60. See Ledger, *New Woman*, 111–18, on Grand's *The Heavenly Twins* in the context of the social purity movement; Chrisman, "Empire, 'Race,' and Feminism at the *Fin De Siècle*"; and Jusová, *New Woman and the Empire*, for a reading of both Grand and Egerton.

61. Work on Victoria Cross is deeply indebted to Shoshana Milgram Knapp's extensive research. Her cluster of work outlines Cross's biography and analyzes her major novels and stories. See Knapp's "Real Passion and the Reverence for Life," "Revolutionary Androgyny in the Fiction of 'Victoria Cross,'" and "Victoria Cross."

62. Knapp, "Victoria Cross," 76.

63. Ibid.

64. M. Brittain, "Erasing Race in the New Woman Review," 75.

65. Melisa Brittain makes a related argument regarding the status of race and empire in *Anna Lombard*, Cross's fourth novel. She argues for a more critical approach to Cross's work than merely a celebratory recuperation of Cross's portrayals of female sexuality: "This type of recuperative project demonstrates a blind spot with regard to the ways the reconstructions of Western female subjectivity, through the figure of the New Woman, participated in the late nineteenth century rearticulation of a white middle class femininity that reproduced dominant ideological formations of race, class, and imperial rule, and the way our current recuperative practices perpetuate this Western feminist legacy" (ibid., 77).

66. In 1903, Cross published *Six Chapters of a Man's Life*, which expands the "Theodora" fragment into a full novel. Here, I consider only the 1895 short story, but it is worth noting that in the novel, Theodora travels to Mesopotamia with Cecil, cross-dressing as his male companion.

67. Cross, "Theodora," 18, 28, 29.

68. Ibid., 9, 12, 15, 16.

69. Ibid., 10, 17.

70. Ibid., 32–33.

71. Ibid., 20, 21, 24.

72. Ibid., 26, 34, 35.

73. Ibid., 37.

74. Hogarth, "Literary Degenerates," 586.

75. Crackanthorpe, "Sex in Modern Literature," 614.

76. Hogarth, "Literary Degenerates," 587, 588.

77. Ibid., 592.

78. Sewell Stokes, quoted in Knapp, "Victoria Cross," 76.

79. Frankel, *Oscar Wilde's Decorated Books*, 54–55.

80. When Oscar Wilde was arrested, in 1895, *Yellow Book* publisher John Lane was confronted with the newspaper headline "Arrest of Oscar Wilde, *Yellow Book* under His Arm." Though the book in question was later proved not to be the *Yellow Book* but merely a book with yellow binding, this headline cemented a widespread public association of Wilde with the *Yellow Book* (already fostered by the connection of Audrey Beardsley to both *Salomé* and the *Yellow Book*). The headline, coupled with some transatlantic miscommunications, resulted in Beardsley's dismissal from the *Yellow Book* and, perhaps, its demise. The Wilde headline "killed the *Yellow Book* and it nearly killed me," Lane recounted (quoted in Katherine Lyon Mix, *Study in Yellow*, 140–47).

81. Weeks, *Coming Out*, 59–60.

82. Bland, *Banishing the Beast*, 262.

83. Weeks, *Coming Out*, 61.

84. Ellis and Symonds, *Sexual Inversion*, 99–100.

2. PUBLIC WOMEN, SOCIAL INVERSION

1. Linton, "Wild Women," 79.

2. Linton's own biography presents a curious juxtaposition with her fiery journalistic prose. Martha Vicinus notes that "one of Linton's most curious characteristics is her flaunting of her own masculinity at the same time as she excoriated it in others" (*Intimate Friends,* 147). On Linton's social Darwinism, see Meem, "Eliza Lynn Linton and the Rise of Lesbian Consciousness." Both Meem and Vicinus classify Linton as a lesbian, drawing on her masculine identification and her veiled, cross-dressed autobiography, *The Autobiography of Christopher Kirkland.* Meem, in particular, equates Linton's personal and narrative exonerations of masculinity as a sign of her "lesbian consciousness." Whatever her interior sexual desires or gendered identification, Linton's series of essays on "the wild women" provide scathing critiques of feminist women occupying masculine public space in their agitation for gender equality, critiques that, I believe, when read in their historical context, are devoid of any implicit, transhistorical "lesbian consciousness."

3. A. Kaplan, *Anarchy of Empire in the Making of U.S. Culture,* 25.

4. Davin, "Imperialism and Motherhood," 10.

5. As I am primarily interested in how the discourses on suffrage participated in the transition from nineteenth-century to twentieth-century ideas and representations of women's gender and sexuality, I will not begin my analysis with the first articulations on women's suffrage in Britain. To do so would lead back at least to John Stuart Mill's 1869 *The Subjection of Women.* Instead, this work begins when women began to organize against, as well as in favor of, women's suffrage. It is at this point, in the late 1880s, that the *debates* on women's suffrage began to address cultural change and transition to modernity, as well as women's positions in relation to those cultural shifts. Similarly, this chapter focuses primarily on the prewar suffrage debates, when they were most visible culturally. This is not to imply, however, that suffrage activism ceased during World War I. For an excellent discussion of wartime suffrage activities and ideologies, see Gullace, *"Blood of Our Sons."*

6. Following the contemporary popular usage, I refer to moderates as "suffragists" and militants as "suffragettes," and I use "suffrage" or "suffrage women" to describe both groups more generally.

7. Dangerfield, *The Strange Death of Liberal England,* 144, 149.

8. In *Sex and Suffrage in Britain, 1860–1914* (1987), Susan Kingsley Kent critiques "traditional historians" (among them George Dangerfield) for invoking lesbianism as a threat or a negative characteristic. In a footnote, she opines that "it is disturbing to find historians raising the specter of lesbianism for early feminists as a way to dismiss or disguise the radical nature of feminism. Veterans of the second wave [of feminism] will not be surprised to discover that charges of lesbianism plagued the early feminist movement, usually leveled at women who were described as 'unsexed' or 'viragoes'" (233–34). Though charges of lesbianism certainly do not

produce good history, Kent's assumption that suffragists were in fact accused of lesbianism during the campaign for women's suffrage between the 1890s and 1920 actually falls in line with Dangerfield's. Kent assumes that being called "unsexed" or a "virago" is the early twentieth-century equivalent of being called a "dyke" in the late twentieth century, an assumption that this chapter disputes.

9. See, for example, Burton, "'States of Injury,'" Fletcher, "'Women of the Nations, Unite!'" Wollacott, "Australian Women's Metropolitan Activism," and Laura E. Nym Mayhall, "The South African War and the Origins of Suffrage Militancy in Britain, 1899–1902," all in Fletcher, Mayhall, and Levine, *Women's Suffrage in the British Empire*; Grewal, *Home and Harem*; Levine, *Prostitution, Race, and Politics*; Mayhall, *Militant Suffrage Movement*; and Tusan, *Women Making News*.

10. Fletcher, Mayhall, and Levine, *Women's Suffrage in the British Empire*, xviii.

11. For more detailed discussions of the rhetoric, history, and politics of antisuffrage movements, see Harrison, *Separate Spheres*.

12. Ward, "Appeal against Female Suffrage," 781.

13. Ibid., 782.

14. Mrs. Humphry Ward, quoted in Trevelyan, *Life of Mrs Humphry Ward*, 231.

15. Corelli, *Woman, or—Suffragette*, 4, 18–19.

16. *Votes for Women*, editorial, November 1907, 13.

17. Owen, *Woman Adrift*, 10.

18. Dicey, *Letters to a Friend on Votes for Women*, 8, 89–90, 91.

19. The hysteric is another favorite characterization of suffrage women by opponents. See Tickner, *Spectacle of Women*, for more on antisuffrage and popular characterizations of suffrage "types."

20. "The Suffragettes" postcard, Donald McGill.

21. Tickner, *The Spectacle of Women*, 202.

22. Ibid., 203.

23. "Militant Suffragist" (cartoon).

24. Evelyn Sharp, "Filling the War Chest," 44.

25. Editorial, *Common Cause*, April 15, 1909, 3.

26. Tusan, *Women Making News*, 163.

27. Just as antisuffragists rallied around figures in addition to the masculine or sexualized suffragists, so too did suffragists deploy rhetoric in addition to that of their central strategy of domestic femininity. Liberal arguments for equality, arguments for the enfranchisement of working women, and positions based on strategic party alliances also flourished.

28. Such appeals for rational equality also have their roots in nineteenth-century political theory. For discussion of John Stuart Mill's influence on constitutional suffrage, see Hume, *National Union of Women's Suffrage Societies, 1897–1914*, 8–20; and Cini, "From British Women's WWI Suffrage Battle to the League of Nations Covenant."

29. Millicent Garrett Fawcett, letter to the *Times* (London), June 6, 1910, 6.

30. "In the Tube,"103.

31. In the nineteenth century, actresses had been far from respectable. "Like the prostitute, the actress could also be seen as a 'figure of public pleasure,' whose deployment of cosmetics and costume bore witness to the artificial and commodified forms of contemporary female sexuality. The motif of the female performer easily lent itself to . . . the generation of modern forms of desire" (Felski, *Gender of Modernity,* 19–20). Even in the nineteenth century, actresses were figures of the modern. As more women entered the profession, however, actresses were increasingly accepted as professional, even moral, women at the turn of the century.

32. Hirshfield, "Actresses' Franchise League and the Campaign for Women's Suffrage, 1908–1914," 130.

33. See Green, "From Visible *Flaneuse* to Spectacular Suffragette?"; Lyon, "Women Demonstrating Modernism"; and Vicinus, "Male Spaces and Female Bodies."

34. See Hume, *National Union of Women's Suffrage Societies, 1897–1914;* and Strachey, *The Cause.*

35. Mayhall, *Militant Suffrage Movement,* 44. See chapter 3 as a whole for a detailed discussion of radicalism and the suffragettes.

36. Fletcher, "'Women of the Nations, Unite!'" 109.

37. Ibid.

38. *Suffragette,* cover illustration and editorial (55).

39. An anonymous letter to the irreverent *New Freewoman* journal (discussed in greater detail in chapter 3) noted, in October 1913, "We have always been accustomed to think of [Christabel Pankhurst] as a heroic but somewhat tedious Joan of Arc."

40. For more on the spiritual component of the militant movement, see Vicinus, "Male Spaces and Female Bodies."

41. This move to a concern with sexual purity profoundly alienated much of the militant movement's working-class support.

42. Marcus, *Suffrage and the Pankhursts,* 14.

43. Pankhurst, *Great Scourge and How to End It,* 188.

44. Lyon, "Militant Discourse, Strange Bedfellows," 118.

45. Ibid.

46. Pankhurst, *Great Scourge and How to End It,* 217–18, 191–92. Pankhurst repeats this strategy in a fascinating section on male "sexual excess," where men continue to be pathologized and rendered the object of medical scrutiny and concern. See p. 192 for an interesting twist on nineteenth-century medicine's concern for "spilt seed" and men's "vital energy," and pp. 208–9 for a discussion of "fallen men."

47. Ibid., 221, 222.

48. Ibid., 219, 221.

49. Ibid., 222. The only appropriate sacrifice for the militants was one for "the Cause."

50. Ibid., 237, 238.

51. Louisa Martindale, *Under the Surface,* quoted in ibid., 239.

52. Though the Contagious Diseases Acts had been formally repealed before the 1913 publication of Pankhurst's text, their central tenets remained in operation throughout much of the British Empire through the early twentieth century. Philippa Levine notes, "In repealing Act V of 1895, the new rules of October 1897 reinstated the right to expel from cantonments women refusing treatment, returned VD to the list of contagious and infectious diseases over which control could be exercised, and allowed the prohibiting of brothels" (*Prostitution, Race, and Politics,* 118–19).

53. Pankhurst, *Great Scourge and How to End It,* 238.

54. "The issue was no longer one of central public concern . . . [and] had lost its drama for the wider metropolitan population" (Levine, *Prostitution, Race, and Politics,* 136).

55. Ibid., 143.

56. Stape documents the start date of Woolf's work on *Night and Day,* through Woolf's letters, diary, and holograph fragments of the novel, in "Virginia Woolf's *Night and Day.*"

57. For readings that argue for a connection between the novel and World War I, see Fox, "Woolf's Austen/Boston Tea Party"; and Wussow, "Conflict of Language in Virginia Woolf's *Night and Day.*" Fox attempts to link Woolf's aesthetic project in the novel with the Great War by arguing that the text opposed "literary imperialism," and thus English military imperialism (260 and throughout); Wussow asserts that "the antipathies of dialogue in *Night and Day* have their social correlative in the First World War" (63).

58. See, respectively, Underhill, "Voyage toward Reality," 112; Mansfield, "Ship Comes into the Harbour," 108; and Burke, "Modern English Novel Plus," 115.

59. *Times Literary Supplement,* unsigned review of *Night and Day,* by Virginia Woolf, 105.

60. Mansfield, "Ship Comes into the Harbour," 110.

61. Malamud, "Splitting the Husks," 162.

62. For readings of *Night and Day* as a modernist text, see Malamud, ibid.; and Squier, "Tradition and Revision." For analyses of the same-sex eroticism between Katharine and Mary, see Cooley, "Discovering the 'Enchanted Region'"; S. Garner, "'Women Together' in Virginia Woolf's *Night and Day*"; Hussey, "Refractions of Desire"; and Smith, *Lesbian Panic,* 37–41.

63. Park, "Suffrage and Virginia Woolf," 127. For a reading of *Night and Day* as a "precursor to [Woolf's] experiments with identity," see Priest, "Between Being

and Nothingness." Zemgulys's work on the novel also places *Night and Day* as a "transition from her traditional to experimental forms" through her work on location ("'*Night and Day* Is Dead'").

64. Woolf, *Night and Day*, 9.

65. Phillips, *Virginia Woolf against Empire*, 85.

66. Woolf, *Night and Day*, 116–17.

67. Phillips, *Virginia Woolf against Empire*, 92–93.

68. Woolf, *Night and Day*, 46.

69. Ibid., 136, 284, 341.

70. Cassandra not only takes up women's suffrage as a fad but, as Phillips notes, also enacts a "private insurrection" against her parents by cultivating silkworms in her rooms, "recalling Gandhi's India, filled with spinning wheels to make homemade cloth and so lessen India's dependence on English cotton mills" (*Virginia Woolf against Empire*, 86). Cassandra's faddish feminism and the possible nod to anti-imperialism stand in stark contrast to more "committed" (as opposed to faddish) reformers in the novel, such as Mary Datchet.

71. The final pairing of feminine William with womanly Cassandra can be read as a queer match. Here, social femininity is associated with the past, so William and Cassandra will "fit" together, both being slightly out of step with a more robust, masculine modernity. William is further feminized when Katharine accuses him of being "such a queer mixture . . . half poet and half old maid" because of his social conservatism (Woolf, *Night and Day*, 68). Again Woolf links conservative social values to unexpected feminization.

72. Zemgulys notes that "'Chelsea' became shorthand for everything Woolf despised about London's literary world. . . . That Woolf placed her 1919 novel *Night and Day* in Chelsea therefore corroborates the widely held view that this novel worked as a transition for her from traditional to experimental fictional forms" ("'*Night and Day* Is Dead,'" 56–57). Of Mary's home, Bloomsbury, Sara Blair notes that in the 1910s, the neighborhood was "marked not just as a zone of class fragmentation and uneven development but as a site of racial instability" ("Local Modernity, Global Modernism," 821).

73. Woolf, *Night and Day*, 48, 49.

74. Ibid., 47.

75. Ibid., 166.

76. Ibid., 433.

77. Ibid., 131. Asquith was England's antisuffragist prime minister between 1906 and 1916.

78. Ibid., 83. Phillips reads Mary's rumination in the British Museum as "an exotic scenario to support [Mary's] belief that [Ralph] is 'not in the least conventional, like most clever men'" (*Virginia Woolf against Empire*, 80). She continues, "Mary's daydream in fact calls into question a familiar literary and cultural paradigm

of quest and conquest, as seen in a long-running battle of male warrior and (often female) monster" (81). Where Phillips reads Mary's colonial fantasy as part of the sex war between Woolf's men and women, I read it as part of the ongoing tension in the novel between, on the one hand, Victorian, imperial gender norms and, on the other hand, markers of women's autonomy through registers of modernity, gender, and sexuality.

79. Woolf, *Night and Day*, 83.

80. Ibid., 243, 350.

81. Ibid., 58, 358, 391, 392.

82. Ibid., 168. Mary is also contrasted to the controlling, antifeminist Mr. Clacton (ibid., 265–66) as Woolf critiques men involved in women's suffrage who continually seek to grandstand and control the struggle. For a history of such men, see Kevin F. White, "Men Supporting Women," 45–59.

83. Woolf, *Night and Day*, 262.

3. "A MORE SPLENDID CITIZENSHIP"

1. Though *feminist* was not used consistently in the prewar period, this chapter uses the term to denote men and women committed to various programs for gender equity or women's cultural, legal, and/or civic freedoms.

2. See Davin, "Imperialism and Motherhood."

3. Soloway, *Birth Control and the Population Question in England, 1877–1930*, 23.

4. Stone, "Race in British Eugenics," 404.

5. Peel, Editor's introduction, xii. See also Ordover, *American Eugenics*.

6. Peel, Editor's introduction, xii.

7. Stone, "Race in British Eugenics," 398.

8. Peel presents a disturbingly sanitized version of early British eugenics. Lauding the absence of negative eugenics appears to erase or ignore the racially abhorrent implications of positive eugenics as well. Peel writes, for example, that "the Eugenics Education Society avoided the unpleasant excesses of its North American counterparts; nor did it become involved with the issue of sterilisation as in Scandinavia" (editor's introduction, xiv). Dan Stone notes that "the idea that there were two strands of eugenic thought, a German one emphasizing race and a British one stressing class, was promoted, after the Second World War, by the eugenicists themselves" (ibid., 402).

9. Soloway, *Birth Control and the Population Question*, 145.

10. Ibid., 151.

11. Mary Scharlieb, "What It Means to Marry," quoted in L. Hall, *Outspoken Women*, 77.

12. Soloway, *Birth Control and the Population Question*, 22.

13. Hall, *Outspoken Women*, 5.

14. Stone, "Race in British Eugenics," 404.

15. Of course, the 1910s were not the first time that men and women engaged in discussions of such topics. Free love was popular in nineteenth-century utopian communal situations in the United States, for example, as it was in Germany. Here, however, I will discuss one example among the intellectual communities of Britain, which took up these issues in the 1910s and 1920s. For more on this topic in Britain, see Bland, *Banishing the Beast.*

16. In 1913, the *New Freewoman* metamorphosed into Ezra Pound's *Egoist.* Some critics view Pound's takeover of the *New Freewoman* as emblematic of "male modernism's" co-optation of female writings, whereas other critics present a more complicated story of philosophical, economic, and ideological shifts. See Joannou, "Angel of Freedom"; Barash, "Dora Marsden's Feminism, the *Freewoman* and the Gender Politics of Early Modernism"; Roberts, "Reading Women Writing Modernism"; Ferrall, "Suffragists, Egoists, and the Politics of Early Modernism"; Thacker, "Dora Marsden and the *Egoist*"; and Jeffreys, *Spinster and Her Enemies.* For a good discussion of Pound's relation to feminist principles generally, and female writers specifically, see the introduction to "Pound" in Scott, *Gender of Modernism,* 353–57.

17. L. Hall, "'Disinterested Enthusiasm for Sexual Misconduct,'" 665.

18. Ibid., 666–68.

19. Ibid., 670.

20. For Marsden's individualist philosophy, see, for example, her bold declaration in the inaugural issue of the *New Freewoman*: "Accurately speaking there *is* no 'Woman Movement.' 'Woman' is doing nothing—she has, indeed, no existence" ("Views and Comments" [June 15], 5). When readers (and, most importantly, subscribers) demanded an explanation of this denunciation, Marsden elaborated in the next issue that "it is an empty concept and should be banished from language. . . . If we take 'female reproductive organs' away from this concept Woman, what do we have left? Absolutely nothing, save a mountain of sentimental mush. . . . But in itself, feeling is sexless" ("Views and Comments" [July 1], 24).

21. Bland, *Banishing the Beast,* 251.

22. Ibid.

23. Marsden, "Notes of the Week."

24. Kennedy, "Psychology of Sex," 15–16.

25. D'Auvergne, "Definition of Marriage," 6.

26. E. S. P. H., "Contemporary Recognition of Polygamy," 9–10.

27. Moreland, "Persian Women," 125, 126.

28. Cicely Fairfield, "The Position of Women in Indian Life,"39.

29. C. Drysdale, "Freewomen and the Birth-Rate II," 90.

30. B. Drysdale, "Foreign Notes."

31. Gaskell, "Unspeakable," 176.

32. Hill, correspondence, *Freewoman.*

33. Pearce, "Marriage and Motherhood," 32.

34. C. Drysdale, "Freewomen and the Birth-Rate," 37.

35. Radical feminist historian Sheila Jeffreys is the most strident defender of the "celibate" spinster as a protolesbian. In *The Spinster and Her Enemies,* she writes of the spinster debates in the *Freewoman*: "There were two fronts to the battle against the spinster. One was to declare against all evidence to the contrary that spinsters suffered from thwarted desires which turned them into vicious and destructive creatures. . . . Another was to promote sex freedom" (97). She goes on to assert that "any attack on the spinster is invariably an attack on the lesbian" (100).

36. "The Spinster, by One," 10, 11.

37. Oliver, "Correspondence: Asceticism and Passion"; Browne, "Correspondence: Who Are the 'Normal'?" 313.

38. Oliver, "Correspondence: More Plain Speaking."

39. Tout Pouvoir, "Correspondence: 'Normal and Abnormal,'" 376.

40. Gideon, "Correspondence: The Love-Child."

41. Oliver, "Correspondence: On the Loose Principle," 399.

42. In *Banishing the Beast,* Lucy Bland reports, quoting Kathlyn Oliver, that she "wrote to [Edward] Carpenter three years [after the *Freewoman* correspondence] with the declaration that she had read his book *The Intermediate Sex* 'and it has lately dawned on me that I myself belong to that class'" (291). See pp. 291–92 for more on this revelation.

43. Browne, "Correspondence: Who Are the 'Normal'?" 313.

44. Bruce Clarke writes of Charles J. Whitby that he was "an invited respondent who debated Birnstingl regarding homosexuality but was otherwise generally supportive of women's emancipation" (*Dora Marsden and Early Modernism,* 83). Like most of the contributors to the *Freewoman* itself, Clarke appears to link women's liberation and homosexual emancipation. The fact that Marsden "invited" Whitby to respond indicates her desire to produce debate and dialogue in the *Freewoman.*

45. Birnstingl, "Uranians," 127, 128.

46. Ibid.

47. Marah, "Correspondence: The Human Complex," 438.

48. The term *bisexual* was an ambiguous one in this time period. In his *Three Essays on the Theory of Sexuality* (1905), for example, Freud used the term to refer to gender variance, not sexual-object choice, signaling androgyny, not the bisexual of today. In Marah's letter, "bi-sexual" appears to refer to a same-sex erotic attachment, not a gender inversion, through the older woman's "extravagant" praise of young Marah's beauty.

49. Marah, "Correspondence: The Human Complex," 438.

50. Northerner, "Correspondence: Knowledge Wanted."

51. Marah, "Correspondence: The Human Complex," 438.

52. Bland, *Banishing the Beast,* 267.

53. For more on the Freewoman Discussion Circles, see L. Garner, *Brave and Beautiful Spirit*, 73–75; and Clarke, *Dora Marsden and Early Modernism*, 73–78.

54. Garner, *Brave and Beautiful Spirit*, 74.

55. Ward, "Religion and the Suffrage." The editors of the *Freewoman* and the *New Freewoman* seemed to regard an attack from Mrs. Ward as good publicity: a quotation from Ward's letter appeared on the back page of the *Freewoman* and the *New Freewoman*, as part of "Some Opinions of the *Freewoman*," for several months. Mrs. Ward's vitriol countered more complimentary comments from Havelock Ellis, H. G. Wells, and others.

56. Ward, "Religion and the Suffrage."

57. Boyden, "Nauseous Publication."

58. Balfour, "Religion and the Suffrage."

59. Margesson, "'Nauseous Publications."

60. Private opinions of feminists were similarly split on the *Freewoman*. For example, Bland quotes a letter from Olive Schreiner to Havelock Ellis: "I think it ought to be called the *Licentious Male*. . . . It is unclean. And sex is so beautiful! It can be discussed scientifically . . . philosophically . . . from the poetic standpoint . . . from the matter-of-fact standpoint . . . from the personal standpoint . . . and it is all beautifully clean and natural and healthy" (*Banishing the Beast*, 265).

61. "The *Freewoman* continued until the distributors, W. H. Smiths, boycotted the paper in September 1912 due to 'the nature of certain articles which . . . render the paper unsuitable to be exposed on the bookstalls for general sale'" (Thacker, "Dora Marsden and the *Egoist*," 183–84).

62. On the demise of the *Freewoman*, see Franklin, "Marketing Edwardian Feminism," 638. For the rise of the *New Freewoman*, see Clarke, *Dora Marsden and Early Modernism*, 90–98; and Thacker, ibid.

63. Carpenter, "Status of Women in Early Greek Times," 68.

64. Ibid.

65. Ibid., 69.

66. Sedgwick, *Epistemology of the Closet*.

67. John Addington Symonds, quoted in Carpenter, "Status of Women in Early Greek Times," 68.

68. Carpenter, "Status of Women in Early Greek Times," 68.

69. Lloyd, "Intermediate Sexual Types." 155, 156.

70. See Carpenter, *Intermediate Sex*.

71. Lloyd, "Intermediate Sexual Types," 155–56.

72. Birnstingl, "Interpretations of Life," 71.

73. The translation of *The Symposium* by Benjamin Jowett (1817–1893) was the definitive English translation in Edwardian England. Jowett's translation of Aristophanes' speech explicitly mentions a female-female possibility: "Now there were these three sexes, because the sun, moon, and earth are three; and the man was

originally the child of the sun, the woman of the earth, and the man-woman of the moon" (line 190b). Once split by Zeus, these three sexes form three possible sexual pairings: male-female, male-male, and female-female. According to Jowett's version, "the women who are a section of the woman don't care for men, but have female attachments" (line 191e). The fact that Jowett was most likely Birnstingl's translation source makes vivid the latter's omission of any possible female-female pairings in Edwardian England.

74. Bland, *Banishing the Beast,* 257.

75. See Soloway, *Demography and Degeneration,* 31–37.

76. Browne, "Sexual Variety and Variability among Women and Their Bearing upon Social Re-construction."

77. Ibid.

78. Browne, "Women and the Race."

79. In 1917, Browne presented "Studies in Feminine Inversion" to the BSSSP.

80. Browne, "Sexual Variety and Variability among Women."

81. Wallace, "Case of Edith Ellis," 14.

82. Bland, *Banishing the Beast,* 270; H. Ellis, prefatory note to E. Ellis, *New Horizon in Love and Life,* xl.

83. Indeed, Havelock Ellis relied on his wife's circle of friends for all of his case studies of female homosexuals (Bland, *Banishing the Beast,* 294). Their marriage was an unconventional one in many ways: "For over half of each year they chose to live separately, although they were regularly in touch; they both had other sexual relationships" (294). Wallace speculates, "It may have been that Edith Lees and Havelock Ellis married in order to explore their mutual interest in experimental marriage, which for her symbolised a commitment to rethinking larger social and sexual relations. . . . Much of the evidence suggests that Edith Ellis saw herself as an *interestingly* (if not happily) married congenital invert" ("Case of Edith Ellis," 24, 26; emphasis in original).

84. These essays were originally published in *The New Horizon in Love and Life,* a collection of Edith Ellis's writings published posthumously, and it is this volume that I cite here. I must, however, note my debt to Lesley A. Hall, whose excerpts from these essays in her volume *Outspoken Women* first whetted my appetite for more Edith Lees Ellis.

85. E. Ellis, "Eugenics and Spiritual Parenthood," 55.

86. E. Ellis, "Eugenics and the Mystical Outlook," 50.

87. Ibid., 42–43.

88. Edith Ellis apparently followed her own prescription: she and Havelock consciously decided not to have children of their own, a decision that Havelock Ellis attributed to "Edith's 'inherited nervous instability' and [his] own 'nervous excess'" (quoted in Wallace, "Case of Edith Ellis," 37n34). In other words, the Ellises appear to have determined that they were not appropriate eugenic stock to

procreate. Indeed, through Edith's framework, the couple's collective oeuvre stands as a voluminous brood of "spiritual children."

89. E. Ellis, "Eugenics and Spiritual Parenthood," 60.

90. Ibid., 60, 62–63, 65.

91. For a discussion of the biographies of both female and male suffragists and sex radicals who formed affectional and erotic bonds with members of the same sex, see Holton's excellent monograph *Suffrage Days*.

4. AROUND 1918

1. This chapter focuses on the representational politics of sexual and gendered transformations on the home front. For an essay engaging similar questions on the *battlefront*, see Doan, "Topsy-Turvydom." Doan seeks to uncover traces of the wartime "lives and experiences of certain women ambulance drivers" (527), focusing on identity and lived experience through private as well as public documents. Doan's text provides a strong conversational partner to my work, which takes up the more public politics of home-front representation.

2. The formation of a public narrative of female homosexuality is the topic of this chapter. I will not argue for the "birth" of a private lesbian subject; I do not claim a date upon which women who sexually desired other women began to conceive of themselves as outsiders or constitutively deviant women for that particular reason. Rather, I am interested in the emergence of a lesbian subject in public culture, in nonsubcultural and nonintimate representations—thus, this chapter does not analyze diaries, letters, or other similarly "private" writings.

3. Hynes, *War Imagined*, 225–26. Note that, in Britain, "public" schools are of the type known in the United States as "private" schools.

4. Ibid., 226.

5. Kettle, *Salome's Last Veil*, 3. Philip Hoare similarly explains the increased attention to male homosexuality through "a number of factors: the legacy of the Wilde trials and attendant cultural notions of decadence; the social reform movements in Germany which were advocating homosexuality; and the mass bringing together of men in [cross-class,] all-male environments during the war" (*Oscar Wilde's Last Stand*, 34–35).

6. The cleavage of homosexual scandal to Germany was a result not only of the national origin of many pioneering sexologists but also of Germany's own public homosexual scandals. James D. Steakley reports, "From 1907 to 1909, Imperial Germany was by turns amused and mortified by a series of journalistic exposés, libel trials, and Reichstag speeches, all of which turned upon the alleged homosexuality of the chancellor and of two distinguished members of the entourage of Kaiser Wilhelm II" ("Iconography of a Scandal," 233–34). This so-called Eulenburg Affair has been compared to England's Wilde trials, and was covered by both the German and international press: "The British response [to the Eulenburg scandal]

was initially quite restrained and even tactful, if only due to prudishness; but as enmity between the countries grew, various English publicists demonstrated that the scandal was by no means forgotten" (247).

7. Lord Alfred Douglas, "God's Lovely Lust," quoted in Hynes, *War Imagined,* 223.

8. Lord Alfred Douglas, "The Rossiad," quoted in Kettle, *Salome's Last Veil,* 15.

9. Arnold White, "Efficiency and Vice," quoted in Kettle, *Salome's Last Veil,* 4–6.

10. For a history of Germany's Clause 175, see Steakley, *Homosexual Emancipation Movement in Germany.*

11. The "rape of Belgian women" by German soldiers in 1914 provoked widespread outrage and protective gestures toward Britain's feminized neighbor, garnering British popular support for the war. For a detailed discussion of the representational politics and home-front impact of tales of German atrocities in Belgium, see Gullace, *"Blood of Our Sons,"* chapter 1.

12. Tylee, *Great War and Women's Consciousness,* 121.

13. Wachman, *Lesbian Empire,* 117–19.

14. For more detailed discussion of Edward Carpenter's influence on Allatini's novel, see Doan, *Fashioning Sapphism,* 153–55; and Wachman, ibid., 105–19.

15. Allatini, *Despised and Rejected,* 52. Dennis's brother complains that his music is unsuitable accompaniment for family theatrics: "'There's no tune in it, however hard you listen for one'" (14). Thus, the music of modernism is linked to an alienation that quickly emerges as homosexual, in addition to artistic.

16. Ibid., 16.

17. Ibid., 31.

18. Ibid., 107.

19. Carpenter, *Intermediate Sex,* 32–33.

20. Antoinette's physiognomy is not as inverted as Dennis's. The only indications that her body does not conform to a wholly feminine model are recurring references to her "boyish curls." Hair is one of the most culturally mutable body parts; it can be grown or cut, whereas thick ankles, another frequently cited marker of female sexual inversion in medical literature, cannot be modified. The social markers of Antoinette's sexual inversion are similarly nebulous. This demonstrates not any "weakness" in her diagnosis as a homosexual but, rather, that in the case of female homosexuality, more factors than the sexological and pathological combine to represent an identity predicated on same-sex desire, particularly at this historical moment of transition.

21. Carpenter, *Intermediate Sex,* 36.

22. Allatini, *Despised and Rejected,* 12. Early in the novel, hints and codes can produce a reading of masculine Hester as homosexual. When Antoinette goes to visit her, however, Hester's sexual secret is revealed to be a mundane affair with a

married man. I found this section unconvincing and was uncertain whether Hester was still "lying" to Antoinette. Hester's possible heterosexuality illustrates that gender inversion does not always indicate sexual inversion; other clearly and unambiguously heterosexual women are masculinized by war, for example. In his discussion of *Despised and Rejected*, David Trotter makes a related point. He highlights Hester's role as "the novel's most memorable event" and reads the possibility of homosexuality into the character of Hester against the novel's narrative: "Some of the book's first readers would have recognized Hester, I believe, and through Hester the nature of Antoinette's love, because they had already encountered her like in Newer Woman fiction" ("Lesbians before Lesbianism," 198).

23. Allatini, *Despised and Rejected*, 50.

24. Vicinus, "Distance and Desire."

25. See H. Ellis, *Studies in the Psychology of Sex*, appendix A, especially 374.

26. Allatini, *Despised and Rejected*, 68, 66.

27. Ibid., 69.

28. Doan, *Fashioning Sapphism*, 154.

29. Allatini, *Despised and Rejected*, 217–18.

30. Wachman, *Lesbian Empire*, 115.

31. Wachman designates one form of representational interdependence of lesbian and gay male subjectivity as lesbian "crosswriting." She defines crosswriting as the representational practice that "transposes the otherwise unrepresentable lives of invisible or silenced or simply closeted lesbians into narratives about gay men" (ibid., 1). Lesbian crosswriting "also reflects the identification with gay men that encouraged lesbians to acknowledge or act on their sexuality throughout the twentieth century. Above all, it is a tool for escape from one's specific, limited location within the rigid frames of imperialist society" (2). Wachman and I share an interest in how representations of female same-sex desire are often written through or in tandem with those of gay male subjectivity, yet she generally sees invisibility or silence where I often locate historical emergent subjectivity. Wachman characterizes Allatini's characters as "coming out" (108) or as full of "deception and self-deception" (115), implying a transhistorical gay identity. I argue, in contrast, that the novel's representation of homosexual subjectivity and gendered differences evinces a representational interplay of history, sexology, subjectivity, and nationalist politics of the Great War.

32. Ibid., 115.

33. Allatini, *Despised and Rejected*, 223, 260.

34. Ibid., 267, 249.

35. Ibid., 250.

36. Trotter notes that "pacifism offered Allatini an analogy for the sexual 'intermediacy' that was one self-definition by then available to gay men and women" ("Lesbians before Lesbianism," 197). My reading builds on this analogy but insists

that it is a gendered analogy into which the slippages for female homosexuals must be read.

37. Allatini, *Despised and Rejected*, 194, 195.

38. Tylee, *Great War and Women's Consciousness*, 124.

39. Allatini, *Despised and Rejected*, 240, 188.

40. For a more detailed discussion of the novel's censure, see Wachman, *Lesbian Empire*, 117–19.

41. V. Woolf, *Diary of Virginia Woolf*, 246.

42. On *The Rainbow*'s banning, see Parkes, *Modernism and the Theater of Censorship*.

43. "'Despised and Rejected': Publisher of Pacifist Novel Fined." All subsequent quotations from the trial of *Despised and Rejected* are taken from this account. As Wachman recounts, in *Lesbian Empire*, the trial was covered in other newspapers as well. Although the transcript of the trial is no longer available, the contemporary newspaper accounts are consistent.

44. Doan, *Fashioning Sapphism*, 155.

45. Allatini, *Despised and Rejected*, 346.

46. Although I generally use the term *homosexual* rather than *gay* or *lesbian* to signal the historical specificity of sexual identities, the word *lesbian*, as well as the term *homosexual*, was used throughout *Rex v. Pemberton Billing*. In the trial's rhetoric, *lesbian* signaled a wide range of sexualized and gendered practices, as well as an emergent identity of female homosexuality. Thus, I use *lesbian* in my discussion of this case not only to accurately mirror the language of the case but also to highlight the word's multilayered, and often ambiguous, meanings in this context.

47. Doan, *Fashioning Sapphism*, 32.

48. Medd, "'Cult of the Clitoris,'" 26.

49. The official trial transcript for *Rex v. Pemberton Billing* appears to no longer exist; see Bland, "Trial by Sexology? Maud Allan, *Salome*, and the 'Cult of the Clitoris' Case." Bland's research, as well as my own, has revealed that a few documents relevant to the trial (the Pleas of Justification, Harold Sherwood Spencer's war record, a [mislabeled] evidence file) are stored at the Public Records Office in England, but trial transcripts are not archived there or, apparently, elsewhere. Previous scholars have relied, as I do, on Noel Pemberton Billing's *Verbatim Report*, which alleges to reproduce the trial verbatim. Daily newspaper reports of the case confirm most of the language in Billing's report, yet the *Verbatim Report* cannot be uncritically regarded as a "true" primary source. I have noticed minor (but significant) inconsistencies between that report and those of daily newspapers (ranging from the *Times* of London to the *Manchester Guardian*, the *Pall Mall Gazette*, and more). I do quote here primarily from the *Verbatim Report*, as that is the closest that we can come to a trial transcript, but I do so with a healthy skepticism and supplementation from other sources when necessary to note significant

inconsistencies. Two recent "authoritative" accounts of the trial include Kettle, *Salome's Last Veil,* which provides an edited transcript of the trial, and Hoare's more recent, book-length study of the history of the case, *Oscar Wilde's Last Stand.*

50. See Bland, "Trial by Sexology?"; Medd, "'Cult of the Clitoris'"; Travis, "Clits in Court"; and Walkowitz, "'Vision of Salome.'" The trial is also discussed in recent monographs by Doan (*Fashioning Sapphism*), Wachman (*Lesbian Empire*), and Tammy Proctor (*Female Intelligence*).

51. Billing's eclectic history already included involvement in theater, as a singer and manager; in aviation (his unsuccessful inventions almost killed him more than once); and in military service (a "rather mysterious" time of his life from which almost no record remains) when he began his political career as an Independent member of the House of Commons, in 1916. His fellow ministers dubbed him the "Member for Air," yet this lightweight label belied the thorn that Billing proved to be in the government's side. He was a consistent embarrassment (among other things, he openly critiqued the Royal Air Force for incompetence and frequently disparaged the government), and the Liberal Party sought to discredit him whenever possible (Hoare, *Oscar Wilde's Last Stand,* 48–49).

52. Ibid., 53.

53. The remaking of this periodical was concurrent with a financial collapse and reorganization of Billing's society. Billing refused any advertising in his periodicals, claiming it was a "corrupting influence." Kettle speculates that the name change was a result of a fight with one of his principal funders, Lord Beaverbrook, as the first issue of the *Vigilante* contains numerous vicious personal attacks against this previous supporter of the organization (*Salome's Last Veil,* 10).

54. Billing, "The First 47,000."

55. Medd, "'Cult of the Clitoris,'" 24. Though the piece alluded to several individuals, this initial article had little impact beyond the newspaper's small readership. The theory of "the 47,000" did, however, slowly disseminate beyond Billing's circle. Hynes notes that "in mid-February Billing made the same claims in a speech in the House of Commons. A few days later an article appeared in a popular newspaper, the *Referee,* in which the list was referred to, not as one man's undocumented fantasy, but as a fact—a classic example of the life of rumour in wartime" (*War Imagined,* 227).

56. Billing, "Cult of the Clitoris."

57. Billing, *Verbatim Report,* 3.

58. Hoare, *Oscar Wilde's Last Stand,* 60, 70. Allan's career consisted primarily of middlebrow dance, emulating Duncan but privileging overt sexual expression (and very minimal costuming) over avant-gardism. For an important and detailed discussion of Allan's dancing career and its relation to "a double-edged cosmopolitanism," see Walkowitz, "'Vision of Salome.'" For a more detailed biography of Allan's early years, see Hoare, chapter 4.

59. Oram, *Her Husband Was a Woman!* 57. Oram reads the coverage of *Rex v. Pemberton Billing* by the popular Sunday newspapers in the context of her outstanding history of mass-cultural representations of women's erotic adventures, female husbands, theatrical cross-dressing, and same-sex love scandals. She also notes a distinction between *People*'s "tantilising but unintelligible" discussions of the libel charge and *News of the World*'s publication of, "in full, the explicit language of the indictment" (57).

60. The Black Book is so mysterious, in fact, that scholars disagree as to whether it actually existed or not. Samuel Hynes calls it Billing's "undocumented fantasy" (*War Imagined*, 227), Kettle assumes its existence (*Salome's Last Veil*, 102–3 and throughout), and Hoare is most convincing when he argues, with Hynes, that it did not ever exist (*Oscar Wilde's Last Stand*, 165–69). The volume was often referred to, but never actually produced, in Billing's trial, and all those who had allegedly seen it (with the exception of Billing's mistress and the mentally ill Spencer) had conveniently died at the front. At the Public Records Office (as of June 2004), a file labeled "Black Book" (HO 144 1498 364780) contains no book but, rather, various Home Office documents tracking Billing in the years surrounding the trial. This confirms further to me the nonexistence of such a document, insofar as one can ever prove a negative.

61. Noble, *Masculinities without Men?* 30.

62. Reports on Mrs. Villiers-Stuart's July statements are located at the Public Records Office, in file no. HO 144 1498 354780.

63. Billing, *Verbatim Report*, 144.

64. Spencer's military record is on file in the Public Records Office (file WO 339/41960 6036755) and contains extensive correspondence regarding his mental instability and the web of lies he wove to talk his way into the British military. See also Billing, ibid., 176–82, for his testimony regarding his interactions with army doctors, as well as his hallucinations and delusions. For more on Spencer, see Hoare, *Oscar Wilde's Last Stand*, 57.

65. Billing, *Verbatim Report*, 185, 188, 163. Spencer later linked the clitoris to sadism: "It [a passage from *Salomé*] is the mutterings of a child suffering from an enlarged and diseased clitoris. And I got that from a medical treatise by a German—" (quoted in Billing, 187–88).

66. Ibid., 317–18.

67. Stopes, *Married Love*, 87. In "Cult of the Clitoris," Medd argues that the concurrence of Stopes's handbook with the trial indicates that the trial "contributes to a revolutionary moment in the knowledge of female body parts and the configurations of female sexuality" (48n42). In addition, I think we must consider the incoherence of definitions and uses of the clitoris in the trial in contrast to the medically sound and discursively coherent discussion of clitoral function in Stopes. To me, this contrast is a reminder that the discourse of the Billings trial must not be

overgeneralized as reflecting dominant cultural understandings of female sexuality and subjectivity. For more on Stopes's impact on literary and cultural discourses, see Chow, "Popular Sexual Knowledges and Women's Agency in 1920s England"; and Peppis, "Rewriting Sex."

68. Billing, *Verbatim Report,* 41, 410.

69. Ibid., appendix 24, 476.

70. Hoare points out that this diagnosis is taken "straight from the pages of Richard von Krafft-Ebing's . . . *Psychopathia Sexualis*" (*Oscar Wilde's Last Stand,* 67). For more details of the Theo Durrant affair, see 65–68.

71. Billing, *Verbatim Report,* 82, 67, 68–69, 74–75.

72. Ibid., 98, 100.

73. Ibid., 286, 288, 294, 295. When asked about Wilde more generally, Douglas responded that his former lover was "the greatest force for evil that has appeared in Europe during the last 350 years. . . . He was the agent of the devil in every possible way" (286–87). Hoare notes that the violence of this attack had as much to do with Douglas's hatred of Robert Ross, Wilde's executor, and his anger at his own lost reputation, as it had to do with his love of virtue and conservatism, both of which were extremely strong at this point in his life (*Oscar Wilde's Last Stand,* 16–24).

74. Two letters did great damage to Douglas's testimony. The first was a love letter from Wilde to him, which Douglas's father used to prosecute Wilde. The second, dated June 9, 1895, was from Douglas in response to a newspaper editorialist; in it, the young Douglas passionately defended homosexual acts through references to Krafft-Ebing and allusions to their widespread practice among men of the professional and ruling classes. For a more detailed discussion of the 1895 Wilde-Douglas correspondence under discussion here, see Hoare, *Oscar Wilde's Last Stand,* 156–59.

75. Billing, *Verbatim Report,* 294, 290, 291.

76. Ibid., 411, 415.

77. Michael Kettle remarks, "This is . . . probably one of the few occasions when the Acting Lord Chief Justice of England . . . had relied, for the definition of a crucial piece of expert gynecological evidence, not on any of the medical witnesses—bent though some of them were—but on the word of a former member of the British Secret Service, who had recently been discharged as insane" (*Salome's Last Veil,* 260).

78. The foreign press also carried reports of the trial daily. For an account of some of the French coverage, see Dean, "Claude Cahun's Double."

79. Siegfried Sassoon, quoted in Hynes, *War Imagined,* 232.

80. Cooper, *Durable Fire,* 67, 70, 62.

81. For example, "The Rossiad," by Lord Alfred Douglas, is reprinted in full on p. 2 of the April 20, 1918, edition of the *Vigilante,* as is Arnold White's "Efficiency and Vice," on p. 4.

82. *Daily News* clipping, June 15, 1918, from file no. WO 339/41960 6036755, Public Record Office, London. This file is Harold Sherwood Spencer's war file, but it also contains various clippings and items related to the Billing case.

83. Published by Sylvia Pankhurst's East London Federation of Suffragettes (renamed the Workers' Suffrage Federation in 1916, and then the Workers' Socialist Federation in 1918), the society's organ, *Women's Dreadnought,* became the *Worker's Dreadnought* in 1917.

84. For discussion of the impact of Sassoon's letter on the *Dreadnought,* see Davis, *Sylvia Pankhurst,* 55–57.

85. This was a letter headlined "The Sassoon Case," authored by Cedar Paul.

86. One possible explanation for this lack of coverage might be Pankhurst's own disinterest in parliamentary politics by 1918. Her disenchantment also, Davis notes, caused her to ignore the 1918 election, in which some women were first allowed to vote (*Sylvia Pankhurst,* 61).

87. *Parliamentary Debates,* House of Lords, March 9, 1921, 424.

88. In chapter 2 of *Fashioning Sapphism,* Laura Doan distinguishes between sexual abuse of girls by women and consensual sexual acts between women. This law would criminalize both, and the Parliamentary debates consistently blurred the distinction between these two areas.

89. Other clauses added in the Commons were rejected *after* rejecting the lesbian clause, often with the comment that the rejection of the lesbian clause had killed the entire bill. It remains somewhat unclear whether the clause was introduced in the House of Commons in good faith, or whether it was added to deliberately kill the entire bill. Doan argues that the latter is more likely: "If the obstructionists [as the MPs who introduced the bill were called in the feminist press] had indeed been sympathetic to the larger bill, they would hardly have introduced a contentious clause, especially one so malicious and calculated to shock. Its very indelicacy undoubtedly embarrassed and humiliated some social purity advocates and feminists (including lesbians) who had campaigned actively for over a year for the CLA Bill's passage" (*Fashioning Sapphism,* 60).

90. As opponents of the lesbian amendment pointed out in debates in both houses, a similar measure was proposed in 1913 but never reached the floor of either house: the home secretary prevented that bill from reaching Parliament for debate.

91. *Parliamentary Debates,* House of Commons, August 4, 1921, 1802.

92. Ibid., 1799, 1800.

93. This confusion reflects a period of ambiguity far messier than Michel Foucault's historical formulations of the transfer of cultural authority over homosexuality from the church to the prison and, finally, to the doctor.

94. *Parliamentary Debates,* House of Commons, August 4, 1921, 1803.

95. Ibid., 1800–1801.

96. See Whitaker, *Almanack,* 222.

97. *Parliamentary Debates,* House of Commons, August 4, 1921, 1801.

98. Ibid., 1804.

99. Doan, *Fashioning Sapphism,* 58.

100. *Parliamentary Debates,* House of Commons, August 4, 1921, 1804, 1805.

101. For a breakdown of the vote, see 145 H.C. Deb.5s, *Parliamentary Debates,* House of Commons, August 4, 1921, 1806. For a complete list of members of the House of Commons, see Whitaker, *Almanack,* 216–22.

102. *Parliamentary Debates,* House of Lords, August 15, 1921, 567–68, 572.

103. Ibid., 574, 572, 573.

104. Homosexuality can still rouse the House of Lords to action. In the summer of 1998, a measure appeared in Parliament to lower the age of consent for gay youth, rendering it equivalent to that for heterosexual youth. After the measure passed in the House of Commons, however, the House of Lords took the unusual step of refusing to sign it.

5. BOY-GIRLS AND GIRL-BOYS

1. "Vulgarity of Lesbianism," 614.

2. Taylor compares Woolf's *Orlando* and late twentieth-century transsexual autobiographies in "True Stories." For readings of *The Well of Loneliness* as a transsexual "body narrative," see Prosser, *Second Skins.* For work on Hall's constructions of "female masculinity," see Halberstam, *Female Masculinity.*

3. Wee, "Trials and Eros," 167.

4. Doan, *Fashioning Sapphism,* 96.

5. Ibid., 96–97.

6. In 1918, British women had won a limited national franchise that still withheld the vote from women under thirty years old and from all unpropertied women. See Pugh, *Women and the Women's Movement in Britain, 1914–1959,* 77.

7. Alberti, *Beyond Suffrage,* 185.

8. For more on the early opposition to women's suffrage, see Harrison, *Separate Spheres.*

9. Pugh, *Women and the Women's Movement in Britain, 1914–1959,* 77–78.

10. Riley, *"Am I That Name?"* 93; Pugh, ibid., 77.

11. McKale, *War by Revolution,* 230.

12. Gikandi, *Maps of Englishness,* 161.

13. Immediately after the Great War, British authorities sought to "solve" both the problem of redundant women workers and imperialist expansion through programs encouraging single British women to emigrate to the colonies. On September 12, 1919, the *Daily Chronicle* reported of "Openings for women in the Colonies": *"The new women of Britain, the women who arose and donned strange garments and turned their hands to unfamiliar work, are to be especially welcome in the Greater Britain overseas. . . .* Women who served their country as Waacs, Wrens,

or Drafs, are expected to make splendid emigrants" (emphasis in original). Clipping in *Scrapbook Relating to Women's Work during the First World War.*

14. Oram, *Her Husband Was a Woman!* 102.

15. Doan, *Fashioning Sapphism,* 119–20.

16. Alison Oram's monograph *Her Husband Was a Woman!* analyzes narratives of female masculinity in the working-class, popular press in the early twentieth century. Oram's investigation presents an important piece of the history of emergent lesbian representations in Britain, which departed from elite representations of female same-sex erotics found in Bloomsbury. Her analysis of the popular press's tepid response to Radclyffe Hall's trial demonstrates the distinctly class-based representations of women's gender and sexual deviance: "In the 1920s and 1930s . . . Sunday papers had a set of discourses to deal with sex between women, which was generally imagined as happening far from the day-to-day world of their readers, occurring among the upper classes, the smart set, and the cultural elite. In spite of the trial for obscenity of *The Well of Loneliness,* this theme still remained largely obscured, and was clearly not a topic which the newspapers wished to investigate" (81).

17. R. Hall, *Well of Loneliness,* 437.

18. Chinn, "'Something Primitive and Age-Old as Nature Herself,'" 303.

19. R. Hall, *Well of Loneliness,* 11.

20. For more on the role of "Celticness," sexual inversion, and femininity in the novel, see Chinn, "'Something Primitive and Age-Old as Nature Herself'"; and Backus, "Sexual Orientation in the (Post)Imperial Nation." For a brief discussion of the racial politics of the "Celtic periphery," see Fletcher, "'Women of the Nations, Unite!'" 115–65.

21. Chinn, "'Something Primitive and Age-Old as Nature Herself,'" 303.

22. R. Hall, *Well of Loneliness,* 12.

23. Jean Bobby Noble makes a similar argument that "in *The Well,* the notion of boundedness includes both the psychic . . . and a political geography referenced by the signifier 'England,' which is coterminous with everything Stephen believes he should be: masculine, aristocratic, patriotic, honourable, and, above all, white" (*Masculinities without Men?* 41). Noble presents an important reading of Stephen's "mirror scene" (Hall, ibid., 186–87) as a production of whiteness, not just Stephen's grappling with issues of sexuality or gender identity, as has been read notably by Esther Newton, "The Mythic Mannish Lesbian"; Prosser, *Second Skins;* and Halberstam, *Female Masculinity.* "These critics fail to see that a racialized body, a white body, has also materialized, although for whiteness to function most effectively as a marker of white supremacy that whiteness cannot be marked and must always be trumped or cloaked by gender" (Noble, 79).

24. R. Hall, *Well of Loneliness,* 201, 202.

25. See, for example, Aguilar–San Juan, "Going Home."

26. Kent, "*The Well of Loneliness* as War Novel," 226.

27. For discussions of the role of the Great War in Hall's novel, see ibid., on female masculinity and the metaphor of war in the novel; and Medd, "War Wounds," for a more psychoanalytic reading and particular attention to shell shock.

28. R. Hall, *Well of Loneliness*, 265, 437.

29. Ibid., 267, 271.

30. Hemmings writes that "it is Mary's *active desire* for Stephen, and her admirable persistence in pursuit of that desire, that marks the emergence of Mary as a femme subject of her own narrative" ("'All My Life I've Been Waiting for Something . . .,'" 189; emphasis in original). Mary's initiation of the couple's sexual relationship contains a possibility for agency that the narrative glosses over as it focuses on the barriers to happiness that such a couple faces: "But Mary Llewellyn was no coward and no weakling, and one night, at long last, pride came to her rescue. She said, 'I want to talk to you, Stephen. . . . I'm going back home to England. I forced myself on you, I asked you to take me. . . . But I want us to part quickly because. . . .' Her voice broke: 'Because it torments me to be always with you and to feel that you've literally grown to hate me. . . . What do I care of the world's opinion? What do I care for anything but you, and you just as you are—as you are, I love you" (R. Hall, *Well of Loneliness*, 311–12). With the same heroic language Stephen used to defend her love to her mother, Mary asserts her passion to Stephen. Mary claims Stephen as her lover, and even after Stephen's warnings of the perils of "what it's going to mean if you give yourself to me" (312), Mary persists and the relationship is finally consummated. For more on Mary's sexuality and its disruptive role, see also MacPike, "Is Mary Llewellyn an Invert?"

31. Chinn, "'Something Primitive and Age-Old as Nature Herself,'" 309.

32. Ibid.

33. Unlike Nella Larsen's African American novel *Passing*, published in 1929, in which Europe is a symbol of class privilege and sexual propriety, for Hall, Europe is always already degenerate, decadent, and diseased.

34. The Great War serves as a vehicle not only for masculine women to express their patriotism but also for effeminate men to be (at least partially) "rehabilitated" back into the national family. After the war, the effeminate Brockett returns a changed man: "His figure was more robust, there was more muscle and flesh on his wide, straight shoulders. And she thought that his face had certainly aged . . . the war had left its mark upon Brockett. Only his hands remain unchanged; those white and soft-skinned hands of a woman" (R. Hall, *Well of Loneliness*, 330). The war has erased most, but not all, signs of Brockett's effeminate homosexuality. In a slightly different argument, Kent argues that manliness is established through Stephen's experience of the war, rather than through Brockett's: "After the war, as Hall makes clear, it is Stephen, and not Jonathan [Brockett], despite his war service, who has proved her manliness" ("*The Well of Loneliness* as War Novel," 221).

35. R. Hall, *Well of Loneliness*, 379.

36. Ibid., 388, 389.

37. Jean Walton, "'I Want to Cross over into Camp Ground,'" 294.

38. Ibid., 295.

39. The racism of the characterizations of the two brothers is critical to Hall's construction of their "natural" affinities for music and sex and their intrinsic cultural distance from Stephen. See ibid.

40. R. Hall, *Well of Loneliness*, 363, 364, 365.

41. Ibid., 437.

42. Martin can also be read as sexually deviant. Unlike other heterosexual men in the novel, he is neither repulsed nor threatened by Stephen but, on the contrary, is her good friend: "Yes, strange though it was, with this normal man [Martin,] she was far more at ease than with Jonathan Brockett, far more at one with all his ideas; and at times far less conscious of her own inversion; though it seemed that Martin had not only read, but had thought a great deal about the subject" (ibid., 416). Further, "Mary would talk to him freely as she did very often . . . of the night life of the cafés and bars of Paris—most of which it transpired he himself had been to . . ." (416–17). Thus, both Mary and Stephen find a kindred spirit in Martin, in great part because of his own independent familiarity with both the literature and the scene of Paris's homosexual communities. This suggests either a former or a latent homosexuality in Martin, and the novel's closing marriage of Mary to Martin could come directly from the case studies of sexologists, many of which noted the tendency for people with some homosexual inclinations to marry one another. Noble provides an extended reading of the masculine homoerotics of Martin and Stephen's early friendship (*Masculinities without Men?* 49–54). Also, Hemmings suggests that "Martin's status as ideal heterosexual male is cast in doubt in a number of ways throughout *The Well*" ("'All My Life I've Been Waiting for Something . . .,'" 183–84).

43. Hemmings suggests the possibility that Mary rejects Martin's offer of a tempered heterosexual future: "Against the existing critical readings of *The Well* that read with Stephen and consign Mary to a certain heterosexual future, I want to insist that there is no evidence for her presumed heterosexuality outside a masculine viewpoint. . . . We must seek out Mary's possible futures in other texts" ("'All My Life I've Been Waiting for Something . . .,'" 194).

44. Allison Wee and I developed similar readings of *Extraordinary Women* simultaneously yet independently. For her discussion of the novel in the context of the rise of lesbian identities under a culture of censorship, see chapter 5 of her dissertation, "Trials and Eros," especially pp. 169–75.

45. Mackenzie, *Extraordinary Women*, 134.

46. Ibid., 40–41.

47. For a more detailed history of the impact of marriage on British women's citizenship, see Bhabha, Klug, and Shutter, *Worlds Apart*.

48. Mackenzie, *Extraordinary Women*, 110–11, 112.

49. Ibid., 231, 232.

50. Ibid., 45.

51. Ibid., 224, 225, 226.

52. Ibid., 288.

53. Ibid., 288–89, 348.

54. Ibid., 391–92.

55. Tea itself, as Urmila Seshagiri reminds us, is a symbol not only of British-ness but also of British imperial culture: "Tea's Eastern origins were overwritten by English practices that burgeoned as the Empire grew stronger. . . . Tea—imported, transplanted, and imposed as a social ritual—signifies the hybrid, culturally divided quality of Englishness" ("Orienting Virginia Woolf," 70).

56. V. Woolf, *Orlando*, 117.

57. Nigel Nicolson, *Portrait of a Marriage*, 202.

58. V. Woolf, *Orlando*, 13.

59. Butler, *Bodies That Matter*, x.

60. Hovey, "'Kissing a Negress in the Dark,'" 398.

61. Phillips, *Virginia Woolf against Empire*, 186.

62. V. Woolf, *Orlando*, 24, 25.

63. Ibid., 29–30.

64. Ibid., 37.

65. Ibid., 117, 46, 47.

66. Ibid., 57, 64, 52.

67. On the importance of Constantinople, see Seshagiri's discussion of Woolf's 1906 visit to that city. Seshagiri argues that "Woolf's Constantinople journals . . . forge an early link between cultural identities and artistic representations, calling attention to the lines separating self from other" ("Orienting Virginia Woolf," 59).

68. Phillips, *Virginia Woolf against Empire*, 188.

69. Hovey, "'Kissing a Negress in the Dark,'" 399.

70. V. Woolf, *Orlando*, 137–38.

71. Ibid., 161.

72. Hovey, "'Kissing a Negress in the Dark,'" 400.

73. V. Woolf, *Orlando*, 153, 154, 162, 163.

74. Johnson, "Giving up the Ghost," 113.

75. V. Woolf, *Orlando*, 221, 219.

76. Ibid., 246, 242, 243.

77. Hovey, "'Kissing a Negress in the Dark,'" 400.

78. V. Woolf, *Orlando*, 250, 251–52.

79. Hovey, "'Kissing a Negress in the Dark,'" 401.

80. V. Woolf, *Orlando*, 264, 258, 288.

81. Douglas, "Book That Must Be Suppressed," 37.

82. Ibid., 38.

83. Though it was well after the writing of *Orlando,* obscenity and censure were much on Woolf's mind in the autumn of 1928. She mused in her diary after returning home from the trial of *The Well of Loneliness,* "What is obscenity? What is literature? What is the difference between the subject & the treatment?" (*Diary of Virginia Woolf,* 207).

84. To compare: in late 1928, Wyndam Lewis's *The Childermass* sold at a price a bit higher than the average novel, at eight shillings and sixpence, whereas Siegfried Sassoon's *Memoirs of a Fox-Hunting Man* was sold at the most common price of seven shillings and sixpence. The least expensive novels I found in this period were sold at six shillings.

85. The U.S. edition, about whose production and distribution I can find little information, sold *Extraordinary Women* at the much lower price of $2.50. I do know that the American publisher (Vanguard Press) printed at least two runs *before* publication. In the United States, at least, the type was not distributed after the first edition.

86. Raymond Mortimer, "Reviews: New Novels," 735.

87. "Vulgarity of Lesbianism," 614.

88. Indeed, the publisher of *Extraordinary Women* took this advice. In April 1929 (after the storm over *The Well of Loneliness* and months of legal silence concerning Mackenzie's novel had passed), a "cheap popular edition" of *Extraordinary Women* was released (Baker, *Our Three Selves,* 254). Allison Wee uncovered a May 1929 advertisement for this less-expensive paperback edition, which advertises the novel as "obtainable everywhere" at the low price of seven shillings and sixpence. Wee notes that the publication of this paperback edition prompted Robert Cust, the "longtime . . . spokesperson for the London Public Morality Council," to write to the Home Office regarding the novel, and additionally that Mackenzie edited out several of the more sexual scenes for the widely available paperback edition (Wee, "Trials and Eros," 184–90).

89. The Harry Ransom Center for the Humanities at the University of Texas at Austin houses the Morris Ernst and Radclyffe Hall collections, both of which contain materials relating to the publication history of *The Well of Loneliness.* In subsequent notes, "HRC" denotes holdings housed there.

90. *The Well of Loneliness* sold out in England immediately after James Douglas attacked the novel in the *Sunday Express* (Scott, *Refiguring Modernism,* 244). Its publisher's attempt to de-emphasize its possibly salacious content through a moderate price was thwarted by sensationalist editorials and press coverage.

91. Clearly, *The Well of Loneliness* was being (re)packaged to sell. Following the novel's seizure in England, a U.S. bookseller claimed that "pretty nearly every brilliant contemporary English writer have [*sic*] come to the defense of *The Well of Loneliness.*" An advertisement by the Golden Hind Press read, "We have 750 copies

of an edition published abroad on special Japanese tinted vellum, and beautifully bound in boards; 512 pages. $10 a copy" (HRC). This advertisement reprinted both a "specimen page" from the novel (featuring the closest thing one can find to a salacious passage in the novel) and an excerpt of a favorable article about the British trial from the *New York World*.

92. Cline, *Radclyffe Hall*, 240.

93. Cline writes, "Knopf planned the American edition to coincide with Cape's [British] publication in the autumn, but in July, again without warning, Cape changed his plans. He now intended to move publication forward to 27 July . . . . He had discovered Secker's scheme to bring out Mackenzie's *Extraordinary Women* in Britain with a simultaneous publication in America by Vanguard Press" (ibid., 239).

94. As Wee reports, the Home Office considered prosecuting the publishers of *Extraordinary Women*, but eventually decided against any action against the novel: "Despite extensive and often heated debates as to whether or not *Extraordinary Women* officially demonstrated the legally binding 'tendency to deprave and corrupt' readers, the Home Office ultimately allowed it to continue to circulate freely" ("Trial and Eros," 151–52). Wee attributes this in part to the unintended consequence of the *Well of Loneliness* trial—the widespread publicity for the novel—as well as to *Extraordinary Women*'s satiric rather than polemic tone and its high price and limited circulation. For a careful and fascinating reading of the Home Office documents surrounding *Extraordinary Women*, see Wee, chapter 5.

95. Noble, *Masculinities without Men?* 19.

96. For further discussions of the importance of the British and American trials of *The Well of Loneliness*, see Emery, "*Well* Meaning"; Parkes, *Modernism and the Theater of Censorship*; Noble, ibid., 18–29; Scott, *Refiguring Modernism*, chapter 12; Wee, "Trial and Eros"; V. Brittain, *Radclyffe Hall*; Doan, *Fashioning Sapphism*; Souhami, *Trials of Radclyffe Hall*; and Cohler, "Gender Inversion and Representations of Female Desire, 1880–1939," chapter 4. For an excerpt of the British court decisions, see Sir Chartres Biron, "Judgment." For press reports, see *Times* (London), "Alleged Obscene Novel" and "Novel Condemned as Obscene."

97. Virginia Woolf supported the novel publicly but dismissed Hall and the novel in her diary, letters, and reported conversations. In a letter dated August 30, 1928, to Vita Sackville-West, Woolf reports on the petition confrontation: "What has caused this irruption I scarcely know—largely your friend Radclyffe Hall (she is now docked of her Miss owning to her proclivities) they banned her book; so now Leonard [Woolf] and Morgan Forster began to get up a protest, and soon we were telephoning and interviewing and collecting signatures—not yours, for *your* proclivities are too well known. In the midst of this Morgan goes to see Radclyffe in her tower in Kensington, with her love [Una Troubridge] and Radclyffe scolds him like a fishwife, and says that she wont [*sic*] have any letter written about her

book unless it mentions the fact that it is a work of artistic merit—even genius. . . . Now we have to explain this to all the great signed names—Arnold Bennett and so on. So our ardour in the cause of freedom of speech gradually cools, and instead of offering to reprint the masterpiece, we are already beginning to wish it unwritten" (quoted in Nicolson, *Letters of Virginia Woolf,* 3:520). Virginia Woolf also co-authored a letter to the editor of the *Nation and Athenaeum* with E. M. Forster, which clearly supported the publication of *The Well of Loneliness* but, equally pointedly, did not mention the literary merit of the novel.

98. Biron, "Judgment," 49.

99. *People of the State of New York v. Donald Friede and Covici Friede,* defense brief, HRC.

100. Parkes, *Modernism and the Theater of Censorship,* 144.

101. Baker, *Our Three Selves,* 254.

102. Knopp, "'If I Saw You, Would You Kiss Me?'" 119.

103. Ruehl, "Inverts and Experts," 174.

104. Jane Marcus makes a similar point with regard to *A Room of One's Own* ("Sapphistory").

105. Parkes, *Modernism and the Theater of Censorship,* 146.

106. L. Woolf, "World of Books."

107. Hartley, "New Fiction."

108. V. Brittain, from a clipping of her review "Facing Facts," sent to Hall's attorney. In a typed note attached to the clipping, Brittain wrote that the review "represents my carefully-considered opinion that the book is restrained and that it would not be liable to corrupt persons likely to read it" (HRC).

109. Ibid.

110. Ibid.

111. C. P. F., "Review of *Extraordinary Women,* by Compton Mackenzie."

112. *Times Literary Supplement,* "New Novels."

113. *Times Literary Supplement,* "Review of *Extraordinary Women,* by Compton Mackenzie."

114. *Times Literary Supplement,* "Review of *Orlando,* by Virginia Woolf."

115. *Saturday Review,* "Wild-Goose Chase."

116. Scott, *Refiguring Modernism,* 253.

117. Gates, "Enchantment," 150.

AFTERWORD

1. Newton, "Mythic Mannish Lesbian."

2. Rubin, "Thinking Sex."

3. See chapter 5 of Grewal, *Transnational America,* especially pages 209–17; Mukherjee, "Between Enemies and Traitors"; and my "Keeping the Home Front Burning."

4. Somerville, *Queering the Color Line,* 176.

5. FTM International was formed in 1986 as a support group; its newsletter began in 1987. On Brandon Teena's murder and the contestations over this young person's identity as lesbian, transgender, or transsexual, see Prosser, *Second Skins,* 175–77; Halberstam's two chapters on Teena in *Queer Time and Place;* and Noble, *Masculinities without Men?* xxix–xxxi. On debates over inclusions of transwomen in lesbian communities, see Boyd, "Materiality of Gender"; Wilchins, *Read My Lips;* Devor and Matte, "One Inc. and Reed Erikson"; and Cvetkovich and Wahng, "Don't Stop the Music."

6. For analyses of the historical and theoretical relationships between lesbian and trans identities and communities in turn-of-the-twenty-first-century America, see Devor and Matte, "One Inc. and Reed Erikson"; Cromwell, *Transmen and FTMs;* and the dialogue between Hale ("Consuming the Living, Dis(Re)membering the Dead in the Butch/FTM Borderlands") and Halberstam (*Female Masculinity,* chapter 5). Boyd also addresses this debate through her analysis of the body politics of lesbian and transgender histories in "Materiality of Gender."

7. In a keynote address at Brown University's "Pride 1994" convocation, Feinberg quoted Una Troubridge's conversation with Radclyffe Hall regarding the writing of *The Well of Loneliness.* Feinberg cited Troubridge's desire to "dwell with [Hall] in a palace of truth" as Hall's impetus for writing her novel (Troubridge, *Life of Radclyffe Hall,* 82). Feinberg also noted that both *The Well of Loneliness* and her own *Stone Butch Blues* have been simultaneously characterized as autobiography and fiction. In describing both texts as "trans-genre," she called attention to the difficulties in representing sexual and gender variations, thereby constructing a historical legacy, though not an equivalence, between Hall's 1928 text and the work of herself and others in the 1990s.

8. Noble, *Masculinities without Men?* 4, xiii.

9. It is a common move in some trans scholarship to draw on the sexual and gender inversions of the early twentieth century to ground analysis of transgender cultural products in the late twentieth century. For example, Taylor compares the portraiture of modernist Sapphist Romaine Brooks to the late twentieth-century self-portraits of transsexual photographer Loren Cameron, in her article "Peter (a Young English Girl)," and draws a similar parallel between Woolf's *Orlando* and late twentieth-century transsexual autobiographies, in "True Stories." Devor and Matte travel back to *The Well of Loneliness* in their discussion of the complex relationship of queer and trans activism: "Early sexologists and their contemporaries commonly assumed that homosexuality was epitomized by females who seemed to want to be men and by males who seemed to want to be women. . . . Similarly, Radclyffe Hall's book *The Well of Loneliness* (1928) about a (transgendered) female who yearned to be a man, almost single-handedly defined lesbianism in the popular imagination for much of the twentieth century and is still widely acclaimed as

a classic of lesbian literature" ("One Inc. and Reed Erikson," 179–80). Whereas Taylor draws an analogy between narratives of gender inversion identity in the early twentieth century and transsexuality at the end of that century, Devor and Matte seek to claim *The Well of Loneliness* solely as a transsexual text wrongly hailed and appropriated by lesbians.

10. Feinberg, like some other advocates of gender pluralism and transgender visibility, uses the neutral pronouns "ze" and "hir" in lieu of "s/he" or "him/her" for individuals whose gender does not fall into the categories of male or female. I am following Feinberg's usage of "hirself" and in regard to the characters in *Drag King Dreams,* some of whom are referred to as "he" or "she" and others as "ze." In the first-person narrative of the novel, Max is never referred to by a third-person pronoun; my use of "ze" for Max is my own best guess.

11. Ibid., 2, 4.

12. Feinberg's novel argues against narratives in which a sudden outbreak of war follows a previous "peace." Such a narrative belies the conditions of everyday violence experienced in many communities in the United States prior to September 11, 2001. As Grewal remarks, "A large part of what happened [following 9/11] was a continuation and a fulfillment of neoliberal practices that had arisen in the last decades of the twentieth century" (*Transnational America,* 197).

13. Feinberg, *Drag King Dreams,* 201, 208.

14. Ibid., 183.

15. Ibid., 41, 175.

16. Ibid., 86–88, 266.

17. Ibid., 160–61.

18. Ashcroft is pointedly named early in the novel at a drag show, connecting gender transgression with national threat. In the introduction to her rendition of "Somewhere over the Rainbow," the performer riffs, "We're Code Lavender tonight, my dears. . . . We had to go to a higher level of security alert because Mister John Ashcroft called us personally to warn us that gender terrorists were plotting to come here tonight to subvert the binary" (ibid., 13).

19. Ibid., 30, 32–33.

20. Ibid., 267–68, 269.

21. Ibid., 219, 224.

22. Ibid., 300–302, 224, 267.

WORKS CITED

Aguilar–San Juan, Karin. "Going Home: Enacting Justice in Queer Asian America." In *Q and A: Queer in Asian America,* edited by David L. Eng and Alice Y. Hom, 25–40. Philadelphia: Temple University Press, 1998.

Alberti, Johanna. *Beyond Suffrage: Feminists in War and Peace, 1914–1928.* London: Macmillan, 1989.

Allatini, Rose [A. T. Fitzroy, pseud.]. *Despised and Rejected.* London: Daniel, 1917. Reprint, New York: Arno, 1975.

"Alleged Obscene Novel: Proceedings at Bow Street." *Times* (London), November 10, 1928.

Backus, Margot Gayle. "Sexual Orientation in the (Post)Imperial Nation: Celticism and Inversion Theory in Radclyffe Hall's *The Well of Loneliness.*" *Tulsa Studies in Women's Literature* 15, no. 2 (1993): 253–66.

Baker, Michael. *Our Three Selves: A Life of Radclyffe Hall.* London: Hamish Hamilton, 1985.

Balfour, Frances. "Religion and the Suffrage: Lady Frances Balfour's Reply." Letter to the editor, *Times* (London), June 22, 1912.

Barash, Carol. "Dora Marsden's Feminism, the *Freewoman,* and the Gender Politics of Early Modernism." *Princeton University Library Chronicle* 49, no. 1 (1987): 31–56.

Barkan, Elazar. "Victorian Promiscuity: Greek Ethics and Primitive Exemplars." In *Prehistories of the Future: The Primitivist Project and the Culture of Modernism,* edited by Elazar Barkan and Ronald Bush, 56–92. Stanford, Calif.: Stanford University Press, 1995.

Bell, Heather. *Frontiers of Medicine in the Anglo-Egyptian Sudan, 1899–1940.* Oxford: Clarendon, 1999.

Benstock, Shari. "Expatriate Sapphic Modernism: Entering Literary History." In *Lesbian Texts and Contexts: Radical Revisions,* edited by Karla Jay and Joanne Glasgow, 183–203. New York: New York University Press, 1990.

————. *Women of the Left Bank: Paris, 1900–1940.* Austin: University of Texas Press, 1986.

Berubé, Allan. *Coming Out under Fire: The History of Gay Men and Women in World War Two.* New York: Free Press, 1990.

Bhabha, Jacqueline, Francesca Klug, and Sue Shutter, eds. *Worlds Apart: Women under Immigration and Nationality Law.* London: Pluto, 1985.

Billing, Noel Pemberton. "The Cult of the Clitoris." *Vigilante,* February 16, 1918.

————. "The First 47,000." *Imperialist,* January 26, 1918.

————, ed. *Verbatim Report.* London: Vigilante Society, 1918.

Birnstingl, Harry J. "Interpretations of Life." *Freewoman,* June, 13, 1912, 70–72.

————. "Uranians." *Freewoman,* January, 4, 1912, 127–28.

Biron, Chartres. "Judgment." In *Palatable Poison: Critical Perspectives on "The Well of Loneliness,"* edited by Laura Doan and Jay Prosser, 39–49. New York: Columbia University Press, 2001.

Blair, Sara. "Local Modernity, Global Modernism: Bloomsbury and the Places of the Literary." *ELH: A Journal of English Literary History* 71 (2004): 813–38.

Bland, Lucy. *Banishing the Beast: Sexuality and the Early Feminists.* New York: New Press, 1995.

————. "Trial by Sexology? Maud Allan, *Salome,* and the 'Cult of the Clitoris' Case." In *Sexology in Culture: Labelling Bodies and Desires,* edited by Lucy Bland and Laura Doan, 183–98. Chicago: University of Chicago Press, 1998.

Boehmer, Elleke. *Empire, the National, and the Postcolonial, 1890–1920: Resistance in Interaction.* Oxford: Oxford University Press, 2002.

Boyd, Nan Alamilla. "The Materiality of Gender: Looking for Lesbian Bodies in Transgender History." In *Lesbian Sex Scandals: Sexual Practices, Identities, and Politics,* edited by Dawn Atkins, 73–81. Binghamton, N.Y.: Haworth, 1999.

————. *Wide Open Town: A History of Queer San Francisco to 1965.* Berkeley and Los Angeles: University of California Press, 2003.

Boyden, A. Maude. "A Nauseous Publication." Letter to the editor, *Times* (London), June 22, 1912.

Bristow, Joseph. "Symonds's History, Ellis's Heredity: *Sexual Inversion.*" In *Sexology in Culture: Labelling Bodies and Desires,* edited by Lucy Bland and Laura Doan, 79–99. Chicago: University of Chicago Press, 1998.

————, ed. *Wilde Writings: Contextual Conditions.* Toronto: University of Toronto Press, 2003.

Brittain, Melisa. "Erasing Race in the *New Woman Review:* Victoria Cross's *Anna Lombard.*" *Nineteenth-Century Feminisms* 4 (Spring/Summer 2001): 75–95.

Brittain, Vera. "Facing Facts: Review of *The Well of Loneliness,* by Radclyffe Hall; *Nightseed,* by H. A. Manhood; *Strangers,* by Dorothy Van Doren; and *David and Diana,* by Cecil Roberts." *Time and Tide,* August 10, 1928. Clipping in the Harry Ransom Center for the Humanities at the University of Texas, Austin.

———. *Radclyffe Hall: A Case of Obscenity?* New York: Barnes, 1968.

Browne, F. W. Stella. "Correspondence: Who Are the 'Normal'?" *Freewoman,* March 7, 1912, 312–13.

———. "The Sexual Variety and Variability among Women and Their Bearing upon Social Re-construction." Paper presented to the British Society for the Study of Sex Psychology, 1915. http://homepages.primex.co.uk/~lesleyah/variety.htm.

———. "Studies in Feminine Inversion." *Journal of Sexology and Psychoanalysis* 1, no. 1 (1923): 51–58.

———. "Women and the Race." *Socialist Review* 14, no. 18 (May–June 1917). Also available at http://homepages.primex.co.uk/~lesleyah/womrace.htm.

Bucknell, Brad. "On 'Seeing' Salome." *ELH: A Journal of English Literary History* 60 (1993): 503–26.

Burdett, Carolyn. "The Hidden Romance of Sexual Science: Eugenics, the Nation, and the Making of Modern Feminism." In *Sexology in Culture: Labelling Bodies and Desires,* edited by Lucy Bland and Laura Doan, 44–59. Chicago: University of Chicago Press, 1998.

Burke, Kenneth. "The Modern English Novel Plus." In *Virginia Woolf: Critical Assessments,* edited by Eleanor McNees. Vol. 3, *Critical Responses to the Novels from "The Voyage Out" to "To the Lighthouse,"* 113–15. Mountfield, England: Helm Information, 1994.

Burns, Edward. "*Salome:* Wilde's Radical Tragedy." In *Rediscovering Oscar Wilde,* edited by C. George Sandulescu, 30–36. Gerrards Cross, England: Smythe, 1994.

Burton, Antoinette. *Burdens of History: British Feminists, Indian Women, and Imperial Culture, 1865–1915.* Chapel Hill: University of North Carolina Press, 1994.

———. "'States of Injury': Josephine Butler on Slavery, Citizenship, and the Boer War." In *Women's Suffrage in the British Empire: Citizenship, Nation, and Race,* edited by Ian Christopher Fletcher, Laura E. Nym Mayhall, and Philippa Levine, 18–32. London: Routledge, 2000.

Butler, Judith. *Bodies That Matter: On the Discursive Limits of "Sex."* New York: Routledge, 1993.

C. P. F. [pseud.]. "Review of *Extraordinary Women,* by Compton Mackenzie." *Nation,* October 10, 1928, 378.

Carpenter, Edward. *The Intermediate Sex: A Study of Some Transitional Types of Men and Women.* London: Allen & Unwin, 1908. Facsimile reprint, New York: AMS, 1983.

———. "The Status of Women in Early Greek Times." *New Freewoman,* August 1, 1913, 68–69.

Casella, Eleanor Conlin. "Bulldaggers and Gentle Ladies: Archaeological Approaches to Female Homosexuality in Convict-Era Australia." In *Archaeologies of Sexuality,* edited by Robert Schmidt and Barbara L. Voss, 143–59. London: Routledge, 2000.

Chan, Winnie. "Morbidity, Masculinity, and the Misadventures of the New Woman in the *Yellow Book*'s Short Stories." *Nineteenth-Century Feminisms* 4 (Spring/Summer 2001): 35–46.

Chauncey, George. *Gay New York*. New York: Basic Books, 1994.

Chinn, Sarah E. "'Something Primitive and Age-Old as Nature Herself': Lesbian Sexuality and the Permission of the Exotic." In *Palatable Poison: Critical Perspectives on "The Well of Loneliness,"* edited by Laura Doan and Jay Prosser, 300–315. New York: Columbia University Press, 2001.

Chow, Karen. "Popular Sexual Knowledges and Women's Agency in 1920s England: Marie Stopes's *Married Love* and E. M. Hull's *The Sheik*." *Feminist Review* 63 (Autumn 1999): 64–87.

Chrisman, Laura. "Empire, 'Race,' and Feminism at the *Fin De Siècle*: The Work of George Egerton and Olive Schreiner." In *Cultural Politics at the Fin De Siècle,* edited by Sally Ledger and Scott McCracken, 45–65. Cambridge: Cambridge University Press, 1995.

Cini, Carol F. "From British Women's WWI Suffrage Battle to the League of Nations Covenant: Conflicting Uses of Gender in the Politics of Millicent Garrett Fawcett." *UCLA Historical Journal* 14 (1994): 78–100.

Clarke, Bruce. *Dora Marsden and Early Modernism*. Ann Arbor: University of Michigan Press, 1996.

Cline, Sally. *Radclyffe Hall: A Woman Called John*. Woodstock, N.Y.: Overlook, 1997.

Cohler, Deborah. "Gender Inversion and Representations of Female Desire, 1880–1939." PhD diss., Brown University, 2000.

———. "Keeping the Home Front Burning: Renegotiating Gender and Sexual Identity in U.S. Mass Media after September 11." *Feminist Media Studies* 6, no. 3 (2006): 245–61.

Common Cause. Cover illustration. January 5, 1911.

———. Editorial. April 15, 1909, 3.

Cooley, Elizabeth. "Discovering the 'Enchanted Region': A Revisionary Reading of *Night and Day*." *CEA [College English Association] Critic* 54, no. 3 (1992): 4–17.

Cooper, Artemis, ed. *A Durable Fire: The Letters of Duff and Diana Cooper, 1913–1950*. London: Collins, 1983.

Corelli, Marie. *Woman, or—Suffragette: A Question of National Choice*. London: Pearson, 1907.

Crackanthorpe, B. A. "Sex in Modern Literature." *Nineteenth Century,* April 1895, 607–16.

Cromwell, Jason. *Transmen and FTMs: Identities, Bodies, Genders, and Sexualities*. Urbana: University of Illinois Press, 1999.

Cross, Victoria. "Theodora: A Fragment." In *Daughters of Decadence: Women Writers of the Fin-De-Siècle,* edited by Elaine Showalter, 6–37. New Brunswick, N.J.: Rutgers University Press, 1993.

Cvetkovich, Ann, and Selena Wahng. "Don't Stop the Music: Roundtable Discussion with Workers from the Michigan Womyn's Music Festival." *GLQ: A Journal of Lesbian and Gay Studies* 7, no. 1 (2001): 131–51.

Dangerfield, George. *The Strange Death of Liberal England.* New York: Smith & Haas, 1935.

D'Auvergne, Edmund B. "A Definition of Marriage." *Freewoman,* November 23, 1911.

Davin, Anna. "Imperialism and Motherhood." *History Workshop Journal* 5 (Spring 1978): 9–65.

Davis, Mary. *Sylvia Pankhurst: A Life in Radical Politics.* London: Pluto, 1999.

Dean, Carolyn J. "Claude Cahun's Double." *Yale French Studies* 90 (1996): 71–92.

"'Despised and Rejected': Publisher of Pacifist Novel Fined." *Times* (London), October, 11, 1918.

Devor, Aaron H., and Nicholas Matte. "One Inc. and Reed Erikson: The Uneasy Collaboration of Gay and Trans Activism, 1964–2003." *GLQ: A Journal of Lesbian and Gay Studies* 10, no. 2 (2004): 179–209.

Dicey, Albert Venn. *Letters to a Friend on Votes for Women.* London: Murray, 1909.

Doan, Laura. *Fashioning Sapphism: The Origins of a Modern English Lesbian Culture.* New York: Columbia University Press, 2001.

———. "Topsy-Turvydom: Gender Inversion, Sapphism, and the Great War." *GLQ: A Journal of Lesbian and Gay Studies* 12, no. 4 (2006): 517–42.

Douglas, James. "A Book That Must Be Suppressed." In *Palatable Poison: Critical Perspectives on "The Well of Loneliness,"* edited by Laura Doan and Jay Prosser, 36–38. New York: Columbia University Press, 2001.

Dowling, Linda. "The Decadent and the New Woman." *Nineteenth Century Fiction* 33, no. 4 (1979): 434–53.

Downey, Katherine Brown. *Perverse Midrash: Oscar Wilde, André Gide, and Censorship of Biblical Drama.* New York: Continuum, 2004.

Drysdale, B[essie]. "Foreign Notes." *Freewoman,* January 11, 1912, 158.

Drysdale, Charles V. "Freewomen and the Birth-Rate." *Freewoman,* November 30, 1911, 35–37.

———. "Freewomen and the Birth-Rate II." *Freewoman,* December 21, 1911, 89–90.

E. S. P. H. [pseud.]. "Contemporary Recognition of Polygamy." *Freewoman,* November 23, 1911, 9–10.

Ellis, Edith Lees. "Eugenics and Spiritual Parenthood." In *The New Horizon in Love and Life.* London: Black, 1921.

———. "Eugenics and the Mystical Outlook." In *The New Horizon in Love and Life.* London: Black, 1921.

———. *The New Horizon in Love and Life.* London: Black, 1921.

Ellis, Havelock. Prefatory note to *New Horizon in Love and Life,* by Edith Lees Ellis. London: Black, 1921.

———. *Studies in the Psychology of Sex.* Vol. 1. New York: F. A. Davis, 1936. Reprint, New York: Random House, 1942.

Ellis, Havelock, and John Addington Symonds. *Sexual Inversion.* London: Wilson and Macmillan, 1897. Reprint, Manchester, N.H.: Ayers, 1994.

Emery, Kim. "*Well* Meaning: Pragmatism, Lesbianism, and the U.S. Obscenity Trial." In *Palatable Poison: Critical Perspectives on "The Well of Loneliness,"* edited by Laura Doan and Jay Prosser, 355–71. New York: Columbia University Press, 2001.

Ernst, Waltraud, and Bernard Harris, eds. *Race, Science and Medicine, 1700–1960.* London: Routledge, 1999.

Faderman, Lillian. *Surpassing the Love of Men: Romantic Friendship and Love between Women from the Renaissance to the Present.* New York: Morrow, 1981.

Fairfield, Cicely. "The Position of Women in Indian Life." *Freewoman,* November 30, 1911, 39.

Fawcett, Millicent Garrett. Letter to the *Times* (London). June 6, 1910.

Feinberg, Leslie. "An Anti-war Message to Pride Marchers from Author and Activist Leslie Feinberg." Broadsheet distributed by International ANSWER Coalition, June 2002.

———. *Drag King Dreams.* New York: Carroll & Graf, 2006.

———. Keynote address, "Pride 1994: Neither Straight, nor Narrow" convocation. Brown University, Providence R.I., 1994.

———. *Stone Butch Blues.* Los Angeles: Alyson, 1993.

Felski, Rita. *The Gender of Modernity.* Cambridge, Mass.: Harvard University Press, 1995.

Ferrall, Charles. "Suffragists, Egoists, and the Politics of Early Modernism." *English Studies in Canada* 18, no. 4 (1992): 433–46.

Fletcher, Ian Christopher. "'Women of the Nations, Unite!' Transnational Suffragism in the United Kingdom, 1912–1914." In *Women's Suffrage in the British Empire: Citizenship, Nation, and Race,* edited by Ian Christopher Fletcher, Laura E. Nym Mayhall, and Philippa Levine, 103–20. London: Routledge, 2000.

Fletcher, Ian Christopher, Laura E. Nym Mayhall, and Philippa Levine, eds. *Women's Suffrage in the British Empire: Citizenship, Nation, and Race.* London: Routledge, 2000.

Foucault, Michel. *The History of Sexuality.* Translated by Robert Hurley. Vol. 1, *An Introduction.* New York: Vintage, 1980.

Fox, Susan Hudson. "Woolf's Austen/Boston Tea Party: The Revolt against Literary Empire in *Night and Day.*" In *Virginia Woolf: Emerging Perspectives,* edited by Mark Hussey and Vara Neverow, 259–65. New York: Pace University Press, 1994.

Frankel, Nicholas. *Oscar Wilde's Decorated Books*. Ann Arbor: University of Michigan Press, 2000.

Franklin, Cary. "Marketing Edwardian Feminism: Dora Marsden, *Votes for Women*, and the *Freewoman*." *Women's Historical Review* II, no. 4 (2002): 631–42.

Freud, Sigmund. *Dora: An Analysis of a Case of Hysteria*. New York: Collier, 1905. Reprint, New York: Macmillan, 1963.

———. *Three Essays on the Theory of Sexuality*. Translated by James Strachey. 1905. Reprint, New York: Basic Books, 1975.

Gagnier, Regina. *Idylls of the Marketplace: Oscar Wilde and the Victorian Public*. Stanford, Calif.: Stanford University Press, 1986.

———. "Women in British Aestheticism and the Decadence." In *The New Woman in Fiction and Fact: Fin-De-Siècle Feminisms*, edited by Angelique Richardson and Chris Willis, 239–49. London: Palgrave, 2001.

Gandhi, Leela. *Affective Communities: Anticolonial Thought, Fin-De-Siècle Radicalism, and the Politics of Friendship*. Durham N.C.: Duke University Press, 2006.

Garner, Les. *A Brave and Beautiful Spirit: Dora Marsden, 1882–1960*. Aldershot, England: Avebury, 1990.

Garner, Shirley Nelson. "'Women Together' in Virginia Woolf's *Night and Day*." In *The (M)other Tongue: Essays in Feminist Psychoanalytic Interpretation*, edited by Shirley Nelson Garner, Claire Kahane, and Madelon Sprengnether, 318–33. Ithaca, N.Y.: Cornell University Press, 1985.

Garrity, Jane. *Step-daughters of England: British Women Modernists and the National Imaginary*. Manchester, England: Manchester University Press, 2003.

Gaskell, Ellen S. "The Unspeakable." *Freewoman*, January 18, 1912, 176.

Gates, Barrington. "Enchantment: Review of *Orlando* by Virginia Woolf." *Nation and Athenaeum*, October 27, 1928, 149–50.

Gideon. "Correspondence: The Love-Child." *Freewoman*, March 28, 1912, 376.

Gikandi, Simon. *Maps of Englishness: Writing Identity in the Culture of Colonialism*. New York: Columbia University Press, 1996.

Green, Barbara. "From Visible *Flaneuse* to Spectacular Suffragette? The Prison, the Street, and the Sites of Suffrage." *Discourse* 17, no. 2 (1994–95): 67–97.

Grewal, Inderpal. *Home and Harem: Nation, Gender, Empire, and the Cultures of Travel*. Durham, N.C.: Duke University Press, 1996.

———. *Transnational America: Feminisms, Diasporas, Neoliberalisms*. Durham, N.C.: Duke University Press, 2005.

Gullace, Nicoletta F. *"The Blood of Our Sons": Men, Women, and the Renegotiation of British Citizenship during the Great War*. New York: Palgrave Macmillan, 2002.

Hackett, Robin. *Sapphic Primitivism: Productions of Race, Class, and Sexuality in Key Works of Modern Fiction*. New Brunswick, N.J.: Rutgers University Press, 2004.

Halberstam, Judith. *Female Masculinity.* Durham, N.C.: Duke University Press, 1998.

———. *In a Queer Time and Place: Transgender Bodies, Subcultural Lives.* New York: New York University Press, 2005.

Hale, C. Jacob. "Consuming the Living, Dis(Re)membering the Dead in the Butch/FTM Borderlands." *GLQ: A Journal of Lesbian and Gay Studies* 4, no. 2 (1998): 311–48.

Hall, Lesley A. "'Disinterested Enthusiasm for Sexual Misconduct': The British Society for the Study of Sex Psychology, 1913–47." *Journal of Contemporary History* 30 (1995): 665–86.

———, ed. *Outspoken Women: An Anthology of Women's Writing on Sex, 1870–1969.* London: Routledge, 2005.

Hall, Radclyffe. *The Well of Loneliness.* 1928. Reprint, New York: Anchor Doubleday, 1990.

Harrison, Brian. *Separate Spheres: The Opposition to Women's Suffrage in Britain.* London: Croom Helm, 1978.

Hart, Lynda. *Fatal Women: Lesbian Sexuality and the Mark of Aggression.* Princeton, N.J.: Princeton University Press, 1994.

Hartley, L. P. "New Fiction: Review of *The Well of Loneliness,* by Radclyffe Hall." *Saturday Review,* July 28, 1928, 126–27.

Heilmann, Ann. *New Woman Fiction: Women Writing First-Wave Feminism.* New York: St. Martin's, 2000.

Hemmings, Clare. "'All My Life I've Been Waiting for Something . . .': Theorizing Femme Narrative in *The Well of Loneliness.*" In *Palatable Poison: Critical Perspectives on "The Well of Loneliness,"* edited by Laura Doan and Jay Prosser, 179–96. New York: Columbia University Press, 2001.

Hill, Margaret E. Correspondence. *Freewoman,* November 30, 1911, 31.

Hirshfield, Claire. "The Actresses' Franchise League and the Campaign for Women's Suffrage, 1908–1914." *Theatre Research International* 10, no. 2 (1985): 129–53.

Hoare, Philip. *Oscar Wilde's Last Stand: Decadence, Conspiracy, and the Most Outrageous Trial of the Century.* New York: Arcade, 1997.

Hogarth, Janet E. "Literary Degenerates." *Fortnightly Review* 57, no. 1 (April 1895): 586–92.

Holton, Sandra Stanley. *Suffrage Days: Stories from the Women's Suffrage Movement.* New York: Routledge, 1996.

Hovey, Jaime. "'Kissing a Negress in the Dark': Englishness as a Masquerade in Woolf's *Orlando.*" *PMLA [Publication of the Modern Language Association of America]* 112, no. 3 (1997): 393–404.

Hume, Leslie Parker. *The National Union of Women's Suffrage Societies, 1897–1914.* New York: Garland, 1982.

Hussey, Mark. "Refractions of Desire: The Early Fiction of Virginia and Leonard Woolf." *Modern Fiction Studies* 38, no. 1 (1992): 127–46.

Hynes, Samuel. *A War Imagined: The First World War and English Culture.* London: Bodley Head, 1990.

"In the Tube." *Votes for Women,* no. 140, November 11, 1910, 103.

"It May Be Life . . . Review of *Orlando,* by Virginia Woolf." *New Statesman,* November 10, 1928, 162–63.

Jeffreys, Sheila. *The Spinster and Her Enemies: Feminism and Sexuality, 1880–1930.* London: Pandora, 1985.

Joannou, Maroula. "The Angel of Freedom: Dora Marsden and the Transformation of the *Freewoman* into the *Egoist.*" *Women's History Review* 11, no. 4 (2002): 595–611.

Johnson, Erica L. "Giving up the Ghost: National and Literary Haunting in *Orlando.*" *MFS: Modern Fiction Studies* 50, no. 1 (2004): 110–28.

Jusová, Iveta. *The New Woman and the Empire.* Columbus: Ohio State University Press, 2005.

Kaplan, Amy. *The Anarchy of Empire in the Making of U.S. Culture.* Cambridge, Mass.: Harvard University Press, 2002.

Kaplan, Caren, Norma Alarcón, and Minoo Moallem, eds. *Between Woman and Nation: Nationalisms, Transnational Feminisms, and the State.* Durham, N.C.: Duke University Press, 1999.

Katz, Tamar. *Impressionist Subjects: Gender, Interiority, and Modernist Fiction in England.* Urbana: University of Illinois Press, 2000.

Kennedy, J. M. "The Psychology of Sex." *Freewoman,* November 23, 1911, 15.

Kent, Susan Kingsley. *Sex and Suffrage in Britain, 1860–1914.* Princeton, N.J.: Princeton University Press, 1987.

———. "*The Well of Loneliness* as War Novel." In *Palatable Poison: Critical Perspectives on "The Well of Loneliness,"* edited by Laura Doan and Jay Prosser, 216–31. New York: Columbia University Press, 2001.

Kettle, Michael. *Salome's Last Veil: The Libel Case of the Century.* London: Granada, 1977.

Knapp, Shoshana Milgram. "Real Passion and the Reverence for Life: Sexuality and Antivivisection in the Fiction of Victoria Cross." In *Rediscovering Forgotten Radicals: British Women Writers, 1889–1939,* edited by Angela Ingram and Daphne Patai, 156–71. Chapel Hill: University of North Carolina Press, 1993.

———. "Revolutionary Androgyny in the Fiction of 'Victoria Cross.'" In *Seeing Double: Revisioning Edwardian and Modernist Literature,* edited by Carola M. Kaplan and Anne B. Simpson. New York: St. Martin's, 1996.

———. "Victoria Cross." In *British Short-Fiction Writers, 1880–1914: The Realist Tradition,* edited by William B. Thesing, 75–84. Vol. 135 of *Dictionary of Literary Biography.* Detroit: Gale, 1994.

Knopp, Sherron E. "'If I Saw You, Would You Kiss Me?': Sapphism and the Sub-versiveness of Virginia Woolf's *Orlando.*" In *Sexual Sameness: Textual Differences in Lesbian and Gay Writing,* edited by Joseph Bristow, 111–27. New York: Routledge, 1992.

Koestenbaum, Wayne. *Double Talk: The Erotics of Male Literary Collaboration.* New York: Routledge, 1989.

Krafft-Ebing, Richard von. *Psychopathia Sexualis.* 1886. Translated by Franklin S. Klaf. New York: Stein & Day, 1965. Reprint, New York: Scarborough, 1978.

Ledger, Sally. *The New Woman: Fiction and Feminism at the Fin De Siècle.* Manchester, England: Manchester University Press, 1997.

Levine, Philippa. *Prostitution, Race, and Politics: Policing Venereal Disease in the British Empire.* New York: Routledge, 2003.

Lewsadder, Matthew. "Removing the Veils: Censorship, Female Sexuality, and Oscar Wilde's *Salome.*" *Modern Drama* 45, no. 4 (2002): 519–44.

Linton, E[liza] Lynn. *The Autobiography of Christopher Kirkland.* 3 vols. London: Bentley, 1885.

———. "The Wild Women." *Nineteenth Century* 30 (July 1891): 79–88.

Lloyd, E. B. "Intermediate Sexual Types." *New Freewoman,* October 1, 1913, 155–56.

Lyon, Janet. "Militant Discourse, Strange Bedfellows: Suffragettes and Vorticists before the War." *differences: A Journal of Feminist Cultural Studies* 4, no. 2 (1992): 100–133.

———. "Women Demonstrating Modernism." *Discourse* 17, no. 2 (1994–95): 6–25.

Mackenzie, Compton. *Extraordinary Women: Theme and Variations.* New York: Vanguard, 1928.

MacPike, Loralee. "Is Mary Llewellyn an Invert? The Modernist Supertext of *The Well of Loneliness.*" In *Unmanning Modernism: Gendered Re-readings,* edited by Elizabeth Jane Harrison and Shirley Peterson, 73–89. Knoxville: University of Tennessee Press, 1997.

Malamud, Randy. "Splitting the Husks: Woolf's Modernist Language in *Night and Day.*" In *Virginia Woolf: Critical Assessments,* edited by Eleanor McNees. Vol. 3, *Critical Responses to the Novels from "The Voyage Out" to "To the Lighthouse,"* 159–73. Mountfield, England: Helm Information, 1994.

Mangum, Teresa. "Style Wars and the 1890s: The New Woman and the Decadent." In *Transforming Genres: New Approaches to British Fiction of the 1890s,* edited by Nikki Lee Manos and Meri-Jane Rochelson, 47–66. New York: St. Martin's, 1994.

Mansfield, Katherine. "A Ship Comes into the Harbour." In *Virginia Woolf: Critical Assessments,* edited by Eleanor McNees. Vol. 3, *Critical Responses to the Novels from "The Voyage Out" to "To the Lighthouse,"* 108–10. Mountfield, England: Helm Information, 1994.

Marah. "Correspondence: The Human Complex." *Freewoman,* April 18, 1912, 437–38.

Marcus, Jane. Introduction to *Suffrage and the Pankhursts,* edited by Jane Marcus, 1–17. London: Routledge and Kegan Paul, 1987.

———. "Sapphistory: The Woolf and the Well." In *Lesbian Texts and Contexts: Radical Revisions,* edited by Karla Jay and Joanne Glasgow, 164–80. New York: New York University Press, 1990.

Margesson, Isabel Hampden. "'Nauseous Publications,'" letter to the editor. *Times* (London), August 29, 1912.

Marsden, Dora. "Notes of the Week." *Freewoman,* November 23, 1911, 4.

———. "Views and Comments." *New Freewoman,* June 15, 1913, 3–5.

———. "Views and Comments." *New Freewoman,* July 1, 1913, 23–25.

Mayhall, Laura E. Nym. *The Militant Suffrage Movement: Citizenship and Resistance in Britain, 1860–1930.* Oxford: Oxford University Press, 2003.

———. "The South African War and the Origins of Suffrage Militancy in Britain, 1899–1902." In *Women's Suffrage in the British Empire: Citizenship, Nation, and Race,* edited by Ian Christopher Fletcher, Laura E. Nym Mayhall, and Philippa Levine, 3–17. London: Routledge, 2000.

McClintock, Anne, Aamir Mufti, and Ella Shohat, eds. *Dangerous Liaisons: Gender, Nations, and Postcolonial Perspectives.* Minneapolis: University of Minnesota Press, 1997.

McKale, Donald M. *War by Revolution: Germany and Great Britain in the Middle East in the Era of World War I.* Kent, Ohio: Kent State University Press, 1998.

Medd, Jodie. "'The Cult of the Clitoris': Anatomy of a National Scandal." *Modernism/Modernity* 9, no. 1 (2002): 21–49.

———. "War Wounds: The Nation, Shell Shock, and Psychoanalysis in *The Well of Loneliness.*" In *Palatable Poison: Critical Perspectives on "The Well of Loneliness,"* edited by Laura Doan and Jay Prosser, 232–54. New York: Columbia University Press, 2001.

Meem, Deborah T. "Eliza Lynn Linton and the Rise of Lesbian Consciousness." *Journal of the History of Sexuality* 7, no. 4 (1997): 537–60.

"Militant Suffragist." Cartoon. *Punch,* June 4, 1913, 437.

Mix, Katherine Lyon. *A Study in Yellow: The "Yellow Book" and Its Contributors.* Lawrence: University Press of Kansas, 1960.

Moreland, R. H. "The Persian Women." *Freewoman,* January 4, 1912, 125–26.

Mortimer, Raymond. "Reviews: New Novels." *Nation and Athenaeum,* September 8, 1928, 735.

Mukherjee, Roopali. "Between Enemies and Traitors: Black Press Coverage of September 11 and the Predicament of National 'Others.'" In *Media Representations of September 11,* edited by Steven Chermak, Frankie Y. Bailey, and Michelle Brown, 29–46. Westport, Conn.: Praeger, 2003.

New Freewoman. Letter to the editor. October 15, 1913, 178.

"New Novels: Review of *the Well of Loneliness,* by Radclyffe Hall." *Times Literary Supplement,* August 2, 1928, 566.

Newton, Esther. "The Mythic Mannish Lesbian: Radclyffe Hall and the New Woman." In *Hidden from History: Reclaiming the Gay and Lesbian Past,* edited by Martin Bauml Duberman, Martha Vicinus, and George Chauncey Jr., 281–93. New York: New American Library, 1989.

Nicolson, Nigel. *Portrait of a Marriage.* New York: Atheneum, 1973.

Noble, Jean Bobby. *Masculinities without Men? Female Masculinity in Twentieth-Century Fictions.* British Columbia: University of British Columbia Press, 2005.

Northerner [pseud.]. "Correspondence: Knowledge Wanted." *Freewoman,* May 2, 1912, 476.

"Novel Condemned as Obscene: Bow Street Magistrate's Decision." *Times* (London), November 17, 1928.

"The Old Bailey Shocker." *New Statesman,* June 8, 1918, 188–89.

Oliver, Kathlyn. "Correspondence: Asceticism and Passion." *Freewoman,* February 15, 1912, 252.

———. "Correspondence: More Plain Speaking." *Freewoman,* March 14, 1912, 332.

———. "Correspondence: On the Loose Principle." *Freewoman,* April 4, 1912, 398–99.

Oram, Alison. *Her Husband Was a Woman! Women's Gender-Crossing in Modern British Popular Culture.* London: Routledge, 2007.

Ordover, Nancy. *American Eugenics: Race, Queer Anatomy, and the Science of Nationalism.* Minneapolis: University of Minnesota Press, 2003.

Owen, Harold. *Woman Adrift: A Statement of the Case against Suffragism.* New York: Dutton, 1912.

Pankhurst, Christabel. *The Great Scourge and How to End It* (1913). In *Suffrage and the Pankhursts,* edited by Jane Marcus, 187–240. New York: Routledge, 1987.

Park, Sowon S. "Suffrage and Virginia Woolf: 'The Mass behind the Single Voice.'" *Review of English Studies* 56, no. 223 (2005): 119–34.

Parkes, Adam. *Modernism and the Theater of Censorship.* New York: Oxford University Press, 1996.

Parliamentary Debates. Official Record, House of Commons. Vol. 145. London: HMSO, 1921.

Parliamentary Debates: Official Record, House of Lords. Vol. 46. London: HMSO, 1921.

Paul, Cedar. "The Sassoon Case." *Worker's Dreadnought,* August 11, 1917, 826.

Pearce, I. D. "Marriage and Motherhood." *Freewoman,* November 30, 1911, 32.

Peel, Robert A. Editor's introduction. In *Essays in the History of Eugenics,* edited by Robert A. Peel. London: Galton Institute, 1998.

The People of the State of New York v. Donald Friede and Covici Friede. Defense brief. Magistrate's Court, City of New York Seventh District—Borough of Manhattan,

January 1929, pp. 11–18. Radclyffe Hall Collection, Harry Ransom Center for the Humanities, University of Texas, Austin.

Peppis, Paul. "Rewriting Sex: Mina Loy, Marie Stopes, and Sexology." *Modernism/Modernity* 9, no. 4 (2002): 561–79.

Phillips, Kathy J. *Manipulating Masculinity: War and Gender in Modern British and American Literature.* New York: Palgrave, 2006.

———. *Virginia Woolf against Empire.* Knoxville: University of Tennessee Press, 1994.

Plato. *Symposium and Phaedrus.* Translated by Benjamin Jowett. New York: Dover, 1993.

Priest, Ann-Marie. "Between Being and Nothingness: The 'Astonishing Precipice' of Virginia Woolf's *Night and Day.*" *Journal of Modern Literature* 26, no. 2 (2003): 66–80.

Proctor, Tammy M. *Female Intelligence: Women and Espionage in the First World War.* New York: New York University Press, 2003.

Prosser, Jay. *Second Skins: The Body Narratives of Transsexuality.* New York: Columbia University Press, 1998.

Pugh, Martin. *Women and the Women's Movement in Britain, 1914–1959.* New York: Paragon, 1993.

"Review of *Extraordinary Women,* by Compton Mackenzie." *Times Literary Supplement* (London), September 6, 1928, 633.

"Review of *Night and Day* by Virginia Woolf." *Times Literary Supplement* (London), 1919. Reprinted in *Virginia Woolf: Critical Assessments,* edited by Eleanor McNees. Vol. 3, *Critical Responses to the Novels from "The Voyage Out" to "To the Lighthouse,"* 105–7. Mountfield, England: Helm Information, 1994.

"Review of *Orlando,* by Virginia Woolf." *Times Literary Supplement* (London), October 11, 1928, 729.

Riley, Denise. *"Am I That Name?" Feminism and the Category of "Women" in History.* Minneapolis: University of Minnesota Press, 1988.

Roberts, Evelyn. "Reading Women Writing Modernism: History in Literature and Literature in History." PhD diss., Brown University. 1991.

Rubin, Gayle. "Thinking Sex: Notes for a Radical Theory of the Politics of Sexuality." In *Pleasure and Danger: Exploring Female Sexuality,* edited by Carole S. Vance, 267–319. London: Pandora, 1984.

Ruehl, Sonja. "Inverts and Experts: Radclyffe Hall and the Lesbian Identity." In *Feminist Criticism and Social Change: Sex, Class, and Race in Literature and Culture,* edited by Judith Newton and Deborah Rosenfelt, 165–80. New York: Methuen, 1985.

Said, Edward. *Orientalism.* New York: Random House, 1978.

Scott, Bonnie Kime, ed. *The Gender of Modernism: A Critical Anthology.* Bloomington: Indiana University Press, 1990.

————. *Refiguring Modernism.* Vol. 1, *Women of 1928.* Bloomington: Indiana University Press, 1995.

Scrapbook Relating to Women's Work during the First World War. Fawcett Library Scrapbooks and Press Cuttings Collection. Ref. code GB 0106 10/6. Women's Library, London Metropolitan University, London.

Sedgwick, Eve Kosofsky. *Epistemology of the Closet.* Berkeley and Los Angeles: University of California Press, 1990.

Seshagiri, Urmila. "Orienting Virginia Woolf: Race, Aesthetics, and Politics in *To the Lighthouse.*" *MFS: Modern Fiction Studies* 50, no. 1 (2004): 58–84.

Sharp, Evelyn. "Filling the War Chest." In *Rebel Women.* New York: Lane, 1910.

Showalter, Elaine, ed. *Daughters of Decadence: Women Writers of the Fin-De-Siècle.* New Brunswick, N.J.: Rutgers University Press, 1993.

"Single, but Undismayed." Correspondence. *Freewoman,* November, 30, 1911, 32.

Smith, Patricia Juliana. *Lesbian Panic: Homoeroticism in Modern British Women's Fiction.* New York: Columbia University Press, 1997.

Soloway, Richard Allen. *Birth Control and the Population Question in England, 1877–1930.* Chapel Hill: University of North Carolina Press, 1982.

————. *Demography and Degeneration: Eugenics and the Declining Birthrate in Twentieth-Century England.* Chapel Hill: University of North Carolina Press, 1990.

Somerville, Siobhan B. *Queering the Color Line: Race and the Invention of Homosexuality in American Culture.* Durham, N.C.: Duke University Press, 2000.

Souhami, Diana. *The Trials of Radclyffe Hall.* London: Weidenfeld & Nicolson, 1998.

Spencer, Harold Sherwood. War file, no. WO 339/41960 6036755. Public Record Office, London.

"The Spinster, by One." *Freewoman,* November 11, 1911, 10–11.

Spivak, Gayatri Chakravorty. "Globalicities: Terror and Its Consequences." *CR: The New Centennial Review* 4, no. 1 (2004): 73–94.

————. "Three Women's Texts and a Critique of Imperialism." In *"Race," Writing, and Difference,* edited by Henry Louis Gates, 262–80. Chicago: University of Chicago Press, 1985.

Squier, Susan Merrill. "Tradition and Revision: The Classic City Novel and Virginia Woolf's *Night and Day.*" In *Virginia Woolf: Critical Assessments,* edited by Eleanor McNees. Vol. 3, *Critical Responses to the Novels from "The Voyage Out" to "To the Lighthouse,"* 126–42. Mountfield, England: Helm Information, 1994.

Stape, J. H. "Virginia Woolf's *Night and Day:* Dates of Composition." *Notes and Queries* 39, no. 2 (1992): 193–94.

Steakley, James D. *The Homosexual Emancipation Movement in Germany.* New York: Arno, 1975. Reprint, Salem: Ayer, 1993.

———. "Iconography of a Scandal: Political Cartoons and the Eulenburg Affair in Wilhelmin Germany." In *Hidden from History: Reclaiming the Gay and Lesbian Past,* edited by Martin Bauml Duberman, Martha Vicinus and George Chauncey Jr., 233–63. New York: New American Library, 1989.

Stoler, Ann Laura. *Race and the Education of Desire: Foucault's "History of Sexuality" and the Colonial Order of Things.* Durham, N.C.: Duke University Press, 1995.

Stone, Dan. "Race in British Eugenics." *European History Quarterly* 31, no. 3 (2001): 397–425.

Stopes, Marie. *Married Love.* New York: Truth, 1918. Reprint, Oxford: Oxford University Press, 2008.

Strachey, Ray. *The Cause: A Short History of the Women's Movement in Great Britain.* 1928. Reprint, London: Virago, 1978.

Suffragette, May 1, 1914. Cover and editorial, 55.

"A Suffragette's Home." Poster. Produced by the National League for Opposing Woman Suffrage. 1900. Women's Library, London Metropolitan University, London.

Sully, Jess. "Narcissistic Princess, Rejected Lover, Veiled Priestess, Virtuous Virgin: How Oscar Wilde Imagined Salomé." *Wildean: Journal of the Oscar Wilde Society* 25 (2004): 16–33.

Taylor, Melanie. "*Peter (a Young English Girl)*: Visualizing Transgender Masculinities." *Camera Obscura* 19, no. 2 56 (2004): 1–45.

———. "True Stories: *Orlando,* Life-Writing, and Transgender Narratives." In *Modernist Sexualities,* edited by Hugh Stevens and Caroline Howlett, 202–18. Manchester, England: Manchester University Press, 2000.

Thacker, Andrew. "Dora Marsden and the *Egoist*: 'Our War Is with Words.'" *English Literature in Translation* 36, no. 2 (1993): 178–96.

Tickner, Lisa. *The Spectacle of Women.* Chicago: University of Chicago Press, 1988.

Tout Pouvoir [pseud.]. "Correspondence: 'Normal and Abnormal.'" *Freewoman,* March 28, 1912, 376.

Travis, Jennifer. "Clits in Court: *Salome,* Sodomy, and the Lesbian 'Sadist.'" In *Lesbian Erotics,* edited by Karla Jay, 147–63. New York: New York University Press, 1995.

Trevelyan, Janet Penrose. *The Life of Mrs Humphry Ward.* London: Constable, 1923.

Trotter, David. "Lesbians before Lesbianism: Sexual Identity in Early Twentieth-Century British Fiction." In *Borderlines: Genders and Identities in War and Peace, 1870–1930,* edited by Billie Melman, 193–211. New York: Routledge, 1998.

Troubridge, Una Vincenzo. *The Life of Radclyffe Hall.* New York: Citadel, 1961.

Tusan, Michelle Elizabeth. *Women Making News: Gender and Journalism in Modern Britain.* Urbana: University of Illinois Press, 2005.

Tylee, Claire M. *The Great War and Women's Consciousness: Images of Militarism and Womanhood in Women's Writings, 1914–64.* London: Macmillan, 1990.

Underhill, Ruth Murray. "A Voyage toward Reality." In *Virginia Woolf: Critical Assessments,* edited by Eleanor McNees. Vol. 3, *Critical Responses to the Novels from "The Voyage Out" to "To the Lighthouse,"* 111–12. Mountfield, England: Helm Information, 1994.

Vicinus, Martha. "Distance and Desire: English Boarding School Friendships, 1870–1920." In *Hidden from History: Reclaiming the Gay and Lesbian Past,* edited by Martin Bauml Duberman, Martha Vicinus, and George Chauncey Jr., 212–29. New York: New American Library, 1989.

———. *Intimate Friends: Women Who Loved Women, 1778–1928.* Chicago: University of Chicago Press, 2004.

———. "Male Spaces and Female Bodies: The English Suffragette Movement." In *Women in Culture and Politics: A Century of Change,* edited by Judith Frielander, Blanche Wiesen Cook, Alice Kessler-Harris, and Carroll Smith Rosenberg, 209–22. Bloomington: Indiana University Press, 1986.

Votes for Women. Editorial. November 1907, 13.

"The Vulgarity of Lesbianism: Review of *Extraordinary Women,* by Compton Mackenzie." *New Statesman,* August 25, 1928, 614.

Wachman, Gay. *Lesbian Empire: Radical Crosswriting in the Twenties.* New Brunswick, N.J.: Rutgers University Press, 2001.

Walkowitz, Judith R. "The 'Vision of Salome': Cosmopolitanism and Erotic Dancing in Central London, 1908–1918." *American Historical Review* 108, no. 2 (2003): 336–76.

Wallace, Jo-Ann. "The Case of Edith Ellis." In *Modernist Sexualities,* edited by Hugh Stevens and Caroline Howlett, 13–40. Manchester, England: Manchester University Press, 2000.

Walton, Jean. "'I Want to Cross over into Camp Ground': Race and Inversion in *The Well of Loneliness.*" In *Palatable Poison: Critical Perspectives on "The Well of Loneliness,"* edited by Laura Doan and Jay Prosser, 277–99. New York: Columbia University Press, 2001.

Ward, Mrs. Humphry. "An Appeal against Female Suffrage." *Nineteenth Century* 25 (June 1889): 781–89.

———. "Religion and the Suffrage: A Protest by Mrs Humphry Ward." Letter to the editor. *Times* (London), Wednesday, June 19, 1912, 14.

Wee, Allison Lorna Elizabeth. "Trials and Eros: The British Home Office v. Indecent Publications, 1857–1932." PhD diss., University of Minnesota, 2003.

Weeks, Jeffrey. *Coming Out: Homosexual Politics in Britain, from the Nineteenth Century to the Present.* Rev. ed. New York: Quartet, 1990.

Whitaker, Joseph. *Almanack.* London, 1922.

White, Kevin F. "Men Supporting Women: A Study of Men Associated with the Women's Suffrage Movement in Britain and America, 1909–1920." *Maryland Historian* 18, no. 1 (1987): 45–59.

Wilchins, Riki Anne. *Read My Lips: Sexual Subversion and the End of Gender.* Ithaca, N.Y.: Firebrand, 1997.

Wilde, Oscar. *Salomé: A Tragedy in One Act.* 1894. Reprint, Boston: Branden, 1996.

"The Wild-Goose Chase: Review of *Orlando,* by Virginia Woolf." *Saturday Review,* October 13, 1928, 474.

Wollacott, Angela. "Australian Women's Metropolitan Activism: From Suffrage, to Imperial Vanguard, to Commonwealth Feminism." In *Women's Suffrage in the British Empire: Citizenship, Nation, and Race,* edited by Ian Christopher Fletcher, Laura E. Nym Mayhall, and Philippa Levine, 207–23. London: Routledge, 2000.

Woolf, Leonard. "The World of Books: Review of *The Well of Loneliness,* by Radclyffe Hall." *Nation and Athenaeum,* August 4, 1928, 593.

Woolf, Virginia. *The Diary of Virginia Woolf.* Edited by Anne Olivier Bell. Vol. 1, *1915–1919.* New York: Harcourt Brace Jovanovich, 1977.

———. *The Letters of Virginia Woolf.* Edited by Nigel Nicolson. Vol. 3, *1923–1928.* New York: Harcourt Brace Jovanovich, 1975–1980.

———. *Night and Day.* London: Hogarth, 1920. Reprint, New York: Harcourt, Brace.

———. *Orlando.* London: Hogarth, 1928. Reprint, New York: Harcourt Brace Jovanovich.

———. *A Room of One's Own.* London: Hogarth, 1929. Reprint, New York: Harcourt Brace Jovanovich, 1989.

Wussow, Helen. "Conflict of Language in Virginia Woolf's *Night and Day.*" *Journal of Modern Literature* 16, no. 1 (1989): 61–73.

Zemgulys, Andrea P. "'*Night and Day* Is Dead': Virginia Woolf in London 'Literary and Historic.'" *Twentieth Century Literature* 46, no. 1 (2000): 56–77.

INDEX

acquired homosexuality, 4, 6, 7, 9–11.
    See also situational inversion
actresses, status of, 51, 224n31
Actress's Franchise League (AFL),
    British, 51
Aestheticism: women of, 22, 220n58
Afghanistan: war in, 198
Aguilar–San Juan, Karin, 241n25
Alarcón, Norma, 216n7
Alberti, Johanna, 240n7
alienation: homosexuality as familial
    and national, 162, 163, 165; as symp-
    tom of homosexual identity in
    Allatini's *Despised and Rejected,* 118
Allan, Maud, xx, 111, 112, 113, 128–43,
    148, 152, 195; dancing career, 236n58;
    interpretation of *Salomé,* 136–37;
    libel trial rising from performance
    in Wilde's *Salomé,* 111, 112, 113,
    128–40
Allan/Billing trial. *See Rex v. Pemberton
    Billing*
Allatini, Rose, xviii, xx, 111, 112, 115,
    135, 141, 147, 216n18, 233n14–15,
    233n20, 233n22, 234n31, 234n36.
    See also Despised and Rejected
    (Allatini)
ambiguity, sexual, 159, 169–70

androgyny, 97, 171; of Orlando,
    utopian perfection of male and
    female in, 179; sexual inversion and
    increasing emphasis on, 98–100;
    Woolf's imperial, 174–84
Anglo-Boer War (1899–1902), 1;
    recruiting difficulties and fears of
    "racial degeneration" during, 76
animalism: sexual experience and,
    86–87
Anna Lombard (Cross), 221n65
anthropology: Ellis's *Sexual Inversion*
    framed within context of, 4–10
antisuffrage rhetoric, 31, 35–47, 223n27;
    absent or bad mother figure in, 40–
    43, 46; absolute divisions between
    men and women posited, 37–38;
    "Appeal against Female Suffrage,
    An," 35–37; British civilization at
    risk, 38–39; Corelli's *Woman, or—
    Suffragette,* 38; decline of British
    Empire linked to rise of modernity
    and gender equality, 39–40;
    emergent possibility of same-sex
    erotics, 46–47; in popular press, 37;
    portrayal of suffragists, 37, 38,
    40–47, 65; "positive" arguments of,
    35; sexually bereft spinster in, 45.